D0543952

30 years

of language teaching

Resources Technician
University of Central Lancashire
Department of Languages
Fylde Building
PRESTON PR1 2HE
Telephone: 0772 893155

The Centre for Information on Language Teaching and Research provides a complete range of services for language professionals in every stage and sector of education, and in business, in support of its brief to promote Britain's foreign language capability.

CILT is a registered charity, supported by Central Government grants. CILT is based in Covent Garden, London, and its services are delivered through a national collaborative network of regional Comenius Centres in England, the National Comenius Centre of Wales, Scottish CILT and Northern Ireland CILT.

30 years

of language teaching

Edited by
Eric Hawkins

1966-1996 **YEARS**

CILT
Centre for Information
on Language Teaching and Research

1966-1996 YEARS

The views expressed in this book are those of the editor and contributors and do not necessarily reflect the views of CILT.

First published in 1996
Copyright © 1996 Centre for Information on Language Teaching and Research
ISBN 1 874016 67 4
A catalogue record for this book is available from the British Library

Cover by Neil Alexander
Cover photography supplied by Sally and Richard Greenhill Photographers Photo Library
Illustrations: Looking glasses (p33); The roper and the cordwainer (p81); Wells (p133); Boys' sports (p153); The mason (p177); Tennis play (p209); The potter (p267); The bookseller's shop (p297); The shoe maker (p319); Swimming (p331) – all from Comenius J A, *Orbis sensualium pictus*
Printed in Great Britain by Bourne Press Ltd

Published by the Centre for Information on Language Teaching and Research, 20 Bedfordbury, Covent Garden, London WC2N 4LB

CILT Publications are available from: Grantham Book Services, Isaac Newton Way, Alma Park Industrial Estate, Grantham, Lincs NG31 8SD. Tel: 01476 567 421. Fax: 01476 590 223. Book trade representation (UK and Ireland): Broadcast Book Services, 24 De Montfort Road, London SW16 1LZ. Tel: 0181 677 5129.

All rights reserved. No part of this publication may be reproduced, stored in a retrieval system, or transmitted in any form or by any means, electronic, mechanical, photographic, recording, or otherwise, without the prior permission of the Copyright owner.

Contents

Preface

It hardly seems possible that CILT is celebrating its thirtieth anniversary. My own career as a university teacher of modern languages is almost exactly co-terminous with the establishment and growth of CILT, and I have watched its development over many years with respect and admiration. Perhaps because CILT's second Director, John Trim, had been my first tutor in Linguistics I was always particularly aware both of the organisation's vast potential and also of the challenges which it needed to overcome, especially in the early years.

It was then with very real delight that I was able to accept the invitation to become CILT's Chairman some five years ago, a period of office which sadly comes to an end just as the Centre rightly celebrates this auspicious landmark. During these years, I have watched with great pleasure the growing realisation through the educational system, and indeed in society more widely, that competence in one or more modern foreign languages is ever more important in the world, particularly as the European Union plays a steadily more significant role in all of our lives. When I was asked, some seven years ago now, to chair the working group on Modern Languages within the National Curriculum, I became aware of just how strongly the tide was running in favour of languages for all, and the almost universal support which our recommendations received confirmed that the climate was more favourable than for many years.

And this brings me back to CILT. I have absolutely no doubt that the Centre, by working constantly with teachers and with all those bodies responsible for stressing the importance, both cultural and economic, of linguistc competence, was to a considerable extent responsible for creating the new positive mood which is now so widely shared. The evidence which came forward in favour of languages for all within our schools was overwhelming, despite the fact that it created new challenges for teachers in presenting a curriculum to young people of all abilities. And here once again CILT came into its own, using its long-established programme of seminars and conferences to explain what was required, and to share best practice, whether in materials or techniques, with all concerned. It is no accident that at a time when public spending is always under scrutiny, CILT has repeatedly been judged to provide excellent value for money.

CILT then has much to look back on with pride – but it is the mark of a successful organisation that it is always looking forward too. The plethora of new initiatives currently underway are striking evidence of what the Director and his colleagues are seeking to achieve. On all past evidence, they will go from strength to strength. Such success cannot be achieved by adopting a single narrowly focused view of complex issues, but rather, as this celebratory volume shows, by being catholic in approach, revelling indeed in diversity. One influence, however, shines through, that of Eric Hawkins, the editor of the volume, acknowledged by so many for so long as one of the true leaders in the modern languages field.

As one thirty-year period finishes and the next thirty years begins, and as my own chairmanship comes to an end, I know that CILT will continue to flourish. The reputation which it has rightly achieved and the talented staff who work for it will ensure this. It is both a pleasure and a privilege to be associated with this splendid volume, which both looks back in celebration and forward in anticipation – anticipation of CILT's ongoing success.

Martin Harris

Professor Martin Harris CBE
Vice-Chancellor, University of Manchester
Chairman, CILT

Editorial

Why this 30 years?

Eric Hawkins

Historians of language teaching have pointed to the year 1641 as the great 'might have been' which could have transformed what a House of Lords Select Committee recently called *the monolingual tradition of British society*. In that year, Bishop John Williams persuaded the Czech reformer, and foremost language educator, John Amos Comenius, to leave his refuge from persecution at Leszno, in Poland, and make the hazardous journey to London. The bishop and his committee of businessmen and MPs, hoped that Comenius, *whose textbooks were in use in half the schools of Europe* (Needham, 1942) might persuade Parliament to back their plan to build a new kind of 'College' for which they had already chosen a site at Chelsea. It was to be outside the existing universities. These had failed to show what Comenius called *freshness of mind*. The aim was to build a *Universal College* such as Comenius had described in *The Great Didactic,* which would be *a living laboratory for schools, lending them sap, vitality and strength.*

Parliament, however, was preoccupied. Civil war loomed and Bishop Williams' imaginative plan was shelved. Language teaching in Britain then fell into a long, if at times unquiet, sleep. In the past thirty years, however, our discipline has awakened from its sleep, and its awakening coincided with the arrival, in 1966, of something very close to that *living laboratory* giving *sap, vitality and strength* to our discipline, that Comenius looked for.

CILT's first thirty years have coincided with a remarkable transformation in language teaching and our publication salutes the drive and direction that CILT has given throughout. Those who have served and presently serve CILT would, of course, wish to stress that the transformation whose story we have to tell has been due to a combination of factors. It has been largely a teacher-driven reform, encouraged by new technology, support from Local Authority Language Advisers, and from a succession of distinguished HM Staff Inspectors, but perhaps most powerfully by a new readiness of universities and the polytechnics to equip language graduates to meet society's needs. The professional attack of teachers has been much strengthened by the coming together of the diverse language interests in one powerful Association for Language Learning (see Chapter 28).

2 In telling the story of thirty eventful years for our discipline we have a dual aim. One purpose is to inform those in the profession who may not have a complete picture of developments in other fields than their own. We hope, however, also to address a wider readership, outside the profession, especially decision makers and administrators at local and national level, school governors, parents, employers and university selectors.

The need to address a wide readership has become clearer as government intervention in curriculum planning has increased. This consideration has been given added point by Sir Ron Dearing's recent proposal to re-shape the National Curriculum, with new targets at fourteen and sixteen and a new alignment of vocational and academic subjects. Where will foreign languages fit into the new alignment? Discussion should begin with a clear picture of the present position.

A curriculum house with a leaking roof?

Modern linguists had good reason to welcome the Education Act of 1988, establishing the foreign language as a foundation subject for all pupils up to the age of sixteen (in Scotland a similar rule came in with the Scottish Office Circular 11/89, effective from 1992). Throughout most of the 1980s, in England and Wales, some two-thirds of all pupils dropped out of foreign language classes at age fourteen, and far more boys dropped out than girls. The downward spiral was partially checked in 1988 by the introduction of the new-model General Certificate of Secondary Education (GCSE). From September 1996, the fourteen-year-old dropout must end completely.

But will this merely postpone the dropout by two years? At present, in England/Wales as in Scotland, of every eight pupils who study a modern language up to age sixteen, seven drop serious study of it. The dropout of boys is specially marked and is uncannily similar in both England and Wales and in Scotland. Of every thirteen boys taking a language to sixteen, twelve drop serious study of it at that stage (see pp78–79).

Pupils who leave school at sixteen find little encouragement in employment or apprenticeship to build on the foreign language begun in school, while those who stay at school get very confusing signals from university selectors. In 1966, just as CILT opened its doors, the universities announced that they were abandoning their centuries-old entrance requirement of a basic competence in a foreign language. This seemed to send a signal to schools (and to parents) that monolingualism was now acceptable at the highest academic level. The message was reinforced by the universities failure to broaden their narrow, three subject, entrance requirements which effectively dissuade many sixth formers from spending time on a foreign language (see the revealing statement by Cambridge University on p79). For so many pupils to abandon their foreign language after five years hard work just at the moment when they could begin to follow their own reading and explore a neighbouring culture, is a great waste of learners' (and teachers') effort. It is to be hoped that the effect of university entrance policies on sixth form courses will not escape the attention of Sir Ron Dearing's committee, lest our language teaching house, so recently refurbished, be left with a badly leaking roof.

A house with insecure foundations

While the roof leaks so wastefully, are the foundations of our curriculum house any more secure? Ours is the only 'foundation subject' in the National Curriculum which is not started until Key Stage 3. We choose the onset of the insecurity of adolescence as the moment to invite pupils to perform, publicly, in a new language and 'go to meet' a strange way of life. Moreover, many eleven-year-olds, perhaps a majority, begin their exploration of the foreign language handicapped by insecure grasp of the mother tongue and lack of awareness of how language works (see discussion, p121).

Repairing the roof and securing the foundations of our curriculum house will call for a dialogue of equals between those who have to deliver the curriculum in the classroom, and those outside who make the administrative decisions. From this dialogue a coherent national languages policy might emerge. A main purpose of this volume is to promote such a dialogue.

Introduction. What kind of a subject are we talking about?

The introduction 'Language Teaching in Perspective', asks three questions:

- what kind of subject are we talking about?
- is it merely a **skill**, or an essential element in the **education** of all citizens?
- how are languages learned under school conditions?

Part one: the national need for languages

Our survey then begins with the question (Chapter 1): why does Britain need linguists? The view of a leading Germanist who has challenged the complacency of employers is followed by a view from business (Chapter 2), and accounts of recent moves in adult education and at university (Chapters 3–5).

Warnings that we neglect foreign language skills at our peril go back a long way (see page 34). However, in 1966 the omens had looked bright. CILT's arrival coincided with the renewed prospect of Britain joining the European Common Market, with its vast potential of 340 million customers. As a Headmasters' Association Working Party commented at the time: *What will be the effect on language teaching when our daily lives and jobs are enmeshed with our European neighbours at all levels of technology, industry and commerce, not to speak of journalism, entertainment, sport and politics?* (IAHM, 1966). In 1975, after a national debate and a decisive referendum that cut across political party lines, Britain finally joined the EEC. The message seemed to be, if ever Britain needed linguists, she will surely need them now!

High hopes were disappointed, however. The story is told in the opening Chapter (and see John Trim's revealing recollection, p328).

In previous generations, employers, accused of neglecting language skills, could argue that university language courses failed to meet the needs of society. This excuse for employers' complacency is no longer valid. University courses now match much more closely the needs of society. With the 1960s, there began a radical reform of degree courses and an explosive growth of 'service-courses' for 'students of other disciplines' (SODS). These now considerably outnumber language degree students (see p70).

A challenging feature, however, that emerges from this part of our survey, is the growing number of adult learners who *choose to learn a language different from the one they were offered at school.* Their adult choice of foreign language could not have been predicted when they were at school and, even if it could be predicted, no school could ever have offered the range of languages needed. For many, perhaps most, pupils, the secondary school foreign language course is increasingly coming to be seen as, in effect, *the first stage of a two-stage process,* an 'apprenticeship' in 'learning how to learn' language, on which the later (adult) stages must build. It would seem logical to plan the course as such. The implications of this are further examined at p19.

Part two: languages for all?

We then address what has proved the major challenge to language teachers in the past thirty years, namely the 'democratisation' of our subject in the secondary school. In Chapter 6, the impact of comprehensive re-organisation in England and Wales is described and the parallel development in Scotland of 'languages for all to 16', following the Scottish Office Circular (11/89). Comprehensive re-organisation was especially challenging for foreign language teaching because throughout history languages had never been offered to more than a small and carefully chosen élite of learners. In 1965, in England and Wales, only 25% of the 11+ age group were offered a foreign language. They were a verbally privileged minority. The 11+ test effectively selected pupils whose grasp of English was most secure, but it also assessed motivation and home background, rejecting those pupils who had been denied the precious 'parental encouragement' identified as decisive for early language learning (Plowden, 1967). The response of teachers, in seeking to help the 75% of eleven-year-olds who were newcomers to foreign language classes, and who lacked not only the verbal skills needed for the secondary course, but also, in many cases, the precious encouragement from home to support them through difficult learning, forms a large part of the recent story of our subject.

There were many who doubted the feasibility of a foreign language for all up to sixteen. At least one comprehensive school staff, in the Midlands, voted to outlaw all foreign language teaching because they found it a 'sore thumb' in the 'child-centred curriculum' to which they were committed. That the policy of a foreign language for all eventually survived was largely due to the resilience and professionalism of teachers, typified by the enthusiasm with which they supported the 'graded objectives' movement (GOML), described in Chapter 7. In all this, teachers had the support of Local Authority Language Advisers, organised in a strong national association, NALA, and backed in several areas by well equipped resource centres, of which the now defunct Inner London Education Authority centre was a shining example. Powerful leadership also came from a sequence of caring HMI Staff Inspectors such as Mervyn Wigram, Peter Hoy and Michael Salter, and, in Scotland, Joe Howgego and Tony Giovanazzi.

Chapter 8 discusses a challenging development of 'languages for all', with the introduction of a foreign language to pupils with 'special educational needs'. Their right to embark on foreign language studies was questioned by much influential opinion, but successful practice has demonstrated how rewarding the experience can be, in the right hands.

In Chapter 9 recent developments in language teaching in further education are examined.

Part two concludes (Chapter 10) with a discussion of two issues which affect the whole secondary curriculum but with which language teachers have been especially concerned.

The uneven language playing field

With comprehensive re-organisation, as we observed above, it became clear how very unequally some eleven-year-olds were equipped for the linguistic demands of the secondary course. The movement that has come to be called 'awareness of language' sprang from a growing realisation that the language playing field of the secondary school was cruelly uneven. Language teachers took the lead in arguing for 'awareness of language' as a 'bridging subject, across the curriculum'. Only limited progress along these lines can be reported, unfortunately, and the playing field remains most unfairly uneven for many pupils.

The boy/girl imbalance

An outcome of comprehensive re-organisation in England and Wales that has been little discussed was the replacement of largely single-sex grammar and modern schools by mainly co-educational schools. With girls now sitting beside boys in unselected classes, the verbal precocity of girls, disguised for generations by selection at eleven, could no longer be hidden. Girls are, on average, over a year ahead of boys in linguistic development, at age eleven. This must underlie girls' consistently better performance across the curriculum in examinations (see Appendix II, Tables 2 and 4). Boys appear to catch up, verbally, after puberty, but the years eleven to sixteen are decisive for many pupils' subject and career choices.

In England and Wales the growth of co-educational secondary schooling has coincided with a marked shift in the overall balance of male and female teachers (see Appendix II, Table 10):

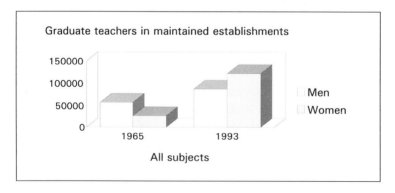

Graduate teachers in maintained establishments

The swing has been especially marked in modern languages:

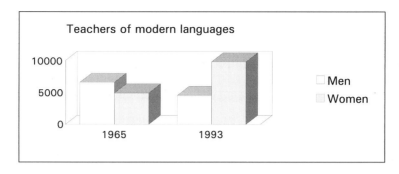

Exactly comparable figures for Scotland are not available but overall there does not seem to have been anything like the same imbalance in the *general* recruitment of men and women to secondary teaching:

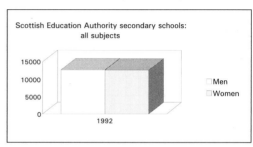

In foreign language class-rooms, however, there is, as in England and Wales, a marked imbalance:

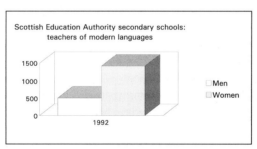

That the male/female teaching imbalance in language classrooms throughout the UK is set to intensify is suggested by the figures of graduates applying to train as teachers:

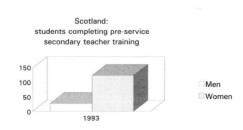

The effect of role models on pupils' career choices has obvious implications for the position of languages post-16, recruitment for university and future supply of teachers (see discussion on p90 and Appendix II).

8

Part three: multilingual Britain

We referred earlier to the House of Lords Select Committee's wish to *sound the death knell of the monoglot tradition of English society*. It is a curious paradox that this 'monoglot tradition' can persist against the reality of a multilingual Britain, whose school children speak, between them, more than 180 different mother tongues, every one of them older than English. It is this reality that is examined in Part three. In Chapter 11 the special position of the two Celtic mother tongues, Welsh and Scottish Gaelic is examined and in Chapter 12, the wider picture of the 'community languages'. Here the question is raised: why cannot multilingualism in Britain be seen as the enrichment it surely is, rather than one more problem for hard-pressed teachers?

Part four: when to start? Early language learning

Chapter 13 gives an account of the Pilot Scheme 'French from Eight', launched, in 1963, by Sir Edward Boyle, paragon of Education Ministers. After a promising start, which attracted world-wide interest, and enthusiastic support from teachers and Local Authority Advisors, the Government lost heart, and, with Sir Edward gone from the scene, the scheme was abruptly abandoned in 1974. The failure of the scheme, despite generous and enlightened financial backing from the Nuffield Foundation, has obvious lessons for present planning. A great number of enterprising local initiatives with early starts have continued and these are described in Chapter 14. In Chapter 15 initiatives in Scotland, with their own important lessons for the future of ETML, are discussed.

Part five: the changing curriculum

The transformation that our discipline has seen during the last thirty years in the way in which the foreign language is presented to learners may be the part of our story least well known outside the language teaching profession. One of our contributors poignantly describes an early lesson, facing

28 pupils, in an empty room, equipped with nothing but a piece of chalk and a cracked blackboard. It is, perhaps, necessary to have lived through the transformation, to appreciate how great have been the changes in materials and methods. Chapters 16 and 17 describe the changes in presentation of the language, in course books and materials from the point of view of the teacher and teacher trainer and as seen by the commercial publisher.

Equally decisive have been changes, during the last thirty years, in the way that languages are tested in schools and this aspect of the transformation is examined in Chapter 18.

Part six: the changing classroom

Part six continues our account of changes in the classroom, beginning with the impact of the increasingly portable and flexible tape recorder (Chapter 19), a marvellous teaching tool whose potential, perhaps, we are even now only learning to exploit fully. Other technological marvels are then examined, such as TV, Video and the Satellite and Information Technology (Chapters 20 and 21). Further aspects of the changing classroom examined in Chapters 22–24 are imaginative ways of maintaining contact with the foreign country, helping to 'make the subject real', strategies for teaching the language 'intensively' and developing pupils' autonomy in learning.

Part seven: who trains the trainers? Towards a new partnership in teacher training

The cascade of innovation examined above has particularly challenged teacher trainers. At initial training level the move to much greater participation of schools offers both challenges and opportunities for a new partnership which are examined in Chapters 25 and 26.

The discussion then moves (Chapter 27) to in-service training and support for teachers, which have changed out of all recognition in the period under review. The role of CILT has been central in giving drive and direction to all forms of INSET. Local Authority Language Advisers (a species unknown before the mid-1960s) have played a capital role here, sadly curtailed by recent developments. But serving teachers have not depended passively on support from outside. Unaided, except for the ready support of CILT throughout the protracted negotiations, they succeeded in unifying their many diverse professional organisations into a single, strong body ALL, the Association for Language Learning, described in Chapter 28. Language teachers now have, for the first time, a single association some 7,000 strong which can represent the profession in national debate with one voice and, through its journals, annual conferences and lively regional activities, support teachers at every stage of their career.

10

Part eight: three decades of research

Part eight reviews research in our discipline over the past thirty years. Francis Mackey (1965) famously likened the history of language teaching to the repeated swinging of a pendulum from one extreme of practice to another. This effect, it was suggested, may be due to the fact that the foreign language teacher's job is always an up-hill struggle and the temptation to look for easier ways is strong. We have seen, during the period under review, some notable instances of the 'pendulum effect' (e.g. in the rush to 'audio-lingual' pattern practice in misnamed 'language laboratories', in the 1960s). Teachers have, perhaps, been too ready to grasp at 'panaceas' which seemed to be offered by successive, but often contradictory, research 'findings'. The role of CILT, through its on-going register of research, consistently well-planned seminars and conferences, and by the flow of well-informed and attractively presented books for teachers, has been a crucial factor in giving teachers balanced reviews of research, and avoiding too violent lurches of the pendulum. Meanwhile, the leading part played by the UK in the research initiatives of the Council of Europe has been a source of pride for all who care for language teaching. These seminal developments are described in Chapter 29.

Part nine: a postscript

Our review of the most eventful thirty years that language teaching has known concludes with a postscript: *A view from the bridge,* by the helmsman who steered the CILT ship through some very stormy seas.

Part ten: Dreams and challenges. CILT looks to the future

As CILT sets out on the next phase of its journey, into the new millennium, the 'Challenges to come' are examined by CILT's present Director, who was also the prime mover behind this volume, without whose encouragement and help the editor's job would have been impossible.

Appendices

In the appendices will be found a calendar of CILT's first thirty years, setting out the main events in its programme, plotted against outstanding landmarks in the progress of education nationally. The statistical tables bring together figures to which some readers may not have easy access. They show the performance of boys and girls in all the main languages, at four points, 1965, 1975, 1985 and 1995 and the numbers of men and women studying languages at post-school level, and applying for teacher training.

Editing this volume has been a great privilege. With a score of distinguished contributors, each an authority in her or his field, some differences of emphasis were unavoidable. The editor has not attempted to smooth out such differences, which are part of the story of thirty eventful years, but has encouraged all contributors to tell their part of the story as they have seen it. Inevitably there are meeting points between the various contributions and wherever possible we have tried to cross-reference these.

The labour of editing has been sweetened by the support and high professionalism of Ute Hitchin and the publications team at CILT.

References

See the bibliography following the Introduction, p30.

Introduction

1966-1996 YEARS

Jean Aitchison (1976) has called human kind 'the articulate mam-mal'. Is it normal for the 'articulate mammal' to be monolingual? Some experts think not. It is common for children to grow up speaking two or three languages, but if they do, it is seldom thanks to schooling.

Whereas up to half the world's children may be fluent in two or more languages without any formal instruction, only a handful of those taught a foreign language in the classroom ever seem to reach a very high level of proficiency in the language regardless of the method of instruction used. (Graeme Kennedy in Oller J W and J C Richards (eds), *Focus on the learner* (Newbury House Inc., 1969))

In the Introduction we ask: what lies behind Graeme Kennedy's scepticism concerning language learning under school conditions?

Language teaching in perspective

Eric Hawkins

A useful exercise, adopted in many teacher training courses, is to attach the trainee teacher to a particular class whose timetable the trainee follows throughout a day, working with the pupils and even doing the homework that they are set. Among the many lessons this offers the trainee teacher is how many *different kinds of learning* pupils must engage with. A typical day for a fourteen-year-old might go like this:

First lesson: *Maths* ('learning' the applications of trigonometry?); then to *English* ('learning by heart' a poem chosen from the school anthology, and going on to 'learn' to distinguish between a poem that is worth memorising and one that is mere pastiche?); then to *History* ('learning' why Parliament voted to execute its king in 1649?) and then to *Physics* ('learning', through experiments, the effects of magnetism? but also 'learning' how school 'confirmation experiments' differ from real discovery by experiment?); in the lunch hour 'learning' to *play the cello* (with its complex mixture of performance skills, careful listening and maturing musical discrimination?); after lunch to the *Woodwork Shop* ('learning' respect for wood and tools and avoidance of short cuts?) And so (perhaps at the end of the day, tired by now and thinking of our tea?) 'learning' *French, German or Spanish.*

So many different meanings of the verb, '*to learn*'! (And we have not mentioned the lessons 'learned' in the other sciences, on the Games Field, in the Art Room, in Religious Education, or, in a difficult but crucial subject now entering the curriculum of a few good schools, Preparation for Parenthood).

A valuable follow-up exercise for the student teacher is to imagine that the English language did not offer this catch-all verb 'to learn'. What verb would be needed to define precisely the mental activity practised in each of these different lessons?

We begin with this reminder, at the outset of our review of thirty years of language teaching, because we want to try to see the subject in perspective. What kind of 'learning' are we talking about? Is mastery of a foreign language simply a useful skill, or is it an essential enrichment of

education? Should it be offered to all pupils or only to those with most aptitude? And, in the light of our answers, how should we teach the subject?

16 It is important to get the questions in the right order. Sometimes, in the
past, debate about how to teach the subject has raced ahead of clear ideas
about its nature. Let us begin at the beginning:

What kind of learning are we talking about?

Language teaching differs from the rest of the curriculum in several
interesting ways:

The model of performance, in the foreign language, is the native speaker

In every other school subject, the model of performance is one who has
followed the same learning route that both pupil and teacher must take. In
our subject the model is the well educated native speaker, whose mastery
neither the learner, nor most teachers, however gifted, can hope to equal.
No other subject in the curriculum invites into the school each year
native-speaking assistants. They offer a unique challenge to the language
teacher's own performance, which teachers of other subjects do not have
to face, but native assistants can be a great advantage too, when properly
prepared for their important role, and imaginatively used.

The rest of the curriculum is not neutral

While other school subjects may be difficult, at least the rest of the weekly timetable is neutral towards them. But, in our subject, from the time the
young learners leave our classroom, until the next language lesson, which
may be several days away, they must survive in the gale of English, reading, writing, discussing in every other lesson, enjoying the playground
witticisms, shouting on the playing field, gossiping on the bus going home,
relaxing in front of the TV. When the next lesson comes, the language
teacher finds the tender seedlings of French, German, etc flattened by the
gale. The teacher revives them and, just when they are restored to where
they were last lesson, the bell goes and the gale of English sweeps in again.
It is a most wasteful process. Experiments have shown that it is possible,
by teaching pupils intensively in 'immersion' courses, stilling the gale of
English, to achieve in a mere two weeks of uninterrupted dialogue in the
foreign language as much progress as is made in six or nine months of
normal school teaching (see Hawkins, 1988).

It should not be forgotten that the 'gale of English' tends, also, to erode the foreign language skills of the teacher. These need to be refreshed constantly by regular access to the teacher's real language laboratory, which is the foreign country. The problems that this poses for language teachers have seldom been faced adequately by those who employ them.

Decline of 'empathy' at puberty

Another unique aspect of our subject, in the present National Curriculum, is that, alone among the 'foundation subjects' it is not introduced until Key Stage 3 (age eleven; twelve in Scotland). Furthermore we choose to introduce it just at the onset of adolescence, when 'empathy', the capacity to share another's feelings, which is so strong in seven/eight-year-olds, gives way to self-consciousness and insecurity. This is especially true of boys. We challenge them to 'go to meet' an unfamiliar language and culture, just when they feel least secure in their own.

Inappropriate comparisons with language skills of foreigners

Yet critics may ask: if language learning is so hard, why are our European neighbours so much better at it than we are? They may cite a study carried out by the European Commission (Young Europeans, 1987). This assessed the **conversational competence** in a foreign language of a weighted sample of 12,000 adults and 5,000 young people aged 15 to 25, across all the member nations of the EC. The UK came in bottom place, jointly with Ireland.

But is the comparison fair? Several factors make the early steps into English easier for our neighbours, than are the first steps into, say, French for our young pupils.

Absence of grammatical gender in English

English is the only language in Europe which has no grammatical gender, and so no 'agreement' of articles, pronouns and adjectives with the gender of their nouns. The verb, in English, too, by comparison with the foreign languages studied in school, is blessedly free from inflexions. These two factors undoubtedly make the first steps into spoken English much easier than our pupils' first engagement with French, German etc.

Of course the English language presents searching difficulties at more advanced stages, in subtleties of usage, enormous vocabulary, and especially unpredictable spelling. But there is no doubt that not only are the early **spoken** steps into English much easier, but the context of the learning, and the motivation to learn, make it a quite different task from that faced by our pupils learning, say, French. The two learning tasks are, indeed so different, that though the growing literature on teaching English as foreign or second language is naturally of interest to foreign language teachers, great caution is called for before applying any of its 'findings' to foreign language learning in our school conditions.

18 'They all speak English'

The fact that the first steps into spoken English are comparatively easy may have helped to make English the world vehicle language. This has been greatly encouraged by the adoption of English as the language of air and sea traffic control, of computer science and technology. English also dominates in much cinema and TV and in the 'youth culture'. So dominant is English that, in many countries, it is studied rather as a 'second' than as a 'foreign' language, eg. in Benelux (Luxembourg came top in the EC Study) and Scandinavia. Outside school, in the pupils' homes, social activities and jobs, a basic level of English is a **sine qua non.** The effect of this on pupils' (and parents') motivation is enormous, especially as learners move through the secondary school and come closer to career choices and challenges.

Increasing recognition of English as the world vehicle language also encourages a short-sighted acceptance of monolingualism. Sadly, even universities, of all places, have, seemed to encourage this complacency (see p78). And, among employers, complacency dies hard.

Which language to choose?

Even if employers and university selectors were more encouraging, however, young English-speaking pupils face another problem, at the outset: which language to choose?

For our eleven-year-olds no one foreign language can ever be 'indicated' as English is indicated for our neighbours. The present distribution of languages in the secondary school owes nothing to planning or to estimates of individual or national needs. It is a position into which we have drifted, and in which we now seem to be locked, by considerations of teacher supply.

In 1995 entries for GCSE in the main languages were as follows. Figures in italics show each language entry as percentage of total ML entry.

(cf Appendix II, Table 2)	Boys	Girls	Total	
Total Modern Language Entries	252,020	295,155	**547,224** *	
Entries for French	163,694	186,323	**350,027** *	*63.9%*
German	60,692	68,694	**129,386**	*23.6%*
Spanish	15,955	24,807	**40,762**	*7.4%*
Italian	1,895	3,715	**5,610**	*1.0%*
Russian	864	1,018	**1,882**	*0.3%*
Other languages	8,920	10,598	**19,557** *	*3.5%*

* Discrepancy in these totals: see note on p383.

But merely increasing the entries for German, Spanish, etc, cannot be the answer. The very pupils to whom we offer the less common languages, in a new, diversified language menu, may turn out, after all, to need some other language as adults. No individual learner's eventual adult language needs can be predicted when the learner is aged eleven or thirteen. It would therefore be logical to plan the primary/secondary language course as an **apprenticeship in language learning**, on which later language learning programmes could build.

The apprenticeship would begin at primary level with an introduction to 'awareness of language', a progressive 'education of the ear' and an opening of young minds to the adventure of learning a foreign language. At secondary level, awareness of language would become a 'bridging subject' drawing together a team of teachers 'across the curriculum' to continue the school apprenticeship in learning how to learn language. (This topic is further developed in Chapter 10).

In sixth forms, colleges and universities, as learners' adult language interests and needs begin to emerge, covering a range of languages that no secondary school could possibly provide for its eleven-year-old learners, it would then be realistic to expect provision to be made for a much wider variety of languages than are currently on offer, exploiting intensive learning strategies.

Meanwhile we should be wary of facile comparisons with countries where the clear advantage of a knowledge of English, for nearly all pupils, can be safely predicted, from the earliest age, with all that means for motivation in the classroom and in the home and job.

Spoken or written language?

One development in our subject during the last thirty years which has not helped some learners has been the swing from study, and examination, almost exclusively of the written language, to far greater concentration on listening/speaking. It was Edison's invention, in 1878, of the wax cylinder phonograph on which speech could be recorded and played back, that encouraged Henry Sweet to argue (Sweet, 1899) for a new emphasis on the spoken form of the foreign language, which he called 'the living philology'. He argued, however, that such an approach would require that the learners be given a serious apprenticeship in 'listening' and he proposed that **20** this must be based on the new science of phonetics. His argument, magisterially supported by such giants as Otto Jespersen, had some initial success. However, teachers qualified to carry on such experiments failed to emerge from the universities, and the dream shared by Sweet and Otto Jespersen, of using phonetic script to help pupils to be better **listeners**, faded.

The marked swing to the spoken language that we have seen in the past thirty years was encouraged by the new accessibility of tape recorder and radio, bringing the native-speaking voice into classrooms in ways previously undreamt of. However there has been little attempt to offer young learners that careful apprenticeship in listening that Sweet envisaged, and there is growing evidence that the slower learners, and especially adolescent boys, have not been helped by this development.

For many adolescents oral performance in a strange idiom in front of classmates does not come easily. Also listening to a foreign language on a tape (or on the telephone) poses special problems. There are no helpful visual signals. It is not only adolescents who are inhibited. Even younger pupils, not shy about performing in public, may find listening to recordings difficult. A striking finding in the Burstall study of French in the primary school (Burstall, 1974) was the frequency of the complaint from the young learners: 'we detest the tape recorder!' They had not been given what Peter MacCarthy called the essential preparatory 'education of the ear' (MacCarthy, 1978).

Emphasis on the spoken language has also had another effect which has been too little discussed. The true 'language laboratory' of the spoken language must always be the foreign country and a serious attack on the spoken language inevitably requires that the language learner must have easy and frequent access to the laboratory where the spoken language lives. The pupil whose home circumstance makes it difficult to get into the foreign country is seriously disadvantaged. Before 1965, when only the written language was tested, learners from modest home backgrounds could readily find the necessary 'immersion' experience in a good library. With the swing to the spoken language the tendency, first noted in Schools Council Working Paper no 28 (SC, 1970), for our subject to become a 'middle class preserve', has accelerated.

Why a foreign language for all?

The vocational argument – national need for language skills

For the UK as a trading nation, competence in foreign languages will be of crucial importance in a rapidly changing and increasingly competitive world (National Curriculum Working Group, 1990, para. 3.6). The vocational argument for our subject at some level in the curriculum is the one most often heard. It was made 100 years ago by the Royal Society of Arts Journal in almost identical terms (see p34). Exactly the same argument has been voiced in the USA. A Commission on Foreign Language and International Studies in 1978 concluded that *American incompetence in foreign language learning was threatening the country's national security and economic development.*

The vocational arguments are strong and amply justify giving our subject a central place in the curriculum for the majority of pupils. But do they justify making the foreign language obligatory for all our pupils? Not all vocations require a foreign language skill. And how honest is it for the teacher of slow-learning pupils, most of whom will work at manual or semi-skilled jobs, to pretend that French or German or Spanish will be *necessary for employment?* And what do we say to school leavers who face the almost certain prospect of unemployment?

And if we do advance the vocational argument, which particular language do we suggest that any given pupil will need? As we recalled above, we can never predict, when a pupil is 11+, which particular language he or she is going to need.

Obviously Britain is going to need linguists in great quantity and variety, especially among its abler young people. In the new millennium it seems certain that a new definition of 'literacy' will be needed, no longer a basic literacy in purely national terms but *a fundamental literacy including mastery of another language.* But since no individual's eventual adult language needs will be identifiable until he or she reaches at least the post 16+ stage, this implies a thoroughgoing reappraisal of the objectives of the secondary school course and of subsequent programmes which build upon it in sixth form, college and university (see pp 19 and 45).

The justification of making the foreign language part of the curriculum **for all** in the secondary school, however, does not depend on vocational arguments. The educational case for a foreign language for all is much stronger and deeper.

The educational arguments

One way to assess the contribution of foreign languages to children's general development ('education' as opposed to 'instruction') is to imagine what a school without any foreign language classes would look (and sound) like. To begin with, there would be no teachers on the staff who, as a normal part of their training, had spent a year in a foreign country, as nearly all language teachers now do. They are unique in the staffroom not only in breaking out of the traditional teacher's somewhat blinkered route from school to college and back to school, but, having braved a year abroad, they are able to report back on the ways in which education abroad is governed and financed, how pupils are taught and examined, the role of parents, etc.

Without foreign languages, school windows and doors would be less open to Europe, with few exchanges bringing learners from overseas back to our classrooms and no incentive to test out our own hard-won language skills, exploring neighbouring lands and cultures.

Most importantly, we would lose a subject which encourages its learners to 'go to meet' difference of language and culture with confidence; its essential lesson is that 'difference' is interesting and worth exploring, not to be feared, or, in self-defence, mocked. It therefore challenges prejudice head on.

The danger of failing to challenge pupils to break out of the monolingual straitjacket was wittily expressed by the eminent American linguist Yuen Ren Chao (1968):

> *Monolingual persons take language so much for granted that they often forget its arbitrary nature and cannot distinguish words from things . . . Persons unused to foreign languages tend to find something perverse in the way foreigners talk. Even Oliver Goldsmith could not get over the perversity of the French, who would call a cabbage a 'shoe' instead of calling a cabbage 'cabbage'. The story is told of an English woman who always wondered why the French call water 'de l'eau', the Italians 'dell'acqua' and the Germans 'das Wasser'. Only we English people, she said, call it properly 'water'. We not only call it water, **but it is water!**

Of course, the foreign language lesson is not automatically mind-broadening. Recent research (Byram, 1989) shows that it is possible for three years' teaching based largely on tourist transactions to have the effect merely of reinforcing some pupils' cultural stereotypes. But when the teaching combines language awareness, cultural awareness and language learning sensitively, it can make an apprenticeship of a kind that our children surely need, especially, in our tense urban areas and housing estates, and wherever prejudice divides communities.

A case history

The relevance of this may be illustrated by asking what can our subject offer to pupils (say) in present-day Belfast? For an adolescent on the protestant side brought up to equate Rome and 'catholic' with all that is hateful, the journey into the Spanish language and poetry may put into perspective, as no other study can, the half-truths of home or pulpit or housing-estate gossip. When the pupil travels abroad to try out the marvellous new linguistic tool the school has given him or her, language learning becomes truly liberating. The experience of a young protestant student of Spanish in the Liverpool of the 1930s, then riven as Belfast is today, by sectarian bigotry, may be relevant. For him the journey to meet the poetry of the wise and gentle Augustinian Fray Luis de León offered a different picture of catholicism from that peddled by the rival marchers. Fray Luis, a devout catholic, professor at Salamanca and one of Europe's foremost Latinists, himself spent five years in Valladolid prison accused by the Inquisition of 'novedades' (innovations). He had illegally translated the 'Song of Songs' out of the Latin into Spanish (he did it as a kindness for his cousin whose Latin was not strong and who wanted to read the songs of David with her fellow nuns in the convent). He was betrayed by a graduate student who found the paper in his desk. During his five years in a prison cell he scratched on its wall, it is said, the famous poem beginning: *Aquí la envidia y la mentira me tuvieron encerrado* (*Here envy and lies held me prisoner*). When Fray Luis was at last prized from the grip of the Holy Office by his friends, he resumed his lectures in Salamanca. On the first day, in front of a crowd who expected fireworks, he began quietly with the customary *decíamos ayer* (*as we were saying last time*). The story is probably apocryphal but it tells something of Fray Luis's reputation and the gentle rebuke has carried down the years more penetratingly than any angry outburst. His classroom is still preserved in the Old Schools building at Salamanca, as it was in his time, next to that of his friend Salinas, professor of music and organist at the cathedral, for whom he wrote one of his loveliest odes.

The journey to meet the integrity of the gentle Fray Luis may be, for a Belfast protestant, or any other schoolboy, not a bad way out of the prison of envy and lies of the graffiti-daubed housing estate.

For the same pupil to go on to point his camera at the marvels of architecture left behind by the Arabs in Andalucía and to see what destruction those of Fray Luis's faith did to the delicate jewels they inherited, may be a further step on the liberating journey. Visiting Seville, for example, he could contrast the loveliness of the moorish Giralda with the mass of the gothic cathedral sprawling against it, and stepping inside the cloister flanking the giralda, read in tiles on the wall the critical comment made by the devout but puzzled Cervantes, on first seeing the cathedral altar, wondrously ornamented with solid gold raped from the Indies: *¡Voto a Dios, que me espanta esta grandeza! (God! This magnificence frightens me!).*

Our protestant student's catholic contemporaries who pursue their German studies into the sixth form might make an equally 'empathic' voyage away from parochialism, when they take their bicycles and seek out one of the protestant churches of North Germany where Johann Sebastian Bach, or one of his gifted sons, sang and improvised on the organ.

24

This is not to make exaggerated claims for the foreign language as education. Of course, other subjects can be liberating. History and Geography, like the sciences, well taught, can challenge parochialism and offer that apprenticeship in *judgement* that is the beginning of wisdom, as opposed to mere cleverness. A good apprenticeship in judgement is through learning to make apt *comparisons* based on careful observation of the evidence. A feature of the apprenticeship in judgement learnt by able pupils in the foreign language classroom is that the pupil does not have to take the teacher's or textbook's word for it. The foreign language programme, properly planned, says, in effect, to the adolescent: the language skills we are now honing in class are *in preparation for your own reading and your study abroad*. They are to be used to ask hard questions: exactly how does the way of life (the newspapers, the school system, local government?) in the foreign speech community compare with what you know at home? And how accurate, from your observation, is the picture that your textbooks offer you? Can other arts subjects claim as much?

But, it may be objected, you are speaking only of able students who will read with confidence and curiosity, and who are fortunate enough to enjoy well-planned study visits abroad. What about the majority of pupils, the 60% perhaps of each age group who throughout the 1970s and 1980s dropped their foreign language at age fourteen, when 'choice' in the curriculum allowed it? What educational argument justifies making the subject obligatory for them?

The foreign language for the slower learner

Educational considerations strongly support the National Curriculum policy of making the foreign language a foundation subject for all throughout their school course.

i.   First, even the slower learner can, and should, be given the chance to escape from Ren Chao's 'magical view of language' and to see the mother tongue afresh from outside.

ii. Secondly, even the early stages of the foreign language course, if planned in cooperation with English, can do much to awaken 'language awareness' and curiosity about how language works, by 'contrastive study' of language patterns and grammar. This can mean a great deal for the whole school learning experience. It can also lay good foundations for a healthy and confident curiosity about language which will go with the learner throughout adult life, and be especially important within the family, in preparation for the linguistic challenges of parenthood.

iii. Thirdly, the foreign language offers a valuable opportunity for careful *listening*, and especially in that matching of sounds to visual symbols which can demystify problems of spelling.

iv. Finally, and perhaps most usefully, for slower learners, the early stages of the adventure into the foreign language give an opportunity for the teacher to revise many elementary concepts and offer a new experience of word play, Jerome Bruner's *operation of thought processes on linguistic representations* but in a new medium. In the foreign language classroom the slower learner may 'recategorise' areas of experience that primary schooling has left imprecise. Those who work with slower learners know how many concepts, that quicker learners take for granted, remain undefined and uncertain for some children as they approach the challenges of the secondary curriculum. Studying a foreign language enables early concept formation to be revisited, but with all learners starting again, if not on equal terms, at least without embarrassment. Equally useful is the chance the pupil gets to appreciate how language works; how sentences are constructed and, in quite basic ways, how particular meanings are conveyed, for example, by prepositions or tenses. Simple 'contrastive' study of mother tongue and the newly met idiom (in sensitively planned 'awareness of language' discussions) has helped many slower learners to explore their mother tongue with new curiosity and confidence. As a teacher-educator at Haifa University in Israel reports:

> *I have found that . . . reading skills, often very poor in the native language, can also be taught and developed via the foreign language. These youngsters, at the sensitive age of 15–17, reject studies of so basic a nature in their own language (interpreted by them as 'childish' and 'old hat'). Yet they exhibit quite a degree of receptivity when the vehicle is new, neutral and recognised as a 'status' subject of study'.* (personal communication)

The contribution of the foreign language to the education of the slower learner is examined further in Chapter 8 by a teacher who has devoted skill and commitment to children with special educational needs. She brings out one lesson that may have resonance for language teachers everywhere, namely how much she has learned from cooperation with non-linguist teachers of SEN children. As the discussion of 'awareness of language' (Chapter 10) suggests, foreign language teachers and their colleagues in other disciplines may have tended too often to retreat into their own sealed-off classrooms, expecting their pupils to make some synthesis out of the discordant messages that they receive about subjects like language, which run through the whole curriculum.

So how should the foreign language be taught?

That British pupils **can** master foreign languages is not in doubt. Anybody who has attended the Young Linguist of the Year Festivals at Warwick University must have been impressed by the enthusiasm and high standard of language skills displayed (see p295). The Festivals, which regularly used to attract up to 8,000 young linguists from all parts of the country, are, sadly, in abeyance, for financial reasons, but they showed that our pupils **can** achieve high standards. Why are comparatively few (especially boys) doing so? Is it the fault of our teaching methods?

Francis Mackey (1965) famously likened the endless debate about language teaching down the ages to the swinging of a pendulum between two extremes of practice, from the grind through grammar at one extreme to immersion in the living language at the other. Adopting Carl Dodson's terms for these two kinds of learning (Dodson 1978) we might call one extreme 'medium orientated' activities, in which the learner's attention is directed towards 'form' (grammatical structure, accuracy of pronunciation, spelling etc.) and the other extreme 'message orientated' activities, where the learner concentrates on using the language with real 'intention to mean' (or understanding the meaning). Dodson stresses, from his observation in Welsh bilingual schools, that immersion alone, without preparation, can be counter-productive. The most effective learning involves a constant interaction between the two kinds of language activity.

One period in the history of language teaching when the need to exploit these two 'levels' of learning was well understood was in Tudor Times. The charters of the Tudor Grammar Schools insisted that both levels be exploited. The charter of Oundle School (1556) was typical in insisting that *boys use only Latin when speaking to each other, as well in the school as coming and going to and from the same.*

Such 'level two' use of Latin became increasingly difficult as the vocational role of Latin outside school declined (Newton was the last British scientist to issue his magnum opus in Latin in 1687). Only 'level one' Latin, 'grammar-translation', continued to be practised. When modern languages began to enter school curricula, in the mid 19th century, insecure teachers of French and German, in self-defence, tended to imitate their more established Latin colleagues and rely solely on 'grammar-translation'.

The need for 'immersion' learning did not disappear, but pupils wishing to experience it found that they had to go abroad. The fact that not all pupils could study abroad was not seen as a problem, since only a small minority of secondary age pupils were offered a foreign language anyway.

These tended to come from more affluent and encouraging homes. Not surprisingly our subject became more and more a middle class prerogative (see evidence in Schools Council Working Paper No 28 1970, and NFER evaluation of the Pilot Scheme, Burstall, 1970).

The comprehensive school brought many challenges to which teachers responded with great resilience. The story is told in Part two. Clear thinking about new challenges was not made any easier by two theoretical debates among psycholinguists which sadly confused teacher trainers.

Confusing debates about language teaching

Language as habit structure?

One of these debates was raging at the time CILT opened its doors in 1966. It engaged proponents and opponents of the view that language learning is acquiring a hierarchy of habits, by repetitive 'pattern practice'. This debate, coinciding with the arrival of tape recorders (and mis-named 'language laboratories') in schools is discussed authoritatively in Chapter 19. We need not pursue it further here, except to note that the rush to invest large sums in new technology, only to have its usefulness questioned, had the effect of shaking confidence both among teachers and among administrators who were asked to find the resources.

Imitate the child?

The second debate is almost as old as foreign language teaching itself and its echoes still reverberate in classrooms. It springs from the fact that all our pupils have learned one language, the mother tongue, simply by using it, without having deliberately to attend to grammar rules. This has prompted the question, by successive 'reformers': why cannot the foreign language be acquired effortlessly, simply by use, in the same way? Why bother with deliberate learning of grammar?

In fact, the extent to which the mother tongue is absorbed without help, simply by use, has been overstated. Children differ widely in their mastery of the mother tongue at the age of 11, especially in mastery of the written language, and the differences correlate closely with the opportunity for dialogue with an interested adult (what the Americans call 'investment of adult time') that each child has enjoyed in the early years (see discussion of research evidence in Chapter 10). This has not prevented foreign language reformers, down the ages, ever hopefully asking: why not imitate the child?

One eloquent advocate of 'imitate the child' was François Gouin, the French philosopher whose plea for the 'natural method' (*L'art d'enseigner*, 1880) achieved brief notoriety, with his claim that learning a foreign language could be *as natural as flying is to a bird.*

Henry Sweet answered Gouin in a magisterial chapter of *The practical study of languages* (1899):

> *The fundamental objection . . . to the Natural Method is that it puts the adult into the position of an infant, which he is no longer capable of utilising, and at the same time does not allow him to make use of his own special advantages.*

28

Two different kinds of language learning

One crucial difference between acquiring L1 and mastering L2 can be grasped by listening carefully to a baby getting the mother tongue and to the adolescent learner in class. The baby's getting its early vocabulary is motivated by urgent human needs (*more pudding! I want mummy!*) and (especially if fortunate to be in an 'encouraging' home) by curiosity about how the world works. To take an example, learning to tell the time is motivated partly by learning at the same time how the passage of time is divided into hours, minutes and seconds. The excitement of such a discovery, once made, cannot be repeated. Learning to 'translate' the clock numbers into the foreign language is not to repeat the excitement of the original discovery. Some other motivation must be found. The imaginative teacher can motivate this different learning, but the two kinds of learning should not be confused.

The Prague linguist, Ivan Poldauf, has expressed this important difference in a pioneering paper (1972) on 'Awareness of Language'. He argued that during the course of normal primary education, children become aware of the mother tongue as a language

> *. . . awareness is the ability, no matter how conscious, to view a language objectively, that is, as a phenomenon . . . When teaching a foreign language to a child before such an awareness of the mother tongue has been formed, the school may attempt a distant simulation of bilingualism. After it has been formed, such a procedure is not only a waste of time but runs more and more against the grain of the learner.*

The LAD is self-sufficient; who needs a LASS?

'Imitate the child' took on a new dimension in the 1960s with the intervention of the formidable Noam Chomsky. He argued (Chomsky, 1959) that the extraordinary intellectual achievement of the baby in acquiring the mother tongue so effortlessly proved that the infant must be born with a set of expectations about language, a 'grammar searching mechanism', commonly known now as the LAD or 'Language Acquisition Device'.

The notion of the innate Language Acquisition Device is now generally accepted by linguists. What psychologists question, however, is the claim that **the LAD is self-sufficient**. Jerome Bruner, who held the chairs of psychology at both Harvard and Oxford, argued (*Child's talk*, 1983) that the LAD needs to be supplemented by a LASS (Language Acquisition Support System) in the family and society, if the child is to go beyond 'communicative competence' and learn 'analytic competence', the mastery of language that the school process will require (see discussion of 'awareness of language', Chapter 10).

'Acquisition' and 'learning'

The Chomsky/Bruner debate, though confined to acquisition of the mother tongue, confused discussion of foreign language learning by suggesting that since the (supposedly self-sufficient) LAD can acquire the mother tongue without any *explicit or conscious* learning of grammar, the foreign language should be acquired in similar fashion and that between instinctive 'acquisition' and conscious 'learning', there is no 'interface' (Krashen, 1981).

This 'no-interface' thesis has now been abandoned by most applied linguists (see Terrell, 1991; AILA Review 11, 1994). The consensus view now is that the two 'levels' of learning interact and enrich each other and both have a proper role in the apprenticeship.

This consensus was succinctly expressed in the Final Report of the National Curriculum Working Group (1990, p54):

> . . . *learners make progress in a second language by continually extending their repertoire of chunks of language, but it is knowledge of the underlying rules which enables them to adapt these chunks to cope with the many and various situations in which they need to use them.*

How does the teacher best help pupils to master these 'adaptive' grammar rules? This is the crucial challenge, for it is at this stage of mastering the rules that most learners fail, often after quite a promising start, when all they had to do was build a repertoire of ready-made chunks of language requiring little 'adaptation'.

Learners differ considerably at this crucial stage. Much depends on their maturity and aptitude. One has seen very able students of English in a Chinese university, isolated by the 'cultural revolution' from contact with native speakers, and brought up on a regime of plodding translation of arid texts about Chairman Mao, acquiring astonishing command of English, especially of its written form, by sheer determination to suspend disbelief.

Need for a balance of 'level one' and 'level two' learning

For the average learner, however, the best way to become fluent in applying the 'adaptive' rules to one's stock of authentic 'chunks' of the language, learned by heart, is by engaging in active use of the language, **for purposes that matter to the user.** This is what makes the new language 'stick'. Most English adults who can speak a foreign language fluently do so because they were fortunate enough to go abroad and use the language for their own individual purposes. Such opportunities have been greatly expanded, thanks to the valuable work of the Central Bureau (CBEVE) (see Appendix III), but they remain the prerogative of a privileged minority. Too many pupils, from less encouraging or less fortunate homes, are still denied such 'level two' language learning experience. They are given free access to the school science laboratories, regardless of home circumstance, but study in the real foreign language 'laboratory', which is the foreign country, is denied them. It is as if we offered our young swimmers exercises on the bank, but denied them the chance to get into the water.

In Chapter 23 we examine a variety of ways in which teachers are meeting this challenge of giving **all** pupils access to 'intensive immersion' sessions. At their best, these initiatives are dovetailed into the normal school programme. They aim to encourage pupils to use the language for their own individual purposes, in an atmosphere where the 'gale of English' is temporarily stilled.

Generous provision of such real 'swimming', supplementing mere 'exercises on the bank', (necessary as these are) will be an acid test of society's concern for equality of opportunity in foreign language learning.

References

AILA Review, *'Consciousness in Second Language Learning'* (Amsterdam: Association de Linguistique Appliquée, 1994)

Board of Education Circular no 797, *Modern languages* (HMSO, 1912)

Board of Education Pamphlet no 47, *Position of French in grant-aided secondary schools* (HMSO, 1926)

Cambridge University Reporter, 17.1.79, 335/109: 223–6 (Cambridge University, 1979)

British Overseas Trade Board, *Report of the study group: 'foreign languages for overseas trade'* (BOTB, 1979)

Bruner J S, *Child's talk* (OUP, 1983)

Bullock A (Lord Bullock, Chairman), *A language for life.* Report of Committee appointed by Secretary of State for Education and Science (HMSO, 1975)

Burstall C et al, *Primary French in the balance* (NFER, 1974)

Byram M, *Cultural studies in foreign language education* (Clevedon: Multicultural Matters, 1989)

Clarendon Commission, *Report of Royal Commission on the (Nine) Public Schools* (1864)

Coleman J A, *Studying languages: a survey of British and European students* (CILT, 1996)

Comenius J A, *The great didactic.* See Keatinge M W (translator), *The great didactic of John Amos Comenius, 1630.* (First edition, 1896; reissued Russell and Russell, 1910)

Comenius J A, *Orbis sensualium pictus.* Facsimile edition of first English edition of 1659 (OUP, 1968)

Crystal D, *The Cambridge encyclopedia of language* (CUP, 1987)

Donmall B G (ed), *Language awareness.* NCLE Papers and Reports 6 (CILT, 1985)

Gouin F, *L'art d'enseigner. The art of teaching and studying languages* (1880; issued in English translation: Philip, 1994)

Green P S, *The language laboratory in school: performance and prediction: the York study* (Edinburgh: Oliver and Boyd, 1975)

Hawkins E W, *Modern Languages in the curriculum* (Revised edition, CUP, 1987)

Hawkins E W (ed), *Intensive language teaching and learning* (CILT, 1988)

House of Lords. Session 1989–90, *European schools and language learning in United Kingdom schools.* 13th Report, Select Committee on the European Communities (HMSO, 1990)

IAHM (Incorporated Association of Headmasters), *Modern languages in the grammar school* (Nuffield Foundation, 1963; revised 1966)

Krashen S, *Second language acquisition and second language learning* (Pergamon Press, 1981)

Leathes S (Chairman), *Modern studies.* Report to the Prime Minister of Committee on the Position of Modern Languages in the Educational System of Great Britain (HMSO, 1918)

Lenneberg E H, *Biological foundations of language* (USA: J Wiley, 1967)

Locke J, *Some thoughts concerning education* (T Basset, 1690)

Luc C, 'Des représentations aux productions en langue étrangère' in *Langues vivantes et français à l'école, REPERES* no 6 (Paris: INRP, 1992)

Luc C and D Bailly, *Approche d'une langue étrangère à l'école,* vols 1 and 2 (Paris: INRP, 1992)

MacCarthy P, *The teaching of pronunciation* (CUP, 1978)

Mackey W F, *Language teaching analysis* (Longman, 1965)

Mattingley I G, 'Awareness of language' in Kavanagh J F and I G Mattingley, *Language by ear and eye* (USA, Cambridge, Mass.: MIT Press, 1972)

N C Modern Foreign Languages Working Group, *Modern Foreign Languages for ages eleven to sixteen.* Proposals of the Secretary of State for Education and Science (London: DES, 1990)

Needham J (ed), *The teacher of nations* (CUP, 1942)

Plowden B (Lady Plowden) (Chair), *Children and their primary schools.* Report of the Central Advisory Council for Education. 2 vols (HMSO, 1967)

Poldauf I, 'Language awareness' in *Language Awareness,* vol 4:1 (Multilingual Matters, 1995)

Powell R, *Boys, Girls and languages in school* (CILT, 1986)

Royal Society of Arts, *Journal* (1879)

Schools Council, Working Paper no 28, *New patterns in sixth form modern language studies* (Evans/Methuen Educational, 1970)

Sweet H, *The practical study of languages* (1899, re-issued OUP 1964)
Terrell T D, 'The Role of grammar in a communicative approach' in *The modern language journal,* 75, 1 (USA: 1991)

32

Part

one

The national need
for languages

1966-1996 YEARS

Over a hundred years ago, in the first edition of its *Journal* (1879), the Royal Society of Arts warned:

Beyond all doubt we suffer in competition abroad from ignorance of foreign languages by our merchants, agents, clerks and mechanics.

The challenge was repeated in the centenary issue of the RSA *Journal,* in 1979. It is this challenge that is addressed in Part one.

It is, of course, a challenge faced by any trading nation, but Britain's language needs are different from those of our trading partners/competitors. They can all safely predict which foreign language their children are going to need as adults. It is English, the world vehicle language. Their curriculum planning (and teacher training) can proceed on this assumption. We can make no such prediction. There is no way of telling, when our pupils are aged eleven, which of a dozen languages they will eventually 'need' as adults. Most adult language students nowadays, whether at university or in further education, find that the language begun at school is not the one they wish or need to pursue.

The logical answer would be to plan the secondary course as an apprenticeship in 'learning how to learn language'. The idea was broached, but not pursued, by the National Curriculum Working Group in its *Final report* (1990):

One of the most valuable general skills which the study of a modern foreign language can impart is the enhanced ability to learn other languages at a later stage. To be fully effective, however, this needs to be a conscious objective of the course. (para 5.21)

Such a planned apprenticeship in language learning would, of course, involve serious study of more than one language (including, as Nigel Reeves suggests on p45, a non-European language). Choice of language(s) and of teaching method would be based on suitability as apprenticeship, to be built on at the post-16 stage, using intensive, immersion techniques.

1

Does Britain need linguists?

Nigel Reeves

UK plc

In business and political circles the British economy is often referred to as 'UK plc'. It is a metaphor which suggests that the UK economy operates in a comparable way to a single corporation with all its usual functions of management – a Board of Directors (the Government?), executive managers (UK companies), logistics (the transport infrastructure), training department (educational establishments) and shareholders (taxpayers), just to name a few of the possible parallels consciously or unconsciously implied.

If the metaphor holds true, we could expect the Board to instruct management to carry out periodical reviews of performance, particularly at this time when we have been members of the European Economic Community for just over twenty years and face the imminent possibility of a Single European currency (no later than 1999 according to the Maastricht Treaty), followed by European Political Union. What might such a review look like in 1996?

Using a modification of the well-known SWOT analysis technique (Strengths, Weaknesses, Opportunities and Threats), and starting with **Opportunities,** the Single European Market (SEM) of January 1993 would be seen as the dominant factor in the immediate past, the present and the foreseeable future, corresponding to the UK's entry into the EEC in 1973 when concern about the UK's foreign language capability began to be expressed. The SEM offers a market of 340 millions, characterised by mobility of goods and services, mobility of people and, most importantly, mobility of capital, for it is this last freedom that drives economic integration most powerfully. It is a market larger than the USA or Japan, embracing, however, fifteen countries and, unlike those competitors, possessing many currencies, not one, and twelve languages, not one mother tongue as in Japan or one vastly predominant mother tongue, also the second language, within a common consumer culture as in the USA.

The UK's main **Strengths** in relation to this opportunity are, as recent major investors in the UK such as Siemens and BMW have said, low labour costs, flexibility of labour, a highly developed capital market – and of course generous incentives. And for investors from outside the EU, such as Japan and the USA, the possession of English, the international trading language, has been an added and important attraction.

36

But the review would also point to **Weaknesses.** Overall a modest rate of productivity improvement and a low Gross Domestic Product – only half that of Germany, barely more than half of West Germany alone – which inhibits the level of investment in the transport and educational infrastructure, as an ageing population with increasing medical expectations, together with a persistent high level of structural unemployment, make their demands on tax revenue. Our review would also have to point to the consequences of the low level of per capita investment in education relative to our wealthier European neighbours, with consequences which included a relative dearth of skilled workers – only 18% of UK's workforce is educated to craft levels, compared with 33% in France, 38% in the Netherlands and 56% in Germany – and lack of people at all levels with adequate language and intercultural skills.

The review would refer to a whole series of reports, surveys and analyses from the mid-1970s to today, assessing the need and comparing the supply of linguistically qualified people, including the pioneering York Report of 1974, the RSA/Betro Report of 1979, the BOTB Report on Languages for Overseas Trade also of 1979, the case studies by Reeves and Liston in 1984, the surveys of foreign language use and need in UK and European industries directed and compiled by Stephen Hagen and, most recently, Colin and Sue Wright's survey of 800 companies in the West Midlands. These reports, spanning some twenty years, reach two recurring conclusions: that there is a correlation between the employment of linguistically qualified personnel and exporting success, and the converse, namely that an absence of linguistic expertise can result in lost business.

Yet awareness in industry of this state of affairs remains patchy. Wright and Wright (1994), for example, were unable to identify a single metal goods manufacturer in the West Midlands that even produced export documentation in the language of the customer – and this industrial branch remains the very backbone of the West Midlands regional economy. And in the autumn of 1995 a survey reported in *Language Matters* found that 74% of calls in French, German and Italian to the UK's top 100 exporting companies were abandoned.

Furthermore, there is a common mismatch between the languages that can be offered within companies and which languages are needed, the overwhelming dominance of French that derives from school provision proving to be inappropriate (Hagen, 1988: xxiif; Wright and Wright, 1994: 8). And most astounding or perhaps symptomatic, the renowned management consultancy company that organised the West Midlands survey even modified Wright and Wright's original questions on languages so that they investigated the capability of individuals to operate in a foreign language, moving away from the intended thrust which was to see whether companies had company-wide foreign language communication policies and thus understood the role of efficient communication at the strategic level (Wright and Wright, 1994: 3f). The management consultancy company had clearly not.

Finally, coming to **Threats,** we might discern the possibility of the UK's marginalisation in European economic development as a non-member of the Single Currency core group, and the potential vulnerability of sterling to speculation when outside the core. This peripheral situation, which could leave scope only for reactive rather than proactive steps on the part of the Government, would exacerbate the linguistic and cultural isolation that the surveys of the past twenty years have illuminated. It is, however, deeply ironical that it is in part precisely the possession of English as a *lingua franca* that fosters the feeling in the UK that foreign languages are not necessary, while blinding us to the profound cultural gaps between ourselves and continental Europe which express themselves not only in the marketplace but more significantly still in political structures and social attitudes. But successful economic integration will depend in the future critically on political partnership. That much is certain from Maastricht. And successful political partnership requires the kind of broadly based cultural insight and empathy that derives from language knowledge rooted firmly in the curriculum at all educational levels.

Inducing change: new curricula, assessment and examinations

Certainly, it is at the level of the curriculum that most attempts have been made since the end of the 1970s to give foreign language learning greater prominence in British education. Prompted by the series of reports and surveys mentioned above, a number of initiatives have been undertaken that have sought to remedy the deficiencies identified in UK plc's foreign language communication systems.

Already in 1979 it was noted that disproportionately few boys continued with languages to the age of sixteen and beyond, resulting, it was felt, in a lack of UK scientists and technologists – and in those days managers – having any command of the languages of our fellow EC member states. To encourage the sixth form study of languages based on pupils' future vocational/professional needs and/or on the study of other school subjects, especially science subjects, the London Chamber of Commerce and Industry Examinations Board (LCCIEB) developed, in conjunction with the DTI and initially Lloyds Bank, the Foreign Languages at Work Scheme (FLAW).

FLAW grew slowly at first, its inception coinciding with severe unrest among teachers concerning the Conservative Government's schools policy. FLAW flourished, however, in the later 1980s and was pioneering in its concept of validating and verifying learner-based, teacher-devised language curricula created within an agreed framework. It has since been adopted in an elaborated form by the Hong Kong Government as the basis for its Vocational English Programme. It also served as one of the models for the concept of National Vocational Qualifications (NVQs).

A later, highly innovative examination scheme – as opposed to a validation/verification model – was the Institute of Linguists' Examinations in Languages for International Communication (ELIC) Scheme, which takes as its assessment basis the cross-linguistic information transfer and communication chains of real-world interaction, assessing candidates against the outcomes they achieve in simulation tests. Both FLAW and ELIC demonstrate a criterion-referenced approach in contrast to the prevalent norm-based approach of the GCE Boards of the time.

We can also have little doubt that awareness of the importance of foreign languages for the UK economy played a major role in persuading government that the National Curriculum should require all pupils to study at least one foreign language to the age of sixteen, the deficiency that FLAW had tried to address in the early days.

However, the most far-reaching development consequent upon the reports has undoubtedly been the creation of a Languages Lead Body, serviced by CILT, to match the other industrial Lead Bodies established at the close of the 1980s. The Business and Technology Education Council (BTEC), the Royal Society of Arts (RSA) as well as the LCCIEB and the Institute of Linguists had long offered interesting vocationally-based language examinations. A particular strength was in the area of bilingual secretarial examinations, for which the RSA was especially renowned. One of the intentions of the Lead Body was to establish proficiency levels or standards against which this range of qualifications could be matched. By means of a detailed description of generic communication tasks, split into the four language skills and ranked in complexity and demand at five proficiency levels, the Lead Body has established standards of achievement (the National Language Standards) for jobs requiring basic foreign language capability through to what should be expected of the professional translator and interpreter. The NVQs in languages now offered by City and Guilds, LCCIEB, the RSA and the Institute of Linguists follow the craft model. They are workplace-based and try as closely as possible, or feasible, to relate assessment to the performance of the real workplace foreign language communication tasks expected of the candidate. The wider importance of the Languages NVQs lies in three features – firstly the establishment of foreign language capability as a vocational and professional achievement to be ranked and measured alongside traditionally recognised vocational and professional skills. Secondly, the Standards provide the first detailed and comprehensive generic description of language proficiency in the context of work. And thirdly they relate the assessment of language proficiency firmly to real-world performance.

At the same time the European examinations board consortium, led by the Cambridge Syndicate, the Association of Language Testers in Europe (ALTE), has set up a similar calibration of existing European language examinations through definitions of proficiency levels and outcome-based profiling that derives from sets of 'can-do' statements.

Inducing change: new teaching and learning provision

Prior even to the publication of the York Report of 1974 a number of universities, specifically the technological universities Aston, Bradford, Loughborough, Salford and Surrey, and polytechnics such as Coventry, Middlesex and the Polytechnic of Central London had offered from the late 1960s and early 1970s programmes in European languages that were linked in their content to social, political, economic and business aspects of the countries of those languages, while also insisting on very high standards of linguistic proficiency in appropriate registers, and offering work placements abroad as well as study opportunities.

There were also Postgraduate Diplomas in languages and exporting with assessed periods of practical experience. Examples were the diplomas of Thames Polytechnic (now the University of Greenwich) and the Buckinghamshire College of Higher Education.

Between 1976 and 1982 the European Commission supported the creation of some eighteen management study programmes taught jointly by UK universities and polytechnics with mainland European colleges. The pioneer was Middlesex Polytechnic where the programme offered dual qualifications, a model followed by colleges such as Trent and Humberside Polytechnics. 1985 saw the emergence of the first integrated languages and business studies programme at a university launched by the Aston Business School and Aston University's modern languages department together with partner universities in Germany and *grandes écoles* in France.

These recipes were to prove remarkably attractive, not only to students but to higher education institutions. According to my own calculations, there were by 1990 already some 46 programmes offering the French language jointly with, or more usually combined with, management related subjects at the 'old' universities. There were 42 offering German in combinations or jointly. By 1993 these figures had rocketed to 86 and 82

40

respectively, still in the old university sector alone. In the 1996 UCAS Handbook, representing the entire sector, I have identified some 160 such programmes in each of French and German. There was a parallel explosion but from a far smaller base-line in Spanish.

How this will impact on British industry cannot yet be assessed, but it does mean that there are now an unprecedented number of graduates of languages and management/business studies coming on to the market. If previous findings concerning the correlation between exporting success and the employment of linguist graduates hold up in the circumstances of the Single European Market – and there is no reason to suppose that they will not – UK plc should be in a much stronger position than at the time of entry into the EEC 22 years ago.

This powerful awareness of the importance of business language teaching was not confined to providers in higher education, though the stimulus was to come from there. A concept which has since had a nationwide impact was the creation of regional commercial language schools linked to university or college language departments. The Aston University project devised by Professor Dennis Ager provided the model for the Language Export Centres. These centres, pump-primed with DTI monies, were established in the UK's major industrial and commercial regions. Later known as Centres of Language Excellence, these schools have added significantly to the professionalism of business language teaching through conferences, training sessions and the production of business language learning materials.

To help publicise this wealth of specialist language providers and to assist companies in making an appropriate and informed choice of teaching and support provision, from language schools, freelance language trainers, translators, interpreters and cultural consultants, CILT has set up the National Business Language Information Service (NatBLIS), a database of registered providers. The database can be consulted directly through CILT or through a network of over 80 business information outlets.

Supporting change: creating business specific language learning materials

Specialist language courses require specialist learning materials. Teachers in all the sectors mentioned have, of course, always collected their own materials from authentic contemporary sources. But here, too, there has been vital outside help. The DTI pump-primed the mixed media course *Making your mark,* produced by the BBC Open University Production Unit in 1987–88. This course filmed the trading transactions of genuine British business men and women in Germany, using their knowledge of the German language in the reality of the exporting environment. The unorthodox approach of using entirely unscripted real-life sequences, together with non-native speakers in transactions with native speakers, opened the way for inter-cultural teaching as well as revealing the way language was actually deployed in business interaction. Inspired by the BBC's *A vous la France,* the series continued in 1990 with *Franc exchange* and in 1992 with *Spanish venture,* when the DTI were joined by the Eurotunnel and the National Westminster Bank as sponsors.

PICKUP money supported in the same period a major project, the inter-active video-disc course, *Expodisc Spanish,* led by Ealing College. Central Lancashire College had already entered the interactive multimedia market with the Vector laser-disc series, a pioneer in this technology and this pedagogic approach.

BBC Television moved to an interest in European business languages with its broadcast series commencing in 1992, *France, Germany, Spain means business,* followed by the sale of specially prepared video, audio and book packs.

Supporting change: the technological revolution in language learning

Dramatic developments in computer-assisted language learning (CALL) using video sequences had been anticipated in the work of Vector and Ealing College, while the Hodder and Stoughton/Mast Learning Systems series *Hotel Europa* edited by Marianne Howarth from 1993 introduced computer-assisted interaction on the personal computer. The extraordinarily rapid increase in the power of personal computers in the early 1990s, the publication of Windows software, digitisation of audio signals and video images and the huge storage capacity of the CD-ROM have led to new possibilities in the incorporation of video, sound and text into learner interactive courses with self-voice recording, written practice and correction, translation into L1 as required, with dictionary and grammar explanation backup of any word in the text. These developments go far beyond the earlier rather mechanistic gap-filling exercises of early CALL and build on the example set, among others, by the Vector company. So far, however, it is English for business that has largely benefited from the technological revolution and the multimedia approach, thanks to the far larger size of the market.

The report edited by Stephen Hagen, *Using technology in language learning,* which referred specifically to the use of technology in technology colleges, was a valuable and practical presentation of feasible technology deployment in an institutional setting. Few companies other than a select number of multi-nationals would be able or wish to invest on the scale of an educational establishment and the way forward in the business sector will in the short- to medium-term be in stand-alone CD-ROM and multimedia workstations. But certainly by the turn of the century we shall see on-line delivery of interactive multimedia language learning offered by cable and telecommunications companies.

The European Commission has taken a lead in encouraging not only the development of materials for languages for specific purposes (LSP) through the LINGUA programme, but also through the more generously funded DELTA programme of the Third Framework. The real challenge, as identified by the DELTA Concerted Action of 1993 on directions for future research and development in technology-based language learning, is to harness the power of the technology to serve the pedagogy, the communicative needs and learning styles of the user, not the other way around.

Within the UK, the Higher Education Funding Councils have launched their Teaching and Learning Technology Programme (TLTP) and have funded a number of language projects, including the ambitious Technology Enhanced Language Learning (TELL) project based at the Computers in Teaching Initiative (CTI) centre at Hull University, the Cambridge, Kent and Southampton (CKS) project based at Cambridge University, developing teaching and self-access learning materials in French and German for scientists and engineers, and the ASTCOVEA project (Aston, Coventry and East Anglia universities) developing software for French and German grammar learning. The software products of all these will be available free to higher education institutions and it is planned that they will be made available commercially by 1997–98.

Assessing change: the language auditing movement

Underlying the emergence of specialist business language curricula, assessment and examinations, specialist business language teaching centres and university degree programmes, and the production of LSP materials, there was an emergent and important philosophy of language curriculum design. Its fundamental concept was not new. Indeed, its origins can be traced back in the literature of curriculum design at least to the 1940s. Interestingly, this concept (while not specifically applied to language curricula) began to come to prominence as the influential American management thinker, Deming, was laying the foundations of the Total Quality Management philosophy. What the pedagogic and the management philosophies shared was a belief in the primacy of the customer (= learner) and the customer's (learner's) needs. Language learners in the adult sector are actually or potentially language users. Language teaching, it was reasoned, therefore had to start by asking what the learner/user needed. This had already been the view that drove the vital work of the Council of Europe in the 1970s and early 1980s, inspired by John Trim, then the Director of CILT, by J A Van Eyk and by D A Wilkins's brilliant concept of function and notion. But the Council of Europe was concerned centrally with the European citizen as a 'lay-member' of a multi-language continent where travel and thus social contact were growing apace. The specific language needs of the corporate and professional sectors were not the focus of attention. The existence of new business language teaching providers, the publication of generic business language learning materials and above all the sheer reality of the impending, then actual, Single European Market all helped to call for the creation of procedures, methods and analytical tools for identifying the usually unarticulated and often misunderstood foreign language communication needs of the business sector in all its specialist technical and management-functional manifestations. Only this identification could lay the foundations for true LSP curricula in the industrial and commercial sectors.

In the UK a milestone had long since been laid by E V Lee's (1972) investigation into how foreign languages were actually used in British industry, an investigation completed by some respondents and later replicated in Germany and Spain. The most prevalent foreign language tasks were identified and distilled into foreign language use profiles for a wide range of business functions.

The idea of the language 'audit' developed from work at Warley College near Birmingham where Ann Stevens, later of CILT and now Director of the Modern Languages Centre at the Open University, played a formative role, and from the study of foreign language use in major West Midlands companies conducted by Dennis Ager and Christine Wilding (now Secretary General of ALL) for Aston University in 1976–77.

A massive boost to the development of the auditing approach to business language curriculum design was given by the LINGUA programme from 1992. Identifying corporate language requirements in the context of the EU's integrating economies has been seen by the LINGUA Bureau of the European Commission (together with its UK branch based at the Central Bureau) as a priority. Projects aimed at designing professional language audit procedures, tools and systems started in that year. The target market was small and medium-sized companies (SMEs), local Government and transport. The principal findings and proposals were published by the Commission in 1994, following a symposium held in Saarbrücken that brought together the co-ordinators of the sixteen funded projects. It was suggestive of the powerful UK interest in business language that no less than five of the sixteen had UK lead partners and that at least two more involved British partners. These projects have led to further LINGUA development work, e.g. the Business Language Workbench Project (at Aston University and Coventry Technical College in conjunction with Mast Learning Systems), and to the publication of **44** both paper-based and computer-based auditing tools and systems. And independently of the EC programme Embleton and Hagen had published in 1992 their edited volume, *Languages in international business* which, as the sub-title states, is a practical guide for industrialists and training officers seeking information on corporate language policies, audits and the pros and cons of the types of language teaching and learning available, together with advice on hiring and using translators and interpreters.

Campaigning for change: the National Languages for Export Campaign

As these advances were taking place under the auspices of the European Commission, the DTI initiated its largest scale campaign to date, opened by Sir Peter Parker at the London Language Show in April 1994. A CILT sponsored report of October 1993 had again highlighted the large number of SMEs, in London and the North of England, that were encountering language barriers in their trading. Flanked by CILT's NatBLIS database of business language providers and by the work of the Languages Lead Body, also based at CILT, the campaign has moved forward on three fronts. Under the guidance of Stephen Hagen at the Open University and Robert Holkham of the DTI, it has published a series of readable and sensible guides on business language strategies, supported by a video.

Secondly, the campaign has set out to encourage and recognise good practice and innovation through National Languages for Export Awards, sponsored by outside bodies, for companies that have developed outstanding language or culture strategies.

The third front is the Languages in Export Advisory Scheme whereby companies can apply for subsidised language needs reviews (the term audit is not being used). The Scheme is being organised on behalf of the DTI by the Association of British Chambers of Commerce, who also undertook initial training of auditors in November 1995, while Hagen and Embleton have developed a software-based 'pre-audit' tool, *Communicado,* for use in companies prior to review.

Culture change: beyond languages for business to languages for citizenship

From this review of an eventful twenty years for foreign languages for business it might be possible to conclude that, even considering the disappointing outcomes of the most recent language use surveys of 1993 and 1994, UK plc has turned the corner in respect of foreign language capability. But this would be to underestimate the nature of the problem.

We face five fundamental challenges. The first is the inherent demand on time and effort which is required to achieve anything beyond the most basic foreign language communication proficiency. The second is the unrelenting growth of technical specialisation and its accompanying language, mastery of which is vital if the UK and Europe are to succeed in the only areas where they can compete with developing giants like China, let alone with the USA and the Pacific Rim, namely in leading-edge, knowledge-intensive activities. The third is the number of languages and cultures with which we are confronted in the EU alone. The fourth is the concomitant and consequent advance of English as the world language. And the fifth is the reality of the European Union, which cannot be wished away, and which is moving inexorably, if painfully, towards a single currency as a prelude to political union.

Technologies such as CD-ROM based and on-line language learning systems, with access to multi-lingual LSP materials databases, will contribute to our coping with the time factor and with the multiplicity of languages. But their strength is unlikely to lie in the area most people regard, simplistically, as communication, namely spoken interaction. Rather, these technologies will prove themselves in assisting reading, translation and information transfer alongside improving listening comprehension, possibly in interchange between speakers using their own mother tongue. Additionally, sophisticated auditing systems, delivered remotely but supported by on-site techniques, will form the base for needs-specific curricula for targeted and strictly instrumental language learning.

Learning at least one Romance and one Germanic language at school as preparation for later extended learning will be essential. The difficulty of learning any foreign language in adulthood without any experience in the formative years is enormous. But it is also a disadvantage to have been exposed at school to only one of the great families of European languages, via say French. Diversification must remain on the agenda, notwithstanding the constraints of the National Curriculum as currently conceived. And even the introduction of a second compulsory language is unlikely to prepare the adult for coping with oriental languages, which the Parker report saw as an essential feature of the portfolio of higher education institutions, a vital weapon in breaking into Far Eastern markets and politically a strategic necessity. It is here that structured courses in language awareness may play their part (see discussion on p19) – which would need not only to look at structures from a comparatist angle but introduce pupils to the issue of different, non-Roman writing systems, which is one of the most persistent challenges in tackling non-European languages.

46

While these remedies are entirely feasible, promoting the motivation to learn foreign languages will remain a challenge as English becomes ever more predominant in international communication. What is needed, in the final analysis, is a culture change on a national scale, a historical shift away from regarding the UK primarily as an island, independent of the European mainland, with the lands of most immediate affinity literally overseas in the Commonwealth and the USA. Perhaps, *mutatis mutandis,* Australia should be our model with its realisation that for it the territories of most immediate importance lie not in Europe but in the Far East and with its consequent enlightened and highly innovative language policies.

The surge in interest in at least parts of UK plc in foreign languages for business is in itself an important achievement. Perhaps we can detect here the beginning of an historical change that could follow a similar pattern to that hoped for by the architects of the European Communities and of the European Union – in their case that a common trading market would lead to an integration of economies, that this would bring about the necessity of monetary union and that monetary union would be the driver not simply of further economic integration but of political union, the declared intention of the Treaty of Rome. In our case, the analogy would be that the habitual use of the languages of the partner states for economic purposes will eventually lead a shift towards greater cultural sensitivity and thus motivation to learn more about the political landscape which those partner states inhabit and the values and attitudes that shape their actions. This strategy, if it is indeed a conscious strategy, could work. The confidence gained through mastery within a defined area of language use can lead to wider curiosity and an increasing range of competence.

But the obstacle to European-wide understanding are mighty. In all spheres of human activity that are the historical product of a society and its culture, such as political systems, special concepts evolve (together with their terms) that have no equivalent in another language and political system or, more deceptively, may appear to have an equivalent but which are in fact *faux amis.* Perhaps the most notorious example currently is the concept of Federalism. In the UK, politicians and press alike appear to believe it is synonymous with Centralism, whereas in the German experience it does not even mean devolution but rather the opposite, namely the system whereby powers of a carefully defined nature are granted by constituent sovereign states to the centre with control exercised not only by an Upper Chamber of representatives of the states but also by the watchful eye of a Constitutional Court. Given the immediate importance of the debates that are occurring within the EU and within the UK on these and many more issues, it is difficult to see how UK citizens can reach informed views and discharge their duties in elections and perhaps referenda without access to dispassionate sources of information. It seems vital that our university courses but above all our schools languages curricula, including those at GCSE level, offer an introduction to the contemporary political systems of our major EU partners and the historical processes that have led to them. Self-evidently, such an introduction would be part of the foreign languages syllabus. We need, in short, foreign languages for citizenship.

Just as UK plc cannot operate optimally in the economic realm without effective performance in the languages of its trading partners and without the strategic insight that such performance is a central factor in business efficiency, the UK as a political entity will not thrive in the face of the 'threats' identified at the beginning of this piece unless we, the citizens of this Kingdom and of the European Union, have knowledge of the circumstances that have shaped our neighbours' historical experience and, through language, gain insight into their consequent ways of interpreting reality, their expectations and their hopes.

References

Ager D E, *Language training at Leyland International* (Aston University Modern Languages Department, 1977) (restricted)

Ager D E, E Clavering and J Galleymore, *Foreign languages in industry, commerce and education. The Aston experience* (Aston University, 1978; 1980)

British Overseas Trade Board Study Group on Foreign Languages, *Foreign languages for overseas trade.* Foreword by HRH Duke of Kent, Vice-Chairman of the Board (British Overseas Trade Board, 1979)

Carrington-Windo T and K Kohl, *German means business* (BBC books, 1993)

DELTA, *Technology in language learning and tutoring. A digest of proceedings and recommendations* (DELTA Concerted Action, European Commission, DGXIII, Brussels, 1994)

Embleton D and S Hagen (eds), *Languages in international business. A practical guide,* with a foreword by HRH The Prince of Wales (London: Hodder and Stoughton, 1992)

Embleton D and S Hagen, *Communicado. An interactive guide to help the international trader plan a language strategy* (DTI, Main Multimedia, 1995)

Emmans K A, E W Hawkins and A Westoby, *Foreign languages in industry and commerce* (York University Language Teaching Centre, 1974)

Gladkow J and C Sanders with C Gordon, *Franc exchange. Effective business communication in France* (BBCOUPC, DTI, Eurotunnel, Pitman Publishing, 1991)

Gould B, L Nogueira Pache and K Bruton, *Spanish venture. Basic business communication in Spain* (BBC Milton Keynes, DTI, Eurotunnel, National Westminster Bank, 1992)

48 Hagen S, *Languages in British business. An analysis of current needs* (Newcastle-upon-Tyne Products and CILT, 1988)

Hagen S, *The foreign language needs of British business: a CTC response* (City Technology Colleges Trust Ltd, 1992)

Hagen S (ed), *Languages in European business* (City Technology Colleges Trust Ltd in association with CILT, 1993)

Hagen S (ed), *Using technology in language learning* (CTC Trust and CILT, 1993)

Howarth M and M Woodhall with C Randlesome, *Making your mark. Effective business communication in Germany* (BBC OUPC, DTI, LCCI, Open College, Open University, Pitman Publishing, 1988)

King A, *French means business* (BBC books, 1993)

The language key in export strategy. Report of a conference held in Birmingham, Monday 12 January 1981 (Aston University)

Language Matters (18) (Guildford: AEB, 1995)

Languages and export performance. A study prepared for the BETRO Trust Committee of the Royal Society of Arts by the P E Consulting Group (London: Royal Society of Arts, 1979)

Lee E V (ed), *The non-specialist use of foreign languages in industry and commerce* (Sidcup: LCCI Commercial Education Scheme, 1972; revised 1985)

LINGUA compendium series (Luxembourg: EC, 1991ff) for details of funded projects

LINGUA – language audits and needs analyses. Symposium proceedings, Saarbrücken 1994 (Luxembourg: EC, 1994)

Liston D and N B R Reeves, *Business studies, languages and overseas trade. A study of education and training* (London: Pitman Publishing and the Institute of Export, 1985; reprinted 1986)

Parker P (Sir), *Speaking for the future.* A review of the requirements of diplomacy and commerce for Asian and African languages and area studies (UGC London, February 1986)

Reeves N B R, 'University language studies and the future of Britain'. An inaugural lecture (University of Surrey, 1976)

Reeves N B R, 'The foreign language needs of UK-based corporations' in *The annals of the American Academy of Political and Social Science* (511): 60–73 (September 1990)

Wilding C, *Languages, education and industry: a survey of reports and conferences* (Aston University Modern Languages Department, 1980)

Wimpory M del R, *Spanish means business* (BBC books, 1994)

Wright C and S Wright, 'Do languages really matter? The relationship between international business success and a commitment to foreign language use' in *Journal of industrial affairs* (3)1: 3–14 (1994)

2

A view from business

Jim Beale

There are no foreign lands. It is the traveller who is foreign. (R L Stevenson)

Change seems gradual to those of us who live through it, but a review of what was happening in 1966 can be quite startling.

The Industrial Re-organisation Corporation was formed; Jaguar and the British Motor Corporation merged; Laker Airways was founded; hemlines were high; unemployment was low (only half a million) with employment in manufacturing standing at a peace-time high of nine million; England won the World Cup at soccer; a 26-year-old electrical engineer called Clive Sinclair invented the world's smallest TV set; the Labour Party was voted back in office; the Government announced its intention of applying for entry into the Common Market; Britain was bottom of the European League in language training; CILT was established.

These last three events are inextricably interlinked. The Government realised that efforts to turn the slow-growth UK into a high-growth, self-sustaining economy were doomed by history and geography. Association with a widening Europe at least had a chance of continuing to provide a full range of employment opportunities, but it was clear that unless we found some means of harmonising with people whose culture, language, and work habits were quite different from our own, these efforts would be in vain. As Nigel Reeves has pointed out, there is a high correlation between the employment of linguistically qualified people, and success in export markets – and of course the converse – absence of linguistic skills results in lost business.

Unquestionably, much has been achieved in the last thirty years, and most of the significant features are identified in later chapters of this volume. From my personal experience, through my association with CILT and the Languages Lead Body, the biggest single change can be seen by contrasting present day teaching methods with my own experience as a language student.

I studied French and Spanish at a traditional university (Edinburgh) in the mid 1950s. For the first two years, teaching in both languages was based on giving access to great literary texts in the original, and on

50

correcting my grammatical and orthographical errors in translation. Thereafter, as was normal in the Scottish system, I spent a year in France, as an *assistant d'anglais,* where I was totally unprepared for the rigours of shopping for provisions in the pre-supermarket era, or debating the Algerian situation in the school staffroom.

This experience caused me to question the whole basis of my early education. In this I was not alone, and neither was I the first. In 1778, Adam Smith, in *The wealth of nations,* said

> *the greater part of what is taught in schools and universities does not seem to be the most proper preparation for that which is to employ them the rest of their days.*

A mere 190 years later, businessmen were complaining about the general standard of young people's skills – not just in languages – after leaving full-time education. Politicians were making statements about the inadequacies of the system, and teachers at all levels were firing off salvoes in response. In retrospect, it seems that many of those involved in teaching didn't understand the major changes which were taking place in the world of work in the latter half of the twentieth century.

CILT's promotion of foreign language training was crucial. Before the establishment of CILT; language training was regarded as a problem. Regarding it as an opportunity, as CILT has done, is the best way to shake off our reputations as the worst linguists in Europe.

CILT has not been alone in this task, and its efforts have rubbed off on other organisations not normally associated with language training. For example, the Chartered Institute of Marketing recognised language training as a major component in its Continuing Professional Development programme – and the emphasis is on foreign language communication in real situations, as it always should have been.

I now write as a businessman who has spent significant periods of his life in mainland Europe, where ability to speak a foreign language (usually English) is seen as a normal management skill. Nevertheless, the majority of the workforce in any Continental European company do not speak English, except in the offices of British or American-owned companies. The everyday language is the local one.

English is the language of everyday speech nowhere in Europe outside the British Isles. Some 82% of European Community members do not have English as their first language, yet critics of the UK emphasis on foreign language training suggest that English will soon become the main language of business communication, because it has for some time been the language of computers, news gathering, airlines and pop music. This logic is difficult to follow.

It seems to me that one of the characteristics of the mid 1990s is an almost complete abandonment of the present day in favour of endless speculation about the future – the Internet, the coming millennium, the composition of the next government, the introduction of a Single European currency. Nigel Reeves has suggested that the UK might be marginalised in European economic development if it does not become a member of the Single Currency core group. As I write, it seems that the Maastricht Treaty signatories face a choice between fudging the economic criteria necessary to make a single currency work, or delaying the creation of the single currency until at least the core countries can be sure of meeting the criteria. But whether you believe that European Monetary Union is the means to deeper political union, or a tool for economic efficiency, it is hard to see how the case for continued promotion of foreign language learning would be affected whether or not the UK is part of the Single Currency. In or out, we will still be trading with the rest of Europe, as members of the Single Market.

This has already been recognised by many companies up and down the UK. Even in the North East of England, an area which, according to a recent report, *appears to experience greater language barriers than other regions,* there are shining examples of companies whose success is based on understanding the cultures and languages of other markets.

Understandably, these companies are reluctant, for reasons of commercial confidentiality, to provide bottom-line details of their performance in specific export markets. Nevertheless, at the Boras Machine Company in Gateshead, which makes textile machinery, export turnover has grown by over 100% in the past five years, and a large part of this increase is attributed to a language strategy which has led to a sales team which has fluent speakers in Chinese, Hindi, Portuguese, Spanish, Italian, German and French.

Less than ten miles away, at Washington (Tyne and Wear), Canford Audio manufacture and distribute audio equipment for the broadcasting industries, studios, hospitals, schools and colleges. Its exports to mainland Europe increased by 30% last year, following the adoption of a four-language strategy, and invoicing and receipt of payments in domestic currencies.

These approaches are typical of the way many dynamic small and medium-sized UK companies are successfully negotiating language and cultural hurdles to make serious inroads into competitive markets.

Europe is now changing economically, politically, financially and demographically, faster than at any previous time in history. Change is high on the agenda of most UK businesses, even of those who currently do little trading outside their home territory, since there is nothing like a real market opportunity or a business threat to inspire corporate action. With growing numbers of joint ventures, international alliances, foreign takeovers and new market entries, more and more UK executives will face **52** difficulties unless they are able to communicate both verbally and in writing in the language of those with whom they have to do business.

In my view, the UK has turned the corner in respect of foreign language capability. We are far better equipped for the next thirty years than we were for the last, and by addressing the language needs of the world of work, CILT, in conjunction with NatBLIS and the Languages Lead Body, will continue to pave the way to improving the country's language skills.

The rich rewards available to the successful in one of the world's three largest markets makes the effort worthwhile, and the rich variety of language, culture and attitudes makes the path to success both intellectually challenging and enjoyable.

3

Adults learning languages

Lore Arthur

It is generally accepted that 26% of the British population is engaged in some form of recognised personal study. This figure rises to 36% if individual learning outside educational institutions is taken into account (Sargant, 1991). Adults have simply more choice than they had thirty years ago. They can enrol in classes organised by adult education centres, further education colleges, universities, even sixth form colleges, or learn independently in open learning centres or via distance learning courses. Some join language training courses available in industry and commerce. Others pay high fees for a course in a private language school or learn on their own at home with an increasingly wide range of audio-visual material at their disposal. But there is also the individual learner who regularly attends either day or evening classes, often against numerous odds. Anyone who has ever attempted to do this will know just how much courage, sacrifice and sheer determination is required.

Historical dimensions

National statistics concerning the provision of, or participation in, foreign language teaching in adult education are hard to find. The influential Russell Report of 1973, for example, refers to the popularity of courses offered in adult education centres such as domestic subjects, music, arts, crafts and foreign languages for leisure-time purposes (Russell, 1973) but provides no foreign language specific data. Other records such as the study undertaken in the years 1978–1981 on behalf of the then Advisory Council for Adult and Continuing Education (ACACE) established that the learning of foreign languages was one of the most popular subjects to be studied in adult education (ACACE, 1982). In 1984 Handy's enquiry into the provision of foreign language courses found that 380 adult education centres, further education colleges and voluntary organisations, at that time about 60% of possible providers in England and Wales, registered 4,719 foreign language classes and 64,529 adult students (Handy, 1984). More recent research undertaken by the National Institute for Adult Continuing Education (NIACE), *Learning and leisure,* confirms foreign language courses to be as popular as ever (Sargant, 1991). These records indicate that a large proportion of the population was and continues to be open-minded, willing to find out about other countries and cultures, keen to accept challenges and 'have a go'!

Adult motivation

Most adult education centres or colleges of further education offer courses in French, German, Spanish and Italian. However, there are noticeable 'fashions' in the popularity of lesser known languages. In the late 1970s, courses in Hebrew, Polish or Esperanto were popular, while the 1980s saw an increase of courses in the 'community' languages such as Hindi, Gujarati, Urdu and even Vietnamese, and nowadays Japanese and Arabic are in demand. One may speculate why this should be so. There may be social and economic influences, often global in their dimension. Other factors such as the location of a centre, the convenience of transport, the fee structure and the nature of the institution itself can determine the type of provision made and influence personal reasons adults may have for joining an adult education course.

A survey of 410 adult education students in a London college taken in 1990 found that 34% had joined because they had friends or relatives speaking the foreign language. Of those questioned, 21% claimed that they had heard the foreign language spoken at home, 11% enrolled because they had previously lived in the country where the chosen language was spoken and 54% had joined for work reasons. Though 89% found travelling to the country concerned a particular motivator, only 25% gave specific holiday reasons (Arthur, 1990). These findings, however, are in sharp contrast to a survey undertaken throughout Lancashire in the same year, where 473 adults were asked to give reasons for joining a foreign language course. Here 80% gave holiday reasons as the main motive, 23% had joined for work reasons and a further 23% had friends or relatives who spoke the same language (Ainslie, 1990). There may be conscious and subconscious, extrinsic or intrinsic reasons. It is not uncommon that a sudden change in personal circumstances or the need to gain self-esteem affect the motivation to learn. Other research confirms that the majority of language learners is likely to come from the upper and middle end of the social scale, with men and women in roughly equal proportion (ACACE, 1982; Ainslie, 1990; Sargant, 1991). Television viewing figures for the BBC's *French experience,* taken for the first ten weeks in the autumn term 1995, on the other hand, indicate a gender balance in favour of women with 53.4% women and 46.6% men, and the Open University enrolled a considerably higher proportion of women (59.9%) for its first French course *Ouverture* than men (40.1%) in the same year.

It is hard to learn a foreign language from scratch to a level where one can speak and understand it with ease and confidence when in contact with native speakers – and hence to maintain one's motivation. The tutor alone cannot prevent students from dropping out of classes. Personal reasons such as pressure of work, lack of time, family commitments are cited much more frequently than course-related reasons (Ryeback, 1980; Ball, 1994). Reasons for a high drop-out rate quoted in other studies include overcrowded and mixed-ability classes at the beginning of the year and poor teaching or classroom accommodation (Hotho-Jackson, 1995). Nowadays, however, the attendance and drop-out rate affects financial resources since colleges dependent on the Further Education Funding Council (FEFC) receive grants geared to course entry, attendance and exit levels.

Legislation and policies

To understand some of the fundamental changes which have taken place in the provision of adult education in recent years it is necessary to refer back to the 1944 Education Act of which Section 4 is particularly noteworthy. It introduced notions such as education as a leisure-time occupation, thereby creating a schism between goal-orientated, purposeful learning and activity-orientated learning for pleasure; a schism considered by many adult educators to have been one of the great weaknesses of British adult education.

This dilemma between what is functional and goal-orientated and what is a leisure-time pursuit has bedevilled adult foreign language learning over many years. The 1992 Further and Higher Education Act effectively removes leisure-time education from government subsidy in favour of goal-orientated learning, that is certification, accreditation and vocationalism. Schedule 2 of the 1992 Act states government educational priorities succinctly since courses funded under Schedule 2 should, among others, lead to either access into higher education, a vocational qualification or to General Certificates of Secondary Education (GCSEs).

Preceding the implementation of the 1992 Act, Local Education Authorities had the choice of either amalgamating most of their adult education services with the further education college in the community – the latter receive grants from the Funding Councils and fall outside a local authority's management control – or to maintain an adult education service without further government subsidies. Since then numerous adult education centres have either been taken over by further education colleges, closed altogether or merged with, for example, the respective local authority's youth and leisure services.

Further education colleges, on the other hand, were able to increase their adult student population to over 51%. All, including a handful of 'designated' adult education institutions, receive state grants via the Funding Councils, provided they offer courses within the remit of Schedule 2 of the 1992 Act. Foreign language courses which are accredited by the Open College Network also fall into this category. Founded in 1985, the National Open College Network (NOCN) consists of approximately 900 organisations, including consortia of colleges, guidance and career services, voluntary and community agencies. The OCNs operate accreditation within the National Credit Framework, that is they award credits for learning achievements within agreed definitions of levels and credits which are recognised on a mutual basis between the Networks and by the National Council for Vocational Qualifications (NCVQ).

The Buckinghamshire Scheme

The Buckinghamshire Modern Languages Scheme presents a good example of operating within the accreditation framework of the Open College. In Buckinghamshire, largely rural, adult education takes place over a widespread area in community halls, schools and adult education centres. Here, long before the Education Act of 1992, foreign language tutors came together and prepared a common curriculum with graded levels suitable for all the adult education institutions in the area. In 1993, the Buckinghamshire Modern Languages Scheme was approved by the local Open College Network. Foreign language courses within that scheme are now eligible for FEFC grants under Schedule 2 and course fees for students are lower than they would have been otherwise. Under the Scheme tutors have to keep records and undertake, with the help of their students, continuous assessment. Classes and tutors are seen by moderators at least once a year. The scheme has been so successful that it is now franchised to other providers (Hilton, 1995)

The BBC

It would be difficult to write about foreign languages in adult education without paying tribute to the BBC which, since the early 1970s, played a significant role in adult education foreign language teaching. From its earliest days, well before the Second World War, the BBC was keen to develop an entirely practical approach (Barnes, 1978). Even now BBC courses emphasise a functional, communicative use of language. Courses are aimed at independent adult learners who may or may not join formal courses. No assumptions are made about previous educational achievements.

Television as a medium for learning had begun to make its mark in the early 1960s. The first television programme, *Parliamo Italiano,* was transmitted in 1963. Subsequent courses for mainly French, German and Spanish followed a conventional pattern in the presentation of their teaching content of grammar and structure. The BBC German course *Kontakte,* launched in 1974, however, broke entirely new ground and was soon to be regarded as one of the milestones in television history. Not only was *Kontakte* the first course based on the communicative, functional approach but it was also the first course which taught language via television, radio and coursebook in an integrated way. For the first time also students were able to sit 'Achievement Tests'. These were devised by the University of Cambridge Local Examinations Syndicate and organised by the local adult education centres (Barnes, 1978). In 1975/76 the first French course, *Ensemble,* developed along similar lines, was broadcast and the Spanish *¡Digame!* followed in 1978/79. Other ground-breaking initiatives followed. The transmitting of German or French news late at night in the target language, copied directly from the respective television programmes via the Eurovision link the same evening but edited, sub-titled and, where necessary, explained, strikes an innovative and adventurous chord even now. From the early 1980s onward other types of foreign language courses were to follow, such as the *Get by in . . .* series covering a wide range of languages. The German course *Deutsch Plus,* launched in September 1996, is likely to be the last television day time 'free' language course. As commercial pressures increase, BBC World-Wide is likely to have to compete at an international level and produce modular, short and long programmes appealing to different markets, across the globe.

Examining bodies

BBC foreign languages programmes are not likely to follow the national trend of accreditation and certification of competence-based learning assumed by the National Language Standards, a vocationally-orientated framework published in 1993. These standards are of particular importance to examining bodies such as the London Chamber of Commerce and Industry (LCCI), the Institute of Linguists (IoL) or the Royal Society of Arts (RSA) in the seeking of NCVQ approval. Here, too, much has changed since 1965. At that time the RSA, for example, offered very traditional examinations although it began already to develop courses for bilingual secretaries which included innovative elements such as the use of real telephones in the examinations and real reference sources. In 1975 the RSA adopted the communicative, functional syllabus initially for English as a Foreign Language but soon for other languages such as French, German and Spanish. A decade or so later the RSA was an early contributor to the development of National Languages Standards of the national competence-based vocational qualifications and is today approved as an awarding body by NCVQ (Ashworth, 1995).

The IoL also contributed extensively to the consultation programme of the Languages Lead Body, particularly in relation to Level 5 for professional translators and interpreters, though the Institute continues to offer a wide range of language examinations, all currently without NCVQ approval. In 1965, the IoL, too, operated on traditional patterns of examining structure based on grammatical accuracy and mainly reading and oral skills, though in 1969 a wider ranging syllabus involving reading aloud, sustained speaking, essay writing and written summaries was introduced. The syllabus for the current Examinations in Languages for International Communication (ELIC), devised during the 1980s and launched in 1990, sought to bring elements of work-orientation and communicative, task-based assessment objectives into sharper focus (Chester, 1995).

The Open University

While the IoL and the RSA can boast international recognition based on long-term commitments to foreign language teaching, the Open University is a relative newcomer. The university itself was founded in 1969, yet its Centre for Modern Languages opened only in 1990 despite previous attempts to introduce foreign languages into the university's academic profile.The Centre's first French course, *Ouverture,* part of a three-year undergraduate Diploma-Programme, was launched in 1995 and attracted an astonishing 2,076 students in its first year. The first German course, *Auftakt,* is planned for 1997 and Spanish will be introduced in 1999. With an anticipated student body of 10,000 adults the Centre expects to be the largest single provider of foreign language courses in the country. Though teaching by distance the OU seeks to tackle verbal communication and personal interaction by a variety of means. Course materials are designed to include the practice of speaking skills on audio cassettes, and computer-assisted interactive-learning programmes are at varying stages of development. Students are registered in one of the university's thirteen regions where they are encouraged to attend eighteen hours of group tutorials during the academic year. Those living further apart receive telephone tuition, a particularly successful venture. From the second year onwards students are also expected to attend a one-week residential summer course either in the country of learning or in this country.

Tutors in AE

The Open University, in common with other institutions offering foreign language courses to adults, is to a large extent dependent on the quality and commitment of part-time hourly-paid tutors. Almost all working in FE or HE or adult education are required to submit and maintain schemes of work, evaluation and assessment records, student profiling and marking schemes as part of current quality assurance schemes (Ainslie and Lamping, 1995). Consequently, tutors are expected to put in many hours of unpaid work – often without adequate training, professional development or career prospects. The lack of a nationally recognised teacher qualification for foreign language tutors in the post-compulsory sector continues to undermine professional status of tutors, though an increasing number of in-service or even pre-service training courses are now available.

CILT

The Centre for Information on Language Teaching and Research (CILT) has long recognised the need to offer professional support to adult education tutors. In September 1984 CILT organised a national conference for teachers of languages to adults with a particular focus on the need for professional support (Moys, 1992). The first CILT Adult Education Working Party was set up around 1985 when the network for adult education language tutors, NETWORD, was established. These are self-help groups which are supported by CILT. The groups meet according to their own needs and circumstances and are linked by the biannual *NETWORD* newsletter for tutors of adults in adult, further and higher education, consultants and tutor trainers. In addition, CILT has published numerous books on practical and theoretical issues of interest to tutors of adults.

Challenges for adult learning

Looking back over the last thirty years it is clear that despite a more recent shift towards certification and vocationalism, the individual adult learner's motivation and commitment to study has remained the only constant factor. During the 1970s and early 1980s, the era of innovation and seemingly unlimited expansion, the adult education environment was particularly suited to the learner-centred functional communicative approach pioneered in foreign languages by the Council of Europe (1971–81). In adult education the learner-centred, facilitative approach, arising out of humanistic psychology and made popular by, among others, Carl Rogers (1968) and Malcolm Knowles (1978), exercised a particularly strong influence in theoretical and practical terms. With the onset of Thatcherism, on the other hand, the later years required a sense of pragmatic realism and a keen sense of survival. Nowadays, the challenge for those in adult education is to combine the best of both: the facilitative, learner-centred approach in the spirit of equal opportunities and access to education with purposeful, goal-orientated learning required by funding arrangements and the current economic and political climate. The determination seems to be there and the dogged British refusal to speak other languages may fast become more of a stereotype than an accurate reflection of reality (Moys, 1992).

60

References

ACACE, *Adults: their educational experiences and needs* (NIACE, 1982)

Ainslie S, *Foreign language courses for adults – the Lancashire survey* (Bootle: Hugh Baird College, 1990)

Ainslie S and A Lamping, *Assessing adult learners* (CILT, 1995)

Arthur L, *Study into independent language learning* (Goldsmiths College, 1990)

Arthur L and S Hurd (eds), *The adult language learner* (CILT, 1992)

Ashworth F, in correspondence with the author, Royal Society of Arts (1995)

Ball C, 'Why the high drop-out rate?' in *NETWORD News* (CILT, 1994)

Barnes N, *Adults learning foreign languages – the role of BBC broadcasting* (Further Education BBC, 1978)

Chester R, in correspondence with the author, Institute of Linguists (1995)

Council of Europe, *Modern languages 1971–1981* (Council of Europe, 1981)

Handy P, *Adult education and the teaching of languages: the current situation in England and Wales* (Brighton Polytechnic, 1984)

Hilton S, in conversation with the author (1995)

Hotho-Jackson S, 'Motivation and group context: tackling the drop-out factor' in *Language Learning Journal*, no 11 (1995)

Knowles M S, *The adult learner: a neglected species* (Houston: Gulf Publishing Co., second edition, 1978)

Moys A, 'The changing context' in Arthur L and S Hurd (eds), *The adult language learner* (CILT, 1992)

National Language Standards (Languages Lead Body, CILT, 1993; revised 1996)

Rogers C, *Freedom to learn* (Columbus, Ohio: Charles E Merril Publishing, 1994)

Ryeback S, *Learning languages from the BBC, research into courses for adults* (BBC, 1980)

Russell L, *Adult education: a plan for development* (Her Majesty's Stationery Office, 1973)

Sargant N, *Learning and leisure: a study of adult participation in learning and its policy implications* (NIACE, 1991)

4

University degree courses

David Nott

Thirty years of change

Modern language departments in higher education are very different places in 1996 from what they were thirty years ago. In 1966, they were distant from the community they served, and enjoyed relatively high prestige for their pursuit of knowledge for its own sake; it was a time of expansion without sanctions, when staff were recruited from a wide field. In 1996, the importance of modern language studies is more widely recognised in the community, but the ethos has changed to one of contracts, efficiency and training; students are seen as units of resource, i.e. money, rather than as intellectual potential.

Students

Since 1966 the student population as a whole has changed enormously, in terms of both numbers and aspirations: in the late 1960s, around 10% of the relevant age group entered HE; by 1993, the figure had risen above 30%. By the early 1990s 'A' levels or their equivalent had replaced the 11+ examination as the means of social promotion through the educational system. Already in 1966, **mature students** – defined as those aged 21 or over at the time of admission – formed 16.8% of overall entry to HE; by 1980 this figure had risen to 24% and to more than 33% by 1995. Numbers of students entering HE modern language courses rose from 3,629 in 1969 to approximately 4,500 in 1990 and approximately 5,600 in 1994 (CREM, 1995). **Single honours** students in modern languages are in a minority: in 1993/94, out of a total of 24,197 students following language courses of all kinds, more than half (13,436) were on **combined** courses (see Appendix II, Table 8). Against a background of a steady increase in the overall number of **women** awarded degrees (from 38% in 1966 to 45% in 1989), the number of men following first degree courses in modern languages in 1982/83 was 25% (Powell, 1986), rising slowly to 28% in 1993/94 (see Appendix II, Table 8).

Courses

Since 1966, the pattern of provision in HE modern language courses has been characterised by diversity: in the 1980s many universities began to offer types of combined or integrated degree courses, e.g. one or more foreign languages with a business-related subject, which had hitherto been a feature of ML studies in polytechnics. There is some evidence (see, for example, Nott, 1990) that the pace of curricular change began to accelerate around 1987–88. In 1966 a typical course description was: *The Honours course and the three-year General course are designed to cover in outline the whole of the history of French literature from the Middle Ages to modern times* (in Stern, 1961 and 1965); Stern points out that *the programme for practically any language will demand some or all of:* the **language**: translation, essays, oral, phonetics; **evolution of the language**, including early texts; intensive/critical study of **literary texts**; wide **reading**, covering all periods; study of **history** and **institutions**; art/music; some time (one month to one year) spent in the **foreign country**.

Since the 1960s, the main trends have been as follows: greater attention paid to the development of **language skills**; increased **use of the foreign language** as the working medium; increased emphasis on **oral skills; less** emphasis on **translation** as a mainstream activity; a widening of the range of the **spoken and written activities** in the foreign language; greater emphasis on **sociocultural, economic** and **political** aspects of the target countries, in both mainstream/core programmes and in options; a **scaling-down** of the range of **pre-twentieth century** literary studies; new courses focusing on contemporary literature, including **women writers** and **writers from outside** the main target country; a proliferation of courses in **film and media studies**.

Courses which eliminate the distinction between 'language' and 'non-language' work, enabling sociocultural, political and economic studies to be conducted entirely in the foreign language, have been introduced, but:

> . . . *departments with a commitment to teaching in the target language are often faced with difficulties as a result of the trend towards multidisciplinary and modular degrees; in a modular Area Studies degree, for example, it is often necessary to teach a course such as German Politics, which may be available to a whole range of students, as well as those majoring in languages, in English, if it is to be viable.* (Rigby, 1991)

This is the central dilemma: the foreign language itself is the key to, and the core of our discipline; if we sacrifice that, we lose our very *raison d'être* as a distinct area of study in higher education.

Languages other than French

The spread of languages on offer to the prospective student in 1996 (see UCAS, 1995) is extensive, but a comparison with the situation over thirty years ago (see Stern, 1965) shows that despite a near-tripling of university institutions, there has been an increase of choice for prospective students in only thirteen languages or groups – including the five main European languages, Japanese, Chinese, Hindi, Korean, African Studies, Asian Studies, Scandinavian Studies and East Asian Studies – while in eighteen cases – including Catalan, Swedish, Polish, Danish, Provençal, Pali, and Semitic Studies – there has been a decrease (see Appendix II, Table 9). It could be argued that there is no national need for more than a handful of institutions to offer courses in most 'minority' languages; it is, however, surprising that in 1996, courses in Arabic and Chinese are offered in only eleven institutions, compared with twelve and five respectively in 1963. The single most dramatic figure is that for Japanese (rising from three to 32), showing that, if trade no longer follows the flag, linguistic opportunities **can** expand to follow the needs of trade.

Ab initio degree courses were available in about half of the institutions offering Italian and Russian in 1963; for Spanish, the proportion was far smaller (seven out of 27), and for German practically unthinkable (four out of 37). Today, provision of *ab initio* courses in these four languages has increased. For most languages other than French, provision at higher education level has always been on the basis of *ab initio* courses.

Teaching, learning and assessment

The most important components of teaching and learning in higher education are the hardest to evaluate, and the least susceptible to influence by public policy: they lie in the quality of intellectual discipleship and the achievement of personal autonomy, and thus depend directly on the integrity and gifts of the teacher, and on the student's commitment to learning and growth. Teaching standards in all HE modern language departments in England, and in the two Northern Ireland universities, were assessed during 1995/96 as part of the Assessment of the Quality of Education procedure of the Higher Education Funding Council. The Welsh and Scottish HE funding bodies have similar exercises. These exercises have proved salutary and worthwhile, helping to concentrate minds on conditions necessary, but not sufficient, for quality to flourish in HE. Failure to formulate appropriate aims and objectives and to ensure adequate conditions for teaching and learning is liable to cause all-round frustration; but good structures, content and methods can only assist good teaching and learning: they cannot guarantee them.

Compared with 1966, more full-time staff in modern language departments in 1996 are involved with language teaching. The need for coherent programmes of language teaching is universally recognised; this often means employment of part-time tutors, many of whom have relevant experience and are dedicated to the task. Foreign **lectors** are as valuable a resource in higher education as they are in schools and colleges; they are no longer called 'colloquial assistants' (Healy, 1967), and far more care is taken over induction and supervision. With the rise in student numbers, not accompanied by an increase in teaching staff, the pressure to reduce contact hours and to increase the size of teaching groups is well-nigh irresistible. As a result, self-instruction schemes, including computer-assisted language learning (CALL), which can be a valuable extension, in private study time, of learning methods carefully nurtured during taught classes, are introduced as an expedient. As one polytechnic reported (Nott, 1990):

> *We are under considerable pressure from above to teach our students less and make more use of self-instruction, but many students give up their time to self-instruction only if there are facts to be learned which are then tested.*

Methods of assessment tend to evolve more slowly than syllabuses and working practices: *many university departments* [of French] *are diversifying teaching methods, but have let examination methods lag behind* (Sewell, 1989). Sewell's survey of 40 university French departments showed that final year assessment involved prose translation both ways and discursive essays in all but one or two departments, and that translation both ways figured in over two thirds of pre-final assessment schemes, and discursive essays in just under half. For teaching purposes, around half used all-French activities such as role-plays and debates, text and video analysis, summary (oral/written), comprehension (oral/written) and non-essay written tasks, but these activities figured in only 20–40% of assessment schemes.

The year abroad

The year abroad was still being described by several university departments in the early 1960s as a period of 'intercalation' (see Stern, 1965), while one German department's arrangements for its students while abroad is, perhaps, not to be recommended: *Each student is placed under a member of the staff who remains in constant touch* (in Stern, 1965). From the course descriptions in Stern (1965) one can work out the extent to which a year abroad was, for Single or Joint Major students, a compulsory part of a modern language degree course in 1963/64: in the case of French, the majority of students spent a full year abroad; for German, about a half spent a term, with most of the rest spending a year; for

Spanish, most spent a term. By 1972, a CILT survey (James, 1973) of four-teen universities and sixteen polytechnics and colleges showed that the year abroad had become an almost universal requirement, but practice varies widely, reflecting differing opinions within and between institu-tions, as to how the year is best spent.

The year abroad provides those who are disposed to widen their intel-lectual and personal horizons with the means to do so: many sixteen- to eighteen-year-olds who are favourably disposed towards foreign cultures gravitate towards higher education courses that include foreign language study, but these favourable attitudes are often based on idealised notions of those cultures. (For a broad and detailed study of these issues, see Opper, 1990.) In many departments, preparation for the year abroad is an important part of the second year programme, and the year itself is close-ly integrated with the degree course as a whole, through projects, disser-tations and other written assignments completed while abroad, and oral presentations and discussions during the final year. Meara (1994), how-ever, working with data from 1986, found that 14% of students were not required to do any written work while abroad, and that *of those that were, 86% were asked to produce this work in English.* According to Meara, there were significant differences between the self-rated improvement scores in three areas (listening, speaking, and employment prospects) depending on whether the year was spent as a student, as a foreign language assistant, or in other work placements: in all three areas, the mean self-rated improvement was lowest among those in study placements; for listening and speaking skills, foreign language assistant placements came out best, while employment prospects were felt to have been most improved by other types of work placement: *This finding suggests that the European Community's emphasis on student exchanges might not be the most effective use of public funds,* though it should be pointed out that many study courses abroad include a one- to three-month work placement. Alas, many of the brightest and most successful products of the year abroad then proceed to teach English overseas.

The number of UK students spending the year abroad as foreign language assistants in schools and colleges more than doubled over the thirty-year period, but most of this increase took place in the early 1970s. By choosing to send their students abroad as assistants, modern language departments in higher education are performing a triple service: they are ensuring work placements for over 2,600 of their students, at minimal administrative cost to themselves, thanks to the Central Bureau for Educational Visits and Exchanges (CBEVE); they are providing those of their graduates who subsequently go into teaching with valid and contrastive teaching experience; and they are, through the reciprocal nature of the scheme, supporting the presence, in UK schools and colleges, of nearly 3,000 units of valuable 'educational hardware': a speaker of the foreign language and emblem of the foreign culture.

Careers

Numerous pleas have been made over the past century for more people in British industry and commerce to be able to speak a foreign language; today, it is not so much the needs that have changed, as public readiness to accept foreign language proficiency as being compatible with British citizenship. Employers' stated needs, except for specialised trades and professions, are expressed in terms of adaptability, flexibility, literacy, numeracy, independence and creativity. There is no conflict between these and the criteria for defining the academically successful student. As Evans (1988) puts it: *the real vocationality of modern languages is at a higher level than the ability to interpret languages. It is at the level of interpreting people to people.* Perhaps we need a car sticker slogan campaign: Modern Linguists Do It Face to Face.

A comparison of Finlay (1969) and Steadman (1987) shows coverage of a similar range of careers in teaching, translating and interpreting, business, travel, media and administration. If anything, the range is widened: clerical work, or posts as telephonists, in films and music or in the armed forces, are replaced by accountancy, banking, insurance, law, diplomatic service, European and United Nations agencies. Sadly, the Government Green Paper of 1985 on *The development of HE into the 1990s* did not include modern languages among the 'wealth generating' subject areas.

The main destinations of language graduates entering employment in 1994 were Business and Marketing, Administration and Management, Accounting and Finance, with few variations for individual languages: for all graduates, the top three were Personnel/Social Services/Medical/Security, Accounting/Finance and Science/Engineering/Research/Design/Development (USR, 1995).

Research

CILT, during the first thirty years of its existence, has provided a forum open to the secondary, tertiary and higher sectors, and as such has played a pivotal role in many developments in modern languages in HE, through: its language teaching library and enquiry service, supported since 1992 by a network of sixteen regional Comenius Centres; its long and distinguished list of publications; its role in servicing organisations and participating in new ventures – CILT's role as midwife in the emergence of the Association for Language Learning as a unitary organisation in 1990 was, in this respect, exemplary – the organisation of conferences; and its research register.

The National Council for Modern Languages in Higher and Further Education (NCML: 1972–94) represented the interests of modern language research and development, following the demise of the Committee on Research and Development in Modern Languages (CRDML: 1964-70). NCML mounted a successful campaign in 1981–82 for an inquiry into modern languages in higher education; through no fault of the NCML, the work of the inquiry was neither completed nor published; some of the material was analysed in three articles in the *Language Learning Journal* (Meara, 1993 and 1994). The Universities Council for Modern Languages (UCML), constituted in 1993, became the accepted forum for the promotion of research, teaching and learning in modern languages, co-operation between institutions, associations and others, the formulation of policies and the pursuit of their adoption by national and international agencies.

Many research projects in modern languages fall into the gap between the remits of the Economic and Social Research Council (ESRC) and the Humanities Research Board (HRB, set up in 1993) of the British Academy, both of which include linguistics but exclude research into curriculum design and teaching methodology. Nevertheless, a number of projects have managed to secure funding: close collaboration between departments of modern languages and departments of linguistics is an essential means of ensuring that some research projects in modern languages are adequately funded. Figures produced between 1990 and 1995 for the Association of University Professors and Heads of Departments of French (AUPHF) show that university departments of French are not turning out postgraduates either in sufficient numbers to meet future demand, or in the specialist areas where staff are needed, such as language-related studies. The provision of research studentships runs way behind the number of postgraduates willing and qualified to pursue research in modern languages: fewer than half of the current number of postgraduate researchers in ML are funded by the HRB. A central problem is the widening gap between the complexity and sophistication of research techniques and preoccupations, and the development and application of these in terms of programmes, materials and methods: according to the rules of the game, an article read by twenty people, or a collection of papers read by 100, constitutes 'publication', but before fundamental research can be of practical assistance to teachers and learners, a great deal of further work needs to be done on it – and funded.

An agenda for modern languages in higher education

As we celebrate CILT's thirtieth birthday we both look back on significant progress made and forward to future priorities. For what it is worth here is a possible agenda for the future:

1. The role of UCML as a **single voice for ML in HE** should be expanded, so that it can become a more powerful champion of our collective interests, and guardian of our common individuality.

2. The technology exists for the establishment of a **national database** on ML in HE: this will be essential for Government planning, for individual universities and ML departments, and for schools/colleges and employers. What is not needed is another 'instant snapshot' which takes years to develop and print. Data on-line could include: student enrolment, courses, starting levels, languages offered, staffing trends: *Any national strategy for MFL needs to be based, among other things, on clear statistical information. This project has shown just how difficult it is to measure, with any accuracy, the trends in MFL across the HE system as a whole, and to identify developments in individual areas* (Rigby, 1991).

3. Expansion of student numbers means that demand for new staff, as those recruited in the 1960s retire, will increase. MA/PhD work is concentrated on further study leading to research; training for the real work of a university lecturer is minimal. There is a need for **a new qualification, a PGCHE**, to be awarded in conjunction with existing MA/PhD arrangements, providing all-round professional training, including teaching practice and courses on administration, finance, etc.

4. Many reciprocal schemes between individual HE institutions are well-established, but ML departments find it costly and time-consuming to match the increase in numbers of students by an increase in **work placements abroad** other than as FLAs. It is time for a Central Bureau for Work Placements and Exchanges (CBWPE), to act as a clearing-house for all exchange and placement schemes between UK institutions and employers, and their counterparts elsewhere in Europe.

5. The universities chose to mark CILT's opening in 1966 by dropping their centuries-old entry requirement of a basic attainment in a FL. This should be restored (along with English and Maths) as part of a general reform of the 18+ examination on a 'group' basis. For the universities to throw their support behind such a reform would make a fitting thirtieth birthday present for CILT.

References

Centre for Research in Educational Marketing (CREM), *Market trends in the demand for ML coursed in HE*, a report for the UCML (University of Southampton, 1995)

Evans C, *Language people: an experience of teaching and learning modern languages in British universities* (Open University Press, 1988)

Finlay I F, *Careers in languages*, (Museum Press, 1969)

Healy F, *Foreign language teaching in the universities*, (Manchester UP, 1967)

James C V and S Rouve, *Survey of curricula and performance in ML 1971–72*, CET, University of Sussex, (CILT, 1973)

Meara P, 'What do students do on a language course?', 'What should language graduates be able to do?' and 'The year abroad and its effects' in *Language Learning Journal* 8, 9 and 10 (ALL, 1993 and 1994)

Nott D O, 'New approaches in ML at undergraduate level' in *ML teaching in the 1990s, Aspects of Education* 43 (University of Hull, 1990)

Opper S, U Teichler and J Carlson, *Impacts of study abroad programmes on students and graduates* (Jessica Kingsley, 1990)

Powell B, *Boys, girls and languages in school* (CILT, 1986)

Rigby G and R G Burgess, *Language teaching in HE. A discussion document*, (University of Warwick, 1991)

Sewell P, 'Survey of language-learning activities' in *AFLS Newsletter* 24 (Autumn 1989)

Steadman H, *Careers using languages* (Kogan Page, second edition, 1987)

Stern H H (ed), *Modern languages in the universities*, Modern Language Association (Macmillan, first edition 1961, second edition 1965)

Universities and Colleges Admissions Service, *UCAS handbook 1996 entry* (UCAS, 1995)

Universities Statistical Record, *First destinations of university graduates* (UCAS, 1995)

5
University courses for non-specialists

James A Coleman

Thirty years ago there were very few university language students outside specialist modern language departments. Today the majority of university language students are specialists in disciplines other than modern languages. A revolution has taken place, but it is not yet complete.

The very establishment of modern languages in universities barely a century ago was a revolution, wrought against strong opposition from disciplines such as classics and mathematics which were viewed as more academically rigorous. Indeed, the study of classics was seen by generations of Victorians as a full education in itself. To gain acceptance, the approach to foreign languages had to reflect the values of the time by adopting the classical model: philology and literature. Despite the growth in number and size of modern languages departments since then, the retention of the redundant 'modern' – originally marking a distinction with 'classical' – in the title of many departments reflects the conservatism of the profession in both its attitudes and its terminology. This conservatism held back and still affects the development of languages for students specialising in other disciplines.

The dominant model of university foreign language studies for two-thirds of the present century ignored their role as a contemporary means of communication, and classroom language exercises aped those of classical studies: prose translation epitomises activities which are designed to be intellectually exacting rather than communicatively useful. Small wonder that in this climate, and despite reiterated criticism that the model adopted for modern language studies was an inappropriate one, scorn for the acquisition of practical language skills, and for that part of a department's teaching force and teaching schedule devoted to developing them – if indeed any resources **were** so allocated – became entrenched in the culture of university language departments. The 1960s brought only a partial change.

For the first and only time in the history of these islands, new universities were created whose mission was as much the social, intellectual and personal development of the individual as any vocational goal. The generation of new, young staff then recruited to the expanded higher education sector has since grown old in post. Perhaps the absence of subsequent new blood recruitment, and even of inter-institutional movement, especially in the humanities, allowed attitudes to fossilise: in a 1993 poll, humanities lecturers were alone in rejecting the view that a university's job is to train students for a career.

But in the 1960s Stern (1964) could write of excitement at *the spread of languages into further and adult education and into industry*, and that *the university language departments are the pace-makers of linguistic activities.* The former Colleges of Advanced Technology (CATs) introduced the first vocational degrees in applied languages. The Robbins Report had recommended developing language provision for those studying technical subjects, and at the ten new universities, which were built on green field sites, the curricula, like the buildings, could be designed from scratch without historical constraints. Some chose to offer a language to all students – at the new University of Kent it was even compulsory. But language was still perceived as merely *an instrument of communication [. . .] not an academic discipline* (Stern, 1964, quoting Peacock, 1948). The provision of such courses was known as 'service' teaching, and the students as 'non-specialists': derogatory terminology has always been part of language provision for specialists in other disciplines (SODs). At Essex, language learning was defined:

> . . . *as a practical skill as distinguished from an academic discipline dependent on the command of the language. [. . .] The Languages Centre [. . .] is envisaged as a kind of service station to other departments.* (Stern, 1964)

Even when its practical value is recognised, the status of language learning and teaching has always been lower than that of other university studies.

My personal conviction is that there is no harder challenge facing staff in university humanities departments than to teach a foreign language successfully. Nor is there a domain in which teaching and research – real scientific research as opposed to scholarship – are more intimately bound together. But the lowly status of language teaching has typically left its advocates short of resources and political influence within institutions, and led to many of the problems now facing SODs language schemes.

Growth of languages for students of other disciplines

Various means have been adopted of delivering foreign language tuition to SODs, and not all waited for the Beatles decade. In Scotland, which for several hundred years had twice as many universities as the rest of this island, a modern language has been, for much of the twentieth century, a compulsory degree component in the older universities, along with a philosophical and a mathematical subject. When I taught at Glasgow in the mid-1970s, the two first-year French courses shared over 700 students. Elsewhere, solutions were found in autonomous learning, Combined Honours, and Institution-Wide Language Programmes (IWLPs).

Many universities of all types – Oxbridge, Hull, Warwick, York, for example – have well-established Language Centres which maintain a tradition of offering largely independent but often certificated language learning to staff and students, over and above their normal curriculum. Such courses suffer more than most from the unrealistically inflated expectations generated by colour-supplement adverts from companies whose language packages are designed to sell, rather than to work. Drop-out rates from drop-in centres tend to be high.

Combined Honours was for a generation the most popular way of combining a language with another discipline, even if, for many years, it was seen as the easy option, suited to weaker students, and even though little or no effort was made initially to adapt the syllabus to students with a broader range of interests. The former CATs pioneered languages with science, and now there are nearly two hundred subjects which can be combined with French (Coleman, 1994a). With nine out of ten British universities committed to modularisation of the curriculum, and many already into their second decade of a unit-based syllabus, study of a foreign language is increasingly allied not only to the culture or literature of a language area, but to a wholly distinct academic discipline.

The European Language Proficiency Survey (Coleman, 1996) shows that, even among specialist linguists, fewer than one in four now opt for Single Honours. The majority, especially of better qualified applicants, are following Joint or Combined Honours courses, with business studies as popular a second major as another language. One in eight specialist language students is on a modularised course. The majority attitude of students, then, whether language 'specialists' or not, is clear: the language is part of a course of study leading to a job. Asked to name their main reason for studying a language, they respond 'my career'.

Probably the most significant development in terms of numbers is the IWLP movement, whose origins lie in a re-evaluation, around 1988-89, by the Standing Council for Heads of Modern Languages in Polytechnics and other Colleges (SCHML) of 'servicing' arrangements in the then polytechnics. Typical schemes, since imitated by many older universities, offer a language as an optional integrated element or a free-standing option with or without accreditation. Teaching is concentrated in the first two years at university, in preparation for possible residence abroad and because timetables then are less rigid. French and German are most popular by far, but up to ten other languages may be available. Language tuition represents 10% to 25% of contact time, at around three hours per week, totalling up to 100 hours of classes and perhaps twice as much independent work. If accredited, the language will represent 10% to 15% of course credits. Courses are offered at between three and seven levels, from beginner (*faux débutant* for French) to post-'A' level. A communicative approach is quasi-universal, with small-group work the norm.

While students of languages generally have been under-studied, SODs have been virtually ignored (Coleman, 1994a). The absence of reliable statistics on language students as a whole has been repeatedly lamented (Rigby and Burgess, 1991; Scott, Rigby and Burgess, 1992; Thomas, 1993; Coleman, 1996). Numbers of SODs are still harder to ascertain. The Universities Statistical Record and its successor the Higher Education Statistical Agency, having failed for three decades to accommodate the complexities of Combined Honours involving languages, have failed so far to register even the existence of these, the majority of university language students. By contrast, the high response rate in the 1991-92 nationwide survey coordinated by Thomas (1993) endows his figures with a degree of authority. He identified 53,564 language students, of whom 29,491 were 'non-specialist linguists'. 47% of institutions sampled then offered the opportunity of learning a foreign language to all students, virtually all of them being certificated. There were also 7,708 students following language courses which were not a formally assessed course component. Principal reasons for **not** offering language training to all were given as lack of resources, lack of timetable space, and the demands of professional bodies. Thomas's snapshot was taken during a period of rapid expansion in student numbers which has since been halted, but the numbers of SODs can only have grown since his data were collected.

Largely as a result of the European Union's determination to increase to 10% the proportion of European students spending part of their university education in another member state through programmes such as ERASMUS, SODs are more likely than before to need the foreign language for their specialist studies. 20% of ERASMUS grants go to business students, and 10% each to social scientists and engineers. They may also end up working abroad: the latest figure is 14% for language graduates but 3% and rising for graduates as a whole.

The psychological challenge of the foreign language

To understand the particular psychological obstacles facing non-specialist linguists requires a brief restatement of what makes language learning unique among university disciplines. Language learning comprises elements of memorisation, of understanding, of analysis and synthesis, even of intensive training of muscles and responses, but what distinguishes it is its psychological component. Our native language is perhaps the most fundamental feature of our personal and social identity, through which all our experience and all our contacts with others have been filtered. To step outside it, to abandon the control which it provides of our immediate environment, to stumble and blunder like a child, to lose the security of native-language communication voluntarily, repeatedly and for several hours a week requires a unique psychological impetus. This is why success depends in large measure on the psychology of the individual learner, and why attitudes, motivation and anxiety have been shown to be powerful predictors of success or failure in language acquisition.

Bringing an inappropriate model of the learning process to the language classroom can prove an obstacle to the science student of languages, all of whose other experience at school and university stresses a purely intellectual apprenticeship, although often the relative informality and student participation of the average language class comes as a blessed relief. Many language teachers report their groups of scientists and engineers to be the most motivated and consequently the most enjoyable to teach. But Evans (1988) cites research showing science students as less mature, seeking certainties and secure boundaries, and coping less well with ambiguity, an analysis echoed in Reuben's discussion (1994) of the mind-set underpinning scientific disciplines. Entwistle (1972), rating students of different disciplines on a range of psychological measures of personality, had previously demonstrated that the pattern of abilities, values and attitudes of science students is diametrically opposed to that of language students. Given the unique nature of language learning, and its in-built provisionality and insecurity, we might expect such students to fare less well in learning a foreign language, even if this were their only handicap.

While the differences between specialist language students and SODs are narrow on such features as travel, language anxiety, and attitudes (Coleman, 1996), there are twice as many men among the SODs (six out of ten) as in specialist language departments. There is also a significant divergence of the types of reasons given for studying the foreign language: SODs are proportionately more likely to cite those motivations which correlate with low foreign language achievement and correspondingly less likely to opt for those correlating with high achievement.

Practical problems

Good practice dictates that all students should have the opportunity to study a foreign language, that appropriate space should be made in their timetable for a 'little-and-often' approach incorporating independent study, that their achievement should be accredited, and that they should be taught by well-qualified and well-motivated staff in an appropriate location. But the low status accorded to language teaching means that those responsible cannot negotiate on a basis of ideal practice. Non-language departments will almost certainly misunderstand and frequently resent the real demands of language learning. Managers negotiating resources will use IWLPs as one element of complex inter-faculty funding deals. As a result, classes too often take place in unsuitable lumps – instead of or even after an afternoon in the lab – in locations wholly unsuitable because of size, acoustics and/or lack of equipment. Under-resourced IWLPs cannot provide adequate coordination, secretarial and administrative support, or staff development. IWLP staff often enjoy the least job security and prospects of any university staff, with temporary and part-time contracts the norm. Their status may be confused by inappropriate administrative groupings involving related but distinct language provision, including English for Academic Purposes – a necessary support for so many fee-paying students especially in Science Faculties – and commercial income generation, incorporating translation and interpreting services and commercial language tuition, often in English as a Foreign Language.

Teaching quality, however, is often **not** a problem: ironically, while specialist linguists are taught by untrained and variously committed individuals whose main interests lie in a non-linguistic domain, SODs may well be taught by trained and experienced language teachers, often poached from secondary or further education. The award of valid and widely recognised certificates of proficiency is still more pressing than for language graduates, but the current multiplicity of systems does not provide it, while language NVQs have not yet provided the hoped-for solution.

Specialists in other disciplines who wish to develop foreign language skills do not, then, have an easy time of it. But I believe that their lot, which has already improved in some respects, will continue to be enhanced, for the following reasons:

In the face of massive cuts in higher education funding, of the staged withdrawal of state funding for students which means that keeping a student at university costs one quarter of a typical income each year, of the average debt of around £5,000 which they nonetheless graduate with, of the historically high levels of unemployment which appear to be becoming permanent, of the job insecurity prevalent in British society, the 'finishing-school' notion of higher education seems to be disappearing, perhaps for good. Students, parents, employers and universities themselves are recognising that graduates need jobs, and that high among the skills employers seek is a competence in one or more foreign languages.

76   There are an increasing number of models of good practice, where a university has seen the importance of languages to its current and future students, and imposed an effective and fully-resourced programme in which part of the weekly schedule for all students is cleared for optional language classes, which are integrated in student timetables and degree assessments.

Those developing institution-wide programmes or similar systems are no longer isolated pioneers but can call on extensive publications and expertise. There are professional organisations: the Directors of University Language Centres (DULC), established in 1981 as a self-help group, has become more active with an expanded membership and links to the rest of Europe through the Confédération Européenne de Centres de Langues dans l'Enseignement Supérieur (CERCLES) and the latter's annual conference. We have already referred to the role played by SCHML. There exist also many personal and institutional links with parallel associations involved in Languages for Special Purposes in other countries, such as the Association de Professeurs de Langues dans les Instituts Universitaires de Technologie (APLIUT), whose annual conference regularly includes British speakers.

Additionally, building on initial studies listed in Coleman (1994a), there are the British Isles conferences at which information exchange takes place, and whose proceedings are published. The annual conference on Institution-Wide Language Programmes began in 1991 at Wolverhampton Polytechnic (Hartley, 1992), and has since been held at Anglia Polytechnic University (Ferney, 1993), Liverpool John Moores University (Archibald, 1994), the University of Central Lancashire, and Nottingham Trent University – the proceedings of these last two are to be published together with a selection of key articles from earlier meetings. A *Science and Language Workshop* at Surrey University led to a useful publication (Parker and Reuben, 1994) in the series *Current Issues in University Language Teaching*, and the proceedings of the most recent in the series, held in the West of Ireland in 1995, are now in press (Royall and Conacher, 1996).

Purpose-designed materials for specialists in other disciplines are now coming on stream, with Scotland, the source of innovative university language teaching materials for the past two decades, once again taking the lead (Dickson, 1993; Taylor, 1994).

There are signs that the entrenched bias against practically-oriented research into language teaching, especially where the outcome is new teaching materials, may be weakening. The European Language Proficiency Survey has shown how much research remains to be done and in what areas.

The current assessment of the quality of the student experience, being carried out for modern languages in 1995-96 under the auspices of the Higher Education Funding Councils for the four countries of the United Kingdom, is drawing attention to any inadequacies of Institution-Wide Language Programmes and similar undertakings – to the extent that their shortcomings can in some instances reduce the grade for language provision as a whole – and to the desirability of having research expertise in all aspects of a department's teaching portfolio, including language.

Lastly and most important is the explosion of demand and the demonstrable success of languages for SODs nationwide. Examples are easily found of programmes which recruit 75% of potential students, or which have shown a four-fold expansion year-on-year. The day may not be far off when a foreign language joins self-awareness, personal transferable skills, information technology skills and intellectual skills as an essential component of all British university degrees.

References

Archibald L (ed), *Conference proceedings of the 3rd national Institutional Wide Language Programmes conference* (Liverpool John Moores University, 1994)

Coleman J A, 'Institution-Wide Language programmes in British higher education: national problems and perspectives' in Parker G and C Reuben (eds), *Languages for the international scientist* (AFLS/CILT, 1994a)

Coleman J A, *Language teaching, language learning, language testing* (University of Portsmouth, 1994b)

Coleman J A, *Studying languages: a survey of British and European students. The proficiency, background, attitudes and motivations of students of foreign languages in the United Kingdom and Europe* (CILT, 1996)

Dickson M, 'Integrating authentic material and new approaches in the teaching of engineers' in Coleman J A and A Rouxeville, *Integrating new approaches: the teaching of French in higher education* (AFLS/CILT, 1993)

Entwistle N J, 'Students and their academic performance in different types of institution' in Butler H J and E Rudd (eds), *Contemporary problems in higher education. An account of research* (McGraw Hill, 1972)

Evans C, *Language people* (Open University Press, 1988)

Ferney D (ed), *Proceedings of the 4th national Institutional Wide Language Programmes conference* (Anglia Polytechnic University, 1994)

Hartley P D (ed), *Institution-Wide Language Programmes. Proceedings of conference held at Wolverhampton Polytechnic September 1991* (Wolverhampton Polytechnic, 1992)

Parker G P and C Ribbon (eds), *Languages for the international scientist* (AFLS/CILT, 1994)

Peacock R, 'Modern languages as an honours school' in *Universities Quarterly*, 2, 2 (1948)

Reuben C, 'Building bridges' in Parker G P and C Reuben (eds), *Languages for the international scientist* (AFLS/CILT, 1994)

Rigby G and R G Burgess, *Language teaching in higher education. A discussion document* (University of Warwick Centre for Educational Development, Appraisal and Research, 1991)

Royall F and J E Conacher (eds), *Issues in languages for special purposes. Theoretical approaches and practical applications* (University of Limerick, 1996)

Scott D, G Rigby and R G Burgess, *Language teaching in higher education. A report to the Training Agency* University of Warwick Centre for Educational Development, Appraisal and Research, 1992)

Stern H H, 'Modern languages in the universities: achievements and present trends', *Modern Languages*, 45, 2 (1964)

Taylor S S B, 'The Nuffield Foundation Science-French project. A research-based linguistic development for students in new and old universities', in Parker G P and C Reuben (eds), *Languages for the international scientist* (AFLS/CILT, 1994)

Thomas G, *A survey of European languages in the United Kingdom 1992* (CNAA, 1993)

―

Editorial footnote: effect of university entrance requirements

As these chapters go to the printer the composition is announced (June 1996) of the *National Committee of Inquiry into Higher Education* under the Chairmanship of Sir Ron Dearing. The committee may draw encouragement from the recent transformation of university foreign language studies, both for specialists and non-specialists, described above. At the same time, it is to be hoped that the committee will address a crucial issue for the future recruitment of language students for HE and eventually of language teachers for the schools. It concerns the adverse impact on sixth form language studies of inflexible university entrance requirements, especially since the abandonment (1966) of the centuries-old requirement of a foreign language for university entrance, and subsequent narrow insistence on high grades in only three subjects. This has discouraged pupils from continuing foreign language study after age sixteen. The dropout of boys has been especially marked. Despite encouraging growth of numbers taking GCSE in languages up to age sixteen, twelve out of thirteen boys drop serious study of their language in the sixth form:

England and Wales

Boys' entries for French and German in GCSE (age sixteen) in 1993:	175,965
'A' and 'AS' entries in 1995:	13,361

See also Appendix II, Table 6, where numbers of eighteen-year-olds taking a ML in General Studies are shown. Only one Board, NEAB, includes a ML element in its GS paper. This tests (by multiple choice questions) a limited reading knowledge of the ML. The ML element counts only 10% of the total paper.

In Scotland the proportionate dropout of boys at age sixteen from serious ML studies is almost identical:

Scotland

Boys' entries for French and German at Standard Grade (age sixteen) in 1994:	25,591
Higher Grade entries in 1995:	1,863

Repeated attemps to broaden university entrance requirements so as to include a foreign language (as was common in Higher School Certificate pre-war) have failed. Cambridge tried harder, perhaps, than any other university to encourage broader programmes but had to confess in 1979:

Cambridge has from time to time tried to ensure some breadth of study by candidates for admission . . . The university gave up such attempts because they tended to discourage applicants from applying to Cambridge . . . The university concludes that no university in isolation could afford to impose entrance requirements designed to encourage breadth of study in the sixth form . . . they would have to be imposed by the Department of Education and Science. (Cambridge University Reporter 335/109, 17 January 1979)

Language teachers in sixth forms will await with interest the Dearing Committee's response to this challenge.

Part

two

**Languages
for all?**

1966-1996 *YEARS*

Comprehensive re-organisation of secondary schooling did not begin with Anthony Crossland's famous Circular (10/65). Already in 1963, 90 LEAs had re-organisation plans and, by 1965, 12% of children were in comprehensive schools (Kogan, 1971). Crossland's Circular merely *'requested' LEAs to submit plans for comprehensive re-organisation of secondary education.* Crossland's Minister of State, Reg Prentice (who later left the Labour Party and became a Conservative minister), pressed for the word *request,* in the Circular, to be replaced by *require,* but Crossland refused this. Although the Circular was withdrawn by Margaret Thatcher in 1970, the swing to comprehensive schooling accelerated and by 1978 over 70% of all secondary pupils were in comprehensive schools.

Maurice Kogan (1971) reports the following exchange with Crossland about the 1965 Circular:

Kogan: . . . *here was a major change, but the Government had done no research on the effects.*

Crossland: *Well this argument had a natural attraction for an ex-academic like myself . . . but it was wrong. It implied that research can tell you what your objectives ought to be. But it can't. Our belief in comprehensive re-organisation was a product of fundamental value judgements about equity and equal opportunity.*

Research might not have altered 'fundamental objectives', but it could at least have averted two decades of muddled thinking which equated *comprehensive schooling* with *mixed-ability class teaching.*

The special problems for foreign language teaching posed by comprehensive re-organisation are examined in Part two.

6

The challenges of secondary education

Alan Moys

The statistics cited in this chapter refer to England, Wales and Northern Ireland. A separate note on developments in Scotland and relevant Scottish examination statistics follows on p94.

The challenge of comprehensive re-organisation

The decade of the 1960s has acquired its own – sometimes negative – mythology, but underlying much of the social and moral ferment of the time was a new confidence and optimism, and a sense of excitement which was evident in education as elsewhere. Much of the confidence stemmed from a belief that science and technology were providing definitive answers to hitherto unresolved questions. Against this background it seemed both timely and logical to launch into the bold enterprise of comprehensive secondary school education, a process which was to accelerate in the late 60s and the 70s. That this fundamental re-organisation of secondary schooling should have happened without coordinated research into its implications and without the systematic retraining of the former grammar and secondary modern teachers may seem irresponsible in retrospect, but the mood for change was strong and a sense of buoyancy prevailed.

In no subject area in the curriculum can the change to comprehensive education have been more fundamental in its demands and aspirations than in modern languages. With some notable and pioneering exceptions, the learning of languages had hitherto been the preserve of the grammar schools, whose teachers had perfected approaches which worked well enough with able pupils bent on examination success. As schools re-organised and merged to form comprehensive units, however, teachers were often and understandably at a loss to know how best to approach the teaching of languages in this new context. In some cases, the grammar school model of provision was simply transferred to the comprehensive school, with less able pupils excluded from language learning or offered a diluted diet, while more able pupils followed programmes inherited from the grammar school. More often than not, however, schools set themselves the target of teaching a language to all pupils at eleven for up to three years, at which point – and sometimes earlier – the subject would become

optional. In most cases a second foreign language was made available at twelve or thirteen, generally to selected pupils.

Teachers also had to find methods and materials appropriate to the whole ability range, especially when, as was most frequently the case, mixed-ability grouping was favoured. Many teachers and their advisers saw potential solutions in a shift of emphasis to the spoken word, as in the newly developed 'scientific' methods of the audio-lingual/audio-visual era, and in the associated hardware of the tape recorder and the language laboratory, but these methods and materials had in most cases been devised for different audiences, e.g. adult learners, and their use in school contexts was largely unresearched. The Nuffield (later Schools Council) funded project based at York sought to correct this mismatch by developing and publishing courses in French, German, Spanish and Russian designed for and pre-tested in our secondary school classrooms. While these courses enjoyed considerable success, it was unfortunate that the use of the later stages of the French course *En avant* in secondary schools was to a degree compromised by the collapse of primary school French in the 70s – the first stages of *En avant* having been designed for eight-year-old beginners.

Thus, in the ten years from 1965–75, teachers of languages faced a twofold challenge, greater than in any other subject area:

- a shift from teaching selected able pupils to teaching all pupils, often in mixed-ability groups;
- a shift of emphasis from written skills to oral skills.

The coincident arrival of these new challenges on the one hand and a host of alluring but untried methods and equipment on the other led unfortunately to this being a period of expensive mistakes. Too many initiatives were insecure, too many models unresearched. The result was that for many pupils the experience of language learning did not incline them to continue once the subject became optional, and around 70% of all pupils abandoned the learning of a foreign language by the age of fourteen. In only a tiny minority of schools was a language compulsory to sixteen.

The low point came in 1977 with the publication of the HMI report *Modern languages in comprehensive schools,* based on a survey of 83 schools in 40 different LEAs. The damning criticisms in the report included lack of planning, inadequate schemes of work, unclear objectives, inappropriate approaches for slower learners, insufficient challenge for able pupils, and lack of leadership by heads of department. The report prompted a sharp reaction, on the one hand from teachers, who felt that it was all too easy to catalogue their failings at the end of a period of great upheaval, where certainties were all too few; and from in-service trainers, advisers and inspectors, who proceeded to give top priority in in-service training to topics such as departmental management, syllabus design, schemes of work, and assessment. The emergence at this time and the subsequent rapid rise of the 'Graded Objectives Movement' underlined the fact that teachers and advisers were working hard to develop language learning programmes tailored to the abilities of all learners. By the mid-1980s there were graded objectives schemes in a majority of education authorities throughout the UK, with increasing numbers of pupils opting to continue language learning beyond fourteen. The graded objectives movement also brought the great benefit of extensive teacher involvement in areas such as syllabus and course design (see GOML, Chapter 7).

In terms of Government policy on provision for modern foreign languages in schools, the DES seemed to be sitting on its hands for much of the 1980s. A long promised policy statement finally emerged in 1986, but offered little that was new, and was grudging in its acknowledgement of the contribution of graded objectives. A much bolder HMI publication in 1987 in the *Matters for discussion* series (DES, 1987) anticipated the National Curriculum by proposing that a language should be compulsory from eleven to sixteen. It also proposed that the second foreign language should be delayed until 14+, but this idea was widely resisted and did not resurface.

The National Curriculum heralded the promise of a major advance in provision, in that a modern foreign language was to be a foundation subject, to be studied by all pupils from age eleven to sixteen. This move was widely supported by the language teacher associations, and there was intensive activity to prepare schools for the phasing in of this significant step forward in provision. However, when Sir Ron Dearing undertook to slim down a National Curriculum which had become overblown and unworkable, the resulting recommendations (Dearing, 1993), though well intentioned, compromised the clear vision of languages for all to sixteen. The statutory requirement that all pupils should follow a full modern foreign language course in Key Stage 4 was replaced by an expectation that most would follow at least a 'Short Course', accredited within a frame of GCSE or GNVQ. As a result, teachers risk finding themselves back to planning a three-year course plus what could easily be a full course for a further two years for the able and a short course for the rest. Let us hope that the expertise and commitment of teachers, together with the pressures of the OFSTED process and the determination of schools to offer high quality education will mean that, in the event, most schools will ensure that all learners follow a full five-year course.

Leaving aside the false starts and changes of direction which have accompanied the introduction of the National Curriculum, its effects on language learning have been largely positive. Schools have generally accepted that a language should be compulsory to sixteen, and pupils are being entered successfully in greater numbers for the GCSE examination, which now closely reflects the content, skills and competencies which pupils acquire in school courses. This positive effect becomes clear if we look at entry levels for public examinations at 16+ over the last thirty years:

16+ examination entries		
	Languages	All subjects
(England and Wales)		
1965, GCE + CSE	225,848	2,400,996 (= 9.4%)
1975, GCE + CSE	361,334	4,946,761 (= 7.3%)
1985, GCE + CSE	415,888	6,297,781 (= 6.6%)
1995, GCSE	547,224	5,431,625 (= 10%)

The message from these figures is a mixed one. While it is gratifying that the number of 16+ entries has more than doubled between 1965 and 1995, for much of the thirty-year period under review the 'market share' of languages – modern foreign languages entries as a proportion of all entries – declined, from 9.4% in 1965 to 6.6% in 1985. However, in recent years the arrival of GCSE and the National Curriculum have led to an encouraging recovery in that modern foreign languages entries in 1995 had risen to 10% of all entries.

Languages 16–19

'Languages for all to sixteen' has understandably been seen over the years as a pre-requisite for improving participation rates in language learning in the sixteen to nineteen age group. It is in this area that our education system has most seriously failed over the past thirty years to provide for generalised levels of foreign language competence among our young people. The year 1970 saw the publication of a truly visionary document, *New patterns in sixth form modern language studies* (Schools Council, 1970). The following assessment from it could, alas, just as easily have emerged in 1996 as in 1970:

One of the most disturbing aspects of the present system of sixth form courses and examinations is the number of pupils who drop their modern language after successfully taking 'O' level . . . The causes are undoubtedly complex . . . Nevertheless the lack of a suitable non-specialist course in a modern language which could be dovetailed in with a pupil's main interest is undoubtedly a strong contributory factor in deterring many able pupils, who have enjoyed their language studies, from continuing them past 'O' level.

The working paper goes on to remind us that until 1950 there existed, alongside the then Higher School Certificate, *a well recognised examination, the Subsidiary, which was taken by the non-specialist linguist in the sixth form.* What is more, it was apparent from available figures that more candidates entered for the Subsidiary than for the principal paper:

1947	No of pupils awarded 'credit' in School Certificate (French)	14,046
1949	No of pupils entering for the subsidiary paper	3,756
1949	No of pupils entering for the principal paper	3, 076

(Joint Matriculation Board)

Furthermore, when the subsidiary paper was dropped in 1950 the proportion of pupils going on from a pass at sixteen to enter for 'A' level remained unchanged, suggesting that those who would have taken subsidiary level were now lost to language study. What was absent in 1970 and is still absent today is the sort of broadly based post-16 curriculum which would avoid the narrow specialisation and imbalance of the 'A' level system. Tinkering with the system by introducing, for example, 'AS' levels has had little overall impact and fails to address the deeper need for reform. Such reform has been widely canvassed by all sectors of society, and when it comes – as come it must – it should lead to a foreign language being considered an essential part of the curriculum of most students in sixteen to nineteen courses.

In the absence of the sort of reform outlined above, the numbers of students choosing to continue a language beyond sixteen declined not only in relative terms but in actual numbers over 25 of the past 30 years. For much of the period only some 12% of language learners at sixteen continued seriously to develop their foreign language competence. Put more starkly, seven out of eight of those language learners who made it to sixteen stopped serious study at that point. In the last few years there are indications that the decline has been halted, since there has been an encouraging upward trend in modern foreign language entries for 'A' level (see Appendix II, Table 3). This is in no small measure a result of the success of GCSE, and may also stem from increasing public awareness of the importance of language skills with the advent of the Single European

Market. It is also a great tribute to teachers who have shown imagination and tenacity in developing more attractive and stimulating programmes within the constraints of the present 'A' level system.

88   The following charts show statistics for England and Wales. The Scottish picture is described in the following section (p94).

Total language entries for GCE 'A' level 1965, 1975, 1985 and 1995
(and see Appendix II, Table 3)

Note: HSC (Higher School Certificate) was replaced by GCE 'A' level in 1950. The figures for HSC in 1938, as the last 'normal' year before World War II, are shown for comparison. The figures in italics show entries for modern languages as percentages of the total subject entries in each year.

	1938	1965	1975	1985	1995
Total subject entries	36,951	370,435	499,883	609,215	730,415
Total entries modern languages	5,894	36,528	37,489	34,999	47,920
	15.9%	*9.8%*	*7.4%*	*5.7%*	*6.5%*

Boys, girls and languages

Within the overall picture as set out so far in this review, one particularly disturbing feature has been the widening gap between levels of participation (and success) by boys and girls. The figures speak for themselves:

Boys and girls examination entries at 16+ compared.

Entries for all modern languages in GCE 'O' level and CSE in 1965, 1975 and 1985, and in GCSE in 1995. (See Appendix II, Table 2).

GCE total entry MLs

CSE total entry MLs

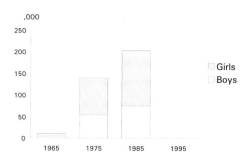

All 16+ exams total entry MLs

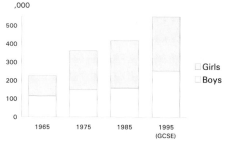

While the total number of 16+ entries has grown steadily to more than double the 1965 level, the percentage of entries from boys had dropped from 50.3% to 38.2% by 1985. The advent of GCSE and the National Curriculum has somewhat redressed the balance, but even if 50:50 parity is ever achieved, there remains the persistent additional evidence throughout the period that girls outscore boys in examination performance across all modern language examinations at 16+ (see Appendix II, Table 2).

At 'A' level, the trends have been similar, but the disparity is more severe, with boys down to 28.4% of the entry in 1985:

Boys and girls examination entries at 'A' level compared

GCE 'A' level: total entry all MLs 1965, 1975, 1985, 1995 (also see Appendix II, Table 4).

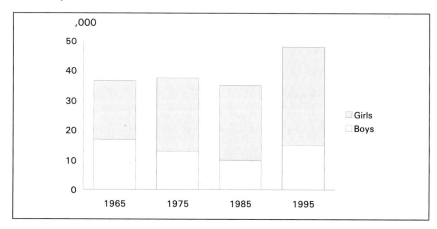

Bob Powell, in his excellent study *Boys, girls and languages in school* (Powell, 1986), charts the presence and progress of this imbalance throughout the pyramid of language learning from its broad base at eleven to its tip in higher education. He advances the very persuasive explanation that boys are disadvantaged from an early stage in languages because key decisions affecting their future progress are made at an age when girls have the advantage of more rapid maturation:

> *British teachers of foreign languages have, generally speaking, rejected the notion of mixed-ability teaching for other than the very early stages of learning. They prefer to set pupils according to proven or assumed linguistic ability. I say 'assumed' because in some schools setting can take place as early as half-term in the first term of the first year. It has been my view for a long time that many able boys fail to take languages seriously or appear to be performing less well than girls because they find themselves relegated too early to ability sets lower than is appropriate. Consequently, those pupils in the school who appear to be linguistically gifted tend to be girls. There is little chance of redressing the balance between boys and girls in the upper school if the imbalance has already been created and fixed during, or at the end of, the first year.* (Powell, 1986)

Powell's thesis is incidentally supported by the fact that the boy/girl imbalance in languages was not present at the beginning of the thirty-year period under review, but seems to coincide with the arrival of the comprehensive school. If his conclusion is correct – and he quotes a survey of 42 mixed comprehensive schools where the ratio girls to boys at 12+ following setting by ability was 65% : 35% – there would appear to be a solution worth trying. The imbalance could be addressed by making up sets containing, for example, the top thirteen girls and the top thirteen boys rather than the top 26 pupils. Since OFSTED inspections look carefully at equal opportunities, there is a potential route to improvement here. Some schools are also experimenting with setting boys and girls separately in the early secondary years.

Choice of languages offered

An innocent bystander reading the *National Curriculum Order for MFL* issued in 1991 might have been forgiven for inferring that our education system had at last faced up to the challenge of a polyglot world and was offering our young people a rich diversity of language learning choices. No fewer than nineteen languages were to be admissible as first foreign language in our schools: the eight working languages of the EC (Danish,

Dutch, French, German, Modern Greek, Italian, Portuguese and Spanish) plus Arabic, Bengali, Chinese (Cantonese or Mandarin), Gujarati, Modern Hebrew, Hindi, Japanese, Panjabi, Russian, Turkish, and Urdu. Did this mean that at last the choice of 'French or French' in schools had been replaced by a broader range of alternatives, and that students would emerge in increasing numbers from our schools with qualifications in a whole variety of languages? In fact, the Government's intention was simply to provide a legal status for these languages if any school chose to introduce them: there was never any question of attempting to resource their wholesale development as foundation subjects. (See Appendix II, Table 7, for entries in 1994 in community languages in GCSE and GCE 'A' level.)

This hint of ambivalence has been present throughout the debate about diversifying the choice of languages offered in our education system, as both policy makers and schools have struggled with the practical and logistic implications of trying to widen choice in this area. It was always clear that market forces alone would never lead to a richer menu of languages being offered: what was needed was a clear and persistent strategy by Government, backed by proper levels of human and material resources. Government policy statements have for the last ten years supported the notion of diversification, but material support has been on a small scale, and such gains as have been secured have been counterbalanced by important losses.

Not that there has been any shortage of serious debate or consideration of the options, either with a focus on the claims of individual languages or from a more global viewpoint. We will consider an example of each. The Annan Report (Annan, 1962) on the teaching of Russian led to an expansion of Russian teaching, resourced to a major extent by a DES teacher retraining programme and by the availability of teachers who had learned Russian during their national service. However, once the immediate effect of these initiatives had passed, and as financial pressures on schools increased, the progress in the 1960s gave way to decline over the next twenty years. From a peak of 800 schools offering Russian in 1971, the figure dropped to just over 300 in 1992. Although there have been signs of recent improvement, nearly 60% of schools surveyed (Muckle, 1988, 1992) have fewer than twenty pupils learning Russian. As schools produced fewer and fewer candidates for public examination at sixteen and eighteen, the falling demand for Russian courses in higher education led to the closure of a number of university Russian departments in the 1980s. Putting all these developments together, as a nation we now have fewer Russian linguists for peacetime activity than for the cold war effort, and tragically we have lost much of the higher education capacity to respond quickly to any increased demand.

At a more global level, there has been a steady consensus in support of the view that secondary schools should offer more than one language, and this has been generally achieved, following the model which already existed in selective and many comprehensive schools in the 1960s, with a second foreign language available as an optional subject from the age of twelve, thirteen or fourteen, and most often only to pupils selected on the basis of their performance in the first foreign language. It is widely accepted, however, that this approach has only a limited impact on the overall picture, and in the last ten years schools have increasingly been encouraged to go further by offering more than one language as **first** foreign language – or more often as joint first foreign language with French. The DES established and funded a pilot project to explore diversification of the first foreign language provision in ten LEAs in 1988–90, and subsequently funded a number of colleges to run linguistic retraining programmes in order that more teachers could offer two languages. However, these provisions have now been discontinued, and the future of diversification now lies with individual schools. Some modest rebalancing of provision has, however, been achieved:

Examination entries at 16+, by language

Figures in italics show 'market share' for each language, as a percentage of all ML entries. (See Appendix II, Table 1.)

	1965 GCE 'O' & CSE	1975 GCE 'O'& CSE	1985 GCE 'O'& CSE	1995 GCSE
French	171,996 *76.2%*	265,440 *73.5%*	310,983 *74.8%*	350,027 *63.9%*
German	33,723 *14.9%*	62,743 *17.4%*	74,471 *17.9%*	129,386 *23.6%*
Spanish	10,011 *4.4%*	16,375 *4.5%*	17,769 *4.3%*	40,762 *7.4%*
Italian	2,895 *1.3%*	4,928 *1.4%*	3,035 *0.7%*	5,610 *1.0%*
Russian	2,393 *1.1%*	2,649 *0.7%*	1,554 *0.4%*	1,882 *0.3%*
Other MLs	4,830 *2.1%*	9,559 *2.6%*	8,076 *1.9%*	19.557 *3.5%*

It can be seen that between 1965 and 1985 German gained ground, largely at the expense of less commonly taught languages, while French and Spanish maintained their market share. The 1995 figures, however, reveal that French has lost some ground to German and Spanish, which are the languages known to have been introduced most frequently as alternative first foreign languages in response to policy pressure for diversification. There has also been a valuable growth in 'other languages' such as Urdu. It may in fact be unreasonable to expect diversification of languages eleven to sixteen to go beyond the 'top three' (French, German, Spanish) on any generalised basis. Certainly it is unfair to argue that it is the responsibility of schools to produce linguists to match the economic and trading needs of this country, and it is unlikely that it will ever be feasible to have widespread school provision in languages such as Japanese or Portuguese (see discussion of the secondary school course as 'apprenticeship in learning how to learn' languages, on pp19 and 45). Nonetheless, it remains a great pity that we have not sought with greater vigour to introduce less commonly taught languages as choices in curricula for the sixteen to nineteen age group, and thus to provide the opportunity and encouragement for older students to start new languages (another recommendation of Working Paper 28 in 1970 . . .). Perhaps then we would have seen a greater flowering of diversification of languages in higher education.

The report of the findings of the TES/CILT Modern Languages Survey (CILT, 1996) provides up-to-date information on the current provision of languages other than French in the early years of the secondary school and on the factors affecting diversification.

References

Annan N (Lord Annan), *Report on the teaching of Russian* (HMSO, 1962)
Burstall C et al, *Primary French in the balance* (NFER, 1974)
DES, *Modern foreign languages to sixteen,* Matters for discussion (DES, 1987)
Dearing Sir Ron, *The National Curriculum and its assessment.* Interim report, York (NCC, 1993). Final report, London, (SCAA, 1993)
Muckle J, *British schools in which Russian is taught* (ATR, 1988; 1992)
Powell B, *Boys, girls and languages in school* (CILT, 1986)
Schools Council, Working Paper no 28: *New patterns in sixth form modern language studies* (Evans/Methuen Educational, 1970)
TES/CILT Modern Languages Survey (CILT, 1996)

Editorial note: The march towards 'languages for all' in Scotland has taken a different route from that in England and Wales described in the foregoing chapter. It does, however, share interesting parallels with experience in the rest of the UK. The following footnote on the Scottish experience has been prepared with the help of Scottish CILT.

Languages for all in Scotland

In Scotland the move towards 'a foreign language for all' has not posed quite the same problems as were faced in England and Wales. Scottish language teachers were spared the trauma of adjustment to an underfunded and unresearched comprehensive re-organisation. Secondary schools in Scotland had been non-selective for many years. That all pupils should at least start a foreign language was accepted. Debate in Scotland turned on the harder question, still not fully resolved in England: should a foreign language be obligatory for all pupils up to age sixteen?

Secondary schooling in Scotland starts at age twelve, not eleven, as in the rest of the UK, and lasts four years. This has a bearing, clearly, on the economics of teacher provision for 'languages for all' up to school-leaving age at sixteen, as it must have done, also, on discussions about the priority to be given to starting the foreign language in the primary school in Scotland (see Chapter 15).

A major step forward in the Scottish march towards the goal of a foreign language for all up to age sixteen came in 1972. In that year the Scottish Central Committee on Modern Languages issued the publication *The place and aims of modern language teaching in secondary schools.* This argued the growing need for foreign languages in industry and commerce, in the explosive expansion of foreign travel and development of the European Community.

This publication was followed, three years later, by a project set up by the Scottish Consultative Council on the Curriculum, aimed at making French accessible to the full range of ability in the early years of secondary education.

A logical consequence of this was the revision of the first examination, the Scottish Certificate of Education, Ordinary Grade, and this came in 1987. The examination, re-named Standard Grade, was completely re-shaped. The new syllabus had as its primary aim the development of communicative competence and confidence. It encouraged the use of the target language in class and assessed pupil performance at three levels –

Credit, General and Foundation – covering six grades. In the new examination all pupils were required to take three parts of the syllabus: speaking, listening and reading. A fourth element, writing in the foreign language, became optional.

The final step on the road to 'languages for all up to sixteen' came two years later with the publication of Circular 11/89 by the Scottish Education Department. This recommended that the study of a foreign language should *normally be pursued by all pupils for the four years of secondary schooling and that this aim should be achieved by the year 1992.*

It is interesting that in England and Wales a comparable regulation was not to become effective until September 1996.

Comparison of the move towards 'languages for all' in England and Scotland, though the historical background differs considerably, yields interesting similarities.

In both countries, despite their very different schooling traditions, a common thread runs through pupils' performance in the secondary stage. It is the marked linguistic precocity of girls compared with boys at adolescence. One effect of this is seen in the difference between boy/girl entries for foreign languages at age sixteen over the years (see Appendix II, Table 2).

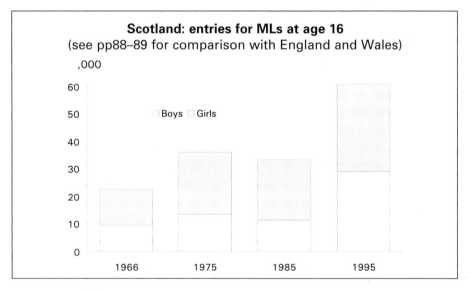

The 1995 Scottish figures show a market reduction in the imbalance between girls' and boys' entries. This would seem to show the effect of Circular 11/89. In the rest of the UK the gap between boys' and girls' entries, while still considerable, also narrowed by 1995, probably reflecting the introduction of GCSE in 1988 which attracted more boys to continue their foreign language beyond the age of fourteen.

In Scotland, as in the rest of the UK, girls' linguistic precocity during the adolescent years is shown clearly in their higher percentage of good passes in first examinations at sixteen:

Scotland: Year 1995. Percentage of boys and girls with good passes (1–3) in Standard Grade:					
	French	German	Spanish	Italian	Russian
Boys	40%	49%	45%	48%	34%
Girls	59%	67%	72%	74%	73%

For comparison, the figures for the rest of the UK were:

Year 1995. Percentage of boys and girls with good passes (A–C) in GCSE:					
	French	German	Spanish	Italian	Russian
Boys	42.9%	47.5%	50.7%	73.8%	76%
Girls	56.2%	61.6%	63.9%	80.1%	83%

In Scotland the performance of those pupils who took the 'writing' option at Standard Grade shows a similar pattern. In 1995 rather more than half of all girl entrants in French took this option (12,386 out of 21,612) against only 8,104 boys out of 20,060. Far more girls scored good passes (1–3 grades):

Year 1995. Percentage of boys and girls with good passes (1–3) in Standard Grade 'writing' option:					
	French	German	Spanish	Italian	Russian
Boys	46%	49%	35%	32%	50%
Girls	60%	64%	51%	52%	73%

Scottish girls' linguistic precocity is further shown in percentage passes in English over the years:

Entries for English and percentage passes (A–C)				
	1966	1975	1985	1995
Boys	16,612	31,982	34,939	30,954
	69.3%	54.5%	51.6%	65%
Girls	15,166	34,488	38,013	30,153
	80.1%	67.1%	62.9%	80%

It would be surprising if this marked linguistic precocity in the mother tongue and in foreign languages at adolescence did not affect pupils' choices of study at the post-16 stage. This is clearly shown in the following table (see Appendix II, Tables 2 and 4).

Entry for Scottish Certificate of Education, Higher Grade (normally taken one year after the Standard Grade, i.e. at age seventeen) Figures in italics show subject entry as percentage of total entries, all subjects				
	1966	1975	1985	1995
All MLs				
Boys	5,180	5,006	2,852	2,127
	6.5%	*3.3%*	*1.6%*	*1.3%*
Girls	7,805	11,591	8,978	6,181
	9.8%	*7.7%*	*5.3%*	*3.8%*

The above table also shows the steady (and continuing) loss of ground of languages, both in absolute terms and as percentage of total entries in all subjects, by both boys and girls. A difference between Scottish 'Highers' and GCE 'A' levels in the rest of the UK, is that 'Highers' total entries, all subjects, have not shown the same steady increase over the thirty years under review as entries for GCE 'A' level. The latter rose steadily in England and Wales each decade by some 110,000 plus:

England/Wales
GCE 'A' level

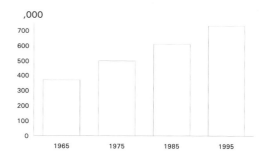

In Scotland there was a dramatic increase in total entries for 'Highers' in the 1960s and early 1970s, but little increase after that and even a falling off in the last decade:

'Highers'

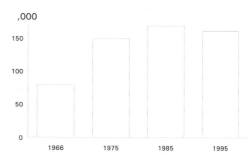

A striking similarity, however, between Scotland and the rest of the UK, is the extent of drop-out from foreign languages post-16. It is significant that Circular 11/89, making foreign language study obligatory up to sixteen in Scotland, does not seem to have arrested the incidence of drop-out post-16, when the study ceases to be compulsory (see Appendix, Table 6 (B)).

Boys and girls entries		
	Standard Grade 1994	Higher Grade 1995
French	39,448	5,111
German	13,932	2,167
Spanish	1,704	652

For comparison, figures in England, Wales and Northern Ireland were:

Boys and girls entries		
	GCSE 1993	GCE 'A' + 'AS' levels 1995
French	283,777	30,530
German	98,516	11,828
Spanish	22,861	5,367

That so many pupils drop their foreign language at age sixteen after years of hard work, just at the point when they might begin to exploit the language, in reading and exploring a neighbouring culture, seems a sad waste of pupils' time and of costly teaching resources. As in the rest of the UK, some important battles in the 'languages for all' campaign have been won, reflecting great credit on resilient teachers and those who have supported them in teacher training and in the Inspectorate, but there is much still to be done. It is suggested elsewhere in this volume that our language teaching house has a wastefully leaky roof. Scottish initiatives and experience have much to teach the rest of the UK, especially in pointing to ways of solving the problems of the earlier start in the primary school (see Richard Johnstone's account, Chapter 15) and in making the foreign language part of the programme for all learners up to age sixteen. Teachers and administrators in the rest of the UK will watch with interest how Scotland tackles the next battle, to construct a less leaky roof for the refurbished secondary curriculum house.

7

Graded Objectives in Modern Languages (GOML)

Brian Page

By the mid-1970s about 90% of eleven-year-olds were learning a modern foreign language. The only official objectives available, however, were GCE/'O' and CSE. In the main, both examinations took a very academic view of language learning. The majority of the marks was given for written work in the modern foreign language and grammatical accuracy was rewarded above all else. Consequently, when learners chose at age fourteen which subjects to take in public examinations, the academically able continued with a foreign language but most of the others did not. Surveys at the time showed that modern foreign languages were among the most unpopular subjects on the timetable. There was, understandably, widespread frustrastion among teachers and taught.

In this new situation, MFL teachers were faced with the question: if this is not what we want, what **do** we want? This led to other questions: If we are going to teach French (at the time it was almost always French) to the mass of the school population, what do we mean by that? What French should we teach? What is French for? Teachers had seldom asked themselves questions like this before. The answers were relatively simple but had far reaching implications and effects that radically changed the teaching/learning scene in the UK.

The main characteristics of GOML

Attainable objectives

What was wanted was a course shorter than five years which would give public recognition to modest achievement and which would encourage learners rather than discourage them. It was soon clear that a short course should be long enough to have some substance but short enough for learners to be able to see the end and so feel they could reach it and, most importantly, earn a certificate. Such schemes were already used for achievement in swimming and gymnastics and were well known in musical instrument learning. Indeeed, appropriately enough, Trinity College of

Music had a test of Spoken English set at twelve levels. Most GOML schemes ended up with three or four levels to cover the five years.

100 Language for communication

Any language exists to enable individuals to do things in the world by communicating their thoughts and feelings to other individuals. This concept was conspicuously absent from school language teaching and examinations at the time. There, French existed in order for learners to display, above all, a knowledge of its grammar. If, in contrast, we were to teach the French required for use in the real world, we must mean the world where French is used; we must assume that our learners will use French in France. There, they will need to get food and shelter, find their way about and make some contact with the inhabitants. These first ideas were soon refined. Young school learners would probably make a first visit with a school party where their most pressing needs would be taken care of. They would want to buy postcards, a present to take home, an ice cream and a coke and use some polite expressions to people they met. Later they might go on an exchange where they would need to converse with the family, exchange some personal information, express likes/dislikes and preferences and possibly use services like a bank and a telephone. Later again they might go independently with their parents and act as interpreters for the rest of the family. These were fairly typical scenarios which produced ascending sets of language behaviours, each wider and more complex than its predecessor. Many others were developed as schemes responded to local needs. These objectives are commonplace today, they were revolutionary then.

Authenticity

From all this came the concept of authenticity which was completely absent from traditional language teaching and examining. First, authenticity of task: what learners were to be asked to do in examinations was to mirror as closely as possible the sorts of activity they could expect to be involved in in the real world. Second, authenticity of material: our learners would need to understand and derive relevant information from public notices, newspapers, guides, advertisements, timetables, etc – actual material meant for French speakers and not concocted for learners. The same should apply to the spoken language. Native speakers using everyday language would have to be captured on tape and used in teaching and testing. This was in marked contrast to then current practice where little or no authentic material was used.

Defined objectives

It was characteristic of traditional foreign language courses that there was no indication of possible content or range of language required. In GOML, objectives were defined clearly. Learners were told exactly what they would be required to do and, if necessary, told what language they would need to do it. In this way, both teachers and taught knew what they had to learn.

All abilities welcomed

GCE/'O' and CSE were aimed at particular ability ranges, GOML were not. They described levels of language proficiency and therefore were not ability related. Ability was shown in how far and how fast learners went up the ladder.

Criterion referencing

Traditional examinations were norm-referenced, designed to produce a rank order showing which candidates were better than others. GOML tests were not concerned with who was better than whom. They were criterion-referenced, designed to see if an individual could successfully accomplish a task. If every one was successful, that meant they had learnt well.

How the ideas spread

After the publication of some early articles the response was rapid. In 1975 two groups of teachers, one in York led by Michael Buckby of the university Language Teaching Centre, and the other in Oxfordshire supported by the local adviser, set about putting the ideas into practice. They set their first tests in 1976. In 1978 alone 25 groups were formed. By the early 1980s there were over 90 in all parts of the UK. Many were derivative of York or Oxford. Others developed ideas of their own. In Lothian, the language adviser John Clarke created a highly sophisticated scheme that relied more than most on research and a deeply thought out language learning philosophy. It was also among the first to recognise its debt to the work of the Council of Europe (see Chapter 29). In Lancashire/Cumbria, LEA advisers working with St Martins College, Lancaster, set up a scheme which, at its height, had a bigger clientele than that of many GCE/'O' level boards. Some groups formed round university education departments, most were led by LEA advisers. A few generous LEAs seconded teachers part- or full-time to help with the work. Most offered facilities and meeting places. The East Midlands CSE board supported a local GOML scheme with a view to giving it official status. The work was formidable and was done by groups of teachers meeting in their spare time in evenings and at weekends. Not only had objectives to be defined and tests devised, but teaching materials had to be created since textbooks of the period were devoted to the GCE/'O'/CSE approach.

102

CILT played a specific and vital role. In 1978 it organised a seminar in which nine groups were represented. A second in 1979 assembled over 40. From this, the GOML National Co-ordinating Committee was set up which CILT supported with a small budget and important staff help, successively Sheila Rowell, Derek Hewett and Lid King. The committee published a regular newsletter, set up research projects (Harrison, 1982; Utley et al, 1983) and responded to the numerous Government and other official initiatives that proliferated at the time. It organised a very important annual workshop where representatives reported on progress in their schemes and discussed and devised activities, tests, teaching materials and methods. Internationally also the GOML idea spread. Interest has been shown from the USA to Malaysia. John Clarke of Edinburgh was seconded for a year to Australia to help with their scheme. The Council of Europe continues to draw ideas from the GOML experience.

The effect on public examinations

Enthusiastic teachers reported equally enthusiastic pupils. Research supported this view (Buckby et al, 1981). In areas where a GOML scheme flourished it was typical to reverse the fourteen plus option drop-out – two thirds chose to stay on rather than give up. The problem of public examinations then arose. GCE/'O'/CSE were, in the main, different in philosophy from GOML. As with teaching materials, teachers would have to make their own examinations. This was possible through the Mode 3 system. When CSE was set up, its founders recognised the need for flexibility in forms of examination in order to accommodate new ideas. Mode 3 allowed teachers to devise and mark their own CSE examination provided the papers, mark scheme and marking itself were scrutinised, monitored and approved by the board. This liberal system enabled teachers to devise official public examinations in harmony with their GOML schemes. Consequently, when the move to amalgamate GCE/'O' and CSE arose again in the early 1980s, language teachers were well placed to influence the debate because they had practical experience of setting new types of objectives and devising and operating new testing techniques for officially recognised examinations.

Although GOML never involved a majority of teachers and learners in the schools, it did engage the most dynamic and reflective fraction and therefore had an enormous influence not only on the GCSE but eventually also on the National Curriculum and the National Language Standards. In the 1990s, the general acceptance of a communicative approach, preoccupations with National Curriculum requirements, the imminence of Key Stage 3 tests and GCSE short courses, and particularly the collapse of the local advisory structure, have, with some notable exceptions, tended to dampen GOML activity, but the philosophy lives on.

GOML was successful because it had the irresistibility of the idea whose time had come. It responded to the immediate needs of a specific situation, but also crystallised aspirations that had been circulating for some time. It radically changed the approach to language teaching/learning by showing, first, that language is not just a body of knowledge to be acquired but a system to be used for a purpose and, second, that to motivate learners we must take their needs into account and reward then for what they can do. It was highly successful in teaching more languages to more people more successfully.

Unanswered questions

But nothing stands still. The communicative approach leaves several questions unanswered.

Grammar

It was long assumed that grammatical accuracy was essential if communication was to be efficient. This is now seen to be untrue. In the famous tiger story (Page, 1990), the message *You run quick, big tiger he come* is crystal clear in conveying the course of action to be taken and the reason for it. But it is not English. This is the *me go sleep now* problem. When we pose efficient communication of the message as the criterion to be achieved we run the risk of teaching pidgin – a *me Tarzan, you Jane* proficiency – effective enough but not the language in question. What has not been realised is that there are two sorts of grammar: a minimum necessary for communication of the facts (all the above quotations rely at the very least on the minimum grammar of an accepted word order) and the rest which enables us also to convey an image of ourselves which affects the way others treat us. We all adopt the grammar (and vocabulary and pronunciation) of the group we wish to be identified with. Most correct grammar fulfils a social function. We need definitions of these two parts so that we can give grammar a communicative value that reflects its dual role. If you merely want to convey raw information then *me go sleep now* is sufficient and should be rewarded as successful. If you wish to be treated more naturally and with more seriousness, then it is not enough, a more sophisticated skill in manipulating the language is necessary.

104 Assessment

Assessment based on communication in simulated authentic situations, vital though it is, cannot sample the linguistic repertoire our learners should acquire in order to be all round communicators. For example, object, relative and demonstrative pronouns pepper the spoken and written production of native French speakers and all appear in GCSE syllabuses. Yet learners of French rarely produce them spontaneously. It is in fact extraordinarily difficult to devise authentic, communicative tasks which oblige a candidate to use, for example, a relative pronoun. So they go largely untested except for recognition. Perhaps we need two sorts of assessment: a test of communication in the real world and a test of knowledge of the language without which communication remains impoverished. There is an enormous danger. We must never go back to learning grammar for its own sake or we shall again end up translating disconnected sentences like the one famously quoted by Otto Jespersen (1904) from a textbook of the time: *your horse has been old.*

Dangers ahead

The new national criteria for GCSE

These abandon authenticity of task and thereby open the door to testing techniques lately discouraged. Current intentions for testing in the target language rely heavily on multiple choice questions and true/false choices, techniques which make no attempt to mirror real life language tasks. The assessment system is in danger of claiming to encourage a communicative approach but in fact of going back to rewarding (and therefore encouraging in the classroom) language behaviours that have no corresponding echo in everyday language use.

Inertia

The revolution in language teaching that took place in the 1970s and 1980s was teacher driven. GOML spread and flourished because teachers found they responded to their needs. They were flexible so that groups and individuals could adapt them to their situations. Through the Mode 3 system these ideas could gain official recognition and eventually affect the national examination itself. In 1996 almost none of this is the case. LEA language advisers, key people in encouraging new ideas, are now rare and, where they exist, no longer have the means to initiate and experiment they once had. The examination system no longer allows a Mode 3 variant. There is no longer any mechanism for new ideas arising in the classroom to be tested in small scale schemes, find wider expression, gain official recognition and influence national policy. Today it would be extremely difficult for the GOML movement to start, grow and flourish. Teachers must use organisms like CILT and ALL to maintain some dynamism. The present system has a built-in inertia which is a recipe for stagnation.

References

Buckby M, P Bull, R Fletcher, P Green, B Page and D Roger, *Graded objectives and tests for modern languages: an evaluation* (Schools Council, 1981)

Harding A, B Page and S Rowell, *Graded objectives in modern languages* (CILT, 1980)

Harrison A, *Review of graded tests, Schools Council Bulletin 41* (Methuen Educational, 1982)

Jespersen O, *How to teach a foreign language* (London: Allen and Unwin, 1904). Translated from the Danish original *Sprogundervisning* by S Yhlen-Olsen Bertelsen

Page B, 'Graded objectives in modern language learning' in Kinsella V, *Cambridge Language Teaching Surveys 3* (CUP, 1985)

Page B and D Hewett, *Languages step by step: graded objectives in the UK* (CILT, 1987)

Page B, 'Why do I have to get it right anyway?' in Page B (ed), *What do you mean, it's wrong?* (CILT, 1990)

Utley D, R Mitchell and J A N Phillips, *Hear/Say: a review of oral/aural graded tests; Schools Council Bulletin 44* (Methuen Educational, 1983)

8
Special educational needs

Bernardette Holmes

For the generation that watched Dr Who defeat the daleks on black and white television, there was no entitlement to learning a modern foreign language. Throughout the 1950s and 1960s, modern foreign languages were the province of the grammar schools. Only the most able learners, about 25% of the school population, studied a modern foreign language from eleven to sixteen.

The coming of the comprehensive school in the late 1960s and 1970s seemed to signal a commitment to a single system of state education where all pupils would have access to a common curriculum, including a modern foreign language. The development, starting in 1965, of the Certificate of Secondary Education (CSE), aimed to offer a meaningful alternative examination to the General Certificate of Education (GCE). CSE gave more emphasis to listening and speaking and offered topics of more interest and relevance for pupils with differing levels of ability. Mode 3 especially was welcomed by teachers of lower ability pupils because it allowed greater involvement of practising teachers in syllabus design. Despite the sincerity of the endeavour, however, CSE did not motivate more pupils to study languages in their fourth and fifth years. Across the curriculum as a whole, the fact of having a two-tier system was a disincentive to many pupils and pupils leaving school with CSEs did not carry the same currency in their pockets as those with GCE, and employers knew it.

The relatively small uptake in languages in Years 4 and 5 led to limited investment from publishers in developing appropriate course material for the full ability range. With the exception of Mary Glasgow Publications, whose pioneering spirit encouraged the development of *Eclair*, resources for the lower ability language learner had very low priority. What little material there was tended to be in French only. In the classroom it was often a case of 'follow the same course more slowly' or 'make your own materials'.

An example typifying the worst features of such an approach may be cited. It was in an urban comprehensive school which would have been bottom of any league table, had they existed then. In this particular school, which now, fortunately, does not exist, the comprehensive ideal of mixed ability teaching had been tried and rejected. In an effort to raise standards pupils were 'colour coded' by ability on entry. Green, Yellow and Pink were slightly better than Brown, Orange and Grey, but the best pupils were arranged in rank order in sets Red, White and Blue. It is not difficult to imagine what sorts of youngsters appeared in 'lower GYP and BOG'. Blatantly labelled in this way from their first term in secondary school, they were highly unlikely to feel good about themselves or the prospect of learning anything, let alone French, which in their eyes was 'worse than useless'. In an empty room with no resources beyond a stick of chalk and a board with a cracked surface, the teacher faced 28 pupils who had pre-vious 'form' in 'getting rid of the French teacher'.

Such pupils clearly had many difficulties which affected their learning but they did not all have the same difficulties. Within the class there were pupils with low reading ages in their mother tongue, hearing and speech difficulties, emotional and behavioural problems. There were irregular attenders, and the 'naughty boys who ought to know better', those who became legends in their own school lifetime. There were pupils for whom English was a second language, one or two children from the Special Unit and a further two or three awaiting appointments with the Educational Psychologist. Indeed any child who did not fit into an accepted pattern of behaviour and learning style landed in this bottom set. The biggest prob-lem was the mismatch between what was expected of the pupils and what they could achieve.

The search for solutions

Teachers across the country were facing the same difficulties, searching for answers, re-appraising their teaching methods in order to meet the needs of all learners. Meeting together and sharing experiences and ideas, they developed Graded Objectives in Modern Languages (GOML) (see dis-cussion in Chapter 7). Targets and materials began to be developed to suit learners of all abilities. GOML offered a form of accreditation which recog-nised success in achieving valid, short-term, achievable goals.

In the best of the Graded Objective schemes, testing materials were similar to teaching materials. The benefits of this were threefold:

i.   the learning did not have to be suspended to facilitate testing;
ii. pupils were familiar with test types;
iii. teaching and learning styles influenced the process of assessment, rather than the other way round.

Through more positive experience of foreign language learning, many pupils, including those with learning difficulties, developed self-esteem and a sense of achievement. Many pupils involved in Graded Objectives could receive an LEA-approved form of accreditation at regular intervals to prove that they were making progress. (At York they even got a certificate from the University!). Whether developments in Graded Objectives were causal or contingent, by 1985 the number of pupils opting to continue their foreign language up to first examination at sixteen had increased to some 40% of the age group. By the beginning of the nineties some 50% of pupils were continuing language study for five years.

The advent of GCSE in 1988 gave a common passport to learners of all abilities which took account of previous developments in examining and of GOML. Discrete skill assessment through the medium of English led to some problems in teaching methodology but had the benefit for the less able that they could compensate for deficits in one skill area by higher achievement in another. Certain Mode 3 initiatives allowed modular assessment, which favoured a wider range of ability and appeared to be a natural development from Graded Objectives.

The Statutory Order for Modern Foreign Languages in the National Curriculum laid before Parliament in autumn 1991, giving foreign languages the status of a Foundation Subject, meant that schools had to make provision for study throughout Key Stages 3 and 4 across the ability range. Emphasis in the Statutory Order on use of the target language as the medium of study caused anxiety, especially regarding teaching pupils in special schools who had not had access to foreign languages and those less able and less motivated pupils in mainstream schools who had previously not continued their language at Key Stage 3.

Advice from the National Curriculum Working Group

The prospect of languages for all was daunting but the Working Group Initial Advice (March 1990) with its famous 'green pages' was an inspired and inspiring document which embodied received good practice with a clear vision of more ambitious things to come.

Although the issue of pupils with special needs was not specifically addressed, there was a clear commitment to entitlement and challenging expectations of both teachers and learners. The Initial Advice described, without seeming to prescribe, the kind of learning environment which would favour all learners, including those with learning difficulties, and put the needs of learners at the heart of the curriculum.

Under the heading 'Opportunities, Competences and Strategies' we read:

Learners should take part in activities which are enjoyable and valid in themselves, as well as those whose primary purpose is to rehearse language. The classroom can thus become a world in which activities and content reflect the wishes of teachers and learners interacting with each other.

It became possible to plan our own schemes of work round learners' abilities, interests and intrinsic motivations. The Areas of Experience proposed were broad, giving scope for teachers and pupils to draw on their own creativity and personal experience. We could explore our own lives and customs and our own environment in the foreign language, as a prelude to comparing and contrasting our world with that of others. We could personalise the curriculum and, in so doing, enable pupils to build conceptual bridges between what goes on in the foreign language classroom and in real life.

The Initial Advice continues: *'What will learners gain from this?'* is the question from which all planning should start. Active response to zany pictures, rhythm, rhyme and mime, varied ways of developing listening acuity and frequent consolidation of language through pair work and games, indeed, all the activities which Lower 3 GYP and BOG had enjoyed were not only encouraged, but were now quasi-legitimate. It was recommended to provide opportunities for pupils to create poems, stories and simple factual accounts for other audiences, including other learners.

The combination of the breadth of Areas of Experience and the non-content-specific nature of the Statements of Attainment allowed flexibility for teachers to pursue cross-curricular work. This was reassuring to teachers in special schools for whom cross-curricular projects are a regular feature.

Teaching a foreign language through music, art, drama and physical education introduces content of a wider, less self-centred nature. This area is one in which teaching MFL to pupils with SEN may have much to teach ordinary schools about delivery of content relevant to low attainers. (Modern foreign languages and special educational needs: a new commitment, NCC, 1993)

The National Curriculum Working Group welcomed comment on the suitability of the Attainment Targets and programmes of study for the different categories of pupils with specific learning disabilities. Many replies were received and by October 1990 the Final Report of the Working Group was able to be largely positive about provision for pupils with special needs in both special and mainstream classes.

In principle, all pupils with special educational needs should have the opportunity to experience a modern foreign language. We are supported in this view by the advice we have received from a large number of sources and by the evidence we have found of active preparation for introduction of a foreign language into the curriculum of special schools. We are also encouraged by the efforts being made by modern languages departments in mainstream schools to accommodate slow-learning and lower ability pupils.

110 Response from teachers

An example of good practice

An instance of successful innovation in developing a scheme of work directly relating to pupils' own experience is offered by a school for boys with emotional and behavioural difficulties. In preparation for a return visit from their German exchange partners, who are also in Residential Education, the class of fifteen-year-old boys designed a storyboard and made a video of school life. Each scene covered a different theme and drew on a topic of language. It was filmed entirely in German over a series of months. Each topic was taught using pair work and games and then the language was consolidated and extended in a new context as each scene from the storyboard unfolded.

Rethinking in the classroom

Unlike the move to comprehensive education, which had not been accompanied by systematic retraining of teachers, the introduction of the National Curriculum was supported by funding for training and for resources. Funds were, naturally, not unlimited, but language teachers, ever resilient and resourceful, generally made a little go a long way, responding energetically to the challenges of the National Curriculum, in both special and mainstream schools.

The period from 1990 to 1992 saw many initiatives involving collaboration between language teachers and teachers of pupils with special needs. Support and advice also came at national level, commissioned by the National Curriculum Council (NCC). Two project reports were published by the National Foundation for Educational Research: *Foreign languages for lower attaining pupils* by Barbara Lee and Peter Dickson (1991) and *Extending opportunities: modern foreign languages for pupils with special educational needs* (1991) by Barbara Lee. The first of these concentrated on the organisation and curriculum for lower attaining pupils in schools where all or most pupils were already studying languages for five years. The second focused on the staffing and in-service implications and the curriculum content and teaching methods being developed in a sample of four LEAs already extending foreign language provision for pupils with special needs. The information on LEA activities collected by CILT was used as a basis on which to select the authorities.

This coincided with an influential project funded by the NCC and managed by CILT. During February and March 1991 existing initiatives involving collaboration between teachers of modern foreign languages and special educational needs in some twenty LEAs became project partners in the CILT/NCC project. The project addressed predominantly the needs of pupils with moderate learning difficulties and those with emotional and behavioural difficulties in special and mainstream education. The project promoted action-research and supported large numbers of teachers through conferences, in-service training and publications.

Support from new technology

Helpful advice also came from the National Council for Educational Technology (NCET) (*Languages for all: IT in modern languages learning for children with special educational needs,* 1991).

New technology offered many ways to re-inforce language and motivate reluctant learners, especially boys. There was increased interest in the use of the concept keyboard. Programmes like *Touch Explorer* allowed different levels of input, to suit a mixed-ability class. Word processing, drafting and redrafting were promoted and pupils with difficulties in handwriting could, for the first time, produce work of the same quality as their peers. Database creation and simple data retrieval were popular with small groups of pupils working round a freestanding computer, working collaboratively. Desk-top publishing applications were widely used. Pupils created flashcards and made signs to display round the school making the environment 'European friendly', or designed menus and school plans.

Emphasis was placed on visual stimuli. The effective use of the overhead projector was promoted. A feature of good practice in many projects was the development of agreed symbols to support the use of the target language and assist recall. The same drawings could be used on the OHP, flashcards, card games and concept keyboard overlays. Care was taken to produce printed and written materials sympathetically, with greater awareness of how difficult it can be for learners with reading difficulties to decode a worksheet or a textbook page. Uncluttered layout was important; size of script was significant; even more important was the nature of the characters used. Were there clear upstrokes and downstrokes? Was the typeface easy to read? How many different fonts or styles of handwriting were presented? How many obstacles were placed between the learner and understanding the foreign language? A fortunate by-product of this was that the lessons learned informed publishers and shaped the coursebooks under development for implementation of the National Curriculum.

Games and multi-sensory learning

New games to rehearse language were invented. There were good examples of learners themselves inventing games and activities, finding out the appropriate language needed, with the help of the teacher or the Foreign Language Assistant.

These classroom developments were reinforced by a new realisation of the value of multi sensory learning – *Rhythm, rhyme and real objects are powerful allies and linked with other stimuli – visual, smell, touch, action – their power is significantly increased. Hear and respond, smell and respond, taste and respond – the message is 'let's get physical'* (Holmes B in McLagan P, *Steps to learning,* 1994). Both conceptual and linguistic development are helped by multi sensory approaches engaging both body and mind. Learning a language is something that learners do for themselves, not something that is done for them. This is specially relevant for pupils with learning difficulties.

The outcome of collaboration at local and national level between language teachers and SEN teachers was that pupils with special needs attained higher priority. At the same time, learning from colleagues in special education, modern language teachers began to analyse classroom activities and materials and become more aware of the many stages and tasks there were in what appeared to be a simple language transaction. There was increasing understanding of their difficulties and a greater readiness to experiment with teaching and learning styles. 'S' truly began to stand for 'special' and not 'second best'.

Positive progress reported

The CILT Project reported in February 1993:

The project has gathered empirical evidence showing pupils enjoying the MFL experience and making positive and noticeable progress. Learning even the rudiments of a foreign language enables pupils to extend and develop linguistically and to demonstrate new skills . . . (improving) pronunciation, progress in reading and listening . . . growing awareness of language in general. Evidence from the project suggests that pupils can operate in a foreign language at the same conceptual and linguistic level as in their own language; this ease of transference promotes general linguistic development. However, while many pupil-centred approaches have been developed in special schools, Project partners report difficulties in ordinary schools . . . it has proved more difficult in ordinary schools to develop integrated and differentiated programmes for many pupils with special educational needs.

Nevertheless by 1993, there was reasonably positive nationwide experience of the first stages of introducing MFL to pupils with SEN.

Recent setbacks

Effect of school league tables

With the introduction (1988) of the Grant Maintained system, allowing schools to operate outside LEA control, there has been increasing competition between schools to improve results by 'poaching' the best pupils. For lower attaining pupils and those with special needs this climate is unfavourable. Foreign languages are especially vulnerable.

The minimum statutory requirement in England at Key Stage 4 is a short course, while in Wales there is no statutory requirement at all at Key Stage 4. The temptation is clear not to enter lower attainers for GCSE.

Will it still be possible to plan the foreign languages curriculum around the needs of learners, as the Initial Advice recommended? Lee and Dickson (1991) observed that the starting point for planning curricula was invariably the form of assessment, greater attention being paid to the aims and objectives of the examination syllabus and less emphasis on methods of teaching and learning. With the Dearing revision of the National Curriculum. the removal of the ten-point scale and with statements of attainment measuring performance over four key stages to be replaced by eight level descriptions measuring performance up to Key Stage 3, the reins are firmly in the hands of the GCSE boards and the council of GNVQ to determine the nature of the curriculum in Key Stage 4. The new GCSE syllabuses will inevitably prescribe content and task types which will exert strong influence on how foreign languages are taught.

Similarly the future of GNVQ is precarious if it becomes synonymous with courses for low attainers. Vocational courses must provide something worthwhile for the full ability range and share the same standing as GCSE, otherwise they will not offer valid currency to pupils at either end of the ability spectrum.

There is less confidence now than there was in 1992. Courses and conferences on lower attaining pupils are less frequent than they were and it is of concern that there has been a dramatic reduction (41%) in the number of LEA advisory language posts between 1992 and 1995.

Liaison between foreign language teachers and colleagues with expertise in special educational needs must be maintained if we are to implement the Statutory Order and keep faith with the spirit of the Initial Advice. To fulfil our aspirations, the needs of pupils with learning difficulties and the support and training of their teachers must become a standing item on the national agenda for education.

References

DfEE and Welsh Office, *Modern foreign languages in the National Curriculum* (HMSO, 1995)

Holmes B, *Communication re-activated: teaching pupils with learning difficulties* (CILT, 1991)

Lee B and P Dickson, *Foreign languages for lower attaining pupils* (NFER, 1991)

Lee B, *Extending opportunities: modern foreign languages for pupils with special educational needs* (NFER, 1991)

McLagan P, *Steps to learning: modern languages for pupils with special educational needs* (CILT/NCET, 1994)

Modern foreign languages and special educational needs: a new commitment (NCC, 1993)

National Curriculum Modern Foreign Languages Working Group, *Initial advice* (DES and Welsh Office, 1990)

NCET, *Languages for all: IT in modern languages learning for children with special educational needs* (1991)

9

Languages in further education

Madeleine Bedford

Then and now

1966 was the year which saw a significant change in the further education sector, with the establishment of the first sixth form college in Luton. Until then, further education colleges had delivered almost exclusively vocational education, often highly specialised. Where foreign languages were included in the curriculum, they were usually an 'add-on' to vocational studies, for example courses in French for catering students.

Most students aged sixteen to eighteen studying languages were still in school sixth forms. GCE 'A' level dominated their curriculum, but even then schools and teachers sought to provide languages to a wider post-16 audience. Given titles such as 'complementary French' – and it was nearly always French– such courses were not universally popular with students. However, these courses often provided a stimulus for the introduction of 'authentic' sources of spoken and written language.

With the increasing move towards comprehensive schools in the sixties, some local authorities began to establish sixth form colleges, as in Luton in 1966. Four years later, in 1970, the first tertiary college was set up in Exeter. Broadly speaking, the sixth form college offered a full 'traditional' sixth form curriculum, while the tertiary college combined both traditional and vocational pathways. I think it fair to say that language teachers viewed these developments with some trepidation. Many of the newly established comprehensive schools made great strides in broadening access to languages for pupils to the age of fifteen/sixteen and in increasing the range of languages offered. But establishing viable sixth form groups was not always easy and the threat posed by the establishment of a new 'sixth form college sector' was keenly felt. In some areas, the local authority simply established 11–16 schools and all sixth form pupils went to the new colleges. One argument advanced was that the new colleges would create viable numbers in minority subjects, including languages other than French, thus saving them from extinction. We shall see later how far this premise has proved well-founded.

Those of us who embarked on a career in modern language teaching in the 60s were in at the start of a period of unprecedented technological and methodological change. Others have charted this in detail. The key changes were the much greater availability of user-friendly audio and later video hardware, soon to be supported by authentic materials of all kinds, as new 'A' level syllabuses in the late 70s and early 80s encouraged a burgeoning of production, often by groups of teachers inspired by a common wish to make language learning relevant for a wider post-16 clientele. Computers would follow, and by the mid-80s no self-respecting languages department was without at least some form of computer and some accompanying software. By the end of the 80s satellite TV was making its appearance, to be followed in the 90s by interactive video and the information superhighway. Throughout this period the language laboratory enjoyed mixed fortunes. In the 80s teachers were inspired by developments such as TVEI to develop work-related courses. In this they were supported by the introduction in the late 70s and early 80s of, for example, work-related modern language assignments for BTEC programmes and the introduction of the Foreign Languages at Work (FLAW) scheme of the London Chamber of Commerce and Industry (LCCI).

The current situation

What is the situation in 1996, thirty years on? The further education sector, which became independent of local authority control in 1993, is generally agreed to have made a successful transition to its new incorporated status. The sector currently includes some 450 colleges, of which 223 are general further education, 114 sixth form, 64 tertiary, and 55 specialist, mainly agriculture and art and design colleges. In all, the further education colleges account for 50 per cent of all sixteen-year-old students and 62 per cent of all seventeen-year-old students, full-time and part-time, that is more than 460,000 students in this age group.

How many of these students are learning a language? Unfortunately it is not possible to put a figure on this, as current published statistics relate only to 'A'/'AS' level and GCSE. These omit of course the many students entered successfully for other qualifications, including GNVQ units and free-standing qualifications from a variety of awarding bodies including the RSA, LCCI, etc and the fact that in FE colleges many and often most students are aged nineteen-plus. However, since 1993, with the introduction of regular inspections by the Further Education Funding Council's inspectorate, the picture has started to become clearer.

Many sixth form colleges offer substantial full-time mainstream provision of GCE 'A' levels and GCSEs, almost entirely for students aged sixteen to eighteen and in the day-time. They offer some restricted vocational provision, primarily some limited GNVQ servicing, and occasionally the Foreign Languages for Industry and Commerce (FLIC), or the Foreign Languages at Work (FLAW) qualifications provided by the LCCI. A few colleges are shifting to FLAW instead of GCSE, 'AS' or GNVQs. 'AS' levels are taught most often alongside 'A' levels, and there is no evidence that their popularity is increasing. Some colleges are using FLAW as an end-of-first year qualification.

The languages offered in sixth form colleges at GCSE and GCE 'A' level consist largely of French, German, Spanish and Italian, in that order. A typical pattern would be: 50 per cent of students studying French, 25 per cent German, 18 per cent Spanish and 7 per cent Italian. A small number of colleges provide less commonly taught languages, including Russian and Japanese. In some inner city colleges, community languages are offered, notably Urdu, Panjabi, Bengali, Chinese and Arabic.

While some general further education colleges still maintain a significant full-time mainstream provision, they are increasingly in the minority. The pattern for general further education (GFE) colleges is usually: a large number of part-time students, mainly adults; an increasing amount of servicing; and a substantial part-time day and evening programme. For example, one college reported 923 students studying MFL, of whom only 20 were full-time 'A' level students; a further 115 were following vocational courses. Servicing occurs in an increasing range of areas. Business studies and travel and tourism predominate, but there is servicing to other areas such as catering and service industries and to engineering and construction. The latter are largely driven by interest in the possibilities of working in the European Union. A number of colleges also provide language activities for students with learning difficulties and disabilities; these are often some of the most lively and enjoyed sessions of all.

Part-time students can be aiming for GCSE, 'A' level qualifications or vocational qualifications. The majority do not intend to take a qualfication but are studying for personal satisfaction, for holidays or work, or for social reasons. Many say they would leave if they had to take an examination and some say they joined an examination course only for the reduced fee level. However, accreditation that is successfully used in this context includes the Institute of Linguists examinations, some business foreign language qualifications and the Open College Network.

Less commonly taught modern languages such as Dutch, Russian, Japanese, Swedish or Greek are provided for part-time study, usually at beginners or GCSE level, where there is a tutor and sufficient demand.

Some colleges are experiencing problems in sustaining their provision. A number of reports comment that numbers of full-time students have declined over the past three years: for example, in one college from 200 to 149. In general, sixth form colleges are more prepared to sustain small non-viable groups in the hope of an upturn or to maintain the breadth of curriculum than general further education colleges. But in both types of college language groups are often small.

Entitlement statements for full-time students, and especially those that give an entitlement to languages, are rarely in evidence, although there is some good practice. In some colleges enrichment programmes or extension studies offer scope for students either to maintain existing skills or more usually to begin a language. Where colleges use General Studies 'A' level for extension studies, the programme frequently includes a language component; however, this is often offered only to those proceeding to the examination in the second year, so not all students have access to it.

Male and female imbalance

The gender balance of students studying modern languages is rarely equal. There is a preponderance of female students at all levels. The ratio of female to male students is more than 2:1 and it is not uncommon to find no male students in a group, whereas the converse is most unusual. In a nationwide in-depth sampling of 135 classes in eighteen colleges of all types, there were 318 male students against a total attendance of 1,025. This figure also underlines the point made earlier about the small size of many language groups: across all the classes inspected the average number of students actually attending was below eight. In a college in the south-east, however, the number of male students outnumbered females; in a sample of twelve classes there were 60 male students out of a total 102 in the groups inspected. Even here, though, average class sizes were small.

Teaching and resources

The teaching and learning in languages in further education is of good quality and, where students stay to the end of the course, results are also good. Students who take a language as a specialist subject often progress to a higher education course which includes a language. However, there is often substantial drop-out, especially where the language is not a key component of the course. Some shining examples exist of colleges which have successfully built in a compulsory and well-received language component to vocational courses.

The resources to support modern language teaching in further education are good. Teachers are well-qualfied. Most language departments have at least acceptable accommodation and good access to texts, audio-visual equipment and cassettes and information technology. The latter is often under-exploited, perhaps understandably so, given the need to train students and teachers to use it and the dearth till recently of really exciting materials. Throughout the years one of the constants has been the excellence of the radio and television output from the BBC, ITV and, more recently, other producers: often their materials provide the essential brightness and good ideas which enliven the more interesting classes. They are not always exploited as well as they could be.

Other enhancements have strengthened languages in further education, perhaps most notably the '1992' factor, when the excitement of the single European market spurred many developments. European Union funding has enabled many students to take part in foreign links and exchanges. These include students from every programme area, and they often receive at least a minimal introduction to the language of the country they will visit before departure.

The growth of courses in community languages is another very positive development. Indeed in 1995 it was only in entries for Urdu that the FE colleges had more entries combined than the schools sector. FE has constantly promoted classes in community languages at all levels. It should not be forgotten that FE has also been a major force in promoting the teaching of English for community groups, often reaching out to offer classes in locations and at times to meet the needs of students.

Issues to be faced

It is sobering to reflect that thirty years on, it is still possible to find post-16 students who spend a substantial proportion of their 'A' level courses studying foreign literature and grammar through the medium of English.

The key issues facing the further education sector, indeed post-16 modern languages as a whole, are standards and recruitment.

Reported standards at 'A' level are generally good, where students complete the course. But a finding of inspection was the difficulty of getting students, particularly girls – who constitute the major proportion anyway – to speak with ease. Colleges report continuing problems of transition from GCSE to 'A' level and evidence from some sources in higher education, particularly Germanists, suggests that all is not well at the transition point from 'A' level to degree courses. Evidence on standards achieved on 'non-traditional' courses is limited. Whether a pass in a GNVQ unit or other non-specialist qualification constitutes a nationally reliable measure of practical linguistic competence remains to be proven. Teachers and students deserve better research evidence and feedback in return for the time and energy they devote to teaching and learning languages.

Recruitment, as we have seen, has slowed in some colleges, while others are experiencing difficulty in sustaining their provision. Despite the great strides made in increasing the number of pupils studying a language in the compulsory sector, only a small proportion continue their study of one or more languages after the age of sixteen. Although there are encouraging examples here and there of colleges which have taken positive steps to make a language part of a broader curriculum, we are still a long way off from the goal of language competence for all students in the age group. Yet we hear, anecdotally but reliably, of companies forced to recruit overseas because they cannot find personnel with the requisite language skills in this country. The end-of-thirty-year report on languages in further education has to be *tries hard, making progress, but could still do better.*

Source for statistics

Examination and other data 1993–5: FEFC/DfEE
Examination entries and results 1966: supplied by CILT
Inspection findings: FEFC

10

An uneven language playing field

Eric Hawkins

. . . linguists and language teachers have seen their task as teaching language: they have not realized that it is teaching students to use language. Thus, they have often ignored the place of language in the wider curriculum of school and in society as a whole. (Bernard Spolsky, University of New Mexico, in Oller and Richards (eds), *Focus on the learner*, 1969)

*Our perception of the educational purposes of foreign language teaching is (inter alia) to **develop an awareness of the nature of language and language learning.*** (National Curriculum Working group on Modern Languages, *Final report*, 1990)

Suppose a visitor from Mars had arrived in the UK thirty years ago, to report back on the hominids he met. How should he describe them? He would know that they liked to call themselves 'homo sapiens'. But half an hour's attention to a radio News Bulletin would reveal the arrogance of that claim. It would be more accurate, he would surely have reported, to call them 'homo loquens', or, following Jean Aitchison, 'the articulate mammal', recognising language as the defining characteristic of humanity.

If our visitor had then gone on to enquire how this central human characteristic of language was treated in the education system, he would have been struck by a curious paradox. At university level, in the 1960s, there raged the most exciting debate about language that had been seen for one hundred years, provoked by Chomskyan claims for language as instinct, overthrowing four centuries of pragmatist denial of innate ideas.

Yet, paradoxically, nothing of this debate was reflected in school classrooms. The most obvious questions about language were seldom raised in school, still less answered:

1. *What is unique about human language? How does it differ from animal communication systems? (Why do human languages change? Do animal systems ever change?)*
2. *How do we acquire our mother tongue? What is the role of parents?*
3. *How does learning a foreign language at adolescence differ from getting the mother tongue?*

4. *Where did English come from? How does it relate to its European neighbours and to the 180+ languages spoken in the UK, every one of them older than English?*

5. *Who decides what English words mean? Is it the same in France?*
6. *How do individuals differ in their mastery of their mother tongue? Are differences in writing skills greater than differences in mastery of spoken language? Why? (see Mattingley, 1972).*
7. *What can 'incorrect' mean in the mother tongue (and in a foreign language?)*
8. *Why is English spelling so illogical? Does it take up to two years longer for an English speaker to learn to read than for a Spanish speaker, other things being equal? (see Stubbs, 1980).*
9. *How does language work to convey meaning? (e.g. what is the effect of word order, and how do English and Latin, say, differ in this respect?)*

Instead of systematic examination of such questions pupils were offered only a haphazard apprenticeship in language. As Her Majesty's Inspectorate noted (HMI, 1977):

Anyone, by following a group of pupils through a day in a secondary school, can prove that their language experiences are largely a matter of chance . . . The pupil's own language may be subject to spasmodic correction . . . (but) many pupils have a view of language as a minefield.

To see the language minefield at work, our Martian visitor needed only to walk down the corridor of any large comprehensive school. He would pass by five different classroom doors, behind which some form of language teaching was going on:

- *English (mother tongue)*
- *A modern foreign language*
- *English as a second language for 'minority' pupils*
- *A 'minority' language (Arabic, perhaps or Panjabi, Modern Greek or Cantonese?)*
- *At the end of the corridor, barricaded in for protection, the teacher of Latin, like the poet Henley,* bloody but unbowed.

These five kinds of language teacher seldom entered their colleagues' classrooms to listen to what the others were saying about language. Only the unfortunate pupil, commuting from one sealed-off teaching-box to the next, heard the discordant messages about language and tried to make some synthesis of them.

Re-thinking school language policies

Our Martian visitor would perhaps have noticed, however, that this haphazard apprenticeship in language was already being questioned. The Central Advisory Council for Education, chaired by the economist Geoffrey Crowther, reported in 1959.

We are all agreed that 'mastery of language' is one of the most important elements of a general education and one where there is little ground for complacency about the effectiveness of present teaching methods . . .

The committee's thinking had been concentrated by the imminent demise of Latin as a university entrance requirement, and therefore as a central element in the secondary school curriculum. The committee was divided as to what should replace Latin (or, as they put it, 'do what Latin does') but agreed in calling for . . . *rethinking of the whole basis of the teaching of linguistics in the schools.*

Reacting to the Crowther call for rethinking, the Schools Council set up a programme in *Linguistics and English Teaching* under the chairmanship of Professor Michael Halliday, eventually published under the title *Language in use* (Doughty et al, 1971).

While the Halliday team were at work, in the 1960s, however, English teachers were distracted by an untidy debate about 'language deficit'. It was a debate that generated more heat than light. It was given special urgency by the drift to non-selective secondary schooling signalled by the Crossland Circular of 1965 (see p82). The selective system had segregated children at 11, largely on a test of *verbal reasoning*. Now, in comprehensive schools, for the first time, children of markedly different verbal skills sat together in the same classes. And they were joined by increasing numbers of pupils from ethnic minorities.

English teaching did not come well out of the 'language deficit' debate. As professor Brumfit has observed: *little in their training had prepared them to look at language objectively* (Brumfit, 1991). This must explain the failure of Halliday and his distinguished team of linguists and teacher trainers to lift the angry, sterile debate about 'language deficit' on to a positive level.

In his introduction to *Language in use* Halliday explained that the aim was:

to develop in pupils . . . awareness of what language is, and how it is used, and at the same time, to extend their competence in using it. He called for a form of language study which can be valued as an end in itself, namely the development of awareness.

New evidence about illiteracy and home background

Before this lead could be followed the debate shifted in the early 1970s to the specific issue of illiteracy. It became increasingly clear that *the debate about selection at eleven had been largely irrelevant for many pupils.* Their careers were being determined long before the age of eleven. The evidence emerged from the National Child Development Study, a vast longitudinal study of a cohort originally consisting of all children born in the third week of March, 1958. News of their progress in the first seven years fell like a bombshell and caused a storm in press and parliament.

The report (*From birth to seven,* Davie et al, 1972) showed that, at age seven, after two years of infant school, *the proportion of poor readers from unskilled manual workers' families was one in two, compared with a proportion of one in twelve of children from the administrative class.* Further study (Bullock 1975: 21) revealed that the gulf between these two classes widened for every year they spent in school. The effect of schooling, therefore, had only reinforced the inequity of home background.

In fact the 1972 figures did not tell the whole story. Later research, (Rampton, 1981) showed that there was an underclass of poor readers, the children of West Indian origin. The Rampton research showed that of every 100 West Indian pupils aged 16+, only nine scored a pass (A to C grade) in English in the school leaving exam, compared with 21% of Asian pupils (for whom English was a second language) and 29% of other school leavers. For 91 out of 100 West Indian school leavers, therefore, the door to further education or the professions was closed, for lack of a good pass in English. The ticking of a time-bomb under the state school system could now be heard very plainly indeed.

The Bullock report – an opportunity lost

The public outcry at the 1972 figures led the Minister of Education, then Margaret Thatcher, to set up the Bullock Committee. Bullock reported three years later and, amid much else, summarised the Plowden Committee's research on the effect of 'parental encouragement' on school achievement. The most powerful variant was found to be the School Handicap Score (SHS) a weighted sum of *Father's occupation, Father's education, Mother's education, Number of books in the home and (minus) Number of siblings.* Bullock concluded: *a child's family background gives a clear prediction of his reading age at age ten and age fourteen* (Bullock: 23).

(The crucial effect of investment of adult time on children's language development has been confirmed by a succession of research studies by Professor J S Bruner and others. These are summarised in the editorial footnote on p129.)

One is reminded of the comment of Comenius in his moving treatise *Schola infantiae* (1646): *by the tales told at their mother's knee do men live or die* (Monroe, 1896). Echoing Comenius, Bullock argued that if parents were to play their demanding role properly they would need preparation:

> *It has to be recognised that many adolescent pupils are simply not ready to cast themselves in the role of future parents and for them the study of language in parenthood . . . through films, demonstrations and practical experience, would lead to an awareness of the adult's role in the young child's linguistic and cognitive development.* (Bullock, 1975: 55)

To help children whose tenuous grasp of English was holding them back, Bullock made two radical proposals:

i. *that the training of all teachers, whatever their specialism, should include a module on language. Possible programmes for such a 'language module' were suggested in an appendix;*
ii. *that all children who had been deprived of one-to-one dialogue with an adult at home should be offered it regularly in school. For this purpose a new kind of 'English assistant' should be recruited to provide individual dialogue in class and the report specified how these new teachers' aides should be trained.*

At York university we were able to test the effect of this proposal. In action research in Yorkshire towns with slow-learning pupils over a period of some twelve years, we were able to observe the marked positive effect on motivation and confidence of arranging for student volunteers to engage in one-to-one dialogue with pupils, both in school time and in vacation 'language camps' and combined school and university 'language summer schools' (Hawkins, 1971; Goodlad, 1975).

The Bullock proposals might have transformed language education in our schools. In the event Government, Teachers' Unions and English Teacher Trainers all lacked the imagination or the will to implement Bullock. As a result, disquiet about English teaching grew. Two subsequent Government commissions, Kingman (1988) and Cox (1989), both advocated the inclusion of knowledge about language in the aims of English teaching, but teachers and teacher trainers again failed to respond. Instead, debate lapsed into a sterile polarisation, which was described by Professor Crystal in the Cambridge Encyclopedia of Language:

> *At one extreme there are those who advocate a wholesale return to . . . traditional parsing. At the other, there are those who avoid anything that*

smacks of grammatical terminology. Fortunately . . . there is . . . a healthy movement arguing for . . . 'awareness of language', aimed particularly at the middle years of schooling. It aims to stimulate the child's curiosity about language, and to integrate the various elements of language training in school, both 'horizontally', in relation to different languages across the curriculum . . . and 'vertically', as the child moves up through the school . . . (Crystal, 1987)

126

'Language awareness' – modern linguists take the lead

The 'healthy movement' of 'language awareness' to which Crystal refers was led by modern linguists. Though they found it hard to build bridges with English colleagues, they found a warmer welcome for 'awareness of language' among teachers of children of ethnic minorities.

The first suggestion that the study of 'language' might be a bridging subject with English came at a joint seminar for English and FL teachers, convened in Manchester in 1973 by George Perren, Director of CILT (see Hawkins in Perren, 1974). Nothing came immediately of this proposal but it was further examined at a series of national seminars and in 1981, George Perren's successor at CILT, Dr John Trim, convened a Language Awareness Working Party, eleven of whose thirteen members were modern linguists. From its Report (Donmall, 1985) there sprang the present Association for Language Awareness with its widely read Journal *Language Awareness* advised by an international Editorial Board.

Meanwhile, at school level, there began an explosive growth of imaginative 'awareness of language' programmes, produced by pioneering modern language teachers at Henry Box School Witney, Hinchingbrook in Cambridgeshire, the Oratory Reading, North Westminster London, and others, whose work and materials became nationally known.

There were several reasons why Modern linguists were drawn into the debate about the 'uneven language playing field'.

i. Boy/girl imbalance in language classrooms

With the arrival of the comprehensive school, language teachers could not fail to observe the marked imbalance in the performance of boys and girls, on average, in language classes. This phenomenon is discussed at several places in this volume and need only be summarised here (see p90 and Appendix II, Tables 2 and 4). On average girls mature physiologically (and linguistically) earlier than boys and this is reflected, *again on average* (there will be many exceptions) in girls' overall school performance in the early secondary years. Girls' linguistic precocity may be reinforced by cultural factors, such as the role models offered in schools by the growing predominance of female teachers (see reference to research in Germany, Appendix II, Table 5). Boys catch up verbally after age sixteen, but by then many boys' career choices have been made. The question this posed was: could not boys' later maturing 'awareness of language' be assisted in some way?

Lessons learned from the Pilot Scheme ('French from Eight') further focused language teachers' attention on how ill-equipped many pupils were for language learning on entering secondary school.

ii. Education of the ear

The NFER evaluation of the Pilot Scheme (Burstall, 1970;1974) revealed that many of the pupils who started early were bewildered by listening to recordings of native French speakers, at normal speed. They told the researchers repeatedly: *We detest the tape recorder!* They lacked what Peter MacCarthy (1978) called *education of the ear, the prerequisite of effective language learning.*

iii. Raising grammatical consciousness

Another lesson was that though the early starters made good progress initially, at the stage of 'listen and imitate', when they were building a stock of 'chunks of language', the later starters soon overtook them when it came to adapting the chunks for new contexts (having internalised the progressively complex 'rules').

Further light on this was shed by work on 'aptitude' for foreign language learning by Peter Green (1975) at York. He showed that eleven-year-olds differed markedly in their grasp of pattern or 'rule' in a language (Swedish) not previously met. Their insight into Swedish language patterns could only have been developed in the mother tongue, since they knew no other language.

The link between mother tongue 'language awareness' and aptitude for foreign language learning was further indicated by research at the Institut National de Recherche Pédagogique (INRP) Paris:

As soon as the child (learning a foreign language) moves out of fairly stereotyped situations, of greetings, introductions, stating wishes . . . in which he repeats phrases already met . . . great difficulties appear . . . what is essential now is an accurate representation of how language works, and specifically how it relates to the way the mother tongue works, because, for most learners the mother tongue is the only reference point available. (Luc, 1992)

The French researchers at INRP put this to the test with their fascinating experiment in raising pupils 'awareness' of the language features likely to be met (see Luc and Bailly, 1992).

This recalls the wise observation years ago of professor Pit Corder of Edinburgh:

> *It is . . . counter intuitive to suggest that the second language learner starts from scratch . . . does the fact that he already possesses language . . . count for nothing?* (Corder, 1978)

It also underlines the importance of the observation of Jerome Bruner (1983) that there are two levels of mother tongue acquisition: 'communicative competence', widely shared by all children, and 'analytic' competence which is not so widely shared. It is not innate, but has to be learned. On it, Bruner suggests, progress in school depends. Bruner's 'analytic competence' is close to the 'insight into pattern' measured by the York aptitude test.

Education of the ear and grasp of pattern linked

Grasp of pattern in the new language and 'education of the ear' are linked in an interesting way. Dr Green's York Aptitude Test was a pencil and paper test. Nothing was spoken. Yet it predicted well pupils' later performance in listening comprehension (in German). To explain this we went back to George Miller's work on Short Term Memory (Miller, 1956). He showed that the average listener could hold only seven (plus or minus two) discrete bits of information in the STM. But if some *pattern* could be observed in the incoming message the capacity of the STM was dramatically increased. So grasping the pattern and listening mutually reinforce each other. Setting up expectations about the linguistic patterns to be met greatly helps the listening and the learning, as in the French experimental language awareness sessions in the primary school described in Luc and Bailly, 1992.

One approach that has been suggested is to start from the language the children already have, encouraging them to trust to observation and careful listening, exploring and seeking out first the simpler grammar patterns, later more complex ones. They can then apply the same careful observation to the patterns in the foreign language, while comparing and contrasting them with their mother tongue. They may thus develop a critical awareness, and confidence in 'induction' from evidence, much as they are taught to do in the best laboratory work in chemistry or biology. It is what

Comenius meant with his guiding principle: *percept before precept*. Henry Sweet (1899) advocated a similar approach with his 'inventional grammar'. We have taken the idea a little further with the notion of 'exploratory grammar' (Hawkins, 1984; 1993).

Why a new element in the curriculum?

The awakening of awareness of language in the curriculum may have had its roots in reaction against unequal linguistic opportunity, but we ought not to overrate the power of schools to correct social injustices, of poverty, ill-health, poor housing and the many factors which hold young learners back. Modern linguists have not rested their case for LA solely on the plea for greater equality of opportunity. They have brought to the debate their own experience of the satisfaction of exploring language. They want that satisfaction to be widely shared, by all children, regardless of what role or status society may have in store for them. As an early plea for AL put it:

> *We are seeking to light fires of curiosity about language which will blaze throughout our pupils' lives . . . seeking to arm our pupils against fear of the unknown which breeds prejudice and antagonism. Above all we want to make our pupils' contacts with language, both their own and that of their neighbours, richer, more interesting, simply more fun.* (Hawkins, 1984)

Our argument for awareness of language to be given a central place in the curriculum rests, then, essentially on the nature of 'homo loquens'. As I A Richards reminded us: *Language is the instrument of everything by which we go beyond the animals.* The fullest awareness of this marvellous instrument is every child's birthright. And this new 'bridging subject' offers foreign language teachers an unrivalled opportunity to cooperate with English colleagues, because they have so much shared interest in their pupils' language development.

Footnote to p125: effect of investment of 'adult time' in child language development

1. *In language development . . . the deciding factor . . . whether or not the child received undivided attention from an interested adult every day.*
Armstrong G, 'The Home Visiting Project' in Smith G (ed), *Educational priority* (HMSO, 1975)
2. *In the breakthrough to reading . . . the first step is . . . conceptualising language – becoming aware of it as a separate structure . . . Some children come to school with this step already taken . . . They come with an enormous initial advantage . . .*
Donaldson M, *Children's minds* (Fontana, 1978)

130

3. *. . . the best single predictor of attainment in literacy (by age seven) was the extent of the children's own understanding of the purposes . . . of literacy at the time they started school. This, in turn, was strongly associated with the interest in literacy that their parents shared with them . . . it was also associated with the quality of the parents' responses to their conversational initiations . . .*
Wells G, *Learning through interaction.* Ten-year Bristol Study of children's language development (CUP, 1981)

4. *In a socially deprived borough of London, involvement of parents in hearing children read, and chatting about reading for ten minutes before going to bed, proved far more effective than extra reading tuition in school in small groups by experts.*
Tizard J, 'Haringey Study' in *British Journal of Educational Psychology,* 52: 1–15 (1981)

5. *. . . in a most deprived sector of Manchester, with highest crime rate in Europe, involvement of parents (mainly unskilled manual) in working with their children's language for twenty minutes per day. Positive results of Tizard Study confirmed. Parents wished to help their children and proved able to do so.*
Beveridge M and A Jerrams, 'Parental Involvement in language development: an evaluation of a school-based parental assistance plan' in *British Journal of Educational Psychology,* 51, 3: 259–69 (1981)

6. *. . . For reading readiness . . . the child must not only be talking with a fair degree of fluency but must have an awareness of what he is doing . . . They show, with tape recordings how mother-child interaction facilitates progress through the 'four grammars' of childhood.*
Bolinger D and D A Sears, *Aspects of language,* third edition (Harcourt Brace, 1981)

7. *. . . the interaction between LAD and LASS (Language Acquisition Support System', i.e. dialogue in the family) makes it possible for the infant to enter the linguistic community.*
Bruner J S, *Child's talk* (OUP, 1983)

8. Crystal D, *Listen to your child,* Penguin handbook for young parents (1986)

9. (On link between early language experience and learning to read/write): 'primary' language activities (largely innate) must be distinguished from 'secondary' activities, which are learned: *Mastering an alphabetic writing system makes heavier demands than a logographic system . . . especially complex in English . . . It calls for a certain level of 'linguistic awareness' (of the primary activity), which is more than merely*

understanding speech. It is learned, not innate, and it depends on the linguistic environment.

Mattingley I G in chapter 'Awareness of language' in Kavanagh J F and I G Mattingley, *Language by ear and eye* (MIT, 1972).

References

Aitchison J, *The Articulate mammal: an introduction to psycholinguistics* (Hutchinson, 1976)

Brumfit C, 'Language awareness in teacher education' in James C and P Garrett, *Language awareness in the classroom* (Longman, 1991)

Bruner J S, 'Language as an instrument of thought' in Davies A (ed), *Problems of language and learning* (Heinemann, 1975)

Bruner J S, *Child's talk* (OUP, 1983)

Bullock A (Lord Bullock) (Chairman), *A language for life.* Report of Committee appointed by the Secretary of State for Education and Science (HMSO, 1975)

Burstall C, *French in the primary school – attitudes and achievement* (National Foundation for Educational Research, 1970)

Burstall C, *Primary French in the balance* (NFER, 1974)

Corder P, 'Language learner language' in Richards J C, *Understanding second and foreign language acquisition* (Longman, 1978)

Cox B (Chairman), *English for ages five to sixteen* (Proposals to the Secretary of State) (Dept of Education and Science, London, 1989)

Crowther G (Chairman), *Fifteen to eighteen.* Report of Central Advisory Council for Education England (HMSO, 1959)

Crystal D, *Cambridge encyclopedia of language* (CUP, 1987)

Davie R et al, *National Child Development Study* (1958 cohort) (Longman, 1972)

Donmall B G (ed), *Language awareness.* NCLE Papers and Reports (CILT, 1985)

Doughty P, J Pearce and G Thornton, *Language in use* (Edward Arnold, 1971)

Goodlad S (ed), *Education and social action* (Geo Allen and Unwin, 1975)

Green P S (ed), *The language laboratory in school – performance and prediction* (Edinburgh: Oliver and Boyd, 1975)

Halliday M, 'Introduction' to Doughty et al (see above)

Harris M (Chairman), *National Curriculum Working Group on Modern Languages, Final report* (London, DES/HMSO 1990)

Hawkins E W (ed), *A time for growing* (Community Relations Commission, 1971)

Hawkins E W, "Language' as bridging subject: modern languages in the curriculum' in Perren G E (ed), *The space between* (CILT Reports and Papers, 1974)

Hawkins E W, 'A possible way forward (a language programme for primary schools as preparation for foreign language learning)' in Hoy P H, *The early teaching of modern languages* (Nuffield Foundation, 1977)

Hawkins E W, *Awareness of language – an introduction* (CUP, 1984; revised edition, 1987)

Hawkins E W, 'Language awareness' in Asher R and J Simpson (eds), *The encyclopedia of language and linguistics,* vol 4: 33–38 (Oxford: Pergamon, 1993)

Hawkins E W, 'On exploratory grammar, 'Percept before precept'' in King L and P Boaks, *Grammar!* (CILT, 1994)

Her Majesty's Inspectorate, *Curriculum 11–16* (HMSO, 1978)

Kingman Sir J (Chairman), *Report of the Committee of Inquiry into the teaching of the English language* (HMSO, 1988)

Luc C and D Bailly, *Approche d'une langue étrangère à l'école,* vols 1 and 2 (Paris: INRP, 1992)

Luc C, 'Des représentations aux productions en langue étrangère' in *Langues vivantes et français à l'école, Repères,* no 6 (Paris: INRP, 1992)
MacCarthy P, *The teaching of pronunciation* (CUP, 1978)
Mattingley I G, 'Awareness of language' in Kavanagh J F and I G Mattingley, *Language by ear and eye* (MIT Press, 1972)
Miller G A, 'The magical number seven – plus or minus two. Some limits on our capacity for processing information' in *The Psychological Review,* 63, 2 (1956)
Monroe W S, *School of infancy.* An essay of the education of youth during the first six years (Boston: Heath, 1896)
Rampton A (Chairman), *West Indian children in our schools.* Interim Report of the Committee of Inquiry into Children from Ethnic Minorities (HMSO, 1981)
Robbins L (Lord Robbins) (Chairman), *Higher education.* Report of the Committee appointed by the Prime Minister (HMSO, 1963)
Stubbs M, *Language and literacy* (Routledge and Kegan Paul, 1980)
Sweet H, *The practical study of languages* (1899; re-issued OUP, 1964)

132

Part

three

**Multilingual
Britain**

1966-1996 **30YEARS**

. . . There is a practical advantage in putting a specific space in the curriculum for discussion of language . . . When the children in a class come from different language backgrounds, or dialect backgrounds, it is helpful to have a regular opportunity for them to tell one another about their language experiences. In this discussion all start level. All feel that they have something to contribute. Experiences that they share, such as the acquisition of language by the baby, can, if properly handled, unite children . . .

. . . (In such discussions) the presence in schools of pupils from the ethnic minorities will become a positive advantage because of the variety of their language backgrounds. The exchange of different language experiences can promote confidence, tolerance of difference and understanding; multilingualism may thus come to be seen as the enrichment it surely is, rather than as one more problem for the hard-pressed teacher. **(Hawkins E W, *Awareness of language* (CUP, 1987))**

11

Older mother tongues — Welsh and Gaelic

Geraint Hughes and Richard Johnstone

WELSH

In 1847, the report of three Commissioners on the condition of education in Wales pronounced that the provision for the majority of Welsh children was 'wretched'. The report further implied that the Welsh language was a hindrance to the educational and intellectual development of the Welsh people. The 'treachery of the Blue Books', as the report was referred to, was instrumental in instigating a call for English-medium education by many ambitious Welsh people. With the passing of the 1870 Education Act, a network of elementary schools was established throughout Wales and English became their medium of instruction.

Indeed, Welsh children were forcibly forbidden from using their mother tongue in school. Pupils who were heard speaking Welsh in school were forced to wear a 'Welsh Not' – a piece of wood or card – around their necks and physically punished at the end of the school day. Many teachers and parents believed that English should be the medium of reading and writing and that the sooner Welsh was no longer spoken by children the better it would be for them.

However, after 1880, following the foundation of an Independent Welsh Party in Parliament, pressure was brought to bear upon the authorities for a fairer status for Welsh in schools. As a result of this pressure, Welsh was allowed to be a 'class' subject in 1883. Sir Owen M Edwards was, during this period, the strongest advocate for the use of Welsh in schools. He campaigned vigorously for Welsh-speaking pupils to be educated through the medium of their mother tongue. In 1907 the Welsh Department of the Board of Education was established and as its Chief Inspector, Sir Owen M Edwards promoted the particular needs of Welsh pupils. There remained, however, a steady decline in the number of Welsh speakers. Many parents still believed that English was the language of learning and culture, of law and administration, of commerce and industry.

The report *Welsh in education and life,* published in 1927 by a departmental committee of the Board of Education, pronounced that the demise of the Welsh language would be a tragedy and that strenuous efforts should be made to give Welsh a prominent place in the school curriculum. During the period 1891–1931, with the growth of the coal mining and other associated industries in north-east and south Wales and the consequent influx of workers, the proportion of Welsh speakers fell from 54.4% to 36.8%. As a result it was realised that more extensive use should be made of the Welsh language in schools.

136

In an effort to stem this tide, the first official Welsh-medium primary school was established in 1939 by a group of parents in Aberystwyth. In 1947 the first Welsh-medium primary school supported by local education authority was opened in Llanelli and the value of these schools was recognised by parents. The first officially designated bilingual secondary school, Ysgol Glan Clwyd, was opened in Rhyl in 1958 and another in Mold in 1961. Ysgol Gyfun Rhydfelen, Pontypridd became the first bilingual school in south Wales. A report published by the Welsh Joint Education Committee in April 1961, noted that only 17.6% of pupils between 5 and 15 could speak and understand Welsh.

The report published in 1977 by the Welsh Language Council, *A future for the Welsh language,* concluded that efforts should be concentrated upon pre-school and formal education with the intention of establishing a flourishing bilingual system of education in Wales.

The implementation of the Education Reform Act in 1988 marked a significant change for the status of the teaching of Welsh in schools. For the first time, Welsh was to be taught as either a Core Subject in Welsh-speaking schools and one of the other Foundation Subjects in other schools in Wales – the main division being between Welsh as a mother tongue (Core Subject) and Welsh as a second language (other Foundation Subject). Although a decision was taken in 1993 to postpone the compulsory teaching of Welsh as a second language at Key Stage 4, it is to be re-introduced in 1999. All pupils in Wales will, in 1999, be taught Welsh as either a first or second language.

Schools in Wales fall into four categories:

1. Traditional Welsh-medium schools in Welsh-speaking areas

These schools are located in the Welsh-speaking hinterland and pupils are taught through the medium of Welsh in primary school. In secondary schools, pupils are taught through the medium of both Welsh and English.

2. Officially designated Welsh-medium schools

Most of these schools are situated in anglicised areas of Wales and have been established by local education authorities in response to the wishes of Welsh-speakers and non-Welsh-speaking parents who wish their children to be taught through the medium of Welsh. In some of these schools, as many as 95% of the children come from non-Welsh speaking homes.

3. Welsh-Medium Units

A unit is a sector of a school and it is administered by the headteacher of the school. Although all teachers in a unit speak Welsh it is unlikely that all teachers in the schools speak the language. These units function in the same way as the officially designated Welsh-medium school – Welsh is the main medium of instruction.

4. English-medium schools

English is the first language of the vast majority of the pupils and Welsh is taught as a second language during a specific period on the primary school timetable. In secondary schools, Welsh is given the same status as any other modern foreign language in the curriculum.

Statistics for 1994–95 issued by the Welsh Office give the following analysis of the provision of Welsh language education:

	No of schools	% of school population
Primary schools		
1. Schools where Welsh is the sole or main medium of instruction	453	26.8%
2. Schools where Welsh is used as part of the medium of instruction	120	7.1%
3. Schools having classes where Welsh is taught as a second language	1,091	64.5%
4. Schools where no Welsh is taught	27	1.6%
Secondary schools		
1. Schools where Welsh is taught as a first or second language	43	21.1%
2. Officially designated Welsh-medium schools	18	7.9%
3. English-medium schools	158	69.6%
4. Schools where no Welsh is taught	3	1.3%

Geraint Hughes

Scottish Gaelic

The 1872 Education Act (Scotland) made no specific reference to Scottish Gaelic, despite the fact that there were over 250,000 speakers of the language at the time. Thereafter, throughout much of the first half of the twentieth century, the use of Gaelic in schools was actively discouraged and the appointment of monolingual speakers of English to teaching posts in Gaelic-speaking areas was common. By the middle of the twentieth century, however, a more enlightened view was gaining ground – in, for example, a series of Scottish Education Department memoranda during the 1950s which supported Gaelic as a medium of teaching at primary and secondary levels in subjects such as geography, music, history and nature study. In 1962 the national 'O' Grade examination, taken normally by pupils at age sixteen in their fourth year of secondary education, became available in Gaelic for both learners and native speakers, and in 1968 the national Higher examination, taken by pupils in fifth or sixth years of secondary, was similarly subdivided. A major influence on these developments was the great Gaelic poet, Sorley MacLean, at the time a primary school headteacher. In 1965 the Primary Memorandum was published, expressing a philosophy of education closely corresponding to that of the Plowden Report and arguing it was the duty of the primary school to maintain and develop Gaelic as a living means of communication and expression.

The governmental Reform of Local Government (1975) which led to the formation of regional and islands councils, including the Western Isles Island Council, has had major and lasting implications for Gaelic. Almost immediately a Western Isles Bilingual Education Project was introduced, funded initially by the Scottish Office. On this bilingual model, pupils at primary school (whether from Gaelic-speaking or English-speaking or bilingual homes) received certain parts of their curriculum through English and other parts, e.g. environmental studies and social studies, through Gaelic. In 1978 a comparable bilingual scheme was established on the Isle of Skye. Interest in Gaelic was reflected in other sectors of education also – e.g. in1978 the first Gaelic-medium secretarial studies course was introduced at Lews Castle College and by 1983 full-time Gaelic-medium Higher National Certificate and Diploma courses were being introduced at *Sabhal Mor Ostaig*, the Gaelic college in Skye.

These welcome advances in Gaelic education were however not immediately reflected in comparable developments in the political arena. Donald Stewart attempted to introduce his Private Member's Bill in the

House of Commons (1980), seeking legal recognition for Gaelic, the definition of Gaelic-speaking areas and the establishment of broadcasting and television services on the Welsh pattern – but the Bill was 'talked out'.

Nonetheless, in the 1980s a number of developments took place that were of great significance. In 1982 the European Commission established EBLUL, the European Bureau for Lesser-used Languages, with a base in Dublin. EBLUL has enabled groups representing many of the indigenous minority language communities of Europe to learn from each other's experiences and to develop common strategies for the maintenance and promotion of their languages and cultures. The year 1982 also witnessed the foundation of *Comhairle nan Sgoiltean Àraich* (Council of Nursery Schools). This has captured the imagination of parents, many of them having no immediate connection with the language, and has flourished to the extent that there are now some 100 Gaelic playgroups in various parts of Scotland, with some 2,000 children. In 1984 the Scottish Office funded an independent evaluation of the Western Isles Bilingual Project, conducted by a research team from the University of Stirling, and in 1986 it introduced its Specific Grant scheme for Gaelic which enabled local authorities to access additional funding for the language, particularly in primary schools. The evaluation report on the Western Isles bilingual project was published in 1987. It generally presented a positive picture, though it identified a need to provide specific teaching in Gaelic as a second language for non-Gaelic speaking pupils, to ensure continuity of effective blingual education. This pinpointed a weakeness inherent in the bilingual formula for Gaelic – if a child from an English-speaking home was experiencing difficulties in a Gaelic-speaking aspect of the curriculum, there was a temptation for the teacher to switch languages. Although there might have been short-term gain in comprehension, this could lead to the Gaelic-speaking part of the curriculum losing some of its force at the expense of the dominant language.

By the mid-1980s a different and much stronger view of Gaelic in primary education was emerging, reflected in the establishment of the first Gaelic-medium units (GMUs) in primary schools in (significantly) Glasgow, Inverness, Portree and Breasclete. This development has tended to be parent-led, strongly indfluenced by parental perceptions of the success of the aforementioned pre-school playgroups. Education in a GMU, unlike the original form of bilingual education, is almost exclusively through the medium of Gaelic for an initial period of some two to three years, after which English is gradually blended in. The stronger GMU model allows children from non-Gaelic-speaking homes to make real progress in the language, without any obliterating effects from English – *gardening with a Gael*, to adapt a well-known phrase. The intention is that by the end of their primary schooling, pupils will be as competent in English, mathematics and other aspects of the Scottish primary school curriculum as their peers educated elsewhere through the medium of English, but possessing the priceless advantage of being bilingual. By the mid-1990s fifty GM units had been establised in Scottish primary schools in areas that are by no means restricted to the Gaelic-speaking heartland. The Scottish Office is now funding independent research into the attainments of pupils in Gaelic-medium classes, to check that pupils do indeed acquire the advantange of bilingualism without any loss of competence in other curricular areas. The 1994 HMI Report on Gaelic in Scottish schools came out strongly in favour of Gaelic-medium as opposed to bilingual education, though – to the dismay of many proponents of Gaelic – it adopted a cautious approach to Gaelic-medium education at secondary, largely on the grounds of a very limited supply of appropriate teachers. Teacher supply for Gaelic-medium education in primary and secondary schools is now a major priority and poses very difficult problems in view of the limited numbers of highly fluent potential teachers.

In 1989 the Government announced the establishment of the Gaelic Television Fund whereby roughly £9 million per annum is made available for the production of television programmes and related initiatives in Gaelic that will complement the provision made already by BBC, STV and Grampian television. This has enabled a number of small companies to develop, has brought an important number of jobs back to the Islands and though a range of imaginative educational and other programmes for young children has strongly supported Gaelic-medium education at primary school.

Developments in Gaelic education serve two major purposes. First, they provide an education for children through the medium of one of Scotland's indigenous languages and thereby give each individual child access to a Celtic culture of inestimable value. Second, they help support the maintenance of the Gaelic speech community. The 1991 national census showed some 65,000 speakers of Scottish Gaelic, compared with some 82,000 in the previous census of 1981. Of these 65,000 speakers there was a weighting towards older age groups. It is calculated that at best the census in 2001 will reveal no further drop, but that thereafter – if the policies for Gaelic in education, television, radio, the arts and the economy achieve their intended impact – then the figures for speakers of Gaelic should begin to rise again. A fascinating prospect of linguistic and cultural revival against the odds.

Richard Johnstone

12

Community languages

June Geach

In the more than 50 years of immigration to Britain since the end of World War II, the language landscape of the country has changed significantly. Language surveys in various education authorities over the years have shown extensive diversity of home languages among the school population; in 1989, the Inner London Education Authority (ILEA) recorded 184 home languages among its pupils. Yet this diversity has only patchily been represented in the school system, despite pressure from these settled language communities. In addition, the emphasis of the National Curriculum (NC) is a further deterrent, even though the NC provides in its schedules for the teaching of some of the languages (see discussion later in this chapter).

Terminology

Part of the difficulty of catering for these languages has been that there has not been a clear understanding of where they fit into the education system. This is reflected in the various terms used to describe the languages: mother tongue, heritage, ethnic minority, community, each of which reflects a social or political attitude, particularly when attempts are made to place them in a multiracial or multifaith context. The problem arises from an imperfect understanding of the nature of the languages, occupying as they do in the British context a middle ground between mother tongue and foreign language. This has allowed interested groups: government, parents, local education authorities (LEA) to interpret the same situation in different ways, with resultant differences in their relationship to the education system. In what follows, bilingualism is understood to mean the ability to use more than one language to a reasonable degree of competence (in Britain, normally English and at least one other language, but it need not include English). Mother tongue is the child's first language of contact, usually in the home, before entering school, and the one to which the speaker may feel the closest emotional attachment, even when it is not the language of which the speaker has the best and most natural command. It may also be the community language. Mother tongue main-tenance may therefore be seen in the context of its cultural/religious connotations; mother tongue teaching, on the other hand, refers to a process of second language learning (perhaps after the language has been suppressed earlier). In this it has some affinity with heritage language, a term which more properly refers to languages supported because of the importance of their linguistic and cultural background, but not in normal everyday use for the most part (Cornish or Manx, for example); it may, as with Gaelic, be revived to become a community language in contemporary use. In these pages community language (CL) will be the preferred term, designating the language of a definable group routinely choosing to use a language other than English in daily life in Britain, or as the language of literacy. 'Community' refers to members of these linguistic groupings. CL touches on the other definitions according to context, and is thus a con-venient portmanteau term which can include Welsh and Gaelic. 'Community' is therefore a useful shorthand for any of these fluid groupings.

The language communities

In 1989 the ILEA identified 184 languages spoken within its jurisdiction, the two largest being Bengali and Turkish. The tables below compare the 1989 position with 1981; figures in brackets indicate percentage of school population.

Number of pupils in the main language groups in ILEA schools				
	1981		1989	
Bengali	5,377	12%	20,113	28.6%
Turkish	4,418	9.8%	4,265	6.6%
Chinese	2,237	5.0%	4,242	6.0%
Gujarati	3,377	7.5%	3,904	5.6%
Urdu	2,778	6.2%	3,821	5.4%
Arabic	1,968	4.4%	3,427	4.9%

In addition, the ILEA noted large increases between 1987 and 1989 in the number of pupils speaking Yoruba (2,031 to 2,941; up 45%) and those speaking Vietnamese (1,028 to 1,573; up 53%). Significant increases in Bengali and Arabic were also noted, although numbers in the other groups remained relatively constant, while Italian and Greek decreased by 14%.

London was and is a popular destination for newly-arrived would-be settlers, and it is interesting to compare these figures with those from the Kingston English Language Service, which monitors its bilingual population annually, in a borough which, because of its proximity to Heathrow Airport, is one register of change in the communities:

Number of school pupils in main language groups in Kingston			
1992/93		**1994/95**	
Panjabi	638	Panjabi	738
Urdu	590	Urdu	636
Italian	260	Bengali	283
Spanish	244	Chinese	275
Bengali	240	Arabic	254
Chinese	224	Italian	238
Gujarati	156	Gujarati	195
Portuguese	75	Portuguese	186
Hindi	67	Spanish	185
		Hindi	94

Although the pattern of settlement shown is different from London's, and numbers not comparable, both surveys show a steady increase in numbers (in Kingston, up from a total of 3,820 in 92/93 to 4,436 in 94/95). Not, then, a situation likely to fade out of the education picture.

Kingston also carried out a one-year research project in community language teaching (CLT), defined as classes to promote the culture of the country with which the ethnic minority community is associated; 710 pupils were recorded overall:

Number of pupils aged five to sixteen in community language schools			
Urdu	142	Italian	185
Arabic	25	Polish	20
Cantonese	95	Spanish	233

Some of these pupils may also be counted among the LEA's totals above, but be learning one of these languages for a specific reason, e.g. an Urdu-speaker learning Arabic as a religious language. Most of these pupils, except for Spanish, were in the eight to thirteen age group. A few (in Urdu and Arabic classes) were under age five. The main needs of the communities were for trained teachers, more teaching materials, funds to pay teachers adequately, public examination syllabuses for CL. These will be considered later in this chapter. Other major centres, such as Birmingham, Leicester, Bedford, Bradford, record a different hierarchy and, to some extent, different languages; Birmingham records Pushto among its major languages; Bedford surveys according to ethnic group supported under Section 11 provision.

Which languages to teach?

The great diversity of languages spoken in Britain is sometimes used to show the impossibility of providing for their teaching in the state system. If not all can be catered for, the reasoning goes, it would be unfair to teach only some. Surveys from various sources carried out in Britain over the years, however, consistently show the same ten or twelve languages represented in substantial numbers, although the hierarchy of languages varies according to locality. An article by John Broadbent (1986) shows a chart (p43) with the main ten languages reported as being taught in classes in the state sector in 1982 in descending order as Urdu, Panjabi, Italian, Gujarati, Spanish, Hindi, Greek, Chinese, Polish and Bengali. *Multilingk*, a committee formed to oversee the development of materials and to participate in the development of examination syllabuses and assessment techniques at GCSE level, identified the same languages, plus Arabic. Within a given LEA, it is probable that two or three could be agreed upon if a choice needs to be made, in the present educational climate. When examination entries are taken into consideration, the spectrum narrows still more.

Examinations

Examination results show a somewhat different picture from surveys of language provision. The entries for Urdu outnumber those for other CL; the returns of the School Curriculum and Assessment Authority (SCAA) show consistent growth in Urdu entries from 3,611 in 1990 to 5,995 in 1994; 1,273 to 1,931 for Chinese; others show smaller increases on smaller entries, a decrease (Bengali) or a cessation (Vietnamese, last examined in 1993; Hindi, last examined in 1994). These figures probably reflect the standing of Urdu throughout a large part of the South Asian population as the language of prestige and/or literacy. The statistics do not show whether CL-tailored examinations, a recommendation of the Swann Committee (see 'Factors in the present situation' below) were offered.

Nor do the statistics reflect teaching provision in the mainstream. With the widespread desire within the communities that their children should attend university, and in the knowledge that a good mark in a CL may count towards entrance qualifications, some candidates are entered through the school who did not study there.

Community language teacher training

This note on the training of teachers of community languages is contributed by Mahendra K Verma, University of York.

There is no Initial Teacher Training (ITT) available for Bengali, Gujarati, Urdu or Chinese within the Education departments in higher education institutions or in teacher training colleges. On the other hand some of these institutions and some LEAs have been organising INSET courses for teachers who are untrained or are perceived to be untrained native speakers.

The two significant initiatives in in-service training have been: the Royal Society of Arts Examinations Board's Diploma in Teaching Community Languages, and the York University Easter INSET courses, both of which attracted community language teachers from 'supplementary' as well as 'mainstream' schools. The RSA Diploma course was launched in 1983. Several colleges and polytechnics in England and Scotland supported the scheme by volunteering to put on the course. The course was unique in that it trained teachers of a range of languages, e.g. Urdu, Greek, Farsi, Turkish and Chinese, and developed methodologies to acknowledge and build on the bi-/multilingual potential of both the trainee teachers and their pupils. The modern foreign language pedagogy and the mother tongue English pedagogy have had to be adapted, and innovative and imaginative approaches created to infuse the scheme with the ethos of bilingual language acquisition and development. Unfortunately, this does not offer qualified teacher status to teachers. In the NCLE research published in Brumfit (1988), the contribution of the RSA scheme became clear:

The major contribution . . . has been to discover significant numbers of good classroom practitioners, good analysts, good co-ordinators and good teacher trainers, so as to build up a genuine national resource in terms of expertise. Unfortunately, much of this expertise remains unrecognised by the British school system, largely because the RSA Diploma does not currently count for anything in the award of Qualified Teacher Status.

The York University INSET was the first of its kind in the country which complemented the RSA initiative, and in 1986 the first Easter residential course for community language teachers was organised. This was preceded by a one-day pilot course, and questionnaire-based research into the needs of the community language teachers across the LEAs. The course attracted a large number of teachers reflecting a good national geographical spread. Although it was predominantly a course for South Asian language teachers, it embraced teachers of Farsi and Chinese too. The main aim of the course was to train teachers in teaching and assessing the four skills of listening, speaking, reading and writing, which are the National Curriculum requirements. In view of the fact that there were few if any commercially produced teaching materials in these languages, the

INSET offered the teachers the opportunity to produce appropriate GCSE-driven materials, including some on cassettes to take back to their classes. In the 1992 INSET further research by Bhatt and Verma (1993) was conducted among the 103 teachers attending the course. A total of 79 questionnaires were completed representing approximately 79% of the participants nationally. An analysis of the data suggested that the position, status, learning and teaching of minority community languages continued to be inconsistent with the presumed spirit of Swann and the National Curriculum. It continued to be haunted by Section 11 funding and the resultant insecurity. Among the needs, 74% listed lack of suitable textbooks, and 45% lack of training opportunities as the real obstacles to delivering the GCSE curriculum.

There has been hardly any new initiative in planning for community language learning and teaching. In our research we found that community language teachers did not consider that the introduction of modules in community languages or in language awareness or in multicultural education as part of BEd or PGCE courses met their needs. The current situation does not seem to be designed to create 'the next generation of experienced teachers'. The final nail in the coffin was the withdrawal in 1994 of GCSE examination facilities in Hindi, a language that continues to be a National Curriculum modern language! The failure to respond to the needs of the bilingual children and adults was signalled by the NCLE research group as early as 1988 and cited in Brumfit (1988):

The failure at the national level to recognise the need for initial training qualifications for community languages has led local education authorities and schools to deploy teachers whose initial qualification has been gained in a main subject other than the language which they are not asked to promote. The lack of purpose-designed courses for teachers of community languages is causing a crisis of credibility within the existing school networks of colleagues promoting community languages.

Other forms of training

Co-operation in the training of teachers is also sporadic within LEAs; but it is now possible to obtain a BA in Community Languages (BACL) leading to qualified teacher status, which presupposes a reasonable standard in the language before entry to university.

It is also encouraging to note that students have come forward to take advantage of a course organised by two Lancashire teaching colleges, Edge Hill and St Martin's, in conjunction with the county council. The course, Access to Primary Teaching for Asian and Black People (APTAB) has attracted a large intake (90%) of Asian women. There will remain the problem of finding a job in competition with other trained teachers. If they do, however, they will constitute a core of qualified teachers already in the school, at a level at which the pupils are still bilingual; many of these teachers will be capable of teaching a CL, and of supporting their pupils' bilingualism.

Broadcast support

The Gaelic Television Service (GTS) was established in 1993 to appeal to Gaelic and non-Gaelic speakers in Scotland. A significant number of viewers (initially 100,000) followed the language course, and a poll showed 75% of respondents thought it important to keep Gaelic alive through Gaelic programmes on TV. The GTS operates in co-operation with the BBC, Channel 4, Scottish TV and Grampian TV. This level of provision contrasts with that for other CLs, which are not regularly budgeted for by the BBC or the commercial stations, although both do from time to time broadcast special programmes or series, for instance the *Hindi Urdu Bol Chaal* series of ten programmes on BBC television, which offered English speakers the opportunity to learn, to a reasonable level, a language with which to communicate with many members of the South Asian community in Britain. During this period, BBC radio broadcast a *Taste of* series aimed at developing understanding of the language and culture of some of the communities settled in Britain; fact sheets produced in association with the broadcasts are available from CILT (*An introduction to . . . Yiddish, Urdu, Spanish, Latin American Spanish, Chinese, Gujarati, Panjabi, Turkish, Greek, Italian, Bengali, Hindi*). It is likely, however, that any regular broadcasts aimed at the communities will be found locally in areas with substantial CL populations.

Factors in the present situation

In the view of many in the communities, a number of opportunities for firm positive statements have been missed or muted over the years: the Bullock Report (1975) published the findings of a committee established to consider, in relation to schools, all aspects of teaching the use of English (although English as a second language did not come within the brief); it famously said that:

> . . . *no child should be expected to cast off the language and culture of*

*the home as he crosses the school threshold and the curriculum should
reflect those aspects of his life . . . (p286)*

148

but it was not precise about how this should be done.

The Swann Report (1985) put forward the recommendations of the
Committee of Inquiry into the Education of Children from Ethnic Minority
Groups, and was thus keenly awaited by the communities, since the terms
of reference:

*. . . to review in relation to schools the educational needs and attainments
of children from ethnic minority groups, consider the value of continuing to
monitor the educational performance of different ethnic minority groups
and to consider the most effective use of resources for these purposes . . .*

seemed to afford the greatest promise up to that time of recognition of CL,
and by extension of the British-based societies which use them. In the
event disappointment was expressed from various quarters; a list of some
of the main community responses to Swann appears in Geach (1986). One
of the most detailed was that of V Saifullah-Khan (1985). She acknowl-
edges the positive aspects of the report: condemnation of withdrawal
arrangements for English as a Second Language (ESL); approval for
including CL within the modern language adviser's brief; developing provision of language awareness courses (Swann particularly commended
the programme developed by Eric Hawkins and described in his book
Awareness of language: an introduction (1984). At the same time, Swann's
analysis is largely made from the point of view of the ethnic (English-
speaking) majority, which immediately distorts any supposed advantage
to the communities.

*To say that nothing should be done that cannot be shown to benefit all,
when the 'all' is . . . the ethnic majority, is profoundly racist. To imply that
the main benefit of the existing multilingualism in Britain is to inform
monolingual pupils of the nature of linguistic diversity is condescending.*

There was also the possibility that language awareness programmes
and knowledge about languages, where the examples were from the CL,
might be considered to be a total answer to the communities' wish for
these languages to be incorporated into the maintained sector.

It was also felt that in his emphasis on ESL needs Swann discounted to
some extent the other side of the pupil's persona which had required ESL
in the first place. Swann identified three types of mother tongue provision:

1   the teaching of the languages of ethnic minorities as part of the modern
    languages curriculum;

2 bilingual education with some of the instruction through the medium of the mother tongue;

3 mother tongue maintenance.

The first was welcomed; on the second there was the feeling that use of the mother tongue was sanctioned only as an aid in the transition from the mother tongue to the full use of English. On the third, there was a suspicion that in its statement, *the linguistic situation in Wales is . . . far from comparable to that of the communities,* political values were being applied rather than the social and educational ones the communities advocated. As naturalised British communities, they were unable to understand how their case should be different from that of Welsh. In short, the communities had hoped for the right of incorporation within the state system on the same basis as English or Welsh; what they got was a compromise between introduction at secondary level as a second language, and relegation to the voluntary sector – an inconsistency possible in part because of the fuzziness of terminology in this field (as mentioned earlier – see 'Terminology', p141). Finally, the Department of Education and Science, having announced (and apparently produced) a statement on CL to parallel its consultative document *Foreign languages in the curriculum (FLIC),* failed to publish it and an opportunity to establish a framework for the place of CL in the education system was lost.

The National Curriculum

In 1989, the National Curriculum established two lists of languages acceptable for teaching in the schools, as shown in the tables below. The first consisted of the languages of the members of the European Community; languages in the second list could only be taught if one of the languages from the first list was already being offered:

Schedule 1	Schedule 2
Danish	Arabic
Dutch	Bengali
French	Chinese (Cantonese or
German	Mandarin)
Greek (modern)	Gujarati
Italian	Hebrew (modern)
Portuguese	Hindi
Spanish	Japanese
	Panjabi
	Urdu

Although the two lists were amalgamated in 1991 into one alphabetical sequence suggesting equal standing, in practice the old divide remains, and should be taken into account in any model of diversification of the second foreign language which is developed. Finally, Local Management of Schools (LMS) has changed the basis of provision and decision, and the consequent changes in the funding patterns of schools and LEAs have tended to militate against CL in the mainstream, except where parents have been strong enough to demand it. This is not seen as a threat to English; parents have always recognised that the key to success in school and post-school is competence in English but, as in Wales, they view officially supported bilingualism as an advantage, whatever the language being paired with English.

150

The way ahead

In two widely separated conference reports, *Bilingualism and bilingual education* (1976) and *Minority community languages in school* (1984), a list of needs and aims for the communities emerged:

1) *Statutory provision of CL as a right in the maintained sector;*
2) *Voluntary provision outside the maintained sector, where felt desirable for cultural or religious reasons; the same child may e.g. learn Urdu for educational or social reasons and Arabic for religious reasons, and thus in effect be a member of two differently-based language communities;*
3) *Contact with parents;*
4) *Development of materials and teacher training;*
5) *Collection of information;*
6) *Monitoring of progress.*

From this menu, much remains to be done on point 1, most reliance being on points 2 and 3; the fourth has been only partially realised, although this was one of the recommendations of Swann for co-operation between the schools and the communities. Another was that local authorities should offer accommodation for voluntary classes; but the adequate and free accommodation which Swann had in mind has not always been made available. Language advisers themselves note the need for materials development, but *Multilingk*, mentioned earlier (p144), was originally conceived as an inter-authority committee for community language materials on the understanding that it would receive a guaranteed portion of its income from co-operating LEAs, but changes in LEA funding patterns are causing it to seek other ways of financing its work. Teacher training has already been discussed.

The last two points remain enduring needs. The National Association for Language Development in the Curriculum (NALDIC) touches on all six points. It is a body of teachers set up in 1993 and formally committed to raising bilingual pupils' achievement in the classroom and to promoting bilingualism and mother tongue development. They also make submissions to the Government on such matters as its education funding proposals, revision of the English curriculum and changes in Section 11 funding, which before 1986 provided 75% of the cost of staff employed by the local authority to meet the special needs of Commonwealth immigrants, including ESL and, sometimes, CL. This funding is gradually being reduced and replaced by new forms of funding which are not targeted at the former Section 11 beneficiaries but require all sectors to submit bids for a share of the available central funds or to bid for money for specific projects.

It has already been noted that CLs fall between the stools of mother tongue and foreign language; this makes planning difficult, particularly if the political will is not there, and the full effects of changes from reliance on Section 11 support to the lottery of bids on the new centralised, undifferentiated budgets are yet to be felt. LEAs, for example, may be limited to the right to be consulted, but with reduced power to affect school-based actions.

Much of this has long been known, but as with economics, it seems that the questions remain the same, only the answers change with changing circumstances. The way forward depends on a basis of accurate information and regular monitoring of demand and provision, based on reliable and wide-ranging statistics. This is a matter of some importance. At present the speakers of community languages constitute some 10% of the population of the UK, a not inconsiderable proportion, and one likely to remain constant.

Ensuring reliability and regularity of return will not be easy. At present the picture is untidy, with the collection of statistics patchy and fragmented and not collected routinely or on a standardised basis. SCAA examination tables, for example, provide clues but do not relate directly to what is happening in the mainstream in terms of actual teaching, and LEAs use different criteria in their collection of statistics. SCAA entries for the main CL in 1994 are shown in the Statistics Appendix.

Since under LMS much funding and therefore power reside at individual school level, it seems reasonable to require schools to provide detailed information following an agreed format – many collect such information internally in any case. School statistics could then be amalgamated with those compiled by the LEAs, the whole to be lodged with a central agency responsible for processing and making them available to interested parties at all levels from individual to national.

This is a difficult task, but it should be attempted, for only then can the policy be developed to give rise to the specific planning at national level which is needed for a co-ordinated language policy within the National Curriculum.

The twin prongs of the way forward are therefore information and statistics, and CILT is continuing to exercise its information function in this field. A start has been made with the establishment of the CILT Advisory **152** Group for Community Languages with a membership widely drawn from the field, which will consider the issues of importance in CL and provide a continuing forum for discussion and expert knowledge and advise CILT on its own services in this area. Thus may we get answers to some, at least, of the perennial questions, not least how to use a valuable national resource, the native bilingualism of many citizens of Britain.

References

Bhatt A and M Verma, *Minority community languages: teachers' attitudes and perceptions.* Paper given at the York Easter Community Language Teachers INSET (1993)

Broadbent J, 'Missing figures: community languages in maintained education' in Printon V, *Facts and figures: languages in education* (CILT, 1986)

Brumfit C (ed), *Language in teacher education* (NCLE, 1988)

Bullock Report, *A language for life* (London: HMSO, 1975)

Geach J (ed), *English as a second language: sources and resources,* CILT Information Guide 1, 2nd edition: 68–9 (1986)

Geach J (ed) with J Broadbent, *Coherence in diversity: Britain's multilingual classroom* (CILT, 1989)

Hawkins E W, *Awareness of language: an introduction* (Cambridge University Press, 1984; revised, 1987)

The mother tongue and other languages in education, NCLE Papers and Reports 2 (CILT, 1979)

Perren G E (ed), *Bilingualism and bilingual education: the dimensions of diversity* (CILT Reports and Papers 14, 1976)

Reid E (ed), *Minority community languages in school.* NCLE Papers and Reports 4 (CILT, 1984)

Saifullah-Khan V, *Education for all?* Working paper no 6, Centre for Multicultural Education, University of London Institute of Education (1985)

Swann Report, *Education for all* (1985)

Part

four

When to start?

1966-1996 **YEARS**

From the Annan Report on the teaching of Russian, 1962 (para. 63):

The attractions in starting to teach a modern language early are that pupils become familiar with the foreign idiom at an age when their imitative faculties are perhaps at their peak. It is, of course, a prerequisite of success that the teachers themselves should have a really fluent command of the spoken foreign language and that the methods they use should be up to date. To find or create such a body of teachers would take a long time and care would be needed to avoid undesirable complications in the presentation of the language in secondary schools, which generally draw their pupils from a multiplicity of primary schools.

In this passage the perceptive Annan Report not only prodded Government to take action but put down marker buoys on the very rocks on which the national Pilot Scheme, launched in 1963, was to founder in 1974.

The Scottish initiatives:

Throughout the world there has been an upsurge of interest in the learning of foreign or second languages by children in primary schools . . . Scotland, which in the past has lagged behind most other countries in its provision of foreign languages, has made serious attempts to implement a variety of measures, including national and regional pilot projects that have been introducing French, German, Spanish and Italian into primary schools, with plans to extend this considerably beyond the initial trials by the mid 1990s. (Johnstone R, *Teaching modern languages in primary school* (SCILT, 1994))

13

The early teaching of modern languages — a Pilot Scheme

Eric Hawkins

We firmly believe that it is now desirable to identify the steps which need to be taken to make widespread teaching of modern foreign languages in primary schools possible, and we have noted the recommendation of the House of Lords Select Committee . . . to this effect. (National Curriculum Working Group Report, 1990, para. 3.13)

The first influential advocacy of ETML in modern times (Comenius had made a strong case for an early start in the seventeenth century) came in the Annan Report on the teaching of Russian (1962). Annan argued that it would be advantageous *if the regular teaching of a first foreign language were started in good conditions and by the right methods in the primary school.* Annan was supported in the same year by a working party of the Federation of British Industries. On 13 March 1963, Sir Edward Boyle announced to Parliament the launching of *a Pilot Scheme to test the feasibility of starting French from the age of eight in state primary schools.*

The scheme met an enthusiastic response from schools and parents and aroused worldwide interest. But it had its critics. One immediate question was: why was it limited to French? The answer given was that only in French could there be any prospect of recruiting sufficient teachers. (Hawkins, 1987: 61ff). Other critics saw the scheme as improper incursion by central Government in curriculum planning. In fact, the 'tradition' that central Government had no right to intervene in curriculum planning was a post-war innovation. The notion would have surprised the Tudor monarchs who founded the Grammar Schools as much as it would the architects of the great Education Acts of 1902 and 1918.

Criticism also came from an unexpected quarter: the 'progressive education' majority on the Plowden Committee, which Boyle himself had set up in 1963 to enquire into primary schooling, was distinctly cool about the scheme because it encouraged 'old fashioned' classroom practices: *the early teaching of modern languages runs counter to . . . developing tradition . . . away from class teaching and formal lessons* (Plowden, 1967: 225).

Edward Boyle was not deflected by carping critics, however, and he was supported by two remarkable allies. The first was Derek Morrell, a civil servant in the Ministry of Education of unusual background. Educated in a French lycée and a sinologue, he was a man of vision and drive who made light of bureaucratic obstacles. Unfortunately he did not remain long in the Education Ministry and was sadly missed when, in the early 1970s, the Pilot Scheme ran into rough water.

Boyle's other great ally was Dr Leslie Farrer Brown, Director of the Nuffield Foundation. He had for some years been advocating reform of foreign language teaching at every level and he was now able to promise the Minister that Nuffield would set aside £100,000 for the development of new 'audio-visual' teaching materials for the Scheme.

Language teaching renewal

New materials were planned not only in French (for the pupils starting at age eight) but also in German, Spanish and Russian for the great numbers of pupils who, it was hoped, would be encouraged, by a successful early start, to begin a second foreign language at eleven.

Four teams, of experienced teachers and native speakers, were recruited and set to work under the direction of Sam Spicer. The new materials were given names like battle cries: *En avant!, Vorwärts!; ¡Adelante! and Yvperyod!* The main project was initially located in Leeds (with the German team in York) but, from 1967, when the Schools Council joined Nuffield as sponsor of the project, the joint SC/Nuffield Materials Unit was established as part of the Language Teaching Centre, York University.

Under Spicer's leadership, the four language teams (led by Don Grant and Mike Buckby – French, Anthony Peck – German, David Rowlands and Robert Clarke – Spanish, and David Rix – Russian) produced language teaching courses which broke entirely new ground. As the units of work were written they were sent month by month (with the accompanying tape recordings) to a network of testing schools (upwards of 100 in all parts of the country) who reported on their suitability in the classroom. The units of material and the schools' criticisms were then considered at regular meetings of expert national advisory committees for each language, representing university researchers, HMI and LEA advisers. The whole project thus developed into a national 'action research' exercise.

Meanwhile the four language teams at York began discussions with the Examining Boards about the kinds of tests that would be appropriate at age 16+ for the pupils using the new materials. This resulted in the acceptance by the Boards of special papers in which at least 75% of the vocabulary tested would be taken from the York materials. This conceded for the first time the principle of **defining the content** of the 16+ examination syllabus. There followed two decades of keen debate as to how the linguistic content of the syllabus should be defined, whether by frequency counting (as in *Le français fondamental*, Gougenheim et al, 1965), or by predicting the 'functions and notions' that learners would need to transact, as in the pioneering work of the Council of Europe team, under John Trim (Wilkins, 1972).

The theory of the 'critical age'

At the time when the Pilot Scheme was launched the idea that there is a 'critical age' for language learning (pre-puberty) was widely accepted. It had been popularised by the Canadian brain surgeons W Penfield and L Roberts in their book *Speech and brain mechanisms* (1959). The authors argued from the effect of brain damage on speech, and from Penfield's experience with his own children, that ***the time to begin . . . a general schooling in secondary languages . . . is between the ages of four and ten.*** This seemed to reinforce a common observation that when an immigrant family settles in a new country, the children soon pick up the new language and speak it like natives while the adults never lose the accent of their first language.

Powerful theoretical support was later given to the 'critical age' by the Harvard biologist Eric Lenneberg in his *Biological foundations of language* (1967). He recalled that brain growth is not an increase in cells, as with the rest of the body, but an expansion of the network of new nerve pathways between the cells ('neuropil'), and that the rapid growth of nerve connections, which ceases at puberty, coincides with the child's acquisition of language. Lenneberg supported his neurological account with evidence from 'feral' children, brought up in the wild until puberty, and so unable fully to master language.

Psychologists have since greatly modified Lenneberg's account (Kinsbourne and Smith, 1974; Clark and Clark, 1977). It is now suggested that children's ways of learning language may change quite radically as they grow up, with different learning strategies appearing about the age of seven and with a further change at puberty.

In the *Reith Lectures* for 1996 Jean Aitchison returned to this idea that learning strategies change as children grow:

The idea of a critical period (for mother tongue acquisition) is now disputed . . . Yet most people find it easier to learn languages when they are young, so a sensitive period may exist . . . A 'natural sieve' hypothesis is one idea put forward to explain this. Very young children may . . . automatically filter out complexities . . . Later learners may have lost this built-in filter . . . A 'tuning-in' hypothesis is another possibility. At each stage, a child is naturally attuned to some particular aspect of language. Infants may be tuned in to the sounds, older children to the syntax, and from around ten onwards the vocabulary becomes a major concern. Selective attention of this type fits in well with what we know about biologically programmed behaviour. (Aitchison, 1996)

Lenneberg, like Aitchison, argued from evidence of acquisition of the mother tongue. So far as foreign language learning is concerned, the 'critical age' thesis advanced by Penfield and Roberts soon came under fire. In the USA, in the wake of the National Defense Act (1958) a number of experimental FLES (Foreign Language in the Elementary School) schemes were begun amid high hopes, but these were soon disappointed.

Objective research evidence . . . offers little comfort to those who main-tain the child superiority thesis. Although children are probably superior to adults in acquiring an acceptable accent in a new language, E L Thorndike found many years ago that they make less rapid progress in other aspects of foreign language learning. (Ausubel, 1964)

J B Carroll found further corroboration for this in the IEA Eight Country Study of learning French (Carroll, 1975):

The study provides no clear evidence that there is any special advantage in starting the study of a foreign language very early other than the fact that this may provide the student more time to attain a desired performance level at a given age.

The debate on the critical age hypothesis has continued. In a masterly summary of the most recent findings, *Teaching modern languages in the primary school*, Professor Richard Johnstone, Director of Scottish CILT, agrees with H H Stern (1976):

We must avoid the danger of creating a false dichotomy between Penfield . . . and Burstall . . . and of having to make a clear choice between them. On developmental grounds each age in life probably has its peculiar advan-tages and disadvantages for language learning . . . in the sixties the mistake was made of expecting miracles merely by starting young. The miracles have not come about. Starting late, as such, is not the answer either.

Johnstone's final conclusion is that all the available evidence strongly sup-ports the introduction of a modern language in all primary schools.

One argument briefly touched on by Burstall (1970) but not widely followed up has more to do with '*attitude*' than with '*aptitude*'. It is that, as the capacity for 'empathy' declines abruptly in children, especially boys, with the onset of the self-consciousness and shyness of puberty, the age of eleven is surely the very worst time to ask the young learner to go to meet a challenging new language (and perform publicly in it).

The Pilot Scheme runs out of control

Whatever initial doubts were raised, the Pilot Scheme quickly caught the imagination of the public. It responded to a wave of optimism in educational planning in the early 1960s. However, the very enthusiasm of its reception was its undoing.

The teaching of foreign languages in primary schools had already begun when Sir Edward Boyle made his announcement. In the Independent Preparatory School Sector, of course, it had been long established, but there was a great deal in the State sector too. A survey commissioned by the Nuffield Foundation (Lazaro, 1963) reported that 58 LEAs in England and Scotland said that a foreign language had been introduced or would be introduced before the end of the session 1962/3, 200 schools in England and 80 in Scotland being involved. However only eighteen of the 58 LEAs were providing support for the teaching; in the other LEAs the impetus came from the schools themselves.

The Pilot Scheme was intended to build cautiously on this experience, given the inevitable problems of teacher supply about which Annan had warned. Unfortunately, national enthusiasm swept aside a cautious, experimental approach. Of the 146 LEAs in England and Wales, 80 volunteered to fulfil the Ministry's conditions (which included taking responsibility for the in-service training of teachers) and from them thirteen Pilot Areas were chosen for the initial, limited feasibility study. Each Pilot Area (part of an LEA) contained an annual age group of about 480 pupils, the total number being 6,702 in 125 primary schools. Within the Pilot Area two conditions had to be agreed: that in the schools concerned **all** eight year old pupils would start French (no selection) and that all would continue until at least the age of thirteen. In 1963 only pupils selected for Grammar Schools at eleven were offered a foreign language, so LEAs in the Pilot Scheme were obviously anticipating having to make a major change in the organisation of secondary schooling. In the event transfer at 11+ proved to be a stumbling block, as Annan had foreseen.

Had the original plan for a limited feasibility study been adhered to, the story might have been different, but at once the scheme ran out of control. The LEAs not selected as Pilot Areas refused to be excluded, and it was (unwisely but perhaps inevitably, since the LEAs could have gone ahead on their own) decided to recognise some 90 'associate areas' which would keep closely to the Ministry's conditions, but not be subject to the detailed evaluation that was planned. As a result the scheme expanded explosively, and by 1970 it was estimated that one third of all primary schools in the country included French in their curriculum (Hoy, 1977). It is interesting that in France a similar thing happened. In 1973 the French Ministry called a halt to experiments with the early teaching of modern languages begun in the 1960s because they had run out of control (Girard, 1974).

The strain on limited teaching resources had, of course, been foreseen though the difficulty of rapidly retraining primary teachers was certainly underestimated. Valiant efforts were made to find more teachers. The number of Training Colleges offering French as a main subject in the teaching Certificate in 1960 was 37. By 1966 there were 63 and, by 1970, 91. A variety of intensive courses for volunteers who had taken their French up to GCE 'A' or even 'O' level were initiated by HMI and by the new corps of Local Authority Language Advisers, whose rapid growth was one of the most positive off-shoots of the Pilot Scheme. However it proved less easy than had originally been thought to convert the holder of a GCE pass in French, by a short intensive course, into an effective teacher of the subject, while most of the increased output of French teachers from the colleges was absorbed by the rapid expansion of French in secondary comprehensive schools which began in the mid 1960s. What was being attempted **simultaneously** was a 'vertical' extension of French down the age range from eleven to eight, at the same time as a 'horizontal' extension across the age range, to the 75% of pupils in secondary schools previously excluded from French classes. This extra hazard faced by the Pilot Scheme has had, perhaps, too little attention.

The NFER Evaluation of the Pilot Scheme

Meanwhile it was planned to make two appraisals of the Scheme. In addition to a detailed, year by year, statistical evaluation of pupils' attainments in French, by the National Foundation for Educational Research, it was promised that Her Majesty's Inspectorate would make an independent general appraisal of the Scheme. In fact, though an appraisal by HMI was included in the interim NFER Report (1970) no final HMI appraisal ever appeared.

The evaluation of the Pilot Scheme by NFER (Burstall C, 1970; Burstall C et al, 1974) was a remarkable undertaking. No other school subject has ever been so closely studied over a period of years. (Indeed had some other difficult subjects been subjected to the same treatment, their place in the curriculum, too, might have been questioned !).

A negative verdict

Besides the main exercise of comparing the progress of 8+ beginners with that of starters at 11+, the final Report also examined other aspects of ETML such as: Does French interfere with other aspects of primary schooling? What methods are most effective at the early age and what organisational problems are posed?

The answers to these questions were by no means negative but they attracted less publicity than the answer to the main question: did the early start result in any substantial gain in mastery ? Here the Report did not mince words: '*This question can be answered unequivocally in the negative*'. This verdict spelt the end of the Pilot Scheme. Government support was withdrawn in 1974.

The Burstall Report did not escape trenchant criticism. Some critics drew attention to the sharp decline in the numbers of pupils tested as they moved up the school:

> *The findings are . . . based on observation of Cohorts (year-groups) 2 and 3, comprising some 11,300 pupils at the beginning of the project and a mere 1,227 pupils in 1973 (Gamble and Smalley, 1975).*

There were other technical criticisms of the evaluation (Buckby, 1976; Bennett, 1975; Nicholson, 1975).

Riposte by Nuffield

The Nuffield Foundation, which had invested enormously in the project, reacted strongly against its abrupt termination. John Maddox, then director of the Foundation, called together a national consultative committee under the chairmanship of G R Potter, a modern linguist, past chairman of CILT and Director of Education, West Sussex, to review the arguments and report on the way forward. The Committee's Report was compiled by Peter Hoy, who had been Staff Inspector for Modern Languages and well placed to observe the later stages of the Pilot Scheme.

One of the aspects of the Scheme brought out by Hoy's Report (Hoy, 1977) was the marked interest it generated in Europe. This was expressed at a Council of Europe Seminar in Copenhagen in September 1976 (Council of Europe, 1977) where a whole day was devoted to detailed discussion of the Pilot Scheme. The Symposium did not accept that the fate of the Pilot Scheme in the UK should point to abandonment of further experiment. It recommended that the Council of Europe should continue to support the early teaching of modern languages and called for further 'pilot experiments' and in particular, for research into possible programmes of 'preparation for language learning' discussed by the Symposium (Hawkins, 1977).

Summing up the Nuffield Committee's findings, Hoy stressed that for the early teaching of modern languages to succeed *we need as a country to decide on acceptable aims and objectives in this area and to create the known and necessary conditions for success.* He appends a useful list of 'conditions for success', in order of importance, at the head of which are *adequate supply of appropriately qualified teachers* and *clear definition of short-term teaching/learning objectives.*

Hoy disclaimed any wish to prolong controversy about the Burstall Report. He concluded, sadly, that:

> . . . *even if Burstall (1974) had urged the expansion of primary French, the implementation of such advice would have been prevented by financial constraints and by the acute shortage of primary teachers who are competent in French*

but he went on to regret:

> . . . *that the researchers confined their conclusions to a 'profit and loss' account . . . without trying to answer the question* What are the conditions for success for primary French? *To have done so would have switched the conclusion from the retrospective to the forward-looking, from the depressing factual statement to the more inspiriting statement that future success was likely to result from the establishment of identifiable conditions.*

The NFER Report is still required reading for informed discussion of the pros and cons of ETML. It should, however, be read in conjunction with Hoy, 1977. The following are its main lessons from the Pilot Scheme contained in the NFER Press Release (1974) and summarised by Hoy:

- early starters showed consistent superiority in listening comprehension;
- early starters showed a consistently more favourable attitude towards speaking French;
- girls scored consistently higher than boys at both primary and secondary stages (in fact one commentator suggested that the logical conclusion from the Report was that primary French should be continued for girls but not for boys!);
- at secondary level the early introduction of French had a negative effect on the position of other foreign languages by reinforcing French as the dominant language in schools and by increasing the number of pupils who reached secondary school convinced that foreign language learning was not for them;
- there was a linear correlation between performance in French and socio-economic status;
- both boys and girls did better in single sex schools;
- pupils in small rural schools did better than those in larger urban schools;
- pupils in the south of England took a more favourable view of learning French than pupils in the north;

- the attitude of the head of the school towards French had a real effect on pupils' achievement;
- an early experience of success positively affected later achievement;
- the most powerful incentive to learn French from the pupils' point of view was the opportunity to go to France. If pupils were convinced that they would never go to France they tended to condemn French as a waste of time;
- children who actually went to France reached higher levels of achievement than other pupils. However they also came from more favoured backgrounds and had better attitudes to French before they visited France;
- high achievers preferred to be taught by more traditional methods. There was universal dislike of the repetitious use of the tape recorder and of reading aloud in French;
- many young pupils soon became bewildered when French was used indiscriminately in class to give instructions without ascertaining whether they clearly understood

The Nuffield/Hoy riposte, valuable as it was for a just appraisal of the Pilot Scheme, could not save the brave project that Sir Edward Boyle had launched. As the Scottish experience of the early start has shown, teaching a foreign language at primary level calls for a combination of language skills *with training in primary methods*. To recruit enough teachers so qualified would have called for a radical solution, such as making a foreign language a compulsory element in all primary teacher training courses (the solution found, for instance, in Sweden when it was decided to teach English in all Swedish primary schools). Central Government lacked the will to adopt (and to find resources for) such policies and men of the calibre of Boyle, Farrer-Brown and Morrell, who might have grasped the nettle of teacher supply, had passed from the scene.

The two following sections of this Chapter describe the current state of ETML in England and of recent well-planned and researched initiatives in Scotland which promise to profit from the lessons of the Pilot Scheme.

References

Aitchison J, 'The language web' in *Reith Lectures*, Lecture no 3, broadcast on BBC Radio 4 (February 1996)

Annan N (Lord Annan) (Chairman), *Report on the teaching of Russian* (HMSO, 1962)

Ausubel D P, 'Adults versus children in second-language learning; psychological considerations' in *Modern Language Journal*, 48: 420–4 [363–4] USA (1964)

Bennett S N, 'Weighing the evidence: a review of *Primary French in the balance*' in *British Journal of Educational Psychology*, 45: 337–40 (1975).

Buckby M, 'Is primary French really in the balance ?' in *Audio-Visual Language Journal*, 14,1 (1976)

164

Burstall C, *French in the primary school: attitudes and attainment* (NFER, 1970)

Burstall C et al, *Primary French in the balance* (NFER, 1974)

Clark H H and E V Clark, *Psychology and language* (New York: Harcourt Brace Jovanovich, 1977)

Carroll J B, *The teaching of French as a foreign language in eight countries* (New York: Wiley, 1975)

Council of Europe, 'Modern languages in primary education' in *Council of Europe: education and culture* (Strasbourg: Council for Cultural Co-operation, CCC/EGT (76) 38-E, 1977)

Gamble C J and A Smalley, 'Primary French in the balance: were the scales accurate?' in *Modern Languages,* vi, 2, 95 (1975)

Girard D, *Enseignement précoce des langues vivantes* (Paris: Ministère de l'Education Nationale, 1974)

Gougenheim C et al, *L'élaboration du français fondamental* (Paris: Didier, 1965)

Hawkins E W, *Modern languages in the curriculum,* revised edition (Cambridge University Press, 1987)

Hawkins E W, 'The relationship between mother tongue and modern language learning with particular reference to disadvantaged children' in Council of Europe, 'Modern languages in primary education' (1977) (see above)

Hawkins E W, 'A possible way forward', Appendix D in Hoy (1977) (see below)

Hoy P H (ed), *The early teaching of modern languages* (Nuffield Foundation, 1977)

Kinsbourne M and W L Smith (eds), *Hemispheric disconnection and cerebral function* (Springfield, Ill: Charles C Thomas, 1974)

Lazaro C M, 'Report of foreign language teaching in British primary schools, January to March' in *Nuffield Foundation foreign languages materials project, reports and occasional papers,* no1 (1963)

Lenneberg E H, *Biological foundations of language* (John Wiley and Sons, 1967)

Nicholson D, *Final report on the French Pilot Scheme,* Mimeograph, Nuffield Materials Project (York: Micklegate House, 1975)

Penfield W and L Roberts, *Speech and brain mechanisms* (OUP, 1959. Re-issued in paperback New York: Atheneum, 1966)

Wilkins D A, *An investigation into the linguistic and situational content of the common core in a unit credit system* (Strasbourg: Council of Europe, 1972)

14

The present position in England

Peter Satchwell

Following the publication of the Burstall Report and the withdrawal of national funding from 1975 onwards, a small number of LEAs and individual schools in the state and private sectors soldiered on with primary French.

Tameside set up a 'pyramid' team of eleven peripatetic French specialists who for several years travelled between a secondary school and its feeder primaries teaching two sessions of French a week. This team produced custom-made materials to suit their situation and these were eventually exported to other LEAs, notably the Isle of Man, which provided substantial funding to introduce primary French throughout the island in the mid 1980s.

The pyramid staffing model of peripatetics was not feasible in other areas of England, especially in large counties where secondary schools might receive pupils from as many as fifteen feeder primaries. It is worth noting, however, that the best practice in the 1980s tended to be found where there was sustained support from advisory teachers (ATs). These ATs were very often able to help teachers in the classroom, advise on appropriate resources and run in-service courses for groups of primary teachers. Common problems were lack of finance, lack of commitment to ETML from headteachers and other primary colleagues, often lack of support from secondary language teachers, and absence of national or regional policies on ETML. Despite all this the enthusiasts battled on.

Examples of advisory teacher work on ETML were the strong initiatives in the early 1980s in East Sussex where peripatetic French teachers were coordinated for several years by a primary trained advisory teacher. This work eventually led to the publication of *Salut!* classroom materials which were designed to provide consistency of experience for Year 6 pupils throughout the county. East Sussex is one of the few LEAs in England which still allocates a substantial budget to supporting ETML.

At various times during the 1980s other LEAs supported primary languages with advisory teachers, but by the mid 80s there appeared to be a serious decline in interest in ETML. The setting up of a Pre-11 Languages Network by Ron Addelman provided a useful forum for the few advisers/advisory teachers still interested to share ideas, experiences and resources. But it was not until 1989, with the beginning of preparations for 1993 and the opening of the European Market, that a sudden groundswell of renewed interest in primary school language learning began to make itself felt, especially among parents. Many heads were unable to find a teacher on their staff who was competent and willing to take on the task. The number of initial teacher training colleges in England offering a French option in the B.Ed course had fallen from some twenty in the early 1980s to only three by 1995.

Where schools were unable to offer a foreign language on the timetable they were frequently persuaded by parents to provide premises for after school French clubs run by individuals or private enterprises. Cottage industries like the '*Club français*' of Linda Ellis and '*La jolie ronde*' of Collette Hallam have developed into substantial commercial enterprises offering French – and now other languages – to children of four to ten years old all over the country.

Requests for the reintroduction of languages into the primary school curriculum, notably in the resolution of the National Association of Head Teachers (NAHT) conference in 1992, have been met with a very muted response from the Government: Baroness Blatch, interviewed by BBC 2 for their *Little Englanders* programme in April 1993, saw no prospect of providing a trained teaching force of linguists for primary schools before the year 2010! However, there have been signs of a possible rethink of the National Curriculum at Key Stage 2 after the year 2000, with some encouraging suggestions from Sir Ron Dearing that primary schools might now consider finding time for a foreign language.

LEA initiatives

Despite this lack of national commitment there have been several encouraging ETML initiatives taken recently by LEAs and individuals. They deserve brief description here (with apologies to any we have inadvertently omitted).

Since 1989 **Kent** has funded the retraining of primary teachers in over 400 schools to enable them to teach French (or German/Portuguese) to pupils in Year 6. The in-service course provided by Keith Sharpe at Christ's College, Canterbury has included days out of school, twilights and an enterprising annual reciprocal element when primary teachers from Kent learn alongside their colleagues from schools in Nord Pas de Calais for a week on either side of the Channel. The retraining of these teachers has been coordinated and followed up by classroom support from an advisory teacher, Glynis Rumley. In 1994 Kent Educational Television (KETV) produced a high-quality set of four teaching/in-service training videos: *Pilote,* to provide the retrained teachers with a year's classroom materials for the full ability range in Year 6. This has been followed in 1995/96 with a German version, *3-2-1 – Los!*

Since 1992 the London Borough of **Richmond** has funded the retraining of teachers in all of its 32 junior schools. The teaching of French is voluntary, but all schools teach it in Years 5 and 6. Again, much of the success of this project is due to the coordination and support of an advisory teacher, Anne Farren. In 1994 Richmond produced its own borough scheme of work for ETML and a set of teaching materials, *C'est facile comme Bonjour!,* aiming to provide consistency of experience for all the children in the borough. A recent interesting development has been the LEA funding of two foreign language assistants who spend one morning a week for seven weeks in each junior school. There is also an invaluable link with primary schools in St. Omer. BT has recently sponsored videophones set up in St. Omer and Richmond.

Since 1993 **Surrey** has provided retraining for fifteen primary teachers a year to enable them to coordinate French in their schools. The course is spread over three terms and combines linguistic and methodological training. This course is taught by an advisory teacher, Richard White, and culminates in a tailor-made two week 'Stage' at the CIEP in Sèvres in June, where the participants work with the Valettes and other CIEP staff. In 1994 Surrey also produced a new set of guidelines for ETML which include audio cassettes to support teachers with a repertoire of basic classroom phrases in French/German/Italian/Spanish.

In 1993/94 **Gloucestershire** ran a small pilot scheme in French and now has the backing of the chief education officer to expand the teaching of foreign languages in all its primary schools on a voluntary basis with support from their advisory teachers Sue Wise and Penny Krucker at the European Development office.

Most of the ETML initiatives have so far been in French, but **Cornwall** and **West Sussex** have in the last three years experimented with German in a handful of pilot schools. An interesting example from these LEA initiatives is the introduction of two languages (French and German) simultaneously in Years 6 and 7 in four Crawley middle schools. Reflections by Sue Mayo on the first year of this pilot can be read in detail in the CILT book *Reflections on modern languages in primary education: six UK case studies* (1996). It is clear from Sue Mayo's evidence that pupils of all abilities have found the learning of two European languages at the age of ten not at all daunting and that the experiment seems to be a success with pupils and parents alike. Again, much of the success of this pilot stems from the constant support from an advisory teacher, Candy Newman, and from Harald Seeger of the Goethe-Institut.

Further work is being done in **North Yorkshire** where the LEA is running retraining courses for primary teachers in cooperation with the College of York and Ripon St John and with sponsorship from Nestlé and in **168** **Manchester** where over 80 primary schools are teaching a foreign language.

Of the many individual school projects across the country one must serve here as a shining example of what can be achieved with very young children if the teacher adopts similar approaches to the partial immersion models developed in Canada. In a private infants school in Croydon, Pascale Bizet has created an impressive programme of French tuition which starts with the reception class in small groups of six and builds up through extra club activities (maths, PE, music, drama) with the five- to seven-year-olds to daily sessions of 40 minutes French with the eight-year-olds. By this stage all curriculum topics are taught in the foreign language in four-week sessions. This programme relies on teaching by two native speakers with quite extensive use of authentic French primary books and materials. It also includes a week in France for all the six- to seven-year-olds!

Published materials, courses and conferences

The last five years have seen a significant increase in the quantity and quality of classroom materials from publishers in the UK, France, Germany and Italy. Indeed, the quality of many of the French and German resources shows that ETML is now being taken very seriously indeed by the leading publishers in Europe. The BBC has also launched new programmes aimed at older juniors with *Le club* on radio and television and the TV *Carousel* of twenty short stories in simple French for beginners. In 1995 Channel 4 is broadcasting *Le petit monde de Pierre,* an entertaining modern 'fairy-tale' for beginners imported from Germany.

Encouraging for primary teachers also is the increase in the number of in-service courses and conferences. The early initiatives of Ming Tsow who launched in 1990 a series of annual ETML conferences at King's College, London, have been followed up by CILT with its first national conference, *First steps in foreign language learning* in Southampton in February 1994. Since then CILT has been inundated with requests for further in-service sessions and these have been run as one-day or twilight in-house events on resources and aspects of primary foreign language methodology. In 1995 CILT launched a new series of books for primary language teachers, *Young Pathfinders,* and primary languages now receive a high profile in the annual *Language World* conferences organised by the ALL.

Lessons learnt

The evidence from recent experience seems to indicate that:

- We have until now seriously underestimated young children's capabilities and enthusiasm for learning foreign languages.
- Young children do not see learning a new language as 'hard' – adults tend to see 'difficulties' which do not occur to children.
- Children as young as five are quite capable of handling quite ambitious topics through the foreign language if the language is presented in an entertaining and enjoyable way.
- We need to rethink our approach to timetabling discrete foreign language lessons in primary schools: French twice a week is not sufficient. We need to follow the Scots' example of trying to 'embed' the foreign language into normal classroom routines and activities so that there is daily reinforcement and constant recycling of language structures, e.g. taking the register/dinner money, mental arithmetic, music, aerobics, art and craft, etc.
- The spin-offs from FL learning for **all** children are undoubtedly improved listening skills, greater awareness of language (mother tongue and foreign language), greater self-confidence and poise as individuals, improved social skills – through cooperative learning: pairwork, groupwork, improvised drama – and greater empathy with foreign people and cultures.
- It is fair to conclude that learning languages is both a valuable experience and a vital part of all children's general education. This has been confirmed by projects in the UK and most other countries in Europe, and especially in Canada and Australia. Young children under ten, respond without inhibitions to a new language, absorb it like a sponge and use it creatively for their own purposes. They are interested in learning about the culture and the way of life of children in other countries and will perform rhymes, raps, songs, playlets with real enthusiasm and amazing accuracy of pronunciation and intonation if they are encouraged to be creative with the new language from the start.
- Not everybody can teach a foreign language to young children! The primary languages teacher does not need to be a languages graduate, but she/he needs both confidence and reasonable fluency in the areas designated so clearly in the 'Competences' drawn up by the Scottish Office for Education (SOED) for their retraining programme (1994). These skills cannot be acquired overnight or by distance learning; they

require intensive work and sympathetic interaction with well qualified tutors and advisory teachers. If our primary pupils are to receive a positive and rewarding first experience of a new language we must ensure that the teachers are confident in their own abilty to sustain most of each lesson in the target language with reasonable accuracy of pronunciation and intonation – and that the structures and vocabulary they use are as up-to -date and as authentic as possible.

To conclude: the quality and success of young children's learning and their attitude to foreign languages for the rest of their life is likely to be dictated by the personality and competence of their primary teachers. If we are going to compete with the rest of Europe and take ETML seriously we need major national and regional initial training and retraining programmes based on the lessons we shall undoubtedly learn from the current Scottish programme.

References

BBC, *Little Englanders* (BBC2, April 1993)
BBC, *Le club,* TV series (1994)
BBC, *Le club,* Radio series (1994)
Channel 4, *Le petit monde de Pierre,* TV series (1995)
Johnstone R, *Teaching modern languages at primary school: approaches and implications* (SCRE, 1994)
KETV, *Pilote,* 4 videos + t. notes (for Year 5/6 and special schools), available from KETV and Language Centre Publications (1994)
KETV, *3-2-1 – Los!* 3 videos + teacher's notes from KETV/Invicta Media, Barton Road, Dover, Kent CT16 2ND
Martin C, *Young Pathfinder 2: Games and fun activities* (CILT, 1995)
Mayo S, 'Teaching two foreign languages in Year 6' in Hurrell A and P Satchwell, *Reflections on modern languages in primary education: six UK case studies* (CILT, 1996)
Richmond, *C'est facile comme Bonjour!* (FCs, cassettes and worksheets) (1994)
Satchwell P and J de Silva, *Young Pathfinder 1: Catching them young* (CILT, 1995)
SCOPE + SOED, *Modern languages in the primary school,* 3 videos + viewing guide (85 extracts from lessons taught in pilot schools filmed in 1993) (1994). Available from SCOPE Picture Productions Ltd, Keppie House, 147 Blythswood Street, Glasgow G2 4EN
SOED, *Interchange no 19: foreign languages in the primary school: the national pilot project in Scotland* (1993)
SOED, *Modern languages in the primary school: competences* (1994)
Tierney D and P Dobson, *Young Pathfinder 3: Are you sitting comfortably? Telling stories to young language learners* (CILT, 1995)

15
The Scottish initiatives

Richard Johnstone

In the late 1960s and early 1970s Scotland experienced the introduction of French at primary school in a manner that had much in common with developments in England. The initiative embraced some 500 primary schools and ran into similar sorts of problem. Although there was not a Scottish Burstall to point these out, an HMI (1969) report, based on visits to106 schools, pinpointed a lack of continuity from primary to secondary and a lack of fluent competence in French among many primary school teachers. A study by Nisbet and Welsh (1972) did however show that pupils who had begun French at primary school retained a positive attitude through the second year of secondary and suggested that there may be benefits in the enlargement of pupils' interests and the development of a more general language skill.

It was not until the late 1980s that a new initiative was announced in the form of a national pilot programme on Modern Languages at Primary School (MLPS). A key factor influencing the decision to go ahead was political will. The Single Market was approaching and Government politicians in Scotland subscribed to the view that the early learning of a foreign language would in due course increase the commercial competitiveness of Scottish businesses. Without this political will it is doubtful if the funds would have been secured for the implementation of what was bound to be a long-lasting and costly enterprise if eventually all primary schools were to become involved.

In Scotland pupils spend seven years at primary (P1 to P7) and they are one year older than their English counterparts when at the age of twelve they go to secondary school. The national pilot scheme was launched in Autumn 1989, consisting of six secondary schools and associated primaries. From the start then the development would proceed on the notion of a 'cluster', each cluster embracing all primaries associated with a particular secondary. This would help with eventual transition to secondary, in that pupils would tend to have had a similar foreign-language experience, irrespective of the primary they had attended. In 1990 an additional six secondaries and associated primaries were added to the national pilot, making twelve secondary and 76 primary schools in total. At the same time there were regional initiatives, the largest by far being in Strathclyde with 24 secondary and over 130 primary schools. In the first year of the national pilots a foreign language was offered to pupils aged eleven in P7, but in subsequent years it was offered to classes at P6 and P7, and in a smaller number of cases to classes at P4 (pupils aged seven to eight). In addition, there were from the start several small primary schools with composite, mixed-age classes.

At the time of the launch, it was made clear that the national pilots would not necessarily lead to an extension of the scheme to all Scottish primary schools. However, as the scheme progressed, a general consensus arose among HMI, advisers, teachers and parents that it was going well. By 1992 the Secretary of State for Scotland was able to announce that within roughly five years all Scottish primary schools would have incorporated a foreign language into their curriculum.

The Scottish pilots cannot be understood without reference to four key assumptions. First, it was not to be 'French for all'. Some clusters would be dedicated mainly to French but others would feature German, Spanish or Italian. This would signal the importance of languages diversification. Second, the ethos would be one of language learning, not language awareness. In several European countries there was a debate between *apprentissage* and *sensibilisation* as the term under which languages at primary should be organised. In Scotland there was some suspicion that an approach based on language awareness might lead to much discussion in English but not much use of the foreign language, and so a view was promoted that pupils at primary should engage in foreign-language activities with the aim of developing a serious level of competence in the language. In the event, however, as a result of experiences gained during the pilot phase, the notion of language awareness has once again come to be seen as supportive of successful language learning. Third, it was considered important that the foreign language at primary should not be taught as a separate subject but instead should find its place in the holistic Scottish primary school curriculum. The term 'embedding' was adopted to describe this process. Fourth, in most clusters the teaching would be shared between visiting specialist languages teachers from the secondary school and the primary school classteachers. The languages competence of the visiting teacher would be complemented by the primary classteacher's knowledge of the pupils and their curriculum.

Since the national pilots represented a major policy initiative, the Scottish Office Education Department commissioned an independent evaluation, the aims of which were prescribed as: assessing the linguistic attainments of children involved in the pilot projects compared with children not having a foreign language at primary, and evaluating the project courses and pedagogical methods that were adopted. Phase 1 of the research began in January 1991 and lasted until the end of 1992. Assessments of pupil performance, conducted towards the end of first and second years of secondary, indicated that pupils who had begun a foreign language at primary had some advantage over those who had not. Their pronunciation was better, they produced somewhat longer utterances, made more use of communication strategies, showed higher levels of motivation and were more ready to initiate and answer in class. The advantage of primary over secondary beginners was evident across the range of abilities, and was particulary marked in the case of slower learners.

In the second phase (1993–95) the research team explored issues that had emerged in the first phase. These consisted of three strands: teaching and learning, pupils' attainments and the professional development needs of teachers. Cutting across these strands were three topics: knowledge about language, learner strategies and transition from primary to secondary. Some differences between primary and secondary were identified that were possible causes for concern. For example, when learning a foreign language at primary school pupils tended to experience a fairly open set of topics and activities, possibly a reflection of the embedding approach, but at secondary school the approach was more controlled by the course materials. At primary, pupils were exposed to a greater range of vocabulary and structure than they received in early secondary. Clearly then there were problems of transition that even by the end of the pilot phase in 1995 were not fully solved.

So far as making progress in the language was concerned, pupils' performance on a common task (a conversation between a pair of pupils and a researcher) increased from P6 to P7 to Secondary 1 and to a lesser extent Secondary 2, though the improvement was in the numbers rather than the range of words they were able to use, and most expressions seemed to consist of set phrases with relatively little manipulation. It was possible to track the first cohort through to their Standard Grade examinations in fourth year of secondary. Although several intervening variables made it impossible to draw clear conclusions from this first set of national examination evidence, the researchers did find that the schools concerned were entering a substantially wider range of pupils than before yet were able to maintain their previous standards of attainment. This suggests that the advantage of primary school learners over secondary school beginners was being maintained up to the age of sixteen.

The pilots are now past, and the process is underway of extending the provision of a foreign language to all Scottish primary schools. This generalisation phase differs from the pilots in one key respect: the main provider of foreign-language input will be the primary classteacher, not the visiting teacher from secondary. To this end a national training programme has been launched with the aim of equipping primary teachers with appropriate knowledge and skills. The numbers of primary teachers receiving training have been: 370 in 1993/94, 800+ in 1994/95 and 800+ in 1995/96. Thus far, responses to the training received seem highly favourable.

The MLPS innovation has prompted fresh thinking on the role of children's first language in the development of their competence in a foreign language. There is now a better understanding that knowledge about language (language awareness) should be seen as a vital ingredient in children's overall language development, and that the primary school classteacher, willing and able to exploit more than one language in class, is well placed to support children in this respect.

What will CILT's next thirty-year review have to say about MLPS in Scotland? At present, many vital questions remain to be answered. How many trained MLPS teachers will be needed for each primary school? What further on-the-job support will they receive? Who will provide this support? Will pupils entering secondary always have the right to continue with the language they began at primary, or will administrative concerns oblige them to change? How will busy teachers cope with MLPS once they are confronted by the next major innovation which probably will be in a different area of the curriculum? How will the links with secondary schools be maintained? What changes will secondary school teachers make to their teaching, in order to overcome the problems of transition that the pilot phase clearly identified?

So long as there is strong political support for languages, reflected in a will to provide adequate funding for an adequate supply of teachers, for their training and their professional development, and so long as it is understood that the process of embedding a foreign language in the culture of primary schools will be a gradual one, the prospects could be good. The pilot phase has ample evidence to confirm that, when the circumstances are favourable, an early start does make a difference.

Athough the introduction of foreign languages into Scottish primary schools has received much national and international attention, mention must be made of another languages innovation at primary that is as important and more fundamental. As a result of parental interest, supported by a special fund from the Scottish Office, there are now over fifty Gaelic-medium units in Scottish primary schools in areas by no means confined to the Western Isles and Inner Hebrides. Children attending a GMU receive their primary school education mainly through the medium of Gaelic, with English being gradually blended in. In many cases they are from families that are not Gaelic-speaking. A recent HMI report testified to the success of GMU education, and a three-year research-based evaluation has been commissioned that will seek to establish not only what GMU pupils' progress and attainments are in Gaelic but also how they compare in English, mathematics and science with children receiving English-medium education.

If I may express a personal hope for the next thirty years, it is that as insights are gained from these two fascinating initiatives – one in foreign languages and the other in an indigenous heritage language – a more integrated national policy on language at school will be developed that will help teachers to support children not only in all of their language activity – first, second, heritage, foreign – but also in their personal development, including their sense of local and international identity.

References

Her Majesty's Inspectorate of Schools, *French in the primary school* (HMSO, 1969)
Low L, J Duffield , S Brown and R Johnstone, *Evaluating foreign languages in primary schools. Interim report* (Scottish CILT, 1993)
Low L, S Brown, R Johnstone and A Pirrie, *Foreign languages in primary schools: evaluation of the Scottish pilot projects. Final report* (Scottish CILT, 1995)
Nisbet J and J Welsh, 'A local evaluation of primary school French' in Entwhistle N and J Nisbet, *Educational research in action* (Open University, University London Press, 1972)

176

Part

five

The changing
curriculum

1966-1996 **YEARS**

Motivating the learner:

A pioneering example of a learner-friendly Latin textbook, using pictures to motivate the learning, was Jan Komensky's attractive *Orbis sensualium pictus (Picture of the visible world,* English edition by Charles Hoole, 1659). The great Czech reformer wrote mainly in Latin and took the pen-name of Johan Comenius (the name Amos = loving was added by his teacher at Prerov, who adopted him after he lost his parents from the plague at the age of twelve). In the moving preface to his *Orbis pictus,* Comenius reveals something of the additional personal tragedy he suffered in the loss (again from the plague) of both his own young children, to whose upbringing he had so looked forward.

This most innovative textbook has a bright picture on every page, illustrating an activity outside the classroom (e.g. playing tennis in the yard, etc). Parts of the picture are numbered to allow close association with the appropriate Latin phrase printed below.

Comenius even expressed the hope that pupils might be encouraged to colour the pictures themselves. Unfortunately, as Charles Hoole, his translator, who used the textbook in his London Grammar School, explains, the cost of the book (5 shillings each, or £25 at present rates) prevented his allowing pupils to do this, and Hoole eventually had to give up using the books because of the expense.

16
Materials and methods 1966–1996

Maurice Whitehead

The period under review has seen a process of 'democratisation' of foreign language learning. It is not quite without precedent. From the 1870s until the beginning of the present century, working class children in higher grade elementary schools and in organised science schools, where French, and to a lesser extent German, held a prominent place in the curriculum, enjoyed opportunities to learn languages for vocational purposes. These beginnings in the democratisation of modern languages were unfortunately short-lived. Despite widespread protest, the Board of Education in 1904 abolished curricular overlap with secondary schools. At a single stroke, the curriculum 'reform' of 1904 both denied the majority of the school population access to the learning of modern languages for the next sixty years and contributed largely to the unfortunate myth, still prevalent today, that the British are innately 'bad' at languages (Bayley, 1989 and 1991).

During the period 1904–1964, the value of modern languages in developing social skills was neglected at the expense of the development of mental cultivation and discipline and the almost exclusive study of their *written* form. With Latin and Greek still pre-eminent in British independent schools and grammar schools in the early twentieth century, modern linguists argued the case for the promotion of their subject area in terms dictated by the classics. This resulted in heavy emphasis on grammatical and literary concerns, with consequent neglect of the spoken language – a state of affairs obtaining at both school and university levels. Even as late as 1965, with some notable exceptions, the predominant emphasis in the teaching and learning of modern foreign languages in the United Kingdom was still on their value in the development of intellectual rather than practical skills.

The year 1965 was to be a momentous one. The publication of circular 10/65, encouraging comprehensive education, also finally brushed aside the scandalous curricular situation of the previous sixty years. At the same time, there was growing excitement at the new possibilities offered by the increasing classroom use of tape recorders, at the advancing emphasis on the use there of the spoken form of the target language, and at the new 'O' level examination syllabuses then being introduced by the AEB and the JMB. If there was now hope for the future, there was still reality to be faced: the learning of modern foreign languages was still an elitist affair, being studied by at most 25% of the 11+ age group. Typically, languages were taught throughout grammar schools, as well as to the ablest third of pupils in about one half of secondary modern schools, with very few less-able pupils ever being allowed such opportunities (Newsom, 1963). There was still a heavy middle class bias in both attitudes and materials. Even the very aims of language teaching were unclear. Here a vicious circle existed. Many teachers relied completely on the published course books for which they opted, and the authors and publishers of these wrote what they *thought* was appropriate, often with previous examination papers in mind. In the absence of a single national association for modern languages, or a national body such as CILT, there was no natural forum available in which to debate the aims of language teaching and learning and how these might best be taken forward.

The one debate then raging, however incoherently, among modern linguists was between the *anciens* and the *modernes*. The *anciens* saw modern languages primarily as a means of training people in 'habits of accuracy' and 'mental gymnastics', in ways similar to Latin and Greek. On the other hand, the *modernes* took a much larger view, arguing that the aim of communication should underlie discussion of method, initial teacher education programmes and the design of courses and materials in schools (IAHM, 1966).

The diversity of outlook of teachers of modern languages was reflected in the very appearance of the classroom in which modern languages were taught. In the grammar schools, even under 'enlightened' head teachers and heads of modern languages, it was still the norm in 1966 for classes to be streamed from the age of eleven, and for most subjects, apart from PE, music, art and handicrafts, to be taught in the same room to a single group throughout the day. Though there were doubtless outstanding exceptions to the general rule, the only concession to modern languages in such general 'form' rooms might be one or two posters – often French ones, from the SNCF – and a map of France, Germany or Spain. In the classroom of an *ancien*, there was not likely to be any decor appropriate to the language being taught. The specialist language room was yet to arrive on a widespread basis, even though many headteachers were already arguing that *language rooms are as essential a part of school equipment as science laboratories* (IAHM, 1966).

The teaching and learning environment for modern languages in 1966 was riddled with variables. Schools were at liberty to devise their own curricula. Though these were to a great extent governed by the public examination system, the background and calibre of modern languages staff in schools played an important part in the process. Even in a single school department of modern languages, staff could vary enormously: graduate and non-graduate; trained and untrained; specialist and non-specialist; some with very little, if any, residence abroad, as the year abroad was only just beginning to be a normal part of a degree course in languages. In an age when individual languages 'departments' were generally very much more loosely knit than the majority are today, the scope for individualism if not idiosyncrasy in teaching methods and materials on the part of the teacher was vast.

In 1966, in terms of materials and methods to be used in the classroom, teachers of modern foreign languages had three or four broad areas to explore with their pupils: 'traditional' courses; BBC radio materials; 'audio-visual' or 'audio-lingual' courses; or any combination of these.

Traditional courses

Taking the example of French, then (as now) the most widely-taught modern foreign language, the textbook market in 1966 was still dominated by the publications of one man – W F H Whitmarsh. His *First, Second, Third* and *Fourth French Book* series, first published by Longmans between 1947 and 1951, had captured the immediate post-war market and, proving popular, had run into numerous further editions and impressions throughout the 1950s and early 1960s. Such was their success in terms of sales that they spawned a wide range of further publications by the same author. Though these claimed to work towards one end – *that the fundamentals of spoken and written French shall become utterly familiar* (Whitmarsh, 1963) – it is difficult to see how the claim was justified through the provision of books alone, without supporting materials, using extremely traditional (i.e. 'old fashioned') methods of presentation, and offering a stylised, idealised and distinctly bourgeois image of France.

BBC radio courses

The role of the BBC in the promotion and development of good practice in the teaching of modern languages, especially in the 1960s, is one which has hitherto received insufficient recognition, partly owing to the fact that it is very difficult to quantify the number of schools which made use of the programmes then available.

In terms of quality, however, the programmes and their supporting materials still stand up to the closest scrutiny, even today. Though more research still needs to be done in this area, it seems clear that some of the impetus for the resumption of language broadcasting to schools in the post-war period – the earliest BBC language broadcasts in French and Spanish date back to 1924 – stemmed from the success of work of the *Modern Languages for the Services* courses developed for use in the British armed forces during the second world war. Courses such as *French from Scratch: Bill et Tommy en France*, and the parallel German course, *Bill und Jock in Deutschland* (1942), with their copious supply of recordings on disc, and their handy pocket-sized supporting students' booklets, were successful in that they featured native speakers using colloquial language in lively, authentic situations, together with cultural background of interest to the adult learners using them.

When BBC language broadcasting resumed in the late 1940s, these principles were adhered to in the devising of new language materials for schools. Under the aegis of the Schools Broadcasting Council for the United Kingdom, new radio courses in French and German were developed by the BBC. Broadcasts in the *Early stages of French* series flourished throughout the 1950s and 1960s and provided a generation of secondary school pupils with their first taste of authentic French. In my own northern grammar school in 1965, an introduction to the weekly *Early stages of French* series, recorded on tape faithfully week by week by an inspired and inspiring French teacher, who ensured that we each had a copy of the excellent BBC *brochure* which accompanied each series, first awakened my interest in, and enthusiasm for, things French. The short programmes, carefully designed to introduce appropriate new vocabulary and structures week by week, also gave ample scope for the proficient teacher who had enjoyed a period of residence abroad to incorporate cultural awareness into the lesson – and every programme ended with a new and memorable song.

Such was the success of these broadcasts that in 1964–65 the BBC launched a new radio-vision course, entitled *French for beginners* relying for its success on the hope that there would be:

> . . . *sufficient teachers of French ready to postpone the use of the grammar text book and knowledge of when to add an e to the past participle of a verb in a written examination at the age of sixteen until after a pupil was able to speak simple French with fluency and confidence* (Schools Broadcasting Council, 1965).

The demand for this new course was such that in September 1965 the BBC discontinued its highly successful *Early stages of French* course and replaced it with a course entitled *Allons-y*, which introduced new speech patterns and grammatical forms more systematically than its predecessor and used a carefully-controlled vocabulary based to a great extent on *Le français fondamental*.

Other audio-visual and audio-lingual courses

If considerable fossilisation of language textbooks occurred in Britain in the 1950s and early 1960s, activity across the Channel in France at this time was frantic. There, at the Centre de Recherche et d'Etude pour la Diffusion du Français (CREDIF), based at the Ecole Normale Supérieure at Saint-Cloud, new audio-visual courses such as the massive *Voix et images de France* course and *Bonjour Line*, with their plethora of filmstrips and audio recordings, were developed. Developed originally for use in Francophone Africa, where the teacher might not know the pupils' native language or might be faced with several native languages in one class, these courses established meanings through the use of pictures. Other courses such as *TAVOR Aids*, developed by Supreme Headquarters Allied Powers in Europe (SHAPE) for children of military personnel of different nationalities and different mother tongues in the immediate post-war period, were soon enthusiastically purchased from the early to mid-1960s onwards by British teachers at both primary and secondary levels eager to escape from the restrictions of traditional coursebooks (Hawkins, 1987). Suddenly there was a change in departments of modern languages: considerable hardware was now needed – film-strip projectors, tape recorders, language laboratories, black-out facilities, and new multi-point electric sockets to operate all the new equipment.

Perceptive and enthusiastic teachers made a success of new audio-lingual and audio-visual courses in the mid-1960s by realising the limitations of the materials available and creating their own supplementary, supporting materials such as exercises, worksheets and workbooks. They were soon to be helped, as will be seen, by developments in the examinations system, which from 1965 onwards both encouraged the use of tape recordings of native speakers and fostered increasing emphasis on the spoken language. But even these teachers had doubts, and others soon became disillusioned and dissatisfied both with the intricacies of technology which the courses demanded and with the methodology underpinning them (Cammish, 1983). With lesser skilled teachers, the effects could be disastrous. Even at their very best, visual aids cannot always convey general concepts, let alone more complex ones expressed in particular forms of language. With some teachers, an excessive trust in the ability of visual aids in new courses in the mid-1960s to convey meaning led in some cases, at best, to routine and dullness and, at worst, to mindless parroting of phrases, with all the demotivation and boredom of pupils which inevitably ensues from such an approach. As time wore on, further problems were to emerge: as David Phillips has reminded us, *visual aids dated [and] the disembodied voices on the tapes lapsed into caricature; method had failed again, despite the convincing enough methodology* (Phillips, 1988).

184

Changes in materials: from 'method' to 'approach', 1966–1996

Such disillusion and disappointment was nothing new: a whole series of experiments with new methods in the teaching and learning of modern languages over the previous two centuries had ended with similar results. What has positively emerged from the period 1966–1996 has been the gradual abandonment of a fruitless quest. Beginning in the mid-eighteenth century and ending only recently, its aim had been to find a universal panacea method for the optimum teaching and learning of modern languages. It is now generally accepted that no one single such *method* exists (Hawkins, 1987; Saunderson, 1992) – but that a communicative *approach*, incorporating *inter alia* many of the best elements of a wide variety of methods, can lead towards success.

The words 'towards success' are used advisedly. Though few today would question the basic tenets of a communicative approach, a number of problems arise in its implementation. First, the teacher has the daunting task of identifying the most appropriate materials with which to teach, with so many courses now boasting a battery of supporting materials beyond the text book and the teacher's manual – cassettes, flashcards, OHP colour transparencies, readers, workbooks, language masters and CD-ROMs. Keeping abreast of such rapid development is difficult for the hard-pressed classroom teacher. In this context, CILT's creation in the period 1992–95 of a national network of Comenius Centres is greatly to be welcomed. In such centres, many of these materials may be previewed by teachers prior to scarce financial resources being allocated for bulk purchases.

Once considerations of materials have been resolved by the teacher, at best, the eleven-year-old embarking on the learning of a modern language in a comprehensive school in 1996 may be taught French, German or Spanish in a specialist language room, festooned with lively, colourful, stimulating, up-to-date and educationally useful authentic material in the target language. At worst, and still too commonly, the language lesson may be conducted in the bleak and featureless environment of a bare, multi-purpose portakabin. The specialist language room, called for thirty years ago, is sadly still not a widespread reality.

Again, at best, our young pupil may be exposed to the wide variety of published materials already mentioned, supplemented by additional material of the teacher's own devising, necessary to varying degrees even in the best-conceived and best-designed of today's courses. The pupil with special needs will receive particular attention and support. At worst, and also still too commonly, in the wake of the reduced budgets of recent years, pupils may have to share a textbook in class and be unable to take books away for homework. Even in those schools where appropriate IT software is available in the foreign language, it will not necessarily be available to more than a few pupils at a time.

The democratisation of language learning happily brought about through recent *languages for all* policies has not been accompanied on a widespread basis by *democratisation of access* to the materials needed today for effective language learning. Though few, if any, would today wish to see a return to a pre-1966 language learning environment in our schools, a key question must be asked. Does today's motivated comprehensive school pupil, particularly one from a socio-economically disadvantaged background, learning a foreign language through a multi-skill approach, enjoy at least the same level of opportunity for self-study outside the classroom as did his or her grammar school or secondary modern school counterpart thirty years ago? The latter, following a more 'traditional' course to first examination level, could resort to a well-stocked public library, particularly in our larger cities, and there find the wherewithal to study. How many of our contemporary pupils can find in the public libraries or school resource centres of today – struggling with much reduced budgets – the necessary materials for effective self-improvement in listening, speaking, reading and writing, or the appropriate IT software in the target language? (Compare discussion, p30.)

The virtual classroom – a glimpse of the future?

Just as even the best informed modern languages teacher in 1966 would have been hard put to guess the type and range of materials for language teaching which would be available in 1996, so it is difficult to anticipate what materials will be available thirty years hence in 2026. However, some indications surely exist already. Daily the 'global village' is becoming a reality. The three years from 1993 to 1996 alone have witnessed a massive increase in usage by schools in the developed world, from the primary level upwards, of electronic mail: the potential this offers for language teaching and learning has yet to be realised widely. Again, daily, the volume of foreign language material on the World Wide Web grows; and though, at present, its suitability for classroom use is limited (Horsfall and Whitehead, 1996), this situation is bound to improve sooner rather than later. Thirdly, the development of telematics, particularly of desktop video-conferencing, offers a whole new world of possibilities as yet large-ly undeveloped. Interactive multimedia terminals already exist and will begin appearing everywhere in the next few years – including in the world of education (BT, 1995).

But what will the classroom of 2026 look like? If the educational visionaries of today (Hargreaves, 1993; Wood, 1993; Beare and Slaughter, 1994) are right – and there is every evidence that they are – the educa-tional world of 2026 will have to be a very different place from what it is today if our young people are to be equipped with the skills to survive and prosper in the next century. The challenge ahead for language teachers and learners, at the European level at least, is perhaps best summed up (with the insertion of my own emphasis) by the words of the European Commission's white paper on education and training of 29 November 1995, *Teaching and Learning: Towards the Learning Society*:

> *It is no longer possible to reserve proficiency in foreign languages for an elite or for those who acquire it on account of their geographical mobility . . . It is becoming necessary for everyone, irrespective of training and educa-tion routes chosen, to be able to acquire and keep up their ability in at least two Community languages in addition to the mother tongue . . . All this pre-supposes* **the availability of top-quality education drawing on modern materials, equipment and methods customised to meet the needs of the diverse groups involved.**

References

Bayley S, "Life is too short to learn German': modern languages in English ele-mentary education, 1872–1904' in *History of Education*, 18: 57–70 (1989)

Bayley S, 'Modern languages as emerging curricular subjects in England, 1864–1918' in *History of Education Society Bulletin*, 47: 23–31 (1991)

Beare H and R Slaughter, *Education for the 21st century* (Routledge, 1994)

British Telecom, *Research and development: delivering the future* (1995)

Cammish N, 'The audio-lingual and audio-visual 'revolution" in Richardson G (ed), *Teaching modern languages* (Croom Helm, 1983)

European Commission, *Teaching and learning: towards the learning society* (1995)

Hargreaves A, *Changing teachers, changing times: teachers' work and culture in the postmodern age* (Cassell, 1994)

Hawkins E W, *Modern languages in the curriculum* (CUP, 1987)

Horsfall P and M Whitehead, 'Exploring the Internet for 'A' level language teaching and learning' in *Studies in Modern Languages Education,* April 1996 (forthcoming)

Incorporated Association of Head Masters, *Modern languages in the grammar school* (1966)

International Bureau of Education/UNESCO, *Modern languages at general secondary schools* (1964)

Newsom J, *Half our future* (HMSO, 1963)

Phillips D (ed), *Languages in schools: from complacency to conviction* (CILT, 1988)

Saunderson B, 'English and the French enlightenment' in Whitehead M, *Education and Europe: historical and contemporary perspectives,* Aspects of Education 47 (University of Hull Institute of Education, 1992)

Schools Broadcasting Council for the United Kingdom, *Bulletin for colleges of education: French for beginners* (1965)

Whitmarsh W F H, *More rapid French,* Book III (Longmans, 1963)

Wood D, *The classroom of 2015,* National Commission on Education Briefing no 20, October 1993

17

New language teaching materials

Louis Greenstock and Rosemary Davidson

PRESENTING THE LANGUAGE IN CLASS

The period 1966–1996 saw the development of an increasingly communicative approach to the presentation of the foreign language in the classroom. Within this movement it is possible to distinguish a number of phases each marked by the appearance of notable new materials.

The Nuffield Foundation/Schools Council Materials Project, which began work in 1963, under Sam Spicer, marked the first major advance out of the traditional 'coursebook' pattern in the UK. New model materials from the USA and France were, of course, already in use in some schools (see discussion on pp183 and 213).

The *En avant* materials produced by the York team were initially intended for pupils taking part in the National Pilot Scheme *French from eight* (see p156). Eventually the materials came to be used with middle school and secondary learners, with an extension course, *A votre avis*, catering for pupils going on to public examinations. The parallel development of German, Spanish and Russian materials (*Vorwärts, Adelante* and *Vperyod!*) were planned to meet the needs of the greatly increased numbers of eleven-year-old pupils of a potentially wide range of abilities who, having begun French at age eight, were expected to start a language other than French on entering their (comprehensive) secondary schools.

The *En avant* materials were 'audio-visual' in format. They exploited the tape recorder and pictures (on filmstrip and in textbook) as well as (initially) the *'tableau de feutre'* (felt board) on which brightly coloured cut-outs could be stuck, to accompany the dialogue. This was not, however, their chief originality. Audio-visual courses from France, *Tavor aids* and (for primary schools) *Bonjour Line* from Crédif, were already in use. Where the Nuffield/Schools Council materials broke new ground was in the commitment of a university Language Centre, generously funded by the Nuffield Foundation, to the production of materials exclusively for schools' use. Later (1967), when the Schools Council came in as joint sponsor, the project came indirectly under government control and funding, with general oversight by the Schools Council Modern Language

Committee, on which HMI had strong representation.

The production of the materials also broke new ground. The teams at York (experienced teachers and native speakers, with artists and designers) produced modules of work which were tested, month by month, in class, by a national network of schools. The modules, and the schools' comments on them, were then further assessed at periodic meetings of national advisory panels, representing HMI and Local Authority Advisers, as well as linguists in university departments.

The multi-media nature of these resources set a pattern for all the major courses which have appeared subsequently. It has been continued in such materials as *Tricolore* (E J Arnold in association with the Nuffield Foundation, 1980), the success phenomenon of the 1980s, and, in Russian, the resilient *Iskra* (Stanley Thornes, 1988–95), with their successors, *Encore tricolore* (Nelson, 1992–) and *Novaya Iskra* (John Murray, 1996–97).

A different pattern was offered by the development of resources in response to local needs which were then brought, by a commercial publisher, to a wider national, and even international audience. Typical of this approach was *Eclair*, which the Inner London Education Authority began to develop in 1974. This also rapidly evolved from a Primary French resource to one which catered for mixed-ability learners in middle and secondary schools, and came to encompass a range of supplementary resources proved in the extensive piloting test-bed offered by the Authority's schools. An equivalent for Spanish, *Claro*, was designed to meet diversification needs, and in the absence of an Italian course within the Schools Council/Nuffield initiative, ILEA also commissioned *Il bocca al lupo*.

It is probably no accident that both the 'stables' of resources mentioned above continued to find their supporters throughout the subsequent decades and stayed in print, to a greater or lesser extent, into the early 1990s. Another important and long-lived product of this era started publishing in 1963. *Longman audio-visual French* offered various permutations of its components for eleven- to sixteen-year-old students and expanded to incorporate a post-16 course, *Au courant.* A few remnants still linger in the publisher's list in 1996, unlike their *Audio-lingual German* course, which faded from the scene much sooner. A significant and characteristic course from the CSE/'O' level years which also 'served its time' in the GCSE period was the four-stage *Deutscher Sprachkurs.* The three earlier stages *Biberswald, Unterwegs* and *Angekommen,* took pupils to their 16+ examinations. They are no longer in print. The fourth stage, *Panorama,* provided for 'A' level, a function it is still performing to this day, despite changes in syllabuses and approaches.

Chapter 7 has dealt with the impact of Graded Objectives in Modern Languages (GOML) on language teaching methodology from the mid-1970s onwards. Over and above the syllabuses and testing materials which the various LEA-based GOML groups developed, and the resources which they offered to local schools to support their operation, a number of the groups also generated teaching materials which publishers recognised as answering pupil and teacher needs on a much wider stage, particularly as GCSE extended a number of GOML principles to public examinations. The **York** group were responsible for *Action!* (with its subtitle: *Graded French*), while the group which brought together teachers in **Cumbria and Lancashire** gave rise to the French, German and Spanish courses *Escalier, Einfach toll!* and *Premio.* On a slightly less ambitious level, the **Oxfordshire** group **(OMLAC)** produced parallel practice resources for French and German in *Entente cordiale* and *Auf ins Rheinland,* while the **Lothian** group produced a battery of resources focussing on discrete skills, and exploiting authentic material in French, German and Spanish. These had generic titles such as *French for real*, the *German writing folio, Corresponding with a Spanish penfriend, Hear-Say: listening tasks for French.*

On the subject of exploiting authentic realia, the publishers' lists of this period, certainly in the latter part, have regularly offered collections of texts and recordings as stimuli for single- and multi-skill activities. In the 1990s this has extended to video recordings from terrestrial and satellite TV channels, increasing the opportunities for pupils to encounter genuine uses of the target language in manageable packages. Some random examples, with varying degrees of sophistication in the levels of their exploitation, include the *Sign language* and *Signposts* series, *French in the news, A la carta, Radio-France, Drucksache – echt Deutsch, Aktuelles aus Radio und Presse,* etc. Of course, published collections of texts lose their topicality, and one attempt to address this problem, by providing regular newspaper-format collections of press-extracts on subscription, incorporating guidance for teachers and exercises for students, has been the Dublin-based *Authentik* operation. Although by no means the first product of its kind, it is probably the best-known to UK teachers currently available, has developed parallel listening resources, and offers material at two levels.

One major area of expansion in resources that has followed the implementation of the National Curriculum has been in the provision of graded reading schemes, to encourage extensive reading for pleasure among pupils. In fact this represents something of a renaissance, in that a number of the courses developed in the 1960s and 1970s, from the Nuffield and Longman courses to others such as *Sprich mal Deutsch,* were supported by integrated sets of readers, which could equally serve as free-standing resources in their own right. In the intervening years, perhaps the most significant resources of this kind have been *Bibliobus* and its German equivalent *Lesekiste*, in their characteristic boxes. Now one can say that all the major National Curriculum courses have generated their own reading schemes, and a number of publishers have also provided dedicated resources which offer teachers and pupils a fair degree of choice in the range and register of reading matter that they can explore. One or two of them have followed the lead set by *Bibliobus* in also offering audio recordings of the stories, read by native speakers, and thus encouraging a much more flexible approach to the reading skill and its integration.

Another related area of classroom practice which has prompted substantial materials development has been the encouragement of a degree of student autonomy in reading and listening, with the aim of motivating students as well as enabling the teacher to maximise that most precious of commodities, contact time. The goal has been resources which, with guidance from the teacher, the student can use alone or with partners, and which can contribute to extension work for the more able as much as to necessary consolidation and practice for the majority of the class. They have also usually involved a facility for self-assessment. Materials have been developed which apply this approach even to pupils at elementary level (e.g. *Here's how in French, Hier steht's*), although GCSE provided a particular stimulus for them. Listening resources have ranged from the trio of individual packages *A ton casque/Kopfhörer auf!/A la onda,* for use at school or at home on the student's personal stereo, to what one could call the 'listening bank' approach, exemplified by *K7: le français sur cassette,* or, catering for French, German and Spanish, *Eurolab.* The latter is also notable in being available at three levels, as is its pioneering reading-card equivalent, *Carte blanche/Kartei/Carta blanca.* Other examples of this approach have been *On y va!* and *Packs an!*

If the preceding paragraphs represent a necessarily cursory glance at some of the trends in materials provision for secondary learners of modern languages over the last thirty years, one constant has been the basic structure of a core coursebook, usually designated either by the generic requirements of course structure (beginners', foundation, continuation, etc), or linked to progressive levels of assessment and the examinations system (CSE/'O' level/'A' level/GOML/GCSE/National Curriculum Key Stages). A wealth of supplementary resources has also been produced, and enthusiastically embraced by teachers, to provide for those circumstances where even the most fully-integrated and all-encompassing package needs enhancing. This might suggest that providing for the needs of the individual pupil lies more in the success of the teacher in applying these multifarious components, than in the nature and content, and/or the intrinsic quality, of the pupil's book. This question has been given current relevance by an observation or recommendation contained in the 'Modern Foreign Languages' section of a recent OFSTED report *Subjects and*

Louis Greenstock
and Rosemary Davidson

standards: issues for school development arising from OFSTED inspection findings 1994/5 – Key Stages 3 & 4 and post-16 (HMSO, 1996).

192

Schools should give priority to providing pupils with adequate support for their learning; usually this will mean providing each pupil with a personal copy of a textbook.

If this is so, are we talking about the pupil's book as usually constituted, or something which incorporates more of the 'add-on' elements referred to above, making them available to all pupils automatically and as of right?

Louis Greenstock

—

PUBLISHING FOR LANGUAGE LEARNING

In the early sixties, for a publisher fortunate enough to have a well established language course on his or her list, life was relatively straightforward. You could count on a course lasting a good ten to twelve years without more than the odd facelift – new cover or new illustrations (black and white of course). Author loyalty was strong in schools (*We always use the green Whitmarsh/Jones/whatever . . .*). Reprint numbers were high and predictable.

That was the solid base from which in the mid-1960s publishers could make forays into ways of supplying the emerging needs of the new comprehensive schools, experiment with sound recordings, try out different forms of supplementary material to liven up what had essentially been a pretty dull diet for the pupil. There was money available to an extent that publishers and schools now find enviable; there were Nuffield/Schools Council projects developing new approaches and bringing with them considerable financial investment.

The thirty-year span on which this book is based moves from the totally print-based course to the complete multimedia learning system; from a target audience of largely grammar and public school pupils, all aiming towards the same examination, to a constituency of all abilities in different kinds of schools and colleges, some working towards one of a range of examinations, others aiming only at an elementary familiarity with basic social language transactions; from individual authors (usually not native speakers) writing in their spare time (more spare then than now) to teams of writers and other specialists seconded from teaching or on special contract.

Each of these aspects of change has affected the way publishers work and their relationship with the creators of language materials and their users.

Lone writer to team member

It was often the would-be writer of a language course, usually male and often teaching in a public school, who made a 'proposal' to a publisher – from the publisher's point of view this was 'in-tray' publishing. Alternatively, some of the more experienced publishers' representatives were astute judges of the teachers they met, developed a good nose for potential writing talent and would report back their discoveries to their publishers. And lastly, there were the more enterprising publishers themselves who got out and about in the schools and signed up teachers.

Once under contract, the author got on with the writing in relative isolation. Neither the author nor the publisher over thirty years ago thought about trialling material in any formal way; some of it in any case was probably based on the author's own tried and tested techniques with pupils and experience in successfully preparing them for public examinations, and that was thought to be enough. Eventually the author would 'deliver' – a manuscript. And sometimes it was literally a manuscript – not all authors had entered the typewriter age. It might have been already 'marked up' for the printer by an established author, with 'LARGE' or 'SMALL' instructions (no nonsense about getting the book typographically designed).

The scene changes to the nineties. The editor is now a 'project manager', and indeed a lot of her or his work is managing, for the team responsible for the material may nowadays comprise not only the in-house editorial, design, production and marketing people, but also members of outside production teams involved in sound recording, video and TV. The actual writing team will include a native speaker and a full-time professional writer or perhaps several teacher-writers who may be on secondment from their schools. There may be on-location recording or filming. Trialling is a must. And when the material eventually sees the light of day, the team will be joined by advisory demonstrators.

Changing financial ballgame

Financially the situation both for the creators and publishers of materials has changed enormously during the thirty years under review. That lone writer expected only a modest advance on royalties, and the publisher's investment in production and marketing was relatively low, relative to the situation later on.

Demands on both parties grew greater as professionalism increased. Teachers could only afford to take time off teaching to gather material in the country of the language and to write if they were paid to do so by the publisher. Publishing budgets had to be bumped up, profits forecast over a longer term, more money invested in marketing to try and outsell the competition.

By far the largest scale research and development projects were those funded by Nuffield and the Schools Council. Competition amongst publishers to publish these was naturally intense. There was also a keenness on the part of publishers to demonstrate what they could contribute professionally, because of an undercurrent of anxiety that, in the euphoria engendered by large grants and well funded trials, both those involved in administering the projects and those in government might increasingly be attracted by the idea of extending research and development into publishing large-scale projects themselves. The prospect of state publishing (the private bogey of British educational publishing) through a kind of Educational Stationery Office was profoundly unattractive not just to publishers but fortunately also to enough people of good sense and influence in the educational world for this danger to recede.

At that time, in the 1960s and 1970s, no individual commercial publisher was willing or financially able to undertake alone publication of extensive course materials in the less frequently taught foreign languages, such as Spanish or Russian, on the scale of what was expected for French. Of course there were bound to be difficulties for both publishers and Schools Council teams working together and not always able to appreciate each others' priorities, but on the whole these difficulties were insignificant (especially in retrospect) in comparison with the unfolding of opportunities for schools and publishers alike to branch out excitingly into 'new' languages and new kinds of materials. For the first time examinations were devised to fit more or less what was being taught, not vice versa.

Quite apart from the influence of the Schools Council projects, there was a general increase in the participation of institutions as providers of writing teams. The newly established Language Centres at universities and the more enterprising of the university and college Departments of Education and the polytechnic and technical college Language Departments (some with their own excellent recording facilities) were potentially very well placed to collaborate with publishers in the production of materials. Many who did so successfully found that producing materials for their own internal purposes meshed with the wider needs that publishers were set up to meet, so a certain amount of subsidy in people and time helped their publication.

But over the years, with more stringent budgeting of time and money, institutions have had to account for their staffs' activities in a much more precise way. So the bread-upon-the-waters attitude, which often brought a difficult to quantify but genuine enhancement of reputation to an institution – and to the individuals who worked in it – as well as a welcome increase in freedom of manoeuvre to the publisher, has died a regrettable death.

Nowadays, with the exception of certain EU-funded projects and the occasional business sponsorship, investment in publishing large-scale new courses has got to come from the publisher, taking a deep breath and a long-term view.

The result has been that now only a small number of large publishers are able to undertake this, as the investment is so big, more so than in many other subjects because of the expectation of materials in a wide range of media. Fortunately it is still possible for small 'niche' publishers to respond quickly to new small-scale needs, in a way impossible for and unattractive to the more ponderous larger organisations.

Another result has been the making of new links between publishers and both BBC and ITV producers of language programmes. On the one hand the TV producers benefit from being able to leave the printed materials to professionals who know how to promote the whole multimedia package to schools, and on the other the publishers do not have to bear the heavy costs of filming and recording in order to have a multimedia system on their list.

Diversity of demand

Because modern languages has been in the past regarded as an elitist subject, unlike English or maths for example, the change in the kinds of materials needed for a much wider clientele, to provide first for CSE and 'O' level, then later for non-examination courses, has been that much greater than in some other subjects. Already in the late 1960s it was common for publishers to produce 'A' and 'B' versions of courses, in an attempt to cater for different levels of ability. But now, with the compulsory study of a language up to sixteen for all pupils, the challenge to provide suitably stimulating material is that much greater. And the temptation for schools to skimp on materials for the less able, relying on a hotchpotch of photocopied worksheets, does not encourage publishers to invest much in this area. Attempts to publish self-standing modules that could be slotted into the teaching process as and when required are not so acceptable to the majority of teachers as material that is based on a sequential progression.

The vocational needs of students in further and higher education have also proved a challenge for publishers. User groups are diversified by their individual subject needs, but each group is necessarily small. The economics of providing highly diversified material for a number of small groups does not work easily for conventional publishing techniques. It is an area where the more flexible and less expensive desk-top publishing techniques, possibly not involving a publisher at all, may be more appropriate.

196

The National Curriculum: recipe for conformity?

In one way the National Curriculum (NC) has made life simpler (if duller) for publishers. Agreed national guidelines give a certain sense of security; there are fewer agonising choices to be made about linguistic content. On the other hand it has put on all producers of NC materials certain unbeneficial pressures and restraints. There have been the pressures of time – trying to get suitable material out in time for the start of a new Stage on the basis of information not provided early enough, or on the basis of changing requirements. After a bad start and considerable pressure from publishers, the School Curriculum and Assessment Authority (SCAA) has become much more aware of the sense of giving information to publishers about intended changes. The Educational Publishers' Council (EPC) has set up regular joint meetings in the main subjects with SCAA which act as proper forums for discussion, with publishers providing useful feedback and suggestions. The restraints of content and curricular time have meant that there is precious little room for the brilliant 'originel', in the French sense, who can stimulate a class with something odd or outrageous. For the same reasons there is little time to devote to free-standing enrichment materials – on language awareness, background, etc – and so there is no incentive for publishers to produce them.

When curricular content was less prescribed, it was possible for a publisher to buy the rights for a language course (particularly in Spanish, Italian or Russian) from another European country with a roughly similar educational approach – Sweden springs to mind – and adapt it successfully for the UK. That gave an increased variety and a freshness of approach. But that is no longer likely to succeed (except in further education).

Redefinition of publishing

With the hectic pace and erratic development of new technology publishers are beginning to rethink and redefine their *raison d'être*. They are having to get back to the basic idea of 'making public', keeping a properly open mind about the most appropriate media, and thinking afresh about what should be left to individual persons and institutions and what can benefit from the skills of the professional communicators.

Rosemary Davidson

18

From 'O' level to GCSE — the impact of examinations

Maurice Whitehead

Examinations, however carefully organized, are at best rough-and-ready measuring instruments, useful enough, as long as their limitations are appreciated. (Newsom Report, 1963, para. 256)

For decades before the creation of CILT in 1966, teachers of modern languages, in common with teachers of other subjects, had to rely for guidance on the curriculum and examinations from the relevant examination board or government department, from a relevant subject-based association, or from a professional body. Adequate machinery for an on-going and discussion on curricular policy, particularly between examination boards and schools, simply did not, as yet, exist.

In 1952, the Incorporated Association of Assistant Masters in Secondary Schools (IAAM) issued a substantial 370-page handbook entitled *The teaching of modern languages*. Published just as 'new' GCE 'O' and 'A' level examinations were being introduced, the handbook argued in the case of modern languages that the old School Certificate and Higher School Certificate examinations had been the outcome of long experience and were 'suited as well as possible to the practice of the majority of teachers'. The 'new' languages examinations retained most of the features of the 'old' examinations, and it was noted that, *failing unforeseen educational discovery, progress can come only from the improvement or development of existing method* (IAAM, 1952).

The introduction of 'O' and 'A' level examinations in modern languages in 1950 simply perpetuated a mode of assessment which had existed since 1918, which continued down to the mid-1960s and beyond, and which still survives in attenuated form, in a few 'A' level examination syllabuses at least, even today. It was a pattern largely dictated by the examination boards themselves. The majority of these bore the very names of, and owed their origins to, the universities which had originally created them for their own two major purposes: to identify as efficiently as possible in general terms those candidates best suited to a university education; and, more specifically, those candidates in any given subject best suited to continuing that study ultimately at honours degree level. If 'A' level courses were meant as a direct preparation for such honours courses, 'O' level courses were themselves a dilution of, and preparation for, 'A' level.

The 1952 IAAM handbook did not question the basic structure of a language examination, which, it was argued, should test a number of key skills: ability to translate both into and from the foreign language; free composition writing; comprehension tests; dictation; reading aloud; and oral conversation. To this list at 'A' level would be added the study of a number of prescribed literary texts. On the one hand, the handbook noted that some examination boards then did not include a compulsory oral test in their examinations, a practice which was strenuously condemned. On the other hand, and surprisingly in view of its positive attitude to oral tests, the handbook was uncompromising with regard to translations into the foreign language, which were seen as essential in any language examination worth its name. If examiners were too often 'pained by the rubbish which they [had] to read', the report argued, the fault lay not in the examinations themselves, but in schools putting forward candidates who were ill-prepared for the examination. The 'prose' test was seen as a way of testing the mastery of grammar and total accuracy, though, as the following extract argued, care had to be taken both in designing passages for translation and in avoiding excessive and obsessive tendencies, then evidently not infrequent in examination papers:

> *Choice of words may impair validity: a candidate who, instead of using the word* bague, *writes* L'anneau qu'elle a trouvé, *may have got his past participle right by accident. Similarly,* the little mouse *fails to test adjective agreement if the candidate thinks that* souris *is masculine: it would be better to say* mice. *It is still more unfortunate if the passage over-emphasizes a particular point of grammar. In French, for example, more than a dozen Past Participle Agreements have at times been set in one* Thème. *Such excessive weighting of one section of knowledge is liable to distort the whole picture of a candidate's achievement.* Thème *can be a test of the very highest validity: every care should be taken to make it so.*

The handbook went on to offer guidelines concerning the content of an 'O' level modern languages examination and the ideal percentage weightings which might be allocated to its component parts. The extent to which the 1952 guidelines were still being followed in the mid-1960s can be measured from the following composite table which contrasts them with the actual practice of two examination boards – the Joint Matriculation Board (JMB) and the Associated Examining Board (AEB) – in their main 'O' level modern languages examinations in the summer of 1965.

Summary of percentage of marks in 'O' level language examinations			
IAAM recommendations 1952		JMB 1965	AEB 1965
Prose translation	20%	20%	Prose not set
Composition	13%	17%	17.5%
Version	20%	30%	30%
Comprehension	10%	8%	20%
Dictation	17%	8%	7.5%
Reading test	10%	3%	Included in oral examination
Oral examination	10%	7%	25%
(Aural comprehension)	—	7%	Test not set
	100%	100%	100%

(Sources: IAAM, 1952; JMB, 1965a; AEB, 1965a)

Of the two boards, the JMB's main 'O' level paper was clearly the more 'traditional' language examination, adhering closely to the 1952 recommendations. However, two significant divergences are worthy of note – the extra emphasis then given to translation *from* the foreign language into English, and the low percentage awarded for the oral examination. The AEB examination, on the other hand, was notable on at least two counts: the substantial weighting given to the oral examination, in line with the recommendations of the 1963 Newsom Report (and in line with the best practice thirty years later); and the absence of prose translation. The abolition of the latter had involved the AEB in a prolonged battle with the Secondary Schools Examination Council (SSEC), which had repeatedly refused to break the long-existing format of modern languages examinations. The AEB had won an important victory in 1964 when it ultimately established that its new papers were of sufficient rigour *without* prose translation to compare with other GCE papers (Hawkins, 1987).

The main 1965 JMB 'O' level paper in French was not the only such examination then on offer by the board. Following the AEB's 1964 victory, the JMB had received permission to set, for one year only in the first instance, a new 'alternative' 'O' level French examination in 1965. The initiative for this had come from the pioneering work and pressure exerted from 1959 onwards by a group of Lancashire and Cheshire headteachers, many of them modern linguists, all of them members of Division XII of the Incorporated Association of Head Masters, under the chairmanship of Eric Hawkins. The new JMB syllabus followed the AEB but introduced important new elements. Alarmed that too little reading appeared to be done before 'O' level by aspiring examination candidates, the headteachers attempted to stimulate reading by asking the JMB to circulate to schools a list of over 100 recommended books. From these, candidates were invited to take two of the books they had read into the oral examination to serve as a springboard for conversation, but in no sense were they intended to be 'set books'. The oral examination itself was revolutionary, being conducted by school staff, monitored by the chief examiner, visits from assessors from other schools, and tape-recordings of candidates' performance (JMB, 1965b; IAHM, 1966).

At the same time a research project, sponsored by the MLA and the Nuffield Foundation under H S Otter, was experimenting with new examination techniques previously unknown in GCE, including multiple-choice questions and oral comprehension tests, using tape recordings circulated to schools. By the time of the creation of CILT in 1966, the mould had been broken, some machinery for discussion between examination boards and schools had been invented and progress was at last possible. As one commentator was to report in 1966:

Schools which take the papers of the Boards which have not so far reformed their papers should now have no difficulty in persuading them to move forward. (IAHM, 1966)

Much of the progress achieved at 'O' level was also mirrored at 'A' level, as the following comparative table indicates:

Summary of percentage of marks in 'A' level language examinations			
IAAM recommendations 1952		**JMB 1965**	**AEB 1965**
Prose translation	15%	15%	12.5%
Composition	15%	10%	12.5%
Version	20%	21%	25%
Dictation	10%	8%	10%
Reading test	5%	6%	part of oral
Oral	10%	10%	15%
Literature	25%	30%	25%
	100%	100%	100%

(Sources: IAAM, 1952; JMB, 1967; AEB, 1965b)

As at 'O' level, the AEB was again forging ahead at 'A' level, allocating to the oral component one quarter of all marks available in the language part of the examination. More fundamental change in the literary aspects of 'A' level was already being called for. In 1966 the IAHM put forward to examination boards two important recommendations:

i) *that all written answers in the literature section be in the foreign language; and*

ii) *that one or more books of those recommended for reading be tested by an oral examination in the foreign language.* (IAHM, 1966)

These recommendations were reinforced in 1970 in the widely-discussed Working Paper no. 28 of the Schools Council, *New patterns in sixth form modern language studies* (SC, 1970). The Working Paper recommended additionally that sixth formers should present a module of 'coursework', preferably based on a well-planned study visit to the foreign country. A generation was to pass before these recommendations were to be taken seriously on a widespread scale by examination boards.

Certificate of Secondary Education (CSE)

The growing power of teachers in shaping examinations in the mid-1960s is best exemplified in the development of the Certificate of Secondary Education (CSE), first introduced in 1965. Fourteen regional boards, with panels of teachers further assisted by advisory panels, worked with chief examiners in designing examinations based on Mode 1 syllabuses which they themselves had drawn up. They were also responsible for approving syllabuses produced by individual schools or consortia of schools and for setting examinations based on them (Mode 2), and for moderating course-work prepared either for an examination or instead of an examination by schools within their area (Mode 3). The examination was intended for those pupils unable to attempt 'O' level, including pupils of 'average abili-ty' (SREB, 1965), though the practice of 'double-entering' borderline 'O' level/CSE candidates quickly grew up. Often, results demonstrated that the CSE was not an 'inferior' examination, as many claimed, chiefly because it employed positive marking, rather than the traditional 'one off for each mistake': numerous were the candidates for modern languages examinations who obtained a grade C pass at 'O' level, and failed to obtain a Grade 1 at CSE level. This can largely be explained by the considerable importance attached to the oral side of the examination, which was commonly allotted as much as half an hour and 30% of the total marks – more than even the most enlightened 'O' level syllabus at that time.

Though the new 'O' level and CSE modern languages syllabuses were an improvement on earlier models, the two examinations remained intrinsically deficient, whatever the nature of their syllabuses, from the mid-1960s to the mid-1980s, in two key respects: they failed to support the needs of the entire spectrum of ability of pupils then being taught in com-prehensive schools, and the very existence of two examinations at 16+ proved divisive. The effective assessment of modern languages was a major concern of CILT from its inception: one of its earliest conferences and publications was devoted to this issue (CILT, 1969) and it continued to pursue a leading role in this area throughout the 1970s and beyond (CILT, 1973; CILT, 1980). Though admirable attempts to overcome these problems were addressed regionally in certain parts of the country by means of common examinations at 16+ , these failed to have widespread national influence.

Likewise, the important and urgent clarion calls sounded in 1974 for alternatives to 16+ modern languages examinations, especially for the least able (Harding and Page, 1974; Page, 1974), were quickly heeded (see Chapter 7). Taking the example of graded examinations in music and the Trinity College grades in English as a Foreign Language, various local education authorities and regional consortia devised and developed graded systems of examinations in modern languages, with the prime aim of providing pupils with short-term achievable goals, rather than the more usual five-year 'marathon' approach to 'O' level and CSE. Though these schemes were open to legitimate criticisms (for example, Byram, 1978 and Byram, 1979) on the grounds that the pursuit of performance competence, with memory-dependent learning, is at odds with the language teacher's crucial role as a teacher of language awareness, these tensions were never resolved. In the same way, a radical draft proposal (Biggs, 1980) for a fully coherent ten-level system of examinations in modern languages, covering the entire teaching and learning spectrum from 11+ beginners to final year undergraduates, failed to leave the drawing board.

Since 1980 much has been achieved. The introduction of the General Certificate of Secondary Education (GCSE) in 1988, with its welcome incorporation of national criteria for modern languages, and its emphasis on assessing the four skills of listening, speaking, reading and writing in a balanced manner, also saw the final demolition of the outdated 'top-down' model of examining, replacing it with a 'bottom-up' approach. Notwithstanding its shortcomings, some of which will be noted below, the GCSE in modern languages has been arguably the most important development in MFL teaching and learning in the past thirty years: the embodiment for the first time of practical objectives for all abilities and backgrounds in the GCSE made the new approach 'official' for all teachers of modern languages, especially for the majority who had not previously been involved with graded objectives.

The introduction of exciting new topic-based modern languages 'A' level syllabuses in the late 1980s and early 1990s opened fresh possibilities to young people otherwise and understandably unwilling to embark on the traditional limiting diet of 'four set literary texts' studied over two years. The introduction of Advanced Supplementary ('AS') level courses in 1987 for first examination in 1989 gave modern languages teachers real hope. This much-needed target for the non-specialist student would perhaps restore, if not surpass, the healthy situation which had obtained from 1918 until the wanton abolition of the 'subsidiary' Higher School Certificate (HSC) examination in 1950: in that year about twice as many science and classics students took the 'subsid', as took the 'main' HSC papers, in French (Hawkins, 1987). More recently, the development of General National Vocational Qualifications (GNVQs) have led to the introduction of new vocational language courses.

But how do all these examination course developments fit together coherently? Though great progress has been made since 1980, a large number of opportunities have also been missed. The 1988 GCSE syllabuses failed to promote extensive use of the target language, including in examination paper rubrics and answers, in line with a fully communicative approach. Other issues were not addressed – the need to foster study skills, including the use of dictionaries; and the desirability of assessing coursework, at least as an option, to allow teachers and learners maximum freedom to pursue particular interests and adopt a personal approach, as well as encouraging the use of information technology.

Though these deficiencies have been addressed (see, for example, NEAB, 1995a) in new revised GCSE syllabuses from 1998 (full course) and 1997 (short course), a whole series of questions remain. The general criteria for the new GCSE impose constraints on the forms of assessment allowed. Will this prevent further development of existing highly motivating modular GCSE examinations (Sidwell, 1990)? Will proposed new GCSE modern languages short courses (NEAB, 1995b) really motivate reluctant pupils fulfilling National Curriculum requirements in the same way that graded objectives did prior to the introduction of the National Curriculum?

GCSE remains the principal assessment instrument at Key Stage 4 and any course offered at the end of that Key Stage must be approved by SCAA under Section 5 of the Education Reform Act. Will the recent development of free-standing vocational language units linked to the GNVQ system, intended as an alternative means of accrediting National Curriculum short course requirements, and to be accredited by vocational awarding bodies, contribute to resolving the long-standing difficulty of motivating reluctant young language learners? And how will the revised GCSE examinations address the already existing, widespread problem of GCSE/'A' level mismatch, which demands that teacher and student 'bridge the gap' before embarking fully on even the most up-to-date 'A' level languages examinations?

Despite the good intentions behind the introduction of 'AS' level examinations, the take-up of them, particularly by non-specialist languages candidates, has been disastrously low (JMB, 1992; ULEAC, 1994). Will Sir Ron Dearing's proposal, contained in his March 1996 review of qualifications for 16–19-year-olds (Dearing, 1996) for the reformulation of 'AS' level – to be renamed henceforth 'Advanced Subsidiary' – do anything to improve this situation in the field of modern languages?

The Dearing Review of 16–19 qualifications provides for the first time a coherent national framework of examinations and qualifications summarised below.

Summary of proposed framework of national awards		
National Award: Advanced Level		
'AS' and 'A' level	GNVQ Advanced Level	NVQ Level 3
National Award: Intermediate Level		
GCSE Grades A*–C	GNVQ Intermediate Level	NVQ Level 2
National Award: Foundation Level		
GCSE Grades D–G	GNVQ Foundation Level	NVQ Level 1
National Award: Entry Level		
Common to all pathways: Three grades A/B/C		

Welcome though this new coherence is, it raises a much larger question. As we face a new century and a new millennium, are we well advised to carry on compartmentalising disciplines and examining them in a compartmentalised fashion? Instead of searching for a new coherent paradigm for examinations and qualifications, should we not first be seeking a new paradigm for teaching and learning (Beare and Slaughter, 1994; Hargreaves, 1994)? In the context of modern languages, what lessons can we usefully learn from the very limited number of (what have also proved outstandingly successful) attempts in the UK at creating *sections bilingues* in state schools (Hawkins, 1988)? Could these provide the much-needed way forward? A recent European report on education (Cochinaux and de Woot, 1995) would suggest so:

The multiculturalism of Europe implies a multilingualism de facto. It is therefore of the utmost importance that a European can converse in the major languages of Europe. [A foreign language] should be taught as early as possible in primary school. This would allow pupils to have some lessons, e.g. history, geography, given in [the foreign language] as a means to practise and to learn the language. The best way to learn a language is when it is used for real like the teaching of a specific course.

As we shift our thinking from yesterday's challenge of developing good national curricula, examinations and qualifications towards tomorrow's challenge of creating not simply a good European, but a good global core curriculum, the need for a global qualifications system becomes apparent. In that context, teachers of modern languages will have to have a highly credible response to a highly challenging question which has already been asked: if, in the next century, everyone will need to learn English, the world language, *what is the rationale for the teaching of second and third languages in English-speaking nations?* (Ball, 1995).

206

References

Associated Examining Board, *Ordinary level GCE papers May/June 1965* (AEB, 1965a)

Associated Examining Board, *Advanced level and scholarship GCE papers May/June 1965* (AEB, 1965b)

Ball C (Sir), *Towards a global core curriculum*, synopsis of the presidential address delivered at the British Comparative and International Education Society conference, Oxford, 23 September 1995 (typescript)

Beare H and R Slaughter, *Education for the 21st century* (Routledge, 1994)

Biggs B C, 'A graded system of examinations in modern languages', in *The teaching of modern languages: a view for the 1980s* (HMC Modern Languages Report no 2, 1980)

Byram M S, 'New objectives in language teaching' in *Modern Languages*, 59 (December 1978)

Byram M S, 'Performance objectives and language learning' in *Modern Languages*, 60 (June 1979)

CILT, *Aims and techniques: language-teaching methods and their comparative assessment* CILT Reports and Papers 2 (CILT, 1969)

Cochinaux P and P de Woot, *Moving towards a learning society: a CRE-ERT forum report on European education* (Association of European Universities/European Round Table, 1995)

Dearing R, *Review of qualifications for 16–19-year-olds: summary report* (SCAA, 1996)

Hargreaves A, *Changing teachers, changing times: teachers' work and culture in the postmodern age* (Cassell, 1994)

Hawkins E W, *Modern languages in the curriculum* (CUP, 1987)

Hawkins E W (ed), *Intensive language teaching and learning: initiatives at school level* (CILT, 1988)

Incorporated Association of Assistant Masters, *The teaching of modern languages* (IAAM, 1952)

Incorporated Association of Head Masters, *Modern languages in the grammar school (Revised Edition)* (IAHM, 1966)

James C V and S Rouve, *Survey of curricula and performance in modern languages*, Centre for Educational Technology, University of Sussex, and CILT (CILT, 1973)

Joint Matriculation Board, *Ordinary level papers Summer 1965* (JMB, 1965a)

Joint Matriculation Board, *Sixty-second annual report 1964–65* (JMB, 1965b)

Joint Matriculation Board, *Papers in advanced and special French, 1963–1967* (JMB, 1967)

Joint Matriculation Board, *Annual Report, 1991–92* (JMB, 1992)

Moys A et al, *Modern language examinations at sixteen plus: a critical analysis* (CILT, 1980)

Northern Examinations and Assessment Board, *Syllabus for 1998: French [draft submitted September 1995 – awaiting SCAA final approval]* (NEAB, 1995a)

Northern Examinations and Assessment Board, *Syllabus for 1998: French Short Course [draft submitted September 1995 – awaiting SCAA final approval]* (NEAB, 1995b)

Schools Council for Curriculum and Examinations, *New patterns in sixth form modern languages studies,* Working Paper no 28 (Evans/Methuen Educational, 1970)

Sidwell P, 'A group mode 3 GCSE: a model to build on' in Whitehead M, *Modern Language Teaching in the 1990s,* Aspects of Education 43, University of Hull Institute of Education, 1990 (Sidwell, 1990)

Southern Regional Examinations Board, *Regulations and syllabuses for the CSE examination 1965* (SREB, 1965)

University of London Examinations and Assessment Council, *GCE statistics June 1993/January 1994* (ULEAC, 1994)

Part

six

The changing
classroom

1966-1996 30 *YEARS*

An early tape recorder?

From 'Voyage dans la lune' ('Lunar travel') in Cyrano de Bergerac's *Histoire comique des estats et empires de la lune*, 1657:

A l'ouverture de la boîte, je trouvai dedans un je ne sais quoi de métal, presque semblable à nos horloges . . .

On opening the box I found inside a sort of metal arrangement rather like one of our clocks, full of all kinds of small springs and tiny mechanisms. It is really a book, but a marvellous book with neither pages nor print; in short a book which you don't need eyes to read; you only need your ears. So when you want to read you simply wind a collection of little springs in the machine, then you turn the dial to the chapter you want to hear and immediately there emerges, as if from a man's voice or from a musical instrument, all the different sounds making up the language of these great lunar folk . . .

It took almost 300 years for Cyrano's perceptive prophecy to become reality, transforming foreign language classrooms.

19
The tape recording revolution

Peter S Green

The tape recorder and the language laboratory

If, 50-odd years ago, you had offered language teachers a machine that could bring the voices of native speakers into classrooms, to be interrupted and reheard at will, that would allow students to hear their own efforts, could capture fugitive radio broadcasts and, finally, would enable learners to listen to lesson material at home, they would surely have thought you were proclaiming the millennium. And yet by the beginning of the 1960s, with the advent of the magnetic tape recorder, almost every language teacher did have access to such a machine, and only a few years later the compact cassette had begun its rapid invasion of almost every home and teenage bedroom.

That was not all:

At this hopeful confluence of glittering streams the technologist has appeared with a gift to the language teachers which has a greater potential than any invention, perhaps, since the blackboard. (Hilton, 1968)

This gift was the language laboratory, which arrived on the scene at almost the same time as the tape recorder, but because of its vastly greater cost was introduced much more slowly. Nonetheless, its spread was impressive enough: the first school language laboratory was installed in Salford where J B Hilton was headmaster in 1962; by 1973 one third of secondary schools teaching modern foreign languages had language laboratories (Green, 1975). The proportion of colleges and universities with a language laboratory was almost certainly higher.

Hilton's words reflected widespread enthusiasm among language teachers in the 1960s. It seemed as if theory and practice had for once come together and, sustained by this exciting new technology, would enable them to produce learners across a wide range of ability who could actually speak the foreign language and use it to express their everyday concerns. It was in this spirit of optimism that the Audio-Visual Language Association was founded in 1962 with the declared aim of *fostering the study and promotion of language teaching by means of audio-visual and audio-lingual methods and the use of language laboratory and other teaching aids.*

The *glittering streams* were the introduction of primary French, audio-visual courses, *Le français fondamental,* and reforms in public examina-
tions. These developments would have been largely impossible had it not been for tape recording. Many of the primary-school teachers had only a basic knowledge of French (often no more than 'O' level) and were heavily dependent on tape recordings for an oral approach. The vocabulary of the audio-visual courses they used was based on *Le français fondamental,* which was largely derived from an analysis of tape recorded conversations. Tape recordings, finally, made it possible not only to introduce standard listening comprehension tests into GCE and CSE, but also to moderate, or indeed assess, speaking tests conducted by the pupils' own teachers.

Whilst teachers were undoubtedly enthusiastic about the arrival of the tape recorder and language laboratory, there were attendant problems, both of equipment and of software.

Handling the early equipment could be quite daunting. Reel-to-reel tape recorders were bulky and heavy; threading the tapes could be tricky; and finding the right place on the tape was a potential nightmare of desperate winding to and fro if the rev counter had not been zeroed. If the spools were of different sizes, tape might spill over at the end of a fast wind, leaving the hapless teacher with a tangle of 'tape salad'. It was a well organised teacher who could get both tape recorder and film-strip projector into the classroom and adjacent to a power point, with the tape at the start of the programme, the film-strip the right way up and right way round, and the blackout adequately darkening the room on a bright summer's day and keep the attention of the class during these preparations and any hitches.

The teacher's console of an early language laboratory could vie with the cockpit of a jumbo jet for switches, coloured lights and dials. Whilst some teachers relished the feeling of power that this gave them, others felt intimidated by the initial complexity of the equipment. Both certainly experienced the not infrequent distraction from monitoring students as one or more booths failed to function properly.

Audio-visual and audio-lingual courses

The new equipment called for fundamental changes in teaching methods and teachers were only too happy to leave the production of software in the hands of the experts – teams of writers and linguists who were guided by clear-cut theoretical principles. What they were offered were audio-visual and audio-lingual courses, which initially were imported from abroad. The audio-visual courses originated in France with the production in the early 1950s of *TAVOR (Teachers' Audio-Visual ORal) Aids* designed for teaching French to the different nationalities working at NATO headquarters. The audio-lingual courses, such as *A-LM (Audio-Lingual Materials),* had appeared in the United States in the early 1960s. By the mid-1960s, however, courses had become available which were based on the same principles but designed specifically for UK classrooms, e.g. the Nuffield Foundation's audio-visual courses *En avant, Vorwärts, Adelante, Vperyod!* or the Oliver & Boyd audio-lingual courses *French/German, a structural approach.*

At the time, the audio-visual and the audio-lingual courses seemed radically different from each other, mainly because the audio-visual courses used the additional technology of the film-strip to present the meaning of new language to learners, thereby apparently offering an up-to-date version of the direct method, whereas the audio-lingual courses unashamedly used the mother tongue to convey meaning. It was easy to forget that the original audio-visual courses had of necessity to find alternative ways of getting the meaning across because they were aimed at learners who did not have a common native language (e.g. in francophone Africa). Further-more, this apparently basic difference applied only to the initial presentation stage of introducing new language. What united audio-visual and audio-lingual courses was in fact far more fundamental than what divided them, namely a belief in the habitual nature of language learning.

The underlying theories

The demand for speakers of foreign languages brought about by the war had led to a new approach to language teaching, which was employed in intensive foreign language courses run by the armed services in both Britain and the United States. After the war, the methods were crystallised and rationalised by a number of writers, foremost among whom was Nelson Brooks in an influential book called *Language and language learning* (1960).

The main tenets of the 'audio-lingual method', as Brooks called it, were:

- the primacy of the spoken over the written language (and the separation of the 'four skills' of listening, speaking, reading and writing);
- the 'target language' seen as a set of new habits to be acquired by mimicry and memorisation ('mim-mem');
- the grammar of the language seen as a set of structures to be induced by learners in 'structure drills'.

The audio-lingual method had a powerful impact on language teaching, especially at beginners' level. This is perhaps to be explained by the apparent strength of its theoretical credentials. American 'structural linguistics' (deriving principally from Bloomfield's *Language*, 1933) provided descriptions of the target language structures, while the 'behaviourist' school of psychology, particularly as expounded by Skinner (1957), provided the theory of how the structures were to be learnt.

214

Further theoretical support came from 'contrastive linguistics', which was initiated as a formal discipline by Lado's *Linguistics across cultures* (1957). Lado's position as regards language teaching was that systematic comparison of native (L1) and target (L2) languages, to identify where they coincided and where they differed, would reveal where learners could be expected to make positive and negative transfer between languages. Points of difference, especially where there was some similarity at the same time, could be expected to be points of learning difficulty. This position chimed in well with teachers' experience of learners' errors, which seemed typically to reveal negative transfer or 'interference from L1'.

The theoretical basis of the audio-lingual method was complemented by the new technology. The tape recorder was ideally suited to classroom presentation and choral repetition of new language, while the language laboratory was the perfect drillmaster for individualising and tirelessly practising the stimulus-response-reinforcement paradigm on which the structure drills were modelled that were popularised by Stack in a book that became known as 'the Gospel according to St Stack'.

*The language laboratory is a drill ground guided by authentic native voices. The exercises presented in the laboratory for practice are systematic, giving intensive active practice in application of structural and phonetic principles **previously presented** in the classroom.* (Stack, 1966)

A Stack four-phase pattern drill could be represented diagrammatically as follows:

	One frame of a four-phase drill			
MASTER TRACK	Stimulus		Correct response	
STUDENT TRACK		Attempted response		Repetition of correct response
	PHASE 1	PHASE 2	PHASE 3	PHASE 4

An example of the content of such a drill might be:

Stimulus:	Do you like classical music?
Attempted response:	Yes, I like.
Correct response:	Yes, I do.
Repetition of correct response:	Yes, I do.
Stimulus:	Can you drive a car?
Attempted response:	Yes, I can.
Correct response:	Yes, I can.
Repetition of correct response:	Yes, I can, etc.

The theoretical foundations shaken

So, the tape recorder and the language laboratory were backed by a powerful new trend in language teaching which they had themselves helped to create. It seemed a highly effective symbiosis. And yet, within little more than a decade after their introduction in the UK, the NFER in its report, *Primary French in the balance,* was registering almost universal pupil dislike of the tape recorder:

> *There are, however, certain aspects of learning French which children of all levels of achievement tend to reject, such as the enforced passivity, repetition and incomprehension associated with the use of the tape recorder . . .*
> (Burstall et al, 1974)

Dorothy Forrester, editing a special edition of the *Audio-visual Language Journal* devoted to the language laboratory, was asking '*Are language laboratories liable to fade out?*' (*AVLJ*, vol 11, no 1, 1973). What had gone wrong?

First of all, audio-lingualism came under severe attack. What had seemed its great strength proved to be its fatal weakness – its theoretical foundations in linguistics and psychology. Both structuralism as an account of the functioning of language and behaviourism as an explanation of how it was acquired came in for fundamental criticism in the late fifties and early sixties, in particular from one man – Noam Chomsky.

Chomsky's slim and innocuous-looking study *Syntactic structures* (1957) was the first of a number of writings that led to a rejection of the structuralist notion that an adequate account could be given of a language from an analysis of a finite set of actual utterances. Instead of proceeding from the outside in, 'transformational-generative grammar', as the new approach came to be called, proceeded from the inside out, attempting to discover the rules that a native speaker must have internalised in order to be capable, using finite means, of producing (and interpreting) an infinite number of sentences which are recognised as grammatical by another native speaker.

In 1959, in a devastating review of Skinner's *Verbal behavior,* Chomsky specifically took to task the attempt to understand human linguistic behaviour in terms of the behaviourist paradigm of stimulus-response-re-inforcement that had been derived from animal experimentation. Chomsky wrote:

216

> *We constantly read and hear new sequences of words, recognize them as sentences, and understand them. It is easy to show that the new events that we accept and understand as sentences are not related to those with which we are familiar by any simple notion of formal (or semantic or statistical) similarity or identity of grammatical frame . . . It appears that we recognize a new item as a sentence not because it matches some familiar item in any simple way, but because it is generated by the grammar that each individual has somehow and in some form internalized.* (Chomsky, 1959)

Thus, against Brooks' idea that acquiring a new language was acquiring a new set of habits, Chomsky set the notion of the creativity of language from underlying rules. Young native speakers or foreign language beginners who say things like *they goed* are unlikely to be demonstrating a habit they have acquired through repeatedly hearing or saying *they goed.* They are much more likely to be demonstrating that they have acquired an underlying rule for generating the past tense that is as yet incomplete.

Chomsky's theories seemed apt to demolish all the principal tenets of audio-lingualism: language was not a set of patterns passively acquired by habit formation in structure drills; it was a set of rules for generating sentences, which learners acquired actively by creating and testing hypotheses. The idea of linguistic universals stressed what languages had in common rather than where they differed and this caused a decline in the fortunes of contrastive linguistics. Even the stress laid by audio-lingualism on the prime importance of spoken language was called into question, since the written form of a language was seen in some respects as a separate system.

A less fundamental critique of audio-lingual methods, though at the time it was seen as a very devastating one, was *The psychologist and the foreign language teacher* (Rivers, 1964). Rivers did not refute the importance of habit formation but she severely criticised the narrow behaviourist approach adopted by the audio-lingualists. The book struck a chord with teachers because Rivers was herself a language teacher and many of her criticisms were aimed at aspects of audio-lingualism that had never been popular with a broad base of teachers: the early emphasis on the spoken at the expense of the written word, the stress on analogy to the neglect of explanation, and the heavy dependence on formal drill to the detriment of meaning, situational context and interpersonal relationships.

The audio-lingual movement was also criticised by the psycholinguist J B Carroll at the International Conference on Modern Foreign Language Teaching held in Berlin in 1964. Carroll brought the controversy into focus by giving names to the opposing approaches:

*Examination of the practices of foreign language teachers and the writings of several theorists suggests that there are today two major theories of foreign language learning. One may be called the **audio-lingual habit theory**, the other the **cognitive code-learning theory**.* (Carroll, 1966)

He criticised both theories for failing to take *adequate account of an appreciable body of knowledge* that had *accumulated in the study of verbal learning*. In particular, he found the audio-lingual habit theory guilty of overstressing frequency of practice and neglecting contrast, of playing down meaningfulness, of leaning too heavily on aural learning and of neglecting conscious attention to the critical features of a skill to be learned.

Carroll, too, was less fundamental in his criticism than Chomsky, who returned to the attack in 1966 at the American Northeast Conference on the Teaching of Foreign Languages. Just as categorically as Brooks had stated the fundamental principle of audio-lingualism:

The single paramount fact about language learning is that it concerns, not problem solving, but the formation and performance of habits. (Brooks, 1960)

Chomsky rejected it:

Linguists have had their share in perpetuating the myth that linguistic behaviour is 'habitual' and that a fixed stock of 'patterns' is acquired through practice and used as the basis for 'analogy'. (Chomsky, 1966)

Empirical studies

Whilst declaring himself not competent to make proposals about language teaching, Chomsky's standing was by this time such that audio-lingualism as a theory was set reeling. It might have recovered from the blow if a number of empirical attempts in the 1960s to establish its superiority over other methods had given it wholehearted endorsement. Such was not the case. The best known and largest scale study of the effectiveness of the audio-lingual method with school learners was the Pennsylvania Project. The results of this research were described as *personally traumatic to the Project Staff, deeply committed to a Functional-Skills* [audio-lingual] *philosophy* (Smith, 1970):

'Traditional' students did better than 'Functional Skills' classes in reading and writing and as well as the more modern approaches in listening and speaking.

218

The audio-lingualists found no comfort either in investigations of the effectiveness of language laboratories. Keating (1963) studied the performance in French of over 5,000 pupils, some using, some not using a language laboratory. The results suggested that the lab pupils were actually at a disadvantage compared with those with no lab experience. These shattering results, appearing just when lab installations were enjoying mushroom growth in the UK, were, however, rather easy to dismiss on many grounds, such as the inadequacy of the tests and the lack of information on the teaching, course materials, kind of installation, pattern of usage, etc.

The study conducted in England at the University of York (Green, 1975) could not be so readily dismissed. It was a small-scale study involving around 100 school pupils but was remarkable for the degree of control achieved over potential variables and the fact that the groups were held constant without significant attrition for three years and the pupils studied overall for five years. The testing of performance and attitude was extensive and thorough. The pattern of language laboratory usage investigated was shown to be typical for school labs throughout the country. The results pointed to no significant difference in performance or attitude over a three-year period between pupils using a language laboratory as a regular aid and those using only a classroom tape recorder.

Whilst the York study was widely accepted to have high internal validity, its external validity could be questioned on the grounds of the representativeness of the pupils involved, who were all boys at the upper end of the ability range (grammar school). However, a replication with pupils of both sexes covering the full ability range (comprehensive school) again found no advantage for the language laboratory (Winter, 1982).

The legacy

The decline of audio-visual and audio-lingual courses (reflected in the decision taken by the Audio-Visual Language Association in the 1970s to change its name to the British Association for Language Teaching) was not accompanied by any decline in the use of the tape recorder as a language-teaching aid – rather the opposite. The equipment itself had become far more teacher-friendly as lightweight cassette recorders replaced ponderous reel-to-reel recorders, with attendant savings in the cost and storage of tapes. More importantly, the way was now open for more imaginative, and motivating, tape content.

What had crucially been missing from the tapes was attention to meaning. Already in 1966, in *The visual element in language teaching*, Pit Corder had stated bluntly: *All teaching of language is the teaching of meaning.* He had also pointed to what he considered a more satisfactory threefold division of language skills than the so-called 'four skills' of listening, speaking, reading and writing, which the audio-lingualists had rather artificially tried to keep discrete. Corder's language skills were the 'motor-perceptive skills' (concerned with the articulation and recognition of speech sounds), the 'organisational skills' (concerned with organising language units into acceptable patterns) and the 'semantic skill' (concerned with the expression of meaning). Of the latter, Corder said:

> *Acceptable words strung together in the acceptable patterns of the language do not by that fact alone have meaning. They still have to be used in the right circumstances to have meaning of an effective sort . . .* (ibid)

In the pattern drill quoted above, the student appears to be answering the question *Do you like classical music?* In fact, the answer has to be *Yes, I do* or it will be contradicted by the tape answer. The student who does not like classical music cannot give a meaningful answer. Even the student who does like classical music will find any sense of reality rapidly fading with the semantic leap to *Can you drive a car?* The drill can only claim to be practising the organisational skill.

Ironically, it was the very sophistication of the language laboratory that led to this mechanical kind of exercise. It was felt that students **must** practise speaking in the lab or the potential of the equipment would not be fully exploited. In audio-lingual doctrine, a model response had to be provided, which meant that the student response had to be predictable. The very essence of real communication, however, is that it is largely unpredictable. However ingeniously the speaking exercise tried to emulate communication, the inescapable fact was that the tape was deaf to what the student was saying. In *The language laboratory and language learning* Dakin recognised the far greater potential of the tape recorder for listening than for speaking exercises, summing it up succinctly in a parody of Polonius, *Give every tape thine ear but few thy voice* (1973). Since the mid-1970s, that has been the way forward.

More authentic language

Now almost every course is accompanied by cassettes with material for listening comprehension, material often of a new kind – spontaneous, unscripted speech. There is a world of difference between scripted spoken language and spontaneous spoken language with its false starts, repetitions, fillers, hesitations and incomplete utterances. Most of what learners hear in face-to-face encounters with native speakers is spontaneous speech and they need practice in listening to it. With the focus on the content rather than the form of language, learners can also be confronted with more complex and therefore more authentic and interesting texts. The difficulty of a passage for listening is not determined solely by its complexity but also by the level at which learners are called upon to comprehend it, which may range from simple gist-listening to identifying specified information and right up to full comprehension of details.

In the quest for more authentic materials, the teacher has been greatly helped by *Authentik*, a regular series of authentic listening and reading materials in French, German and Spanish originating from Trinity College, Dublin. In some ways, the most authentic materials of all are the tapes made specifically for a class by the teacher, or the tapes arriving from a linked class abroad with content addressed specifically and personally to the class.

Learners are not merely passive listeners but are required to demonstrate their comprehension by some kind of active response. That may, at the simplest level, be no more than deciding whether an assertion is 'true or false', or ordering items in a sequence, or filling in a table, or matching spoken text to visuals. At the highest level, it may be answering detailed questions on a text or summarising, interpreting or even transcribing it. Such a response may be oral or written, but attempts by the tape to stand in for the teacher and provide model answers after a pause on the tape are now largely confined to beginners' courses designed for independent learning. For teacher-guided learning, too, the ubiquitous cassette recorder and the high-speed cassette copier have meant that teachers can give learners cassettes to take away and work on independently.

Language teaching nowadays is almost unthinkable without cassette tapes for pronunciation and listening practice. That is a development which owes much to the huge commercial success of 'musicassettes' and the widespread availability of machines for playing them, such as portable radio-cassette recorders and so-called 'personal stereos', which are often not much bigger than the cassettes they play back. The fact that virtually everyone now has access to some kind of machine for playing back cassettes has no doubt also contributed to the decline in the fortunes of the language laboratory. One purpose of the lab after all was to provide every learner with an individually controlled tape recorder. The unique feature of the audio-active-record laboratory which enabled learners to record on a tape at the same time as they listened to it became much less valuable with the passing of audio-lingual materials. Above all, perhaps, the lab was costly not only in terms of money but because it occupied premium space. Particularly in schools, teachers found themselves timetabled to the laboratory at a fixed time in the week, whether or not that time fitted in with their teaching, and then more or less forced to use the equipment for the whole of the lesson because the fixed furniture made the room unsuitable for other teaching activities. The early equipment was furthermore notoriously unreliable. Faced with stringent resources of money and space, it is not surprising that schools have tended not to replace worn-out lab equipment but to look instead to the demands of more sophisticated technology such as Satellite TV and computers.

The recording revolution then has shifted to new frontiers leaving behind, however, the now humdrum cassette recorder firmly established as a basic language teaching aid.

References

A-LM (Audio-Lingual Materials), *French, German, Italian, Russian, Spanish* (United States: Harcourt, Brace & World, 1961–66)

Authentik, Authentik Language Learning Resources Ltd, 27 Westland Square, Dublin 2

Bloomfield L, *Language* (United States: Holt, 1933)

Brooks N, *Language and language learning* (United States: Harcourt, Brace & World, 1960)

Burstall C et al, *Primary French in the balance* (NFER, 1974)

Carroll J B, 'The contributions of psychological theory and educational research to the teaching of foreign languages' in Valdman A (ed), *Trends in language teaching* (United States: McGraw-Hill, 1966)

Chomsky N, *Syntactic structures* (Netherlands: Mouton, 1957)

Chomsky N, review of Skinner's *Verbal behavior* (1959) reprinted and abridged in De Cecco J P (ed), *The psychology of language, thought, and instruction* (Holt, Rinehart & Winston, 1969)

Chomsky N, 'The utility of linguistic theory to the language teacher' (1966) reprinted in Allen J P B and S P Corder (eds), *The Edinburgh course in applied linguistics, vol 1: Readings for applied linguistics* (Oxford University Press, 1973)

Corder S P, *The visual element in language teaching* (Longman, 1966)

Creese K J H and P S Green, *German, a structural approach* (Oliver & Boyd, 1966–68)

Dakin J, *The language laboratory and language* learning (Longman, 1973)

Green P S (ed), *The language laboratory in school: the York study* (Oliver & Boyd, 1975)

Hadley C G and B Howson, *French, a structural approach* (Oliver & Boyd, 1966–69)

Hilton J B, 'Using the language laboratory in the secondary school' in Turner J D, *Using the language laboratory* (University of London Press, 1968)

Kamenev V Y, *Cours audio-visuel préliminaire de français* (France: TAVOR Aids, 1955)

Keating R F, *A study of the effectiveness of language laboratories* (United States: Columbia University Teachers' College, Institute of Administrative Research, 1963)

Lado R, *Linguistics across cultures* (United States: University of Michigan Press, 1957)

Nuffield Foundation/Schools Council, *Adelante, Vperyod!* (Macmillan/Lund Humphries), *En avant, Vorwärts* (E J Arnold, 1963–72)

Oliver & Boyd – see Creese and Hadley

Rivers W M, *The psychologist and the foreign language teacher* (United States: University of Chicago Press, 1964)

Skinner B F, *Verbal behavior* (United States: Appleton-Century-Crofts, 1957)

Smith P D Jr, *A comparison of the cognitive and audio-lingual approaches to foreign language instruction: the Pennsylvania foreign language project* (Harrap, 1970)

Stack E M, *The language laboratory and modern language teaching* (United States: Oxford University Press, revised edition 1966)

TAVOR – see Kamenev

Winter R F, *The effectiveness of the language laboratory in the mixed-ability teaching of German in the initial two years of the secondary school* (Unpublished PhD thesis, University of Sheffield, 1982)

222

20

Moving text — TV, video and satellites

Brian Hill

About thirty years ago Noel Coward was reflecting in a TV interview on his life. The question was posed: *What are your favourite television programmes?* Sir Noel leant back in his chair, fingered his lapels and remarked disparagingly: *Television is for appearing on and not for watching.* The opinion that television was somehow not serious and had no real role in a genuine educational experience was also often heard in common rooms and behind the scenes at conferences. It is a tribute to the BBC and, to a lesser extent, to ITV companies that the important role played by television in language learning is widely recognised today.

Few would now argue against the premise that television is inherently attractive and motivating, that it is able to introduce 'real' language in 'real' situations, that it contextualises language with a variety of paralinguistic clues, that it is topical and adaptable. During the last thirty years, television has contributed fully to providing material which stoked the fires of the communicative revolution outlined earlier by Peter Green. We want, indeed we are expected, to produce linguists who can comprehend accurately, speak with confidence and who are aware of the cultural, social, economic and political factors embedded in the target language. Without the judicious application of television and its associated technologies, it is difficult to see how this can be achieved.

Changing technology

In 1966, few schools had television and, anyway, the only language programmes on offer were series such as *Komm mit* and *Parliamo Italiano* which were popular but were designed for adults viewing, often in black and white, at home. Shortly afterwards, Philips began marketing a large video recorder with open reel one inch tape. It was cumbersome, noisy, heavy, unsophisticated, but immensely exciting. Those of us fortunate enough to have access to these magnificent beasts began recording the early schools TV masterpieces such as *La Chasse au Trésor*. The tension and excitement generated by the 'baddie' Luciani was experienced by thousands of children throughout the country and new vistas were suddenly opened. There soon followed more compact videos with unfamiliar names such as Shibaden and Sony and these open reel E1AJ (a video standard common in the 1970s) machines were in turn replaced by cartridges and cassettes. Today, there is hardly a language class in the country that does not have access to sophisticated videos complete with shuttle search, memories, freeze frames and timing devices.

So who would have imagined that fast forwarding thirty years from the struggles with those early machines we would be living in a world where children in a Rochester secondary school are sitting in their classrooms using Asymetrix's 'Toolbook' in a Microsoft PC Windows environment to produce their own televisual guide to Kent in French on CD-ROM? Or that departmental discussions would currently revolve around when we can be connected to Ethernet which will allow us to transfer and download television programmes from around the world? Or again that wafer-thin disks just 4fi" in diameter would now carry video programmes together with graphics and text in an interactive multimedia medium which is revolutionising (again) the possibilities for individuals learning languages alone.

When CILT was founded, it is true that sputniks were already circling the globe, but those early ventures into space led to the establishment of a world-wide satellite network that has added an exciting new dimension to language learning. At the flick of a button our classrooms can be in contact with the sounds and sights of countries thousands of miles away and we are faced with decisions on how best to use the day's news from Paris, a game show from Bonn, a documentary from Rome or even an advert for Persil from Tokyo – all to enhance the learning of languages.

In 1966, Giorgio Marini and Giulia were in the *Parliamo Italiano* bank:

Sig: Mi scusi signore. Che ore sono?
Giorgio (looking at his watch): Sono le dieci.
Sig: Le dieci soltanto?
Giorgio (looking at his watch again): No, No, mi scusi. L'orologio non va.

If you wanted to learn Italian from television, your only option then was to share with Giorgio the frustrations of having an unreliable wristwatch. Now, in addition to BBC courses and commercially available videos, there are some 40 hours of Italian beamed into our satellite dishes each day and the main problem is not the availability of materials but, conversely, the Niagara syndrome of trying to select appropriate materials to fill a thimble from the mass pouring over us.

To produce a television programme in 1966 required hundreds of specialists and pantechnicons of equipment. In another exciting technological development which has taken place over the three decades, language learners can now take their camcorders abroad and return with their own television programmes, having had the enriching and immensely useful experience of interviewing French people, filming and giving commentaries on French cities and even writing and producing scripts on aspects of life in France.

So, whether we like it or not, there are, have been and will be amazing advances in technology which provide us with many new exciting ways of presenting and practising foreign languages, but which at the same time force us to confront a plethora of awesome problems in order to exploit these possibilities effectively. It may be we decide that many of these possibilities are not appropriate to our particular circumstances, but whatever happens in the next thirty years, we cannot afford the luxury of being struthious – if we reject, it must be with knowledge and not from ignorance.

Language learning programmes

Although technological advances are of great importance, they are of no value if the material produced for delivery is poor. Over the last thirty years, we have been well served and television programmes have often been at the forefront of pedagogical advance. The roll call of landmark series is impressive. In schools the advent of *Tout compris* (1972) which used ordinary young people in France talking about their lives, or *Dès le début* (1979) which introduced the concept of television as a 'resource' rather than a 'course'; the gripping dramas from Thames TV such as *Le mystère de Valbec* (1972) or *Le Butin de Colombert* (1973) or, more recently, series such as *The French collection* (1993) which drew on authentic programmes from francophone countries, all in their own way both reflected or promoted innovation.

In the world of continuing education television has played a major role since the 1960s. In 1968, ATV produced a series called *Deux Mondes* in conjunction with the *Daily Mirror* (the book for which cost five shillings), but for the most part learners have looked to the BBC. *Wie bitte?* (1969) ventured out of the studio and was filmed on location in Hamburg. *Reportage* broke new ground in 1973 by compiling programmes based on authentic excerpts from French and German television. Another landmark was the introduction in 1975 of *Ensemble* which for the first time combined television, radio, coursebooks and gramophone records in one integrated course. *Russian language and people* (1980) moved the focus partly from language to promoting an understanding of the country and its inhabitants and still in 1996 the BBC is breaking new ground with series such as *Sueños* which talks to people around the Spanish-speaking world.

There have then been major advances in the number and type of programmes available – the move from studios to location recording, the use of authentic television from overseas networks, the introduction of a range of minority languages, the focus on the country as well as its language, the integration of television with other media. It should also be noted that many BBC series are now available on video which supplement the video course lists being developed by publishers such as Macmillan and Longman.

Success or failure?

Nobody can look back over the last thirty years of television production and associate with those years the word 'failure'. The consistent quality of the productions and, indeed, the contributions of many talented producers ensure that the history of television since 1966 has been marked by substantial successes. Nevertheless, problems have arisen which any even-handed reflection should consider.

If success is judged by achievement, there is some evidence to suggest that, whilst programmes are generally enjoyed, they do not always meet the learning objectives of either producers or students. Surveys conducted in the 1980s, for instance, indicate that well over half the students who started the courses for adults stopped learning before the end. This was partly to do with the stamina needed for regular work over a long period of time and partly a feeling among some students that they had got what they needed after only a few weeks. As a reaction to this situation, the policy changed to providing some shorter series of only five or six programmes to enable learners to 'Get by in' a country or to give them a taste of language learning and the confidence to take on a more substantial course.

It is a similar story in the classroom where, in spite of the ever increasing availability of video recorders, only a relatively small percentage of teachers consider themselves as regular users of television. Again, the reasons given are usually unrelated to the quality of the programmes themselves and more to the logistics of the use of technological equipment in schools or colleges, but it is disappointing that such an important and potentially seminal resource is not making a more substantial contribution to enriching the experience of learners.

Although most of the reasons expressed for any disappointments in the use of television are not related to courses, it must be said that there have been examples over the years where those producing programmes have misjudged the level of learners, the rate at which new language can be acquired and the amount of new material that can be presented in any programme. Crucially, some producers have also confused gist comprehension (listening for the 'what') with 'listening to learn' (where the focus is on 'how'). As a result of this, learners have often been presented with too much material, too fast, with insufficient reinforcement, so that short term comprehension relying heavily on the visual element is achieved, but with little informed acquisition to form the base for processing and the subsequent re-use of language.

Learning and teaching from television is not easy and it is not a skill which automatically exists or that is automatically acquired. Often independent learners have been given insufficient guidance on how to learn and, in their turn, teachers have been given insufficient guidance on how best to exploit the materials.

It is not the function of this short contribution to start apportioning blame nor, happily, to undertake to provide solutions. Suffice it to say that one of our biggest failings throughout education has been our consistent inability to manage innovation successfully. It is the biggest challenge to be faced as we look towards the millennium. It has its roots not just in questions such as the selection, financing and introduction of equipment, but, even more importantly, in the need to improve our understanding of how people learn effectively from video, CD-ROM or satellites and in the need to provide more effective training for those who are asked to participate in the process of innovation.

These few words have sought to celebrate the considerable achievements of all those concerned with television and its associated technologies. If we can pay as much attention to the management as to the production of innovation, there is every reason to believe that the sixtieth anniversary of the founding of CILT will be able to reflect on the determining role of technology in realising the fruits of the communicative revolution.

Some recommended further reading

Allan M, *Teaching English with video* (London: Longman, 1986)

Baer E (ed), *Teaching languages* (London: BBC, 1976; revised 1979)

Barnes N, *Adults learning foreign languages. The role of BBC broadcasting* (BBC Publications, 1978)

Bates A W, *Media and technology in European distance education: proceedings of the EADTU workshop on Media, Methods and Technology* (Heerlen, The Netherlands: European Association of Distance Teaching Universities, 1990)

Bates A and W Prescott, *Le télé-enseignement.* EGLI (Paris: Hachette, 1992)

Doyle T and P Meara, *Lingo: how to learn a language* (BBC Books, 1991)

Feldman T, *Multimedia* (London: Chapman and Hall, 1994)

Hayter C G, *Using broadcasts in schools: study and evaluation* (BBC/ITV, 1974)

Latcham C, J Williamson and L Henderson-Lancet, *Interactive multimedia: practice and promise* (London: Kogan Page, 1993)

Lonergan J, *Video in language teaching* (Cambridge: Cambridge University Press, 1984)

Rogers J, *Adults learning* (Open University Press, 1977)

228

21

Information technology

Sue Hewer

What is IT?

When we talk about IT we are talking about a medium for solutions rather than something which might be a solution in itself. As with print, the medium is neutral. It is what people do with it that determines its worth. Like other media such as print, audio and video, IT has certain characteristics which have to be understood and exploited by software developers and subject specialists in order for it to be appropriately exploited (Horrocks and McBride, 1994).

Unlike other media, IT is, in many of its forms, interactive in that it 'responds' to the input of the user. Again, in contrast to other media, IT is constantly changing and, as it changes, so do its characteristics. (Seedhouse, 1995)

A solution seeking a problem

To many language teachers in the secondary sector in the early eighties, the arrival of computers in languages classrooms looked more like a solution looking for a problem, than a solution to the kind of problems that they were grappling with. The communicative approach to language teaching was gaining widespread acceptance and the criteria for assessment at 16+ were based on the extent to which the message was communicated, rather than on the accuracy of the language used. There was also a change of emphasis from written to spoken language.

At that time, the most obvious characteristics of the computer to be exploited were its ability to compare the written input made by the student against the 'correct' answer stored in its memory, and to give immediate feedback. This led software developers down the road of text-based drill and practice activities reminiscent of discredited language lab techniques and they did not find favour. The current renewed interest in grammar in the secondary sector has caused an upswing in the sales of such software.

IT, HE and EFL

To some extent, the mismatch between what was needed and what the computer appeared to be able to provide, was inflated by the fact that early software developments were largely undertaken by teachers in higher education and those working within the private EFL sector. Such developments sprang from the interests of individuals and reflected the diversity of courses and approaches to be found in the two sectors. Not unnaturally, these needs were sometimes at odds with those of teachers and students in the secondary and FE sectors.

With the advent of a 'languages for all' policy in many universities, and the disappearance of the binary line in HE, the needs of all three sectors have to some extent converged in the nineties. Both schools and further education colleges watch with interest the work of the Computers in Teaching Initiative Centre for Modern Languages (CTI CML) at the University of Hull and await the publication of the products of the three languages projects funded through the Teaching and Learning Technology Programme (TLTP) by the UK Higher Education Funding Councils which include specialised translation training packages, software to build up the student's knowledge of the grammar of the target language, and multimedia packages designed to support the non-specialist language learner (HEFCE, May 1993).

Making the most of the medium

Despite the apparently unpromising software available for language learning in the early eighties, those few teachers who were able to observe students working with computers were struck by the intensity of concentration and the length of attention span achieved by learners across a wide ability range. The willingness to do the same drill many times through the keyboard was in marked contrast with the response to requests to correct written work in a traditional way, and learning undoubtedly took place.

The medium appeared to be able to motivate through its ability to offer instant feedback and also to respond to student requests to follow one of a number of possible paths through a set of learning materials. It also had the benefit of being able to conceal and reveal information and, thereby, to provide surprises.

Inspired by student reaction to computers and by their own fascination with the medium, a number of dedicated individuals set about the task of implementing innovative approaches to software development which contrasted with computerised versions of activities such as cloze tests and multiple choice. Two such developments made significant but very different contributions to the future direction what is now known as CALL (Computer-Assisted Language Learning).

Granville

Having recognised the potential of branching in response to student input, Barry Jones and his colleagues embarked on the creation of *Granville* (Jones et al, 1987), a microworld within which 'real world' interactions could be simulated. This was an altogether more promising innovation for the language teacher concerned with communicative competence.

The package enables students to make a surrogate visit to Granville during which they engage in role plays connected with shopping, eating, sports and leisure activities actually available in the town. They are required to ensure that they do not get too hungry or thirsty, and to keep a check on their spending money. The unexpected is never too far away and changing factual information is conveyed to the students through a daily on-screen newspaper. All student activities are recorded in their 'diary' which they are able to print out and take away, and which provides the teacher with a record of their work at the computer.

The concept, content and facilities responded to the needs of teachers and students. The technology was made to serve those needs. The design concepts which underpin *Granville* are as valid now as they were in the early eighties and should inform the future development of multimedia microworlds.

While *Granville* relied largely on text and required accurate input, it was found by many teachers to motivate students, to enable them to consolidate and make active use of previously learned vocabulary and structures and to provide the stimulus for related oral and written activities away from the computer. This view was not shared by Legenhausen and Wolff (1990) who undertook a contrastive study of the use by students of *Granville* and of a very different kind of package, *Storyboard* (Jones and Higgins, 1983). The latter, despite coming best out of the German study, did not always have immediate appeal for teachers in UK secondary schools.

Storyboard

The essential structure of the original *Storyboard* package is simple. The teacher types in a text of up to eighteen lines and saves it. From within the student programme, the learner chooses the appropriate file and is required to reconstruct the text, each letter of which, by now, has been replaced by an asterisk. Students type in a word which they believe might be in the text. The computer checks the input against the text in memory.

If it finds the word, it displays every occurrence of it in the text. If it cannot find the word, it simply indicates 'word not found' and clears the input window. Students build up the text, drawing on their own world knowledge, their knowledge of the vocabulary related to the topic area of the text and of the form of the words which they want to try out. The more successful they are, the more clues they can get from the developing context.

Despite the simplicity of the structure of the software, the cognitive processes which text reconstruction software causes students to engage in are far from simple (Hewer, 1993). Those who dismiss this genre of software as 'merely a test of memory', or concerned only with form, are missing the point, as are those who believe that the programme should accept a wide range of correct words for single gaps in the text.

Storyboard originated from the collaboration of John Higgins and Tim Johns who saw the computer as having the potential to release the *creative, investigative abilities of our students* (Higgins and Johns, 1984). Johns has pursued his interest in this approach in his concordance package *Micro-Concord* (Scott and Johns, 1993) which provides a valuable tool for the exploration of syntax, morphology and lexis at all levels (Johns and King (eds), 1991).

It is important that the intensity of linguistic activity which *Storyboard* and similar packages simulates is not disregarded as we move towards the 'point, click and drag' of multimedia which might well result in learning environments rich in sensory input, but which fail to force the learner to engage in deep linguistic processing and, as a result, fail to promote lasting learning (Decoo, 1994 and Rüschoff, 1993).

IT utilities

Driven by the IT requirements of the National Curriculum in England, Northern Ireland and Wales, traditional CALL was supplemented in the secondary classroom in the early nineties by the use of the facilities of the word processor and, to a lesser extent, databases (NCET, 1995).

While word processors cannot provide the kind of programmed feedback available within CALL packages, their editing facilities encourage writing because mistakes can be so easily and invisibly corrected. In a word processed assignment, mistakes are not indications of failure but stepping stones to success.

The use of on-line dictionaries, grammar help, style and spelling checkers from within word processors ought to enable students to improve the quality of their written work, but, as with so many IT applications, classroom research is needed which takes into account the nature of the application itself, pedagogy and second language acquisition theory (Garrett, 1991).

Databases provide a reason for students to acquire information in a pre-planned and structured way. In turn, the data which has been collected and stored becomes a resource which can be interrogated. The information retrieved as a result of interrogation can then be used by students and teachers as a prompt for oral information gap activities and a stimulus for written work away from the computer.

Multimedia content

If the eighties was the decade when software developers and teachers explored text on-screen, the nineties is that of multimedia and the Internet. The two are not unrelated. The Internet is being seen as a delivery medium of the future. Indeed it is already possible with some high speed networks to distribute full multimedia applications to remote computers from a central distribution point, opening up exciting possibilities for classroom practice, self-access centres and distance language learners but providing developers with significant design problems (Hagen, 1995) and causing publishers to consider future distribution strategies.

Increases in computing power and data storage capacity have brought sound and authentic images to software. TV quality, full screen video will soon be available, with the kind of user control facility which was possible in early experiments in disc-based interactive video. These facilities bring into language classrooms a multi-sensory, interactive environment, under the control of students and within which they can explore, learn and use the target language, and receive immediate feedback; something not readily achieved through more traditional media.

En route (Nelson, 1995) provides such an environment which contains a wide range of interactive, multimedia activities to complement the conventionally produced course, *Route nationale. Autolire* (Berwick et al, 1992), *Lesen* (Alder et al, 1995) and *Lectura* (Atkinson et al, forthcoming) take advantage of the storage capacity of CD-ROMs to provide for each language some 700 graded, authentic texts for the 14–19 age group, an on-line dictionary, helpful advice on appropriate reading strategies and activities to check comprehension.

The increase in power and in data storage capacity has also given hope to those developing intelligent language tutoring systems, although much work still remains to be done. Such systems require the machine to emulate aspects of natural language processing in order to be able to respond to student input, by identifying needs, offering suitable activities, analysing errors and providing appropriate feedback and remedial activities. For the same reason, teachers will have to wait sometime for computer-based assessment of anything other than very predictable and limited student input and multiple choice testing (Meunier, 1994).

The area in which computer-based technology has even further to go is speech recognition and production in response to student input. The existing facility for students to record their own spoken input within a software tutorial can give pronunciation practice (Hillier et al, 1994). However, no one should hold their breath waiting for the day when it will be possible to have a free dialogue with a computer!

On-line communications

Language learners, whether working in classrooms, in their offices or at home, do not only require content, whether that content comes via CD-ROM, the Internet, textbook, audio or video tape. They need to communicate with other students, with a tutor or a sympathetic native speaker. It is important that those engaged in the delivery of distance learning courses recognise the different contribution that the various communications media can provide to improve the quality of the learning experience.

The use of electronic mail (e-mail) for distance learners and their tutors has the bonus of enabling them to share their views with a number of people through a single 'mailing', at a time and, given the hardware and a phone line, at a place convenient to themselves. With regard to language learners in particular, e-mail appears to encourage informal written communication which, in its discourse structure, resembles the spoken language. If used as a rehearsal for actual spoken communication, this could prove a valuable support not only for distance learners, but for any group of students with access to a network (Chun, 1994).

E-mail can also provide a useful 'publication' medium for students' written work as well as enabling collaborative writing tasks. Its value in putting students in direct contact with their peers in the target language country has yet to be fully realised but the potential is widely recognised (Austin and Mendlink, 1993). Spoken e-mail is technically possible, but it remains only a possibility awaiting exploration and evaluation.

Text-based computer conferencing has been in use in higher education for some time. It enables like-minded people to contribute to an asynchronous debate about clearly defined issues, with the help of a conference moderator who attempts to confine contributors to the agreed topic. The fact that contributions can be prepared off-line, using the editing facilities of a word processor, and that there is a guaranteed audience, again makes this a medium which ought to have something to offer the language learner, but which requires a skilled moderator if learning is to take place. Findings from the Elnet project support the view that this tool could be of benefit to language learners (Mason, 1993).

The use of video conferencing in distance language learning has been explored by major players such as the Berlitz organisation, not least because it enables one teacher to work with a number of learners grouped together at different sites (Jennings, 1994). This is of particular importance for the teaching of a foreign language for specific purposes and of lesser taught languages. The medium provides more of the message than in audio and text conferencing and goes some way to enabling students and their teacher to judge when to interrupt and to ask questions. When desk-top video conferencing becomes commonplace, a teacher will be able to work remotely with learners at individual sites, all of whom will be able to see each other and their teacher. They will be able to communicate through the spoken and written medium and to share text based documents, still images, sound and moving video.

In addition to the communications media discussed above, all of which anticipate an exchange of spoken or written language, the World Wide Web now brings into the classroom easily accessible and up-to-date target language documents at low cost. New web sites become available daily and offer resources for every level of language learners. However, as is the case with Satellite TV, whilst there is no disputing the wealth of materials available, much of the output needs to be in some way mediated by a teacher before it can provide meaningful input for the learner unless the materials are specifically designed for language learning purposes.

The tail or the dog

In the discussion above, the assumption has been made that IT should be harnessed to the needs of the language teacher and learner within the context of existing pedagogical models and curricula. However there are those who are beginning to question whether the fundamental changes in communications currently taking place should influence, rather than respond to, the content of language courses and the pedagogical models on which their design and delivery are based.

Ought we, for example, to re-assess our views on the nature of input and re-consider the level of difficulty of computer-based textual, audio and video input with which our students can cope, given the fact that the medium is very attractive to them and and that it provides software developers with facilities to build in activities to develop de-coding strategies and increase accessibility? And what of on-line communications? Will they prompt us to provide a curriculum centred in part on the learner's immediate communication needs?

A final thought. The Internet is unique in that it offers low cost, international communications to anyone with a reasonably fast computer. Anyone minded to 'publish' on the Internet is free to do so. Which language are they likely to choose for worldwide readership? With all the benefits which IT promises for language learners, might it not also threaten the very existence of the linguistic diversity which we all value so much?

Further reading

Hardisty D and S Windeatt, *CALL* (OUP, 1989)

Higgins J, *Language, learners and computers* (Longman, 1988)

Thompson J and J Parsons, *ReCALL software guide* (CTI Centre for Modern languages, University of Hull, 1995)

Scrimshaw P (ed), *Language, classrooms and computers* (Routledge 1993)

Pennington M and V Stevens, *Computers in applied linguistics* (Multilingual Matters, 1991)

Hagen S (ed), *Using technology in language learning* (CILT, 1993)

Atkinson T et al, *Hands off! It's my go – IT in the languages classroom* (CILT and NCET, 1992)

Fox J et al, *New perspectives in modern language learning* (Employment Department, 1992)

References

Alder J et al *CD-Lesen* (Collins Educational, 1995)

Atkinson T et al, *CD-Lectura* (Collins Educational, forthcoming)

Austin R and F Mendlink, 'E-mail in modern languages development' in *ReCALL*, no 9 (1993)

Berwick G et al, *Autolire* (Collins Educational, 1992)

Chun D M, 'Using computer networking to facilitate the acquisition of interactive competence' in *System*, vol 22, no 3 (1993)

Decoo W, 'In defence of drill and practice in CALL – a re-evaluation of fundamental strategies' in *Computers and Education*, vol 23, no 1–2 (1994)

Garrett N, 'Where do we go from here – and who is leading the way?' in Savolainen H (ed), *Eurocall 1991* (Helsinki Schools of Economics and Business Administration, 1991)

Hagen S, 'User preferences in open and distance learning' in *ReCALL*, vol 7, no 1 (1995)

Hewer S, *It doesn't interrupt when I'm thinking – and you do!: an evaluative study of text reconstruction software in foreign language learning*, unpublished MPhil thesis, University of Nottingham (1993)

Higgins J and T Johns, *Computers in language learning* (Collins, 1984)

Higher Education Funding Council for England (HEFCE), *Teaching and learning technology programme* (May 1993); *Phase II* (November 1993)

Hillier S et al, 'An automated system for computer-aided pronunciation learning' in *Computer-Assisted Language Learning,* vol 7, no1 (1994)

Horrocks G and N McBride, 'Mimic the tutor or the book' in *Computer-Assisted Language Learning,* vol 7, no 1 (1994)

Jennings C, 'Delivering interactive distance learning using advanced communication technologies' in the *CTISS file,* no 17 (University of Oxford, July 1994)

Johns T and P King (eds), 'Classroom concordancing' in *ELR Journal* (University of Birmingham 1991)

Jones B et al, *Granville* (Cambridge University Press, 1987)

Jones C and J Higgins, *Storyboard* (*Wida* Software 1983)

Legenhausen L and D Wolff, 'Call in use – use of CALL: evaluating CALL software' in *System,* vol 18, no 1 (1990)

Mason R, 'Computer conferencing and the new Europe' in Harasim L (ed), *Global networks and international communication* (MIT Press, 1993)

Meunier L E, 'Computer adaptive language tests (CALT) offer great potential for functional. Yet, why don't they? in *Calico Journal,* vol 11, no 4 (1994)

NCET, *Modern foreign languages: approaches to IT capability, Key Stage 3* (NCET, 1995)

Rüschoff B, 'Language learning and information technology: state of the art' in *Calico Journal,* vol 10, no 3, 1993)

Scott M and T Johns, *Micro-concord* (Oxford University Press, 1993)

Seedhouse P, 'Communicative CALL : focus on the interaction produced by CALL software' in *ReCALL,* vol 7, no 2 (1995)

22
Contacts with the foreign country

Barry Jones

Making a reality of the foreign country

In 1965, when foreign language learning was almost exclusively limited to 25% of the school population, the range of visits and contacts with the foreign country was fairly restricted. Whilst home-to-home exchange visits were being organised by teachers in grammar schools, home-to-home exchange visits in secondary modern schools were almost unheard of. Study visits, as such, were much less frequent even in grammar schools. Pen-friend correspondence undoubtedly took place, but few examples of anything other than a periodic, unstructured exchange of letters are described in the language teaching journals of the time.

The 1970s and particularly the 1980s saw several significant initiatives which showed a shift of attitude amongst modern language teachers. The work of the Central Bureau for Educational Visits and Exchanges (CBEVE) was instrumental in encouraging and sponsoring a rapidly increasing variety of teacher visits, amongst its many and expanding activities. Writing in *Educational Exchange* in Spring 1980, Tony Male, now Director of CBEVE, then Deputy Director, commented:

We are faced with a choice of study visits and exchange opportunities which extend from a five-day option to the one-year exchange or the two year contract. These opportunities . . . include EEC study visits for which the Central Bureau acts as the clearning house for the nine member states, inten-sive study visits, reciprocal study visits and teacher exchange programmes. All this adds up to a very comprehensive choice offered to those who feel they would like to introduce a more adventurous or a more peaceful inter-lude into their teaching career. (Male, 1980)

These initiatives were synchronous with and complemented the rapid expansion of the Certificate of Secondary Education (CSE) and teaching a foreign language across the ability range. The shift towards a more communicative syllabus, especially with the development of the Graded Objectives movement (see Chapter 7) and its new types of test, encouraged:

. . . the ability to use the language for realistic purposes rather than, for example, the ability to manipulate the grammar of the language irrespective of meaning, or use it in ways which the actual user would rarely need to employ: (. . .) Objectives should be communicative and behavioural, that is, they should be defined in terms of what communicative tasks a candidate would be able to perform in the language. (Page and Hewett, 1987)

Modern language teachers also began to look to areas of the secondary school curriculum where teachers of other subjects were successfully teaching pupils of all abilities. The experience of history, geography and humanities teachers appear to have had particular relevance. Such cross-curricular initiatives began to influence a foreign language curriculum and widen the scope of visits and contacts abroad. Language learning was increasingly placed in the context of the country in which it was spoken. An example from the county of Avon serves to illustrate this.

In 1983 language and humanities' teachers in seven Bristol schools experimented with the idea of introducing environmental education in order to enrich the experience of both French and English pupils participating in local school-to-school, home-to-home exchanges. The exchanges were not just the reserve of the most able linguists; they were planned to cater for pupils of all abilities. Mary Ryan, then of Hanham High School, writing in the County of Avon's first Modern Languages' *Inset Newsletter*, in September, 1983, saw that environmental studies could:

. . . add an extra dimension to exchange visits, creating a sense of purpose, forcing pupils to work together on common tasks involving the families and also creating a spirit of cooperation within departments in school (Gathercole (ed), 1983).

The way in which these home-to-home exchanges was organised was indicative of a broader approach to such an experience which, even today, provides a principled and highly imaginative approach to visits like this. In the Avon schools' scheme French and English pupils were paired. Together, they conducted town trail surveys and 'discovery walks', each partner helping the other linguistically, and taking photos as they walked. One original task included noting, on tape or in writing, impressions at stages during the walk, focusing on one or two senses (smell and touch, for example). In their bilingual pairs pupils discussed and compared as they progressed. They decided between them which photos to take and the host pupil helped the visitor to prepare a few sentences about the walk and a few questions to ask people in the street. British children worked with worksheets in French, and French children had worksheets in English. In their families each pupil conducted a survey in the appropriate target language on shopping habits (what was bought and where) as well as questions about where they came from originally, what their leisure and sporting interests were, and where they went on holiday.

Such a cross-curricular approach was relatively novel. Different departments in each school worked very closely together. In humanities lessons, before the visit, pupils looked at the language in English needed to describe streets and buildings, outside and inside. Records were made about age, number of floors, size, building use, building materials used, state of repair, signs, street furniture outside and roof furniture. In their French lessons learners were taught or revised this and other language necessary to describe places and people. They also learnt how to make enquiries about shopping habits, daily routine, holidays, etc.

Initiatives like this were intent on exploiting more fully the home-to-home exchange so that it encorporated elements of the study visit and a focused use of the foreign language. Sometimes, however, study visits involved little or no contact with families but were nonetheless of considerable value in promoting language use and an awareness of the daily lives of others. Eric Hawkins describes a visit to France made by a class of fifth form (Year 11) pupils, accompanied by student-teachers from York who acted as group leaders. Together pupils and students made a comparative study of the cost of living in France and in Britain. (Hawkins, 1987)

Visits such as these could not, however, by their nature involve all the pupils in a class. Other initiatives adopted full class participation as their goal.

Contacts sans voyage

Pen-friend correspondence could and often did involve all pupils in a class. A conventional way to start such an initiative was for every pupil to be given the name and address of a partner in the other country. Letters were then written in the mother tongue of each participant and exchanged as and when they were received with little or no intervention by the teacher. The advantage of this procedure was that correspondence remained private. The disadvantages could, however, become disincentives; the language which each participant used was often too complex to be understood without the help of the language teacher and the privacy of the letter exchange was destroyed; sometimes one or other partner failed to reply and one person was disappointed; the frequency of the exchange of letters was unpredicable. Different schemes sought to overcome these problems.

In one such project (Jones, 1981; 1984) personal letters were included in exchanges of parcels timetabled by agreement between French and

English teacher partners to take place on five agreed dates during the school year. Each letter and the contents of each parcel were written within language parameters set out in advance by the language teacher in the other country. In this way both participating groups of teachers and pupils could be relatively confident that the messages would be understood without the pupils having to reveal the contents of their private mail to their teacher. In fact, in one exchange one fourteen-year-old boy never showed anyone else what he received from his French girlfriend during the year the exchange took place!

Linguistic parameters helped motivation as well as allowing access to the information, feelings and opinions of the children in the other country. Because each teacher made the parcel exchange a part of the teaching programme and ensured that everyone participated, no one was disappointed. Pupils were paired if numbers permitted, or at least worked with three named other children in the other country. Partners were chosen from personal descriptions written in the foreign language. At this stage no photographs were sent so that the physical appearance of the pupils did not influence their choice; it was only the written autobiography which counted! Common experiences were created by making the themes of the five parcels common to all by agreement of both the teachers on each side of the Channel and the pupils in their classes. Popular themes were 'Personal introduction and family', 'Christmas', 'School', 'Family Life', 'Home town/village'. On receipt of the parcel from the participating country information was compared, although the contents of each individual's letter were only made public with his or her consent. The choice of and contents for common themes allowed for group discussion and class preparation of the material to be exchanged. All kinds of authentic documents and goods were included in the parcels; sweets, photos, wrappers, tickets, magazines, Christmas cards, drawings, timetables, recipes, school menus, diagrams and instructions showing how to make things (example: Christmas candles), brochures, labels from tins and bottles, packets of food (example: jelly, desserts), shop till receipts, cinema programmes, sports programmes, newspapers, school reports, school absence notes . . . the list is extensive. Contacts with learners in the other country were thus very much guided by the pupil participants. All members of a class were involved and all had something to contribute.

Accounts of other group projects show that similar aims were, and are still realisable. In 1984–85 a *projet-recherche interculturelle et interscolaire* involved fourteen- and fifteen-year-old children in two countries exchanging four mini research projects on how each group of teenagers celebrated Christmas, Easter and their birthday, and a description of school, local and regional celebrations. These projects included written descriptions, poems, recipes, audio and video tapes, cartoon stories, photographs (of, for example, decorations in the home, in school, in the town, for Christmas, to mark birthdays, for special events) and the production of posters using materials received from the participating schools in the other country. (Wilke, 1983)

Other projects involved a haphazard mix of realia in a *Jeu des poubelles* (Dustbin game). Inspired by an article in the *Sunday Times Supplement*, five teachers in Cambridgeshire, coordinated by the author, asked pupils in their third year of learning French to piece together the life style of five French households based on the evidence of the (paper)contents of their dustbins (Jones, 1978). In the project pupils were asked to say what kind of household was represented, what they ate, drank, how they passed their time, what their life style was like and any other hypotheses the pupils felt they were justified in drawing from the evidence of the dustbin contents. The five households in France, two in Paris, one in Nantes, one in Normandy and one in Clermont-Ferrand were genuine. Each had been asked to collect during a week (paper) rubbish which otherwise they would have thrown into their dustbin, and which had been used in their daily living. Unsolicited paper rubbish (like junk mail) was not included. Based on this 'evidence' pupils were asked to draw their own conclusions. In the ensuing class discussion as much was revealed about the British learners as was about the French. One comment, audio-recorded during class discussion, illustrates this tellingly. On finding two (empty) camembert cheese boxes one thirteen-year-old in a Cambridgeshire fenland school declared that the French family was undoubtedly well-off. When challenged by one of the other pupils she said that her family could only afford a little 'fancy' cheese once a week and that the French family had been able to afford two boxes of camembert within the same period. Another fourteen-year-old was worried that the mother in a French family with a *maison secondaire* (second home) was seeing an unknown (gentle-man?) friend in a secret meeting place because she had two houses, a phenomenon unknown to an entire class in Cambridgeshire in 1978.

The production of class newspapers has been a source of both formal and informal news which, when exchanged between classes in two countries can also provide some telling insights. Pupils in South Shields, for example, produced newspapers in both French and German entitled *Escargot Nordique* (1989) and *Kunterbunter Jugend Spiegel* (1989). French and German readers could read about how three sixteen-year-old boys saved a man from drowning, how the weather in France compared with local weather over a period of time, what a tourist should visit in South Tyneside, how the Youth Enterprise scheme worked, as well as announce-ments, advertisements, and a 'lonely hearts' column.

During the last few years contacts with contempories in another countries has been facilitated by fax. John Lemon must have been amongst the first to have produced a bilingual French and German two-page newsheet contributed to by classes in Halifax schools called, appropriately, *Allez fax!* (1990).

Contacts with other countries are becoming faster, with responses being more immediate and resembling more genuine communication. Video exchanges have been organised by some schools, so that learners in both countries during the period of a class-to-class link can be seen in their home or school surroundings, participating in sporting activities, or even enjoying a birthday party. When, hitherto, all that has been seen of a partner abroad is a passport photo, a video image can have a strong motivating force!

E-mail is a reality for some classes and can involve both young and older learners. Initiatives such as that of the *Service Culturel* in the French Embassy who put up-to-date news on-line, make access to French news and events easy, especially when it has direct access to Minitel and some of its information services. Some schools, such as those in the Limousin and Staffordshire, have already enjoyed e-mail contacts.

Electronic communication also allows very rapid communication of personal information. Recently a Year 9 group in a local school conducted a survey on the class's favourite foods and most popular pets, then sent the results to a participating school in France by fax. Within two days a similarly focused survey was received from the French partner school. This immediacy was exciting and within a short timescale created real interest. The greatest and most appealing benefit of fax and e-mail is that exchanges of information can take place rapidly not just between a school in Britain and a school in Germany, or France, or Spain, or Italy, or anywhere else, but between one in any part of the world speaking German, French or Spanish, or Italian.

Contacts with the target language world through e-mail, using the Internet and the World Wide Web, look set to offer all kinds of as yet only partially explored possibilities. In the UK the Schools' On-line project and the Superhighways project already use the Internet for daily classroom practice, supporting teachers as well as learners. Teachers have begun to appreciate the value of hitherto unimaginable contacts. One group of children, about to leave with their teachers for a ski trip to Quebec, had their final briefing in their Surrey school. During this briefing they accessed the Internet, looked through the Canadian cameras as the conditions on the ski runs were being transmitted at regular intervals, saw there was plenty of snow, went home and packed appropriately. After their transatlantic flight and a sleep they were on the same slopes dressed to cope with the conditions they had seen a few hours previously!

The native-speaking assistant

Learners of any language have today inexpensive and rapid means of communicating in the language they are learning and in their mother tongue, with any part of the world. They have access to a new and fast growing technology. We should not forget that they have increased contact with people, too. The Foreign Language Assistant may be for some learners the first contact with a real person from the target language community. We should ensure that he or she is an integral part of lessons for all ages of learner, not just for those needing examination practice. Assistants can be interviewed, compared with former Assistants (on cassette, from written descriptions) , asked to be the other part of role play pairwork activities, as well as native speaker informants. Local teachers in Cambridgeshire have access to banks of materials written by over 40 Assistants at their first briefing sessions. These describe differences and similarities between living in their country and in the UK. They also include their Christmas menus, Christmas shopping lists (prepared to enable them to decorate their homes or for the appropriate festive shopping), first impressions of Peterborough, likes and dislikes, descriptions of house and home, family photos, etc. The school's own Assistant can situate him or herself within the group of fellow nationals, using descriptions which others from the same country have produced in writing or on cassette. This is an important aspect of cultural awareness which language learners need to see. Who better than the Assistant and others to illustrate this for them. People and technology can now combine to make the other country real. Language practice can thus become bilingual communication.

References

Gathercole I (ed), *County of Avon Modern Languages Inset Newsletter,* no1 (September 1983), RLDU, Bishop Road, Bishopston, Bristol BS7 8LS

Hawkins E, *Modern languages in the curriculum,* revised edition (Cambridge University Press,1987)

Jones B, '*Le jeu des poubelles*' in *Journal of the National Association of Language Advisers* (1978)

Jones B, 'Communication is about something or studies of French life through structured class-to-class links' in *Journal of the National Association of Language Advisers,* no 12 (1981)

Jones B (ed), *Using authentic resources in teaching French* (CILT, 1984)

Male A H, 'Improved rates of exchange' in *Educational Exchange,* no 33, Spring 1980 (Central Bureau for Educational Visits and Exchanges, 1980)

Page B and D Hewett, *Languages step by step: graded objectives in the UK* (CILT, 1987)

Wicke R E , *A trip to England. Ein Ratgeber für die Durchführung von Studienfahrten und Austauschreisen nach Großbritannien* (Fuldatal/Kassel: Hessisches Institut für Lehrerfortbildung, 1986)

23

Intensive language teaching

Do Coyle and Eric Hawkins

*The most significant feature of intensive language teaching is **the use of the language for some other purpose than merely learning it**.* (George Perren, first Director of CILT, 1978)

'Intensive' foreign language teaching has a long history. In Roman times, when the foreign language that every well-bred young citizen had to know was Greek, a common practice was to take into the family a Greek slave of decent education who spoke Greek with the children in the nursery and the school room. A similar practice is described by Montaigne in his *De l'institution des enfants* (1580). He and his brothers were compelled by an enlightened father to use only Latin in the nursery: *nor man nor maid-servant were suffered to speak one word in my company except such Latin words as everyone had learned to chat and prattle with me.* We might note that Montaigne's early use of Latin in the nursery did not make him the scholar he became. It was followed by years of hard work in College, just as the young Roman's nursery games in Greek did not suffice if he wished to read the Greek historians and philosophers.

Underlying successful 'intensive' teaching down the ages has been the recognition that mastering a foreign language involves learning activity at two levels. Carl Dodson (1978) has called the one level 'medium orientated' activities, concentrating on accuracy of pronunciation, grammar, spellings, etc, and the other level 'message orientated' activities, use of language with real 'intention to mean' or to effect some result that matters to the user. The two levels have sometimes been likened to 'rehearsal' as opposed to 'performance' and in an earlier discussion (see p26ff) they are called simply 'level one' and 'level two' learning. Dodson, from his observation in Welsh bi-lingual schools, concluded that both 'levels' are equally necessary. Simply immersing the learner in the language, without preparation, can be counter-productive. But, similarly, exercises on the bank do not by themselves make effective swimmers.

These two levels of language learning were recognised and prescribed in the curriculum in the heyday of the Tudor Grammar School, for the teaching of Latin. The Tudor Grammar schools capitalised on the fact that

Latin was widely used outside school, and while the grammar was beaten into pupils unmercifully, the Royal Charters insisted on meaningful use of Latin, for all pupils' purposes, once the rudiments were learned.

Such meaningful use of Latin became increasingly difficult in the late seventeenth and eighteenth centuries and Latin teachers came to rely solely on 'level one' activities, concentrating on the grammar. In the nineteenth century, when modern languages were introduced in the public schools, teachers at first adopted similar methods. The 'great debate' in our subject, a century ago, in which the giants like Henry Sweet and Otto Jespersen gave the lead, was a reaction against relying solely on 'level one' or 'rehearsal' only.

There is obviously a proper place for 'rehearsal'. Beginners need to rehearse (and enjoy playing repetitive games with) numbers, telling the time, the currency, the calendar, the parts of the body, colours, shapes and positions of objects, etc. Experienced teachers will not apologise for playing such games, in the early stages of the learning, to help pupils to make their recall automatic. Beginners also need to listen, at their own speed, to unaccustomed new speech sounds, and have time to practise making them. Anyone who has tried to discriminate, and pronounce, the difficult 'tones' of Mandarin Chinese, will not dismiss 'mere rehearsal' as having no place in the apprenticeship. Moreover the usefulness of 'medium orientated' work is not confined to the earliest stages. Even advanced learners usefully combine 'medium orientated' work with meaningful use of the language, the two 'levels' constantly interacting and reinforcing each other.

Nevertheless, it remains true that 'rehearsal', by itself, can only carry beginners a short way. An early attempt to explain the true difference between the two levels was made by the Leipzig linguist Otto Tacke, in a paper published in 1923, 'Der Sprachunterricht muß umkehren!' ('Language teaching must change direction!'). He borrowed the title from the famous paper of 1882 in which the young Wilhelm Viëtor, then lecturing at the University College of Liverpool, had launched his attack on traditional language teaching methods. Tacke's paper is discussed by Butzkamm and Dodson (1980) who take up Tacke's principle *a will to mean must always underlie the learning of expressions in the foreign language, otherwise the foreign expressions do not stick.*

This anticipated what the philosophers Austin (1962) and Searle (1969) have told us about the 'true speech act'. The 'speech act', Searle claims, is the 'basic unit of communication' (not, as Chomsky had assumed, the sentence). The essential feature of the Speech Act is 'force' or '**intention to**

do something with words'. Language devoid of such intention is, for Searle, 'non-serious language' and as an example of 'non-serious' language, Searle cites **'teaching a foreign language'**.

How can the teacher move from Searle's 'non-serious' language to transacting real 'speech acts' with intention to 'do something with words'? Teachers have made valiant efforts to do so. Butzkamm and Dodson (1980) in their interesting discussion of Tacke, give examples of imaginative dialogues in which pupils are encouraged to transact real 'speech acts'.

Earl Stevick, in *Memory, meaning and method* (1976) addresses the same point and shows how a simple technique like getting pupils to **disagree** with what the teacher says, can make an exchange more meaningful. However, with only four short lessons per week, facing a class of 30 pupils, there must always be strict limits to the amount of individually directed dialogue that the teacher can transact with **any one pupil**. Many teachers are now finding that, in the transition to effective 'performance', intensive sessions have a valuable role to play.

In two CILT symposia (Hawkins and Perren, 1978 and Hawkins, 1988) descriptions are given of a number of early intensive initiatives at school level. Many of these persist and they have since been joined by others which fall broadly into five categories.

'*Sections bilingues*'

The most radical kind of intensive language teaching (which exactly meets George Perren's definition quoted in our epigraph) is teaching another subject through the medium of the foreign language. Whilst a small group of pioneering schools in the UK set up '*sections bilingues*', these have until recently remained isolated examples. Immersion programmes have made most progress in bilingual countries (Wales, Canada) where the purpose is, in effect, to teach a **second** as opposed to a **foreign** language. There has been impressive progress, however, in the last twenty years in many European countries. The European Schools set up as a European Union venture in 1958 incorporated '*sections bilingues*' from the beginning and the Franco-German treaty of 1969 gave further impetus to '*sections bilingues*' and '*sections européennes*'.

In Britain, the 1977 Department of Education Circular (DES/1977/CEE) recommending that at least one school with a substantial '*section bilingue*' be established in every major community passed largely unnoticed and received no further Government support. There were, however some pioneering examples of highly successful '*sections bilingues*', notably at Mill Hill, an independent school in North West London, and at Goff's School, a maintained (formerly selective) secondary school in Hertfordshire (these schemes and others are described in Hawkins, 1988). Following the

Education Reform Act (1988), however, teachers' preoccupation with implementing the National Curriculum led to some promising '*sections bilingues*' being abandoned.

248   In 1990 the National Curriculum Modern Foreign Languages Working Group (MFLWG) reopened the debate concerning the role of languages in cross-curricular work. It advocated a three-tiered approach, i.e. initiatives **within** Modern Foreign Language courses, **between** Modern Language and other school departments and **through other subjects taught in the foreign language.**

Though teaching another subject in the foreign language must seem to many teachers an unattainable ideal, there has been a resurgence of interest in it in the UK. The work of the European Movement for Language Medium Teaching is proving effective (see Council of Europe Workshop 12A in Germany, 1993, and 12B in Luxembourg 1996). Embassies, LEAs and CILT have given support and the recent Department for Education and Employment initiative promoting Language Colleges, albeit targeted at a very small number of schools, actively encourages language medium teaching and means that the UK is becoming integrated into the European 'language medium' network.

Current examples of schools with '*sections bilingues*' are:

- The **Hockerill Anglo European School** (Bishops Stortford) an 11–16 GM comprehensive school where Year 9 pupils learn Geography and History through French.
- **Millais School** (Horsham) an 11–16 girls comprehensive school where pupils take GCSE Business Studies in Spanish
- **William Ellis** (London) an 11–16 boys comprehensive school where pupils study GCSE Geography in Spanish.

The current failure of the Examining Boards to offer appropriate GCSE papers in the foreign language (with the single exception of Business Studies in Spanish) is a major problem. In the absence of external recognition, and with school initiatives restricted by preoccupation with league-tables based on examination results, further expansion of '*sections bilingues*' is in the balance. Grounds for optimism are offered, however, by the growing evidence of the benefits of intensive programmes, increasing opportunities for in-service training and more flexible interpretation of the National Curriculum requirements.

Content Oriented Language Teaching (COLT)

Some schools, unable to operate a full-scale *'section bilingue'* have provided immersion opportunities on a smaller scale but for a wider range of learners, by exploring the other two tiers of cross-curricular activity set out in the NC Working Group model referred to above.

'Content Oriented Language Teaching' (COLT) involves **using language to learn** as well as **learning to use language**. Since the aim is to 'do things with words' it is essential to link the activities engaged in with some specific interest that matters to the learner. Typical examples are:

- **Heathside Grant Maintained School** (Weybridge) an 11–16 comprehensive school, prepares Year 7 pupils by teaching a series of geography lessons in French before the pupils visit France. Pupils then carry out geographical surveys combined with language work. There are also links between the Foreign Languages and Design Technology Departments, where Year 8 pupils carry out a packaging project in French/German.
- **Ashfield School** (Kirkby-in-Ashfield, Nottinghamshire) an 11–18 mixed comprehensive school, prepares science modules for Year 8 pupils in French (e.g. on the solar system, gravity, etc.) each module lasting one term. Pupils afterwards work at La Villette as part of a French visit. There is also a French café once a week where pupils must speak French. It will soon become a 'cyber café'. The teacher responsible workshadowed a French science teacher for two weeks in order to set up the programme.
- at **St Peter's RC Comprehensive School** (Guildford) an 11–18 mixed comprehensive school, pupils in Years 7/8 followed National Curriculum Technology through the medium of French or German.
- at **George Abbott School** (Guildford) pupils in Year 9 followed a module of Geography map work through the medium of French.
- at **Howard of Effingham School** (near Leatherhead) pupils in Year 9 studied a History module on the rise of the Nazi Party in 1933 in Germany, using first-hand documents.

Intensive study abroad

As with 'COLT' schemes, the aim is to provide opportunity and incentive to use the foreign language for purposes that matter to the learner. As in all intensive courses, detailed preparation is the key, but for the short, intensive session abroad, minute preparation of every aspect proves to be especially needed.

Some pioneering examples of such projects are described by Barry Jones (see Chapter 22). Further interesting schemes are described in the National Curriculum Working Group Report, 1990. In one scheme (p65) pupils in Year 10/11, from an urban comprehensive school, all taking French in GCSE, made an exchange with a school in Nantes. They spoke French with their exchange partners and their families but, in addition, those taking GCSE Geography carried out a shopping survey in Nantes as part of their course work while other pupils taking History used their French to collate historical information for presentation and discussion on their return home.

During exchange visits between a Nottinghamshire comprehensive school and its partners in Alsace, where successful links have been developed over a period of time, an entire village becomes involved in simulating GCSE role-plays. Pupils have a real opportunity to shop, buy petrol, book into a hotel, organise social events etc.

At **Hockerill School** (see above) whole classes exchange and spend two to three weeks in their partner school following the normal timetable.

At *La Villette, Cité des Sciences et de l'Industrie*, the Paris multimedia hands-on Science Museum, school groups have benefited from '*les classes européennes*' and '*la classe Villette*' (Science in French). Pupils who have been studying a topic such as the environment, the universe, health or energy, spend a period of time (a day, a week) studying the topic in French with French teachers and students.

Intensive sessions in a local language centre

A disadvantage of sessions abroad will always be that participation depends on the willingness or ability of parents to pay. While European funding is beginning to open some doors, pupil participation still largely depends on home circumstances. Schools' ability to help disadvantaged pupils has not been helped by recent developments in school financing.

A possible answer to this challenge is for schools to have access to specially equipped local (or national) language learning centres. One possible model is suggested by the Euro Tunnel Exhibition Centre in Folkstone which provides intensive workshops based on cross-Channel transport involving seeking information, planning, telephoning and using database.

Another example is the Havering Centre in London where a 'cultural island' mimicking the environment of the foreign country can be created for intensive sessions. Dick Capel-Davies (in Hawkins, 1988) outlines a plan for an LEA language centre in which single-day, week-end or longer sessions can be arranged, catering for pupils at specific levels. Groups of schools, by pooling staffs, native assistants, other native-speakers, sixth formers and university students who have spent some time abroad, can offer younger pupils opportunities for one-to-one dialogue in the foreign language, in intensive sessions, which no single school could provide.

It may be possible to secure funding for such centres from local industry and commerce, in return for access to the centres for adult learners in the evenings.

The publications of the Central Bureau (see Appendix III) offer further examples of initiatives by teachers involving elements of intensive language learning, as do the European Curriculum Awards. In some LEAs, also, European Awareness Development Officers have played a leading role in encouraging school projects involving some degree of 'immersion' in foreign languages.

The rapid expansion of information technology is also providing valuable encouragement for intensive language work (see discussion by Sue Hewer in Chapter 21). From fax machines to video conferencing and via the Internet, learners are being given many opportunities to engage in real communication (see National Council for Educational Technology. For current up-date contact NCET, Science Park, Coventry CV4 7EZ).

A useful source of teaching materials is the Association for Science Education. '*Science across Europe*' (produced with British Petrolium) offers materials by an international team in all European languages on science themes, e.g. *What we eat; Environment; Waste; Drinking Water; Electricity*. Schools throughout Europe choose a topic and a language and link with each other via a database for the duration of a series of lessons on the theme and share their results.

TACADE 'Directions' are module materials in German, French and Spanish for teaching about drug use in 'personal and social education' (PSE) courses. They allow language teachers to extend topic work or to teach PSE through the medium of the foreign language.

Initiatives in partnership between schools and Colleges of HE/FE

Another possibility, of which the CILT 1988 volume referred to above offers successful examples, is for FE and HE institutions to lay on intensive sessions for local schools. For example, pupils beginning Spanish from scratch in Year 10 who attended an intensive course laid on by a HE College in the North West, at the start of the school year in September, made as much progress in an intensive fortnight as would normally be made in six months of normal classroom work at four short lessons per week. Unfortunately recent developments in the financing of HE institutions actively discourages them from giving any such lead to schools, because giving unselfish help to schools does not count for points in the 'league tables' which now determine HE funding.

Intensive sessions and teacher training

A most valuable resource (and one often under-exploited) in both the intensive session abroad, and in local intensive sessions, is PGCE students. For the students themselves, nothing can be more useful than acting as tutor in a well-organised intensive session, observing what works best and how to avoid pitfalls. It is not too much to claim that a PGCE or College training course that does not include the valuable experience of *intensive tutoring* denies future teachers an essential element in their preparation.

The training programme should include not only intensive **teaching** but intensive **learning**. There may be many ways of including this in the programme.

Starting a new language from scratch during the PGCE year

In one example, graduate students (with degrees in French/German/ Spanish or Russian), who were accepted for the PGCE year at York, in the 1960s and 1970s, had to agree to learn Italian from scratch. This was to remind them of the initial learner's problems, to enable then to experience a new kind of teaching, and, incidentally, to encourage the revival, in schools, of Italian, a richly rewarding and unfairly neglected language.

The PGCE students (some 30 to 40 each year) came up to the university before the October term began and learned Italian intensively from morning to night for fourteen days. Once term began they continued with Italian for a couple of hours each week, until November, when they all entered for GCE 'O' level. No student ever failed the exam and it was rare for anyone to score less than grade A.

Many of the students later went on to an intensive course in Italy, run by their tutor, Dr Trudie Berger, and subsequently many of them were able to introduce Italian as a sixth form option in the schools to which they were appointed. The relevance of this for 'diversification', and the introduction of less common languages into the school curriculum in the future, is clear.

While some PGCE courses still offer short intensive sessions in learning a new language to encourage students to empathise with learners, such initiatives as those mentioned have been discouraged by the DFE regulations (9/92) which require students to spend two thirds of their course in schools. However, as opportunities increase for transnational training institutions to forge partnerships, supported by ERASMUS funding and a genuine desire to collaborate, reciprocal exchanges of students ranging from weeks to months have added linguistic and cultural dimensions to many HE courses. The potential for intensive language work at all levels is greater than ever.

The 'reciprocal course'

Intensive methods have also been used in in-service courses for serving teachers. One technique is to bring together equally matched groups of learners from two different countries who wish to learn from, while teaching, each other. As a form of 'in-service' *'perfectionnement'* for serving teachers it has been found to work admirably, since each participant can offer his/her partner well honed teaching expertise.

The students are grouped in pairs, and the pairs in teams of eight, with two experienced tutors (native speakers) from each of the two languages, directing each team's progress. The teams work on alternate sessions in the two languages, each individual acting in turn as learner/tutor. In a typical exercise, a difficult dialogue on tape is listened to by the whole team and a question paper is distributed, testing comprehension and references (political, historical, cultural, social, geographical). The students then split up and work in pairs, the non-native speaker seeking help from the native-speaking partner in answering the questions posed. When the whole team assembles later, the non-native speakers are encouraged to take the initiative in discussing the text, utilising the prompts given them by their (native-speaking) partners. On the following day, of course, the roles of learner/tutor are reversed.

The success of the reciprocal technique may point the way forward towards its exploitation by adult language learners in the professions (doctors, say, accountants or engineers?) wishing to acquire the special vocabulary in the foreign language which few conventionally trained language teachers would be equipped to teach.

Another advantage of the reciprocal course is that it offers opportunities to practise the neglected skill of 'bilingual' communication, in which each speaker/writer uses his own language. This form of exchange is predicted to become far more common, in Europe at least, than it has been hitherto and intensive reciprocal courses may have an increasingly important role to play in the training of professionals of all kinds.

New directions

The new joint *'Maîtrise Français Langue Etrangère*/PGCE' set up in 1993 by the University of Lancaster now involves three UK universities (Homerton College in Cambridge; Lancaster and Nottingham) and eight French universities. Students from UK and France on this eleven-month course follow both a PGCE course in the UK and the Maîtrise FLE in France. This initiative not only gives students a double qualification, but immerses them in the language and culture of both countries.

Gaining the two qualifications in a single year demands very hard work and careful organisation but it is without doubt a most worthwhile experience at every level, pedagogic, linguistic and cultural. (Thoughts of a

254 *Maîtrise/PGCE student. Course brochure: Maîtrise FLE. and PGCE, 1990)*

As part of the *Maîtrise*, UK students have to learn a new language intensively. Having experienced intensive learning these future teachers will, it is hoped, be well equipped to develop COLT and offer intensive language opportunities in their schools, whether these take the form of two- to three-lesson mini projects, intensive study visits abroad or a full-scale '*section bilingue*'.

As a logical extension of this work, looking to the future, the University of Nottingham is soon to train future teachers of Geography, History and Science in French and German, as a start to the creation of a bilingual teacher force in the UK.

The UK may have lagged behind, initially, in provision of 'intensive' opportunities for language learning, but recent developments have been encouraging and there is a growing basis of successful experience on which to build for the future.

References and further reading

British Council, Crédif, Goethe-Institut (ed), *Subject learning and teaching in a foreign language* (Triangle 13, 1994).

Butzkamm W and C J Dodson, 'The teaching of communication; from theory to practice' in *International Review of Applied Linguistics*, 18 (4) (1980)

Council of Europe Reports, *Workshops 12A, 12B* 1993 on content medium teaching and learning (1993, 1996)

Dodson C J, *Language teaching and the bilingual school* (Schools Council, 1978)

Estébanez S and A Feltham, '*Section bilingue:* GCSE Business Studies in Spanish' in *Language Learning Journal* (ALL, March 1994)

Fruhauf G, D Coyle and I Christ (eds), *Teaching content in a foreign language: practice and perspective in European models of bilingual education* (European Platform/European Commission, 1996)

Hawkins E W and G Perren (eds), *Intensive language teaching in schools* (CILT, 1978)

Hawkins E W (ed), *Intensive language teaching and learning – initiatives at school level* (CILT, 1988)

Mackey W F, *Language teaching analysis* (Longman, 1965)

Montaigne M de, *De l'institution des enfants. Essais* (Paris: Langlier, 1580)

National Curriculum MFL Working Group, *Final report* (HMSO, 1990)

Searle J, *Speech acts* (CUP, 1969)

Stevick E W, *Memory, meaning and method* (USA, Rowley Mass: Newbury House, 1976)

Tacke O, see Butzkamm and Dodson above

Viëtor W, *Der Sprachunterricht muß umkehren* (published in 1882 under pen name 'Quousque tandem?' and under author's name, 1886, Heilbronn). For summary of the paper see Hawkins E, *Modern languages in the curriculum:* 122–4 (CUP, 1987)

255

24

Developing pupil autonomy

Vee Harris

Autonomy in modern language learning: an impossible combination?

The changes in modern language teaching methods that swept through British classrooms from the 1960s to the 1980s could on one level be described as dramatic. The traditional emphasis on written grammatical accuracy gave way to the audio-visual approach, where pupils worked their way through oral drills, often in the language laboratory. The advent of comprehensives and the Graded Objectives in Modern Languages (GOML, see Chapter 7) movement saw further transformations to cater for the wider range of pupils studying modern languages. On another level, however, it could be said that little changed. Classrooms remained largely teacher-centred. Whatever the methodology, it was still the teacher who decided what was to be learned and how. It was the teacher who chose the activities that pupils would undertake and the pace at which they would work. And it was the teacher who assessed the pupils' progress.

In other subject areas, the notion of the teacher-dominated classroom was challenged during the 1970s and early 1980s. The work of Barnes, Britton and Rosen (1969) emphasised the notion of exploratory talk, of pupils making new knowledge their own by relating it to their own experiences, talking it through in their own way and learning from the insights of their peers. English, science and history lessons were transformed as pupils worked in small groups on problem-solving tasks and projects of their choice. These radical new developments faced modern language teachers with a problem. How could they be applied to our classrooms, when the situation of learning a new language was so very different from any other subject area? How could we put pupils into groups to discuss a particular issue, when they did not have the language they needed to discuss it? Where was the 'input' to come from, if not from the careful presentation and practice of the language by the teacher with the class as a whole? What would happen if the teacher was not there to correct immediately the inevitable errors that would arise? It seemed that it simply was not possible to shift towards a more pupil-centred approach within the unique constraints of modern language teaching.

The mid-1980s saw a number of developments that challenged this view and allowed us to move forward. As research into first and second language learning showed (Krashen, 1982; Littlewood, 1984), mistakes were part and parcel of the language learning process. It was argued that constant error correction by the teacher was not only unnecessary but might also inhibit pupils from beginning to express themselves in the language. With the advent of the communicative approach, this ability to convey and understand meaning had become a key aim in modern language teaching. Mistakes could be tolerated, provided they did not interfere with the message. Indeed, the popularisation of the communicative approach lead to some use of pair and group work, where pupils were free to carry out information gap activities and class surveys without direct teacher supervision. These activities still tended to come towards the end of the lesson, however, and the majority of the time was still devoted to whole class 'input' of the new language, which had been carefully selected by the teacher.

It was at this point that recent initiatives within adult education in Europe began to shape developments in Britain. Within the Council of Europe, there had been a concern to provide the EEC workforce with the tools they needed not just to learn a particular language but to acquire the skills to learn any new languages they might need in the course of their professional careers; in other words to make them autonomous language learners. The model of learning adopted turned the traditional teacher-centred approach on its head. Holec (1983) defined autonomy in this way:

Autonomy is when the learner is willing to and capable of taking charge of his own learning; i.e. independently:
- *choosing aims and purposes;*
- *choosing materials, methods and tasks;*
- *exercising choice and purpose in organising and carrying out the chosen tasks;*
- *choosing criteria for evaluation and using them in evaluation.*

Autonomy and self-directed learning: present fields of application (Holec (ed), 1988) presented a number of projects from across Europe, in which learners were encouraged to assess their own needs, work out their own learning programme, and evaluate their progress in fulfilling those needs. It was clear that there was much in these projects that related to the problems that we were facing in our own classrooms. Whilst the Graded Objectives movement had done much to improve extrinsic motivation, many pupils failed to identify with some of the topics and tasks that were presented to them. Had they had some control over their learning programme, they may well not have opted to learn to book into a hotel room or change travellers' cheques at the bank. Thus, however carefully we presented and practised the language in one lesson, by the next it had been forgotten. Pupils simply failed to engage with it in any meaningful way and as Stevick (1980) reminds us, for language to be retained, it has to 'strike deep'.

The fact that it was teachers who controlled what was to be learned, and how, had other implications apart from motivation. Johnstone, in a seminal publication in 1989, pointed out the dangers of presenting and practising language in neat, tidy packages. He warned that we were, albeit with the best intentions, protecting pupils from the reality and complexity of real language use and were failing to prepare them to handle the demands of genuine communication:

> *If learners are to cope with unpredictable obstacles that are somewhat beyond their competence at the time, inevitably an element of risk-taking is involved. This may imply quick thinking, imagination, initiative.*

How could pupils develop those skills as long as we were too scared to 'let go' and allow them to grapple with the language for themselves?

Over and above concerns about pupils' language learning, the notion of autonomy resonated with more general educational aims held by many of us. As Trim points out in his introduction to *Autonomy and self-directed learning* (Holec, 1983):

> *It is this willingness and ability to act independently as a socially responsible person, to take charge of one's own actions and one's own learning in the service of one's needs, that characterises autonomy. The person who achieves it has gone a long way to realise the Council of Europe's aim of a democratic European citizenry.*

The majority of the projects described in the book, however, were based on university students. To what extent could they be transferred to the secondary school context?

In January 1990, CILT organised a conference to bring together teachers who had been grappling with these issues. It generated so much enthusiasm and so many ideas, that a follow-up workshop was held in November of the same year. The resulting publications, *Autonomy in language learning* (Gathercole, 1990) and *Letting go – taking hold* (Page, 1992), suggest that modern language teaching is not unique; that we too can move towards more pupil-centred learning and, furthermore, that our secondary school pupils welcome the challenge.

Making autonomy work: a step at a time

What can be learned from the wealth of examples from practising teachers that the two books present? A recurring theme is that if pupils are to take over responsibility for their own learning, then it cannot be achieved overnight. Both we and they need time to adapt. As Nunan (1995) suggests:

It is a mistake to assume that learners come into the language classroom with a natural ability to make choices about what and how to learn.

Pupils then may need to be introduced to autonomous learning through a number of gradual steps. It may be helpful to locate those steps on a continuum, moving from one end where pupils have very little control over their learning to the other where much of it is in their hands. Some concrete examples may be useful at this point. The first steps may not necessarily be far removed from what is being done already.

Let us imagine, for example, a Year 8 class where the teacher introduces the topic of hobbies by inviting pupils to suggest vocabulary they feel is relevant, so that they will not be limited to those presented in the textbook. Playing darts or collecting posters of pop groups take their place alongside the more mundane (and somewhat middle class) tennis and horse-riding. Later, when the class is to answer orally questions on a reading passage, the teacher does not work through them from one to ten, but allows pupils to select which question they want to answer, inviting them at the end to make up additional questions for the class. For homework, pupils may choose from two to three tasks the one which seems most interesting or most within their capabilities.

The potential for differentiation is extended in the classroom next door, where Year 9 pupils, instead of working through the same tasks at the same pace, can choose from a menu of activities, with easier or more difficult tasks in each of the skill areas.

In the third classroom, we find a class of Year 11 pupils who have been discussing what to do about their mock GCSE results. They have decided that they need to revise the tenses and that each group will select a different tense and teach it to each other. As the teacher walks in, they are already at work, preparing the presentation of 'their tense', choosing from a range of textbooks and grammarbooks to get their ideas and devising worksheets, information gap activities and role plays for the rest of the class. The only constraints imposed by the teacher is first in terms of the deadline for the project and secondly that they should also produce a poem illustrating their tense in use. This same class is already familiar with taking charge of their own learning. On an exchange trip to France the previous year, they had been set the task of comparing the cost of living in France and Britain. It had been up to them to decide on the most useful information to collect, to research how to formulate their interview questions in French, and how best to present their evidence.

Levels of independence

These steps to autonomy can be considered as different degrees or levels of independence, as in table 1, where level 1 indicates modest beginnings and level 4 more developed opportunities for pupils to take charge of their own learning. The table also includes relevant page references from the two CILT publications. Based on Holec's definition, the key criterion for defining the levels is the degree of choice offered to pupils; choice over the aims or project to be embarked on, the outcomes or end products, the materials and tasks to be used and the pace of working. The descriptions under level 4 are highly ambitious and indeed may not be wholly appropriate in a secondary school context. It is worth noting however that any project undertaken by teachers can operate at a number of levels, according to what they judge is suitable for a particular class and in their particular school. Thus, in the example given earlier where pupils taught each other the tenses, although the pupils had control over the choice of project (level 4), the teacher had judged that there should be some constraints on the timetable and the pace at which they worked (level 3).

Table 1

CHOICE	Level 4	Level 3	Level 2	Level 1
Aims	Pupils determine what topic they are going to do and why, e.g. teach each other a tense.	Teacher determines broad scope of project, e.g. a magazine. Pupils choose themes within that, e.g. horoscope, problem page, etc.	Teacher determines project.	No long-term aims.
Outcomes	Pupils determine outcomes of project, e.g. report, oral presentation, etc.	Pupils and teacher may negotiate outcomes or teacher specifies several broad outcomes, e.g. prepare two role plays, a vocabulary list, etc	Teacher determines outcomes, e.g. brochure on school.	No long-term outcomes.
Materials	Pupils bring in or select from a wide range of materials.	Pupils choose from a range of materials provided by the teacher. They may switch materials if they are too easy.	Pupils choose from a limited menu, e.g. easy/harder materials or according to skill.	Carousel where all materials must be used.

CHOICE	Level 4	Level 3	Level 2	Level 1
Tasks	Pupils decide how they want to work on the materials. They may provide tasks for one another or across groups.	Pupils and teacher may negotiate how to work on the materials.	Task sheet with teacher-designed tasks, either over several weeks or over a term.	Teacher-designed tasks.
Pace	Pupils draw up own timetable.	Pupils draw up timetable within a deadline from the teacher, e.g. complete project in three weeks.	Pupils have some control of pace but within time constraint of each lesson.	Teacher moves pupils on at regular intervals in each lesson.
Homework	Pupils decide on appropriate home-work tasks. No checks from teacher required. Results shared with peers.	Pupils decide on appropriate home-work tasks within some general sugges-tions from the teacher. Teacher often checks tasks have been completed.	Pupils choose from a menu of possible homework tasks. Teacher regularly checks tasks have been completed.	Teacher sets home-work and always checks it's been completed.

Evaluation

The role of evaluation needs to be mentioned in its own right, since it is central to developing autonomy. The issue of the possible assessment criteria to be used in the autonomous classroom will be discussed later. Here the focus is on the complex relationship between assessment and the subsequent opportunities provided to the learner, since the more the pupil is invited to assess their own progress, the more choice they must have over the materials and tasks to be used in subsequent lessons. As Thorne and Corney point out:

> *A student is not well-served if assessment shows he/she needs more prac-tice with ordering railway tickets, whereupon the topic of railway stations is put aside and students are plunged into dealing with the chemist.*

The right to decide what to learn and how, however, assumes that pupils will make sensible and responsible choices based on an accurate assessment of their own strengths, weaknesses and needs. Again how-ever pupils cannot acquire overnight the ability to assess their own progress and devise appropriate remedial measures; it has to be built up through small steps.

Table 2

CHOICE	Level 4	Level 3	Level 2	Level 1
Evaluation	Pupils mark own work according to own criteria. They check accurately, keep their own record of marks, regularly log their own strengths and weaknesses in a diary and plan next lessons accordingly. They can evaluate the success of the project as a whole.	Pupils mark own work according to general criteria suggested by teacher. They keep a record of their marks. If prompted by teacher, they can evaluate their own strengths and weaknesses accurately. Teacher may test but at a time decided on by pupil.	Pupils mark own work using teacher's answer sheets. Some initial 'cheating'/copying. They keep a record of marks on teacher's 'chart' and assess each other's role plays. Teacher may use structured questionnaire to encourage self-assessment of strengths and weaknesses.	Teacher marks all work and directs what is to be done next lesson. Any pupil self-assessment is vague and undirected. Teacher tests all pupils together at a time he or she chooses.

The more advanced end of the continuum is evident in Steven Fawkes' account of his work with a Year 11 group, again preparing for their examinations. Resources were organised under the GCSE topic headings and a database provided, so that if, for example, pupils felt that they needed more work on 'speaking' in the context of 'the campsite', they could easily find the support materials they needed. Pupils undertook to cover all the skill areas in the course of a week, logging what they had covered in their *journal de travail.*

Although the two tables may be useful in indicating the small steps on the road to autonomy, they cannot do justice to the rich and detailed accounts of the teachers, who were willing to 'take risks' and 'let go' of control in their classrooms.

Within British universities, too, there have been similarly innovative developments, since Holec's pioneering work. The publication, *Promoting learner autonomy in university language teaching* (Broady and Kenning, 1996) provides an exciting account of the way university language teachers have responded to the recent widening of access to higher education and the resulting broader range of learning needs, styles and interests. To take just one example, students can now use *Le Monde sur CD-ROM* to access a wealth of newpaper material whether to investigate a political or social topic they have chosen to work on or to explore a particular lexical domain, such as differences in style and register across journalists' accounts.

Emerging problems

It would be misleading to suggest that the process of developing autonomy has been successfully accomplished. Certainly, the National Curriculum has provided additional impetus within the secondary school context. The initial draft recommendations (1990) heightened awareness by including in the Programmes of Study two key areas: 'Co-operation and interaction' and 'Intrinsic interest and independent learning'. The emphasis on differentiation and on Information Technology also encouraged us to move away from a teacher-dominated approach, since it seemed impossible to meet these requirements through whole class teaching. Yet many teachers who 'take the plunge' have at times felt disheartened at the results. Motivation may initially improve, but as the 'novelty value' wears off, recurrent difficulties emerge. There may be problems in group dynamics, with groups who do not 'jell', or pupils who 'opt out', leaving the others to do the work. Faced with reading longer pieces of authentic material without teacher support, some pupils panic and rapidly lose interest. They appear to lack basic reading strategies like looking for cognates or making sensible guesses based on the context, and it cannot even be assumed that they know how to use a dictionary (Grenfell and Harris, 1993). To make autonomy work, then, it may not be enough for the teacher to organise the classroom, offering a range of choices and resources. Pupils need the strategies and skills that will allow them to take advantage of the opportunities autonomy offers, to manage their learning without constant teacher support and to work collaboratively with their peers. It is interesting to note that even within the university context, problems may otherwise occur. Marshall in his chapter 'The rewards and pitfalls of autonomy' (Broady and Kenning, 1996) reports that:

> Individuals anxious to profit from the opportunities presented by autonomy found themselves frustrated by the inefficient workings of their group. This created tensions.

The last twenty years have seen a growth in research into such learner strategies. In the early days, it focused on identifying the strategies successful language learners use; the kinds of things that we, as successful aspiring linguists in school, probably did without thinking. We cannot assume, however, that our less successful pupils will automatically acquire them. It is possible that they may make greater progress if we 'let them in on the secret'; if we make explicit to them the tools that allowed us to become confident and competent language learners. Recent research (O'Malley and Chamot, 1990; Wenden, 1991) has begun to explore the effects of such strategy training. Many of the findings, however, relate to university students often learning English, rather than our own secondary school pupils learning German, French or Spanish. This was one of the reasons why an MA module was set up in 1994 by Goldsmiths College, working in collaboration with CILT. Participants on the module have set about teaching pupils either reading or memorisation strategies and evaluating their responses. A more detailed account of how they went about it can be found in a recent publication by Scottish CILT (Harris, 1995). Although it could be argued that there is insufficient time within an already overcrowded timetable to embark on strategy training, the results of their projects suggest that pupils have much to gain, provided strategies are systematically taught and extensively practised.

Use of the target language

A final problem is the use of the target language, both within strategy training and more generally when pupils are working in groups. It seems that discussions with younger pupils on strategy use may well have to take place in English, the 'pay off' being the eventual improvement in their ability to access authentic material, memorise words, etc. In terms of group discussions, it is undoubtedly difficult to ensure that these pupils do not resort to English to negotiate who is going to do what for the project and when. However, the video *In focus* (Bromidge and Burch, 1993) does suggest an initial step forward, where pupils are first taught the language they will need for planning their work before embarking on the project itself. Moira Edmunds (1995) suggests a further step which both develops target language use and fosters collaborative skills. Members of each group are assigned clear roles with specific areas of language to use; for example the discussion leader says, *on commence, à toi maintenant,* the time-keeper says, *il reste cinq minutes* and so on. Again, this takes time to teach but if our aim is communication, there is surely no more real communicative context than the classroom itself.

Additional levels of autonomy

Table 3 attempts to describe these additional aspects of autonomy in terms of the degrees or levels. Along with Table 2, it might be used not just to indicate the small steps that can be taken towards achieving autonomy but to suggest additional criteria that may come into play in assessing pupils in an autonomous classroom; their ability to assess their own strengths and weaknesses accurately, to select appropriate learning strategies, to work effectively in groups, or to use the target language throughout the lesson. Alongside the criteria of linguistic accuracy and fluency associated with the teacher-centred classroom, we may also need to chart the development of these other skills. How else can we compare a pupil with a limited grasp of the language, but who is open and honest in evaluating strengths and weaknesses, with a more able linguist who is reluctant to acknowledge and work on areas of difficulty? And how do we reward and recognise the pupil who shows initiative in setting up and organising a project, while at the same time being careful to support and encourage others in the group?

Table 3

CHOICE	Level 4	Level 3	Level 2	Level 1
Strategies	Pupils can readily identify and use the most appropriate strategies to complete a task.	With some general prompting, pupils are able to use a wide range of appropriate strategies.	Pupils are taught some basic strategies for accessing reading/listening materials, e.g. dictionary use, reading skills. They need constant reminders to use them, e.g. checklists.	Strategies have not been taught and pupils may or may not use them.
Participation	All pupils participate fully throughout the lesson, without any intervention from the teacher. They find extra materials/tasks for themselves when they are ready.	Most pupils are 'on task' throughout most of the lesson.	Pupils settle down quickly to the tasks. Teacher may need to intervene with some pupils who are 'off task' at various points in lesson.	Pupils may waste time, especially 'getting started'. Teacher may need to intervene at regular points in lesson.
Effective group work	Pupils are able to collaborate effectively with all members of the class.	Some pupils may facilitate the learning of 'weaker' members of the group.	Teacher makes explicit the 'ground rules' for collaboration. Pupils begin to work effectively with unfamiliar members of the class.	Pupils may collaborate with friends but may sometimes use the opportunity to 'mess about'. Some resistance to working with unfamiliar members of the class.
Use of target language	All pupils use the target language with each other throughout the lesson for a range of functions including the negotiation of tasks.	Teacher teaches the language needed for group discussion. Some pupils begin to use it when prompted. Pupils have assigned roles and language to use for group work.	All instructions in target language. Most pupils attempt to use the target language with each other at some points in the lesson for limited functions, e.g. borrowing pens, etc.	Pupils use English when working together. Some instructions may be in English.

Adapted from Harris V, *Letting go — taking hold* (p7), Huttunen I, *Autonomy and self-directed learning* (Chapter 2) and Dickinson L, *Autonomy and foreign language learning* (p5)

The high level of participation and collaboration indicated for level 4 may seem like an unattainable goal, especially within a secondary school context. However, thirty years ago, it seemed impossible even to embark on the journey towards developing autonomous learning and yet we are now well on the road. There are many challenges that still lie ahead but they may not be insurmountable, if we can keep in mind Brian Page's (1992) timely reminder that *teachers can teach as much as they like but only learners learn.*

References

Barnes D, J Britton and H Rosen, *Language, the learner and the school* (Penguin, 1969)

Broady E and M-M Kenning, *Promoting learner autonomy in university language teaching* (CILT, 1996)

Bromidge W and J Burch, *In focus: the languages classroom – learning to communicate* (CILT, 1993)

Department of Education and Science, *Modern languages for 11 to 16* (HMSO, 1990)

Edmunds M (1995) 'Problem-solving using classroom research: some experiments in improving writing, motivation and learning' in *Modern languages policy and practice,* 1 (Scottish CILT, 1995)

Gathercole I (ed), *Autonomy in language learning* (CILT, 1990)

Grenfell M and V Harris, 'How do pupils learn? (Part 1)' in *Language Learning Journal,* 8: 22–25 (1993)

Harris V, 'Developing communicative competence through learner strategies' in *Modern languages policy and practice,* 3 (Scottish CILT, 1995)

Holec H, *Autonomy and foreign language learning* (Pergamon, 1983)

Holec H (ed), *Autonomy and self-directed learning: present fields of application* (Council of Europe, 1988)

Johnstone R, *Communicative interaction, a guide for language teachers* (CILT, 1989)

Krashen S D, *Principles and practice in second language acquisition* (Pergamon, 1982)

Littlewood W, *Foreign and second language learning; language acquisition research and its implications for the classroom* (Cambridge University Press, 1984)

Nunan D, 'Closing the gap between learning and instruction' in *TESOL Quarterly,* 29: 133–158

O'Malley J M and A U Chamot, *Learning strategies in second language acquisition* (Cambridge University Press, 1990)

Page B (ed), *Letting go – taking hold* (CILT, 1992)

Stevick E, *A way and ways* (Newbury House, 1980)

Thorne S and K Corney, 'Give pupils autonomy' in *German Teaching,* 10: 2–5 (1994)

Wenden A, *Learner strategies for learner autonomy* (Prentice Hall, 1991)

Part

seven

**Who trains
the trainers?**

1966-1996 **YEARS**

had been appointed, typically, on the strength of some ten years of successful teaching including, usually, some experience as a head of department. The authority they quoted for their injunctions was normally that of their own experience. Few had higher degrees in education and in many places there was little opportunity to obtain such a qualification. The cliché of the time was that our ideas about teaching method were essentially 'pre-theoretical'. In so far as it was supposed that research would provide guidance to modern language teachers in their classroom practice it was expected that this would be in the field of Psychology or the emerging discipline of Linguistics rather than in the rigorous study of classroom activity itself.

Though most tutors would no doubt have given lip-service to the goal of communication, there were certainly some who saw little beyond the aim of achieving good examination results, and it was not at all uncommon for Modern Language Methods sessions to bear such titles as 'Teaching prose composition', 'The 150-word essay', 'The Literature paper' or 'Preparing for the 'O' level examination'. The value of assessement was generally agreed to be 'keeping pupils on their toes' or 'giving them something to aim at'.

It is true that there were tutors in some departments of education who challenged the prevailing grammar-translation approach. In all but the best of such cases, however, the positive injunction that language was to be learnt in the process of meaningful communication tended to be transmuted into the negative one of simply avoiding the use of English. Little attention was given to the actual techniques of presenting new material in the target language, dealing with the question of meaning or organising intensive practice or genuine communicative activity, so that, once in the classroom even the most idealistic students had little to fall back on but the methods they themselves had experienced as pupils.

Separation between periods in the training institution and school experience was all but hermetic, both chronologically and in terms of the pedagogic messages conveyed. A period of pre-course experience was normally completely unsupervised. Students then typically experienced a period, often the whole autumn term, in the department itself interrupted only by staged demonstration lessons or visits to schools where particularly good or innovative activities were taking place. The school experience, again often lasting a whole term, was usually one of total immersion in which the less robust were in danger of sinking without trace, followed by a return to the university in the summer to prepare for the 'theory' examination in the four 'disciplines' of education (Philosophy, Psychology, Sociology and History), Health Education and Teaching Method.

Arrangements between university departments and schools were essentially informal and mutual responsibilities undefined. Schools gained no obvious or tangible benefit from receiving a student and regarded doing so as a favour to the university. Students were regarded as 'guests' in the school, being expected to show due appreciation and give as little extra trouble as possible. There was usually no role corresponding to that of the modern professional tutor, and the task of 'looking after' a student would fall to the head of department who did not usually feel able to delegate it to a colleague. The responsibility was often accepted willingly, in the same spirit as organising the annual visit to France or Germany. Seeing the extra commitment as a quasi-voluntary one, however, the head of department did not expect it to be onerous or to be overseen in his or her manner of discharging it, least of all by the university department for whom the favour of accepting a student was being done.

Relations between tutors and school modern language departments were often less than cordial, particularly when the tutor was thought to favour such undignified novelties as using the target language to communicate with pupils or employing visual aids of any description. Tutors were often disparaging of school staff, especially the more established and experienced heads of department whom students might reasonably have been expected to regard as proper role models. By the same token, many former students, now colleagues of some thirty years' standing in the profession, will recall being told quite explicitly to forget what they had been told in the university department, now that they were 'in the real world'. School staff were, nevertheless, often highly protective towards 'their' students on the occasion of the tutor's visit or dreaded 'examination lesson'. On those occasions students were given full liberty to employ the methods required by their tutors and classes were adjured to good behaviour on pain of death. After the tutor's departure the student's lessons would naturally return to 'normal'.

Relations between tutors and schools tended, in fact, to be more social than professional. Drinking coffee and engaging in small-talk with the head teacher while missing the greater part of the lesson one had come to see was an experience suffered by many tutors. Many, however, would hope to escape being 'caught' at the end of the lesson by the head of department who, for his or her part, would often seek to avoid the encounter, either for diplomatic reasons or because they simply had a class to teach and no time to waste. Discussion of the student's lesson was most comfortably done in the absence of the head of department or class teacher who might be expected to find the tutor's views at variance with their own.

Under the circumstances, Modern Languages tutors in university departments of Education, like their colleagues in other subjects, often felt that with the best will in the world they were sometimes less than fully effective in influencing the future classroom practice of their students.

The process of change

In the period falling roughly between the signalling of comprehensive re-organisation (1965) and the introduction of GCSE (1988) three important factors have affected both the importance and the manner of initial teacher education in modern languages. These have been the need to develop and train our students in the use of teaching methods appropriate to pupils of a much wider range of ability, the development of recording technology and its various attempted applications in language teaching, and the coming of serious research in language acquisition and learning.

When the schools in which our students were to teach ceased to resemble those which they themselves had attended, it was no longer sufficient for them to model themselves on the attitudes and conduct of their own teachers. They needed to be taught new approaches and techniques, many of which were yet to be devised. Both they and their tutors lacked the resources of reflection and experience possessed by those working in other subjects already taught across the full age and ability range.

In this connection the Primary School French Pilot Scheme launched in 1963 was of signal importance. Certain French native speakers with primary school training and experience demonstrated beyond doubt that a foreign language could be taught without recourse to traditional grammar translation methods. At the same time the Nuffield Foundation/Schools Council Materials Development Project based at York University set about developing teaching methods and materials (*En avant*) for children of primary school age and all abilities. Tutors and others with an interest in language teaching at all ages were for a time swept along by the prestige and momentum of the Pilot Scheme in its early stages. Though their own experience had for the most part been in traditional schools using mainly traditional methodology, many tutors became involved in the training of Pilot Scheme primary school teachers and were thus brought into contact with the underlying approaches and assumptions generated by the Nuffield team. Foremost among these assumptions was the view that a foreign language not only should but perfectly well could be taught to children of all abilities.

In the belief that Primary French was here to stay and encouraged by government, a number of Colleges of Education instituted BEd courses in French many of which contained strong audio-visual/language laboratory components in both their subject knowledge and their methodology elements. In 1960 a main French course had already been offered in 37 colleges. By 1966 the number had risen to 63 and by 1970 to 91. By 1977, however, this had declined to 58 (Hoy, 1970) and continued to fall rapidly during the 1980s. Though this development was relatively short-lived, one important aspect of its significance lay in the fact that it provided a timely injection into the language teaching profession of a number of trained teachers whose ethos and commitments were those of the colleges of education and the primary school rather than the grammar school and the traditional university.

The inclusion in the various Nuffield packages of audio-visual elements and related technology, not to mention the ferment of excitement surrounding the many in-service courses by which the scheme was supported, endowed those tutors and rapidly increasing numbers of language advisers committed to the scheme with considerable prestige. Though the behaviourist psychology and brand of descriptive linguistics upon which audio-visual and, somewhat later, audio-lingual and other language laboratory courses were based were soon to be transcended, the die was cast. The new approach to modern language teaching was seen to be backed by theory, with the result that tutors, having previously been little more than dispensers of wise saws and anecdotal instances, were able to become experts in their own right, with a genuine body of knowledge and specific skills to impart.

The pervasive hold of audio-visual theories and teaching methods on progressive modern linguists at that time is indicated by the fact that, when a new association of modern language teachers was founded in 1969 it was called the Audio-Visual Language Association (AVLA), though it was later to be renamed the British Association for Language Teaching. Many of the most progressive and influential modern language tutors in the seventies were leading members of the newly formed association, and key articles from the *AVLA Journal* provided a ready source of up-to-date prescribed reading on Modern Languages for initial teacher training courses. In the new situation of rapid educational change, successful tutoring was felt by many universities to require a measure of intellectual and educational sophistication beyond that provided by successful teaching experience alone, and this need was met by an increase in the number of courses for the MEd and other higher degrees in education.

During the 1970s and early 1980s important changes took place in the theoretical background upon which language teaching, and therefore the training of language teachers, was premised. Crude frequency counting, as the means of establishing the content of language courses, was replaced by the concept of communicative competence leading to the elaboration of notional-functional syllabuses (Wilkins, 1972 and 1976; Trim and others, 1973), while behaviourist notions of repetition, reinforcement and over-learning as the basis of language learning gave way to an appreciation that language is naturally acquired when it is employed for the purposes of genuine communication, ideally in conditions of reduced stress (Krashen, 1981).

The idea of notional-functional syllabuses, and particularly that of language functions, was to prove exceedingly helpful in presenting new approaches to language learning to students whose own language learning experience and views of acceptable language performance had been formed in the grammar-translation tradition. Once it was perceived that language was not so much an academic performance as a form of goal directed behaviour, it became easier to accept that utterances which, whatever their grammatical shortcomings, achieved a measure of communication, merited at least some positive credit. The Graded Objectives movement (Page and Harding, 1974; see also Chapter 7 in this volume) made it possible to recognise the validity of the language learning achievements of the least able pupils in the lower forms of comprehensive schools. Five television programmes, produced by the BBC in collaboration with CILT and broadcast in early 1979 (BBC/CILT, 1979), were widely recorded in departments of education and found invaluable by tutors in presenting the rationale and methodologies of this movement to students.

The conclusions of the Strasbourg Studies of notional-functional syllabuses and the related threshold level, and the resultant thinking that lay behind the Graded Objectives movement, were widely welcomed by teachers and ultimately became the basis of GCSE language syllabuses and thus, indirectly, of the present National Curriculum for Modern Foreign Languages. The implications of language acquisition theory underlie not only our present concern with the use of the target language as the principal medium of communication in the classroom, but also many of the pair and groupwork activities, language learning games and other activities involving the genuinely meaningful use of language which we train our students to use today.

Training to teach modern languages today

Present-day tutors in university departments of education find it hard to recall that if, in the past, an institution chose to offer a Certificate of Education qualifying holders to teach in schools, the length, content, structure and objectives of that course were largely a matter for the institution itself.

The scenario for the present situation was set as early as 1983 in the White Paper *Teaching quality* (DES, 1983) in which it was proposed that the Secretary of State should promulgate criteria against which courses for accreditation should be reviewed. Those criteria were set out in the following year in DES Circular 3/84 (DES, 1984) along with arrangements for the establishment of the Council for the Accreditation of Teachers (CATE) by which the application of those criteria was to be overseen. Though CATE has come and gone and Circular 3/84 has been followed by a string of further documents – the White Paper *Better schools* (DES, 1985), the 1988 Education Reform Act itself and, following it, the two Circulars 24/89 (DES, 1989) and 9/92 (DES, 1992) – the main thrusts of Government policy are already present in Circular 3/84 (DES, 1984).

Among other things the policy has aimed at closer co-operation and partnership between teacher training institutions and schools, ensuring a higher proportion of teacher trainers with recent and relevant teaching experience, ensuring a closer match between methods work at the training institution and practical classroom teaching in accordance with the National Curriculum, and increasing the length and value of school experience.

Two further direct effects have been to ensure that institutions set out the aims, content, procedures and staffing of their courses in specific detail and to empower the Office for Standards in Education (OFSTED) to inspect and appraise courses of teacher education in terms of their quality and conformity with government policy. Courses which are deemed to be below standard or not to comply must either be put right or closed down. DES Circular 9/92, the current document governing initial teacher training, lays down certain requirements with respect to students' school experience and lists the competences they must achieve in order to qualify. It also requires that a substantial proportion of the budget which institutions receive for the purposes of initial teacher training must, in one way or another, be transferred to schools in respect of their contribution to the students' training.

The precise manner in which this takes place varies somewhat between institutions and much discussion and experimentation is at present taking place to find the most successful format. Schools normally receive a down-payment in keeping with their contribution to each student's training, supervision and eventual assessment. It is common for institutions to buy in part of the time of a number of teachers from local schools to act as part-time tutors. The essential requirement, however, is that there should exist a quasi-legal partnership agreement between the institution and the schools with which it works that spells out explicitly the respective responsibilities of the various institution and school personnel involved in the training process. In particular, nominated members of school staff, usually referred to as mentors, are now expected to undertake the main responsibility for teaching students their classroom skills and assessing their competence. During periods of school experience the role of the university tutor is, in the main, to monitor and ensure that this is being done, and to provide support and advice for the mentor as necessary. One unfortunate side-effect of requiring HE institutions to develop formal partnership arrangements with particular schools, under which the school may receive as many as ten or a dozen students in all subjects, has been to put pressure on the training of students to teach the less widely taught languages. Many tutors now find it extremely difficult to arrange school experience in these languages within the limited circle of their institution's partner schools.

As it became clear that the staffing resources of institutions would become increasingly limited a number of long established tutors were persuaded to retire. Where these colleagues have been replaced this has usually been by staff on short-term contracts or by colleagues on a part-time secondment basis from school, because of uncertainty about the future role of institutions of higher education in initial teacher training.

From the students' point of view the immediate effect of this will be that they will receive much less methods tuition at the institution – sometimes as little as one session a week – and this will often be provided by some-one appointed locally on an ad hoc basis rather than someone recruited to a permanent post by national competition probably with higher qualifica-tions in education, a research record and intellectual interest in the nature and potentialities of language acquisition and learning. In the short term this may be a change for the better in that the increased period of school experience and more systematic supervision by the school mentor will undoubtedly produce teachers who at least at the start of their careers are more confident and street-wise than their predecessors.

As against this, it is feared by some that it may produce teachers whose interest is narrowly focused on skill-based classroom teaching, ill equipped either to carry forward the development of more valid approaches to language teaching or evaluate judiciously changing fashions in the subject, or later shifts in government policy. Others have expressed the more profound anxiety that if the new-style teachers produced by the present arrangements appear adequate to the purposes of whatever government happens to be in power in the future, the question may be raised as to whether it remains expedient to maintain the link between the training of teachers and institutions of higher education.

References

BBC/CILT, *Modern language teaching: five case studies in comprehensive schools*, five twenty-five minute television programmes produced by the BBC in conjunction with CILT and broadcast in February–March 1979 (London: BBC, 1979)

Department of Education and Science (DES), *Teaching quality* (London: HMSO, 1983)

Department of Education and Science (DES), Circular 3/84, *The accreditation of courses of initial teacher training* (London: Department of Education and Science, 1984)

Department of Education and Science (DES), *Better schools* (London: HMSO, 1985)

Department of Education and Science (DES), Circular 24/89, *Initial teacher training* (London: Department of Education and Science, 1989)

Department of Education and Science (DES), Circular 9/92, *Initial teacher training (secondary phase)* (London: Department of Education and Science, 1992)

Harding A and B Page, 'An alternative model model for modern language examinations' in *AVLA Journal*, 12/3 (1974)

Hoy P, *The early teaching of modern languages* (London: The Nuffield Foundation, 1977)

Krashen S, *Principles and practice in second language acquisition* (Englewood Cliffs, N J: Prentice-Hall, 1981)

Trim J M L and others, *Systems development in adult language learning* (1973)

Van Ek J A, *The threshold level* (Strasbourg, Council of Europe, 1975; also published in London by Pergamon, 1980)

Wilkins D A, *An investigation into the linguistic and situational content of the common core in a unit/credit system* (Strasbourg: Council of Europe, 1972)

Wilkins D A, *Notional syllabuses* (London: Oxford University Press, 1976)

277

26
Towards a new partnership

Cathy Pomphrey

It cannot be said that government policy alone is responsible for the substantial changes which have recently taken place in initial teacher education (ITE). As Margaret Wilkin (1992) states:

Professional initiatives and government measures have both contributed to the restructuring of the balance of control and influence in the relationship between training institutions and schools.

Colin Wringe (see Chapter 25) shows how the preparation of languages teachers for the profession has been affected by such factors as comprehensivisation, new technology and research into language acquisition and learning. He goes on to demonstrate that factors such as these have caused the professionals to rethink how theory and practice are linked and what the content of school placement activities during the training period should be.

Effects of the National Curriculum

The arrival of the National Curriculum meant a change in the needs of those entering the teaching profession. The statutory framework implies a different view of what might constitute the professional judgement of a languages teacher. Some methodological decisions such as teaching through the target language, classroom assessment as an integral part of the teaching process and use of communicative language teaching activities are no longer left to the discretion of the modern languages department or the individual teacher. Professional judgement post National Curriculum is now more concerned with the interpretation of the Programme of Study with reference to the teaching context or relating levels of achievement to pupils' responses and performances during classroom tasks and activities. In addition, future languages teachers must be prepared to deal with the range of texts, topics, and audience which feature in the National Curriculum. Languages for all (11–16) implies a need for Equal Opportunities understanding to be integrated with classroom practice so that access to the National Curriculum for all, including those pupils with Special Educational Needs, is assured. Teaching the National Curriculum in modern languages involves considerable skill in, for example, use of technology, promoting independent learning, developing cultural and linguistic awareness within a communicative approach or the assessment and recording of pupil progress.

Thus preparation for teaching implies developing in the future teacher a complex interrelation of judgement, knowledge, skills and personality.

The statutory framework of the National Curriculum has enabled a more uniform identification of the skills involved in teaching a modern language in this country. This has contributed to a movement towards a skills-led (training) approach to ITE programmes and away from an emphasis on a theory-led critical awareness (education) approach.

The effects of teacher shortages

The languages for all (11–16) policy of the National Curriculum brought with it concerns about teacher shortages. One solution of government policy-makers was an increase in the number of routes into teaching, particularly in shortage subjects such as modern languages. Thus the 1980s and 90s have seen a proliferation of new schemes such as the *Articled teachers* (the first cohort was in 1990 and the scheme ran for three years in the secondary phase – see DES, 1989), *Licensed teachers* (see DES, 1988) and *Overseas teachers* schemes (introduced in 1991). The training for these schemes was usually coordinated by LEAs, although higher education institutes (HEIs) were often involved, particularly in accreditation. These schemes provided employment-based training with an emphasis on skills development rather than on education in theoretical principles. The concept of the 'school mentor' arose from such initiatives, along with an apprenticeship model of training involving observation of experienced teachers and **learning on the job.** Although there were criticisms from many quarters and on the whole these routes into teaching have so far made only a small contribution to teacher recruitment in shortage subjects, much was learned from them about the mentoring role and the potential of school-based training. This was particularly true of the *Articled teachers'* scheme, which was found to be a costly model of training and was discontinued in 1993 in the secondary phase. There were also new initiatives among the more traditional routes into teaching, with some HEIs introducing shortened (usually two year) BEd courses or part-time PGCEs and later the Open University distance learning PGCE. Of particular importance was the Oxford Internship programme (see Benton, 1990) which contributed some useful findings on school-based training and was to have an impact on later government policy.

National policy for Initial Teacher Education

The 1989 DES circular 24/89, calling for **recent and relevant** school teaching experience by HEI tutors involved in ITE programmes, led to further reviews of school and HEI roles. However, the most radical policy change was brought about by DFE circular 9/92.

This circular implied legislation which included the following requirements:

- formal ITT partnership agreements between HEIs and schools;
- school-based training for two-thirds of PGCE courses;
- major changes in the balance of roles and responsibilities between HEIs and schools, with schools taking a major training and assessment role as well as involvement in recruitment and course planning;
- a framework of competences with explicit criteria relating to subject knowledge, subject application, class management, assessment and recording of progress and further professional development as a basis for assessment of school experience.

For most ITE courses the principles of collaboration between HEI and schools, the addressing of the skills (or competences) associated with the National Curriculum and the application of theory to practice through activities such as micro teaching, classroom (action) research, profiling and reflection on practical experience were already evolving before the appearance of circular 9/92. However, the speed of the statutory changes, the extent of the required school responsibility and the resource implications for HEIs of transferring funding to schools for school-based work were at first devastating to HEIs and to some schools. Some HEIs which previously collaborated locally now find themselves in competition with each other for partnership with schools who want to streamline the extra administration associated with partnership ITE courses by working with only one institution. Some schools withdrew from participation in what they saw as an additional burdensome pressure, especially in areas with higher staffing turnover, such as inner cities. Staffing cuts in HEIs were often an unwelcome consequence of the new legislation.

In addition to partnership schemes which share responsibilities for ITE provision between HEIs and schools, new legislation means that teacher training can now be provided as School Centred Initial Teacher Training (SCITT). In SCITT schemes, schools are fully responsible for the organisation of the training programme, although most have maintained some links with HEIs and receive accreditation from HEIs. To date there are four SCITT schemes which provide for modern languages graduates.

Problems of partnership

Now that the dust has settled a little after the explosion of national policy change of the late 1980s and early 1990s, it is possible to get a clearer picture of the consequences, both negative and positive, for the initial preparation of modern language teachers. Schemes range from exclusively school-based training to partnership arrangements with a variety of models for HEI and school collaboration. The most common problems seem to arise from the need for formalised partnership agreements which are usually made at whole school level across a range of subject areas. This has affected the choice and flexibility of placement available for student teachers in specific subject areas. In some cases the quality of placement can be an issue, where a school regarded as strong overall (and hence suitable for partnership) may have weaknesses in individual subject areas. Such problems often become more acute for modern language teaching placements because of the range of languages for which placements are sought. The survey of the CILT Teacher Training Working Group, carried out in Autumn 1995, reports:

Because of the great variability in the quality of placements, teacher trainers expressed concerns about the comparability of the experience offered to the students. (Hansford and Hurman, 1996)

In particular there is concern for languages other than French.

Italian (with one or two exceptions) and Russian were reported as particularly problematic . . . The less widely taught the language, the more difficult it was to find placements. Institutions up and down the country reported increased difficulty in finding placements for Spanish, even though there was a supply of trainees and a demand for trained teachers. (Hansford and Hurman, 1996)

In some cases partnership requirements are having to be interpreted more flexibly to provide placements in non-partnership schools.

Another concern is the danger of narrowing the focus of future teachers to skill-based classroom teaching devoid of theoretical principles on which to base wider professional judgements (see Colin Wringe, p276). Michael Grenfell (1996) discusses the question of what we mean by theory in relation to initial teacher programmes and suggests that professional development in the course of a teacher's career involves a progression in terms of rationalisation of practice and theoretical underpinning. He reminds us of the importance of a personal theoretical rationale derived from reading of research as a basis for owning practical competence: *Developing a personal theoretical perspective is at the heart of developing as an independent professional* (Grenfell, 1996). A critical enquiring attitude is a vital aspect of the language teacher's professionalism. This is a useful warning of the dangers of moving too far in the direction of an exclusively apprenticeship model of teacher development, where an over-literal emphasis on teaching strategies, competences and practical experience without any theoretical basis could result in a mechanical view of teaching which belies the teacher's professionalism.

282

Tailoring the partnership

As they implement the requirements of circular 9/92, teacher educators in schools and HEIs are shaping their own interpretations of partnership in relation to ITE programmes. While many problems have still to be solved, the benefits of partnership are also emerging and some exciting challenges coming into view. The highly successful CILT conference *Partners* in 1993 at the West Country Comenius Centre in Exeter enabled HEI-based and school-based providers of modern languages ITE courses to share experiences, hopes and worries in an atmosphere of optimism and creative energy. Further conferences and publications have followed, including the development of the LINKS bulletin 'for all involved in the training of language teachers', which has grown from a small newsheet to a professional journal with articles from a range of contributors. Such events and publications continue to highlight the problems encountered in partnership schemes, but also provide a forum for professional debate. As a result, ITE providers are more able to tailor partnership schemes to the specific needs of modern languages and to the strengths and priorities of the individual schools and HEIs involved. While the main emphasis of circular 9/92 is on enhancing school responsibility, many schools and HEIs prefer to give more priority to the relationship between partners and the potential of that relationship to enhance the coherence and consistency of the student teacher's experience. As Vee Harris (1993) states:

> *Although it is institutions and schools who set up and administer the partnership schemes, it is the individual tutors, teachers and trainees who must make it work, since they are key members of the partnership.*

Benefits of partnership

As well as the potential dangers already mentioned, changes in approaches to the theoretical content of ITE courses are showing some beneficial effects, not least in increasing coherence of experience for the student teacher. Following Schön's concept of the reflective practitioner (Schön, 1983), the

ITE providers of the 1990s attempt to break down the processes involved in applying theory to practice. In doing so they avoid the assumption of an over simplistic connection between theory and practice and enable student teachers to construct their own interpretations. This is inevitably more possible with current communicative language teaching approaches which are more broadly linked to theory than with the specifically theory-led methodologies of the past. Coherence is achieved in a number of different ways. Closer school and HEI cooperation can enable ITE course structures to allow analytical reflection to be linked in a very immediate way with specific classroom experiences such as observation, team teaching or investigations. Trainers in the HEI often model appropriate classroom practice while teaching about theory, for example by teaching a new language to student teachers who can analyse their own learning in the light of theoretical principles at the same time as they experience the practical strategies used.

Another way into these processes is via the profiling of teaching competence. Profiling of student teachers helps to make reflection, target setting and application of principles to practice a reality. It can also provide an effective communication tool for partners. While the competence list is often criticised as an assessment measure, many find it a useful basis for dialogue and reflection in the formative profiling of developing teachers.

Perhaps one of the most notable benefits of partnership has been the professional development available to the mentor. This new role is a key aspect of such an arrangement. Barry Jones (1993) lists the range of functions in which the mentor is likely to be engaged from modelling good practice to teaching, facilitating, managing and appraising the whole developmental process. This enables mentors, by articulating their own practice in training student teachers, to develop as practitioners themselves – the old adage that teaching something is the best way to learn more about it seems to apply very well to teaching how to teach. The collaboration with HEI means greater access to reading and research issues for practising teachers than has formerly been the case. Most partnerships have derived much benefit from mentor training and the need for continuing the dialogue generated by initial mentor training experiences is now being felt. Sarah Fletcher and Mike Calvert (1994) state:

Mentor development after the initial period of training is having a very positive and modifying effect on old boundaries and practices inside schools.

The future of partnership

A more continuous relationship between theory and practice during the training period could mean that teacher education and training does not have to stop at the end of the PGCE. The newly formed government agency, the Teacher Training Agency (TTA), has already demonstrated an interest in teacher effectiveness and continuing professional development for teachers as well as classroom-based research by practising teachers. Continuous professional development implies in-service training which is not just adding to the teacher's repertoire of teaching strategies and materials but access to theory, research and analytical evaluation of classroom practice. The growing interest in action research could be enhanced by clearer communication channels between HEIs and schools:

A collaborative action research framework can lend a greater degree of credibility to the interpretation of evidence than a lone classroom-visiting researcher necessarily achieves, however skilled or experienced that 'outside' researcher may be. (Peck and Westgate, 1994)

The challenges of achieving a dynamic collaboration between HEI and school partners in ITE courses must not be underestimated. However, with appropriate national commitment and resourcing, the productive dialogue emerging in Initial Teacher partnerships could be extended to include further professional development for teachers, particularly in the area of collaborative classroom-based research. If this were to happen, the struggle to redefine roles and relationships between schools and HEIs for Initial Teacher Education could lay the foundations for some exciting future challenges.

References

Benton P (ed), *The Oxford internship scheme* (London: Gulbenkian Foundation, 1990)

DES, *Qualified teacher status: a consultation document* (DES, 1988)

DES, *Articled teacher pilot scheme: invitation to bid for funding* (DES, 1989)

DES circular 24/89 59/89 (Welsh Office), *Initial Teacher Training: approval of courses*

DFE circular 9/92 35/92 (Welsh Office), *Initial Teacher Training (secondary phase)*

Fletcher S and M Calvert, *Working with your student teacher* (Cheltenham: Mary Glasgow Publications, 1994)

Grenfell M (1996), 'Theory and practice in modern language teacher training' in *LINKS* no 14 (spring 1996)

Hansford R and J Hurman, 'The CILT/Teacher Training Working Group survey: teaching practice in languages other than French' in *LINKS* no14 (spring 1996)

Harris V, 'Partners are people – relationships in partnership schemes' in Thorogood J (ed), see below

Jones B, 'How trainers can help trainees achieve competence' in Thorogood J (ed), see below

Partners! Report on the 1993 Initial Teacher Training Conference at the West Country Comenius Centre, Exeter (CILT, 1993)

Peck A and D Westgate (eds), *Language teaching in the mirror* (CILT, 1994)

Schon D, *The reflective practitioner: how professionals think in action* (London: Temple Smith, 1983)

Thorogood J (ed), *Partners – a guide to school-based initial teacher training in modern languages* (CILT, 1993)

Wilkin M, *Mentoring in schools* (London: Kogan Page, 1992)

27
In-service training and support for
teachers

Alan Moys

In a generation which has been dominated by the information revolution, it is not surprising that the acronym has become a central (if often inelegant) element in everyday communication. Every field of activity seems to have its own acronymic repertoire, more often than not impenetrable to the outside world. In the language teaching field, the 1960s produced a modest but interesting crop, including some acronyms which did not outlive the period under review, such as CRDML and AVLA. These both gave birth to distinguished offspring, which in turn were known best by their acronymic titles. It was the government-funded Committee for Research and Development in modern languages which prompted the establishment of CILT in 1966; and the somewhat oddly named Audio-Visual Language Association rapidly developed into a much more broadly based association for the professional development of language teachers under yet another acronym, BALT, the British Association for Language Teaching. Language teachers had to come to terms with CREDIF, SCMLP, GOML, CALL, FLAW, ALL and the onward march of bodies such as CILT, CBEVE, NCET and NALA (see Appendix IV). For the truly masochistic *The dictionary of acronyms and abbreviations in applied linguistics and language learning* (Jung H and UOH, Peter Lang, Frankfurt, 1991) runs to 800 pages and 13,000 entries over two volumes.

Among these acronyms, INSET may not have been coined in 1966 as the standard term for the professional in-service development of teachers, but it was the explosion of organisational and methodological change from about 1960 onwards which created the need for the expansion of provision of teacher support and training. This was particularly evident in the case of languages, the teaching of which was moving into new territory with developments such as primary French and, at secondary school level, the extension of language learning into the curriculum of all pupils as comprehensive education gained ground. It is worth looking more closely at the principal topics and themes of in-service training programmes over the years. The following list is based on personal recollections of the changing priorities and professional concerns of teachers – a shopping list of areas where help **was** needed at particular moments.

1965–75

primary French – methods, materials and linguistic retraining
mixed-ability teaching
European studies
audio-visual methods, including the use of the language laboratory.

1975–85

syllabus definition
schemes of work
graded objectives and tests
reform of 16+ examinations
communicative approaches

1985–95

National Curriculum, especially course planning and assessment
languages and the world of work
linguistic refreshment and cultural updating for teachers
diversification
autonomous learning
learners with special needs
computer-assisted language learning

The emphasis from 1965–75 was firmly on methods and approaches, with a particular focus on teaching languages to pupils of below average ability. This arose principally from the development of the comprehensive school, which confronted language teachers with the need to find ways of presenting their subject to pupils in mixed-ability classes. The introduction of European Studies into school curricula (and the attendant in-service training) was another – and ill-fated – outcome of our attempts to reduce the difficulty of language learning, in this case by diluting the mix of language and **civilisation.** For similar reasons much effort was directed to familiarising teachers with the technical and organisational demands of the audio-visual course and the language laboratory, which seemed to offer ways of developing the oral skills which were now to be given priority.

From 1975–85 there was a growing concern for clearer syllabus definition and more appropriate assessment, prompted in no small measure by the Council of Europe's modern languages project, but also by the need to provide a new impetus after the frustrations and disappointments of the previous ten years. The resulting movement to develop graded objectives schemes locally and regionally, largely driven by teachers and local advisers, was to have a profound and lasting influence on 16+ examination reform and subsequently on the National Curriculum requirements in languages (see GOML, Chapter 7). The graded objectives movement also achieved a major and decisive change in teacher attitudes to in-service professional development, in that large numbers of teachers up and down the country became involved in, **and had control over,** collective development of teaching and assessment materials in their own area. Drawing heavily on international developments such as the Council of Europe modern languages project, the graded objectives movement also led teachers and in-service trainers into a long overdue recognition of the need to draw on developments in the field of EFL (English as a Foreign Language), where they discovered and enthusiastically adopted the communicative approaches to teaching which are now widely accepted.

The National Curriculum has dominated the last decade, and has prompted a dramatic increase in in-service courses (and in participation rates by teachers) as schools have struggled to follow the evolving obligations in their subject area. Although much of the thinking behind the National Curriculum Order for Modern Foreign Languages is in tune with teachers' views, there has been great demand for in-service training in areas such as the use of the target language, teaching languages to pupils with special needs, provision for the 14–16 age group, and the use of information technology in language learning. Another factor has been the publicity surrounding the advent of the European Single Market at the end of 1992. There has been a positive change in public attitudes to competence in languages, and schools have endeavoured to reflect this by introducing pre-vocational strands into their language teaching programmes. INSET and other support for all these themes has come from a variety of sources over the years, and the picture in 1996 is very different from that of 1966. If the underlying concerns and purposes remain broadly similar, there have nonetheless been radical changes to the context and the mechanisms of teacher support. It is worth charting those changes in some detail.

The LEA adviser

The most significant and radical change in education in this country over the past thirty years has been the shift of power from local to central Government, and the effects of this process on the provision of professional support for teachers can be well illustrated by looking at the role of the LEA adviser then and now.

The period 1965–1975 saw a rapid expansion of LEA advisory services as schools faced major changes in curriculum, organisation and approach. In 1969, when the newly formed National Association of Language Advisers (NALA) held its first Annual Conference, at Buxton, its membership had climbed quickly to around 40. Five years later it had 150 members, and practically every LEA had an adviser with specialist skills in this field. At that time the LEA was the prime source of in-service training and support, both through locally organised courses and through school-based activity prompted or led by the adviser. It was often through this networking of experience among advisers that good practice and the development work in individual LEAs fed through into the in-service training programmes of other LEAs and organisations up and down the country.

In the last ten years much of the adviser's role as trainer, curriculum developer, and source of material and professional support has been suppressed by events. Local authorities have been obliged by statute to delegate most of their budgets direct to the schools, which in turn are free to buy in advisory and in-service support as required. Yesterday's advisers are through force of circumstance today's entrepreneurs, often obliged to fund their own salaries by selling their services to schools or by operating as inspectors within the OFSTED system. It is a great tribute to their resilience that so many advisers are still in post – 100 of NALA's 1995 membership of 230 were still listed as LEA adviser or inspector (85 in England, 4 in Scotland, 7 in Wales, 4 in Northern Ireland) though their role may be very different and the future remains uncertain.

INSET is one area in which central Government involvement (at least in England and Wales) is now much less than it was thirty years ago. In the sixties and seventies, DES short courses run by HMI were the flagship training provision for teachers, and HMI had a prominent role in shaping professional development programmes organised by other agencies, or on a collaborative basis. As an example, for some six years, from 1973 to 1979, HMI in co-operation with the Language Teaching Centre at York ran Anglo/French reciprocal courses for teachers of French and English (24 from each country, selected by HMI and the French *Inspectorat* respectively). The two groups of teachers worked together for two-and-a-half weeks, in intensive sessions of *enseignement mutuel.* Besides helping to organise these innovative courses, HMI supplied two of the tutors on each course. HMI also played a major role in regional DES courses, which were a prominent feature of the 1970s.

However, during the eighties, the DES Short Course Programme – and thus the involvement of HMI in in-service training – was run down. After the eventual dismantling of HM Inspectorate and its re-emergence as OFSTED (the Office for Standards in Education), the latter was given no role in the in-service training of teachers. The role of inspectors working within the OFSTED frame (and of the remaining HMI who oversee the process) is to make judgements on the standards of achievement and the quality of education provided by schools. It is for the schools themselves to remedy any deficiencies which are identified, drawing on any advisory or consultancy service they may be able to call upon or buy in.

The Central Bureau for Educational Visits and Exchanges

290 Among the most popular of DES/HMI courses for language teachers were the short courses abroad, which provided opportunities for cultural, pedagogical and linguistic refreshment in a single frame. When the DES short course programme was discontinued, it was found possible to maintain the short courses abroad through collaboration between HMI and the Central Bureau for Educational Visits and Exchanges, which has been running its own courses with HMI since 1981. The Central Bureau, with funding from central Government, has over the last 40 years given consistently high priority to providing opportunities and grants for language teachers, advisers, and teacher trainers to enable them to improve their linguistic skills and to update their knowledge of other countries. When the EC Lingua Programme was launched in 1989, with the aim of improving foreign language competence in member states, it was the Central Bureau and CILT which jointly set up the UK LINGUA Unit, which through its work in administering the programme in this country, made a substantial contribution to teacher training, and to the development of materials and methods. Some of the Bureau's schemes, such as the Teacher Exchange Programmes offering post-to-post exchanges with teachers in the major European countries, have attracted less support from teachers than they merited, in spite of their relevance and flexibility. Overall, however, the Central Bureau's role in helping teachers to 'bring the foreign country into the classroom' has been and continues to be indispensable and immense. (See Appendix III.)

CILT's role in INSET

Although very different, CILT and the Central Bureau have always considered themselves to be sister organisations, and have enjoyed a close and constructive working relationship in their dealings with the language teaching constituency. It is in the INSET field that some of the most dramatic changes in CILT's role have occurred over the past thirty years. CILT's original remit was (and remains) to provide information, and over the first dozen or so years of its existence it developed a range of information services and publications dealing especially with teaching materials and approaches, as a service to teachers, advisers and other in-service trainers. The Government's crusade against quangos in the early eighties threatened CILT with extinction, a threat from which it saved itself by demonstrating that it could generate an increasing proportion of its own running costs by earning income from services. A range of INSET programmes had been developed and were being successfully marketed to LEAs as part of a more pro-active approach by CILT to its role as an information provider. INSET, along with publications, was to become the major growth area in CILT services until the present day. By 1990 the provision of INSET packages to individual LEAs had given way to an intensifying programme of regional and national courses and conferences to which individual teachers could subscribe. The CILT INSET programme for 1995 reflects the continuing priority and success of this role, with 7 national conferences, 20 regional one-day conferences, 3 courses abroad, 39 on-site events at CILT, and 28 inputs to INSET programmes arranged by others. These events were attended by some 3,500 teachers.

The other major growth area for CILT's activity in support of teachers has been in its publications, which in the last decade have reached a greatly expanded readership, particularly through initiatives such as the *Pathfinder* series, which takes the form of short, accessible and authoritative booklets sharply focused on key teaching topics and have achieved great popularity as a result of their practicality and variety. The series, which already includes well over twenty titles, has now been joined by *Young Pathfinders* (for primary language teachers) and the *Netword* series for tutors in adult and further education.

The Comenius network

In 1992 CILT launched the Comenius Centres initiative, which now provides a network of fourteen host establishments across the country through which INSET and other support for language teachers can be provided, not only by CILT but also by all the other agencies which are active in this field. National centres for Scotland, Northern Ireland and Wales have also been successfully inaugurated since 1992. The Comenius Centres are intended to provide a 'one stop shop' where teachers of languages can obtain access to information, publications and training programmes available from the many organisations which together offer such a wide range of in-service professional development opportunities.

The strength and quality of these services stems in no small measure from the variety of providers. These include national bodies whose remit includes but is in no way restricted to languages, such as the BBC, which has a long and highly respected record of in-service support for languages both in school and beyond; and the National Council for Educational Technology, which has undertaken important development work in the use of Information Technology in language learning and has trained many advisory teachers and other INSET providers in the languages field. The list also includes major contributions from the cultural services of other

European countries, which have been generous in their support of the professional development of language teachers.

A lead from universities

A lot of development work in methods, materials and assessment, together with the associated in-service training of teachers, has been undertaken by modern language specialists in higher education, particularly (though not exclusively) in initial teacher training departments. The trend was set in the sixties by the modern language materials project at York, funded initially by the Nuffield Foundation and subsequently by the Schools Council. This project produced major courses in French (*En avant*), German (*Vorwärts*), Spanish (*Adelante*) and Russian (*Vperyod*). The Language Teaching Centre, of which it was part, organised national in-service courses, and the University of York has continued ever since (even in the face of destructive cuts in recent years) to offer support and training opportunities which have been a constant stimulus to progress. Many other universities, polytechnics and colleges have made major and often unique contributions to the INSET effort. Let us hope that in particular those specialists in the initial training of teachers of languages will not be lost to the system as a result of the current move to school-based initial training. Human resources of this quality are easily dispersed but very difficult to re-assemble.

The Association for Language Learning (ALL)

Some of the most influential and rewarding in-service training of teachers takes place in their own schools through work organised on a self-help basis and focused on needs identified within the school. Teachers working together in this way draw their support and inspiration not only from the agencies already mentioned, but crucially also from membership of associations dedicated to the support of their work. One of the most remarkable and significant achievements during the period covered by this survey has been the creation in 1990 of the Association for Language Learning, through the combined efforts over several years of the former Modern Language Association, the British Association for Language Teaching, and the separate associations of teachers of Dutch, German, Italian, Russian, Spanish and Portuguese. This important development is described by Brian Page in the next chapter.

What emerges above all from this review of INSET over the past thirty years is the dedication and resilience of teachers faced with and facing up to the many challenges which have emerged from our changing view of Britain in the world and of the response of our education sytem to our changing role. The way forward has often been far from clear, and there have been a number of false dawns, setbacks and reversals, but the professionalism and expertise of language teachers are now higher than ever, and there can be no better investment in our pupils' future.

28

The Association for Language Learning (ALL)

Brian Page

The beginnings

According to the minutes it was five days before Christmas, 1892, that the decision was taken to found the first organisation of UK-based teachers of modern languages, the Modern Language Association (MLA). Immigrant French teachers had formed their own *Société Nationale des Professeurs de Français en Angleterre* ten years earlier, in 1882. MLA quickly established a reputation for its serious concern with the teaching and study of foreign languages and literature at all levels. Over the years, teachers of particular languages founded their own associations for German, Italian, Spanish and Portuguese, Russian and Dutch. The introduction of new technology produced the Audio-Visual Language Association (AVLA) which, in 1974, became the British Association for Language Teaching (BALT). The MLA had always run an important annual meeting for its members, an opportunity for the exchange of ideas. In 1963 the language associations formed an umbrella organisation, the Joint Council of Language Associations (JCLA), to run the annual conference on behalf of them all. As the political climate of the eighties produced many new policies for education, JCLA began to find itself having to respond on behalf of language teachers. It was clear that a more powerful and united voice was required. With considerable courage and imagination, the seven independent associations of JCLA decided to dissolve and found one single organisation, the Association for Language Learning. CILT's involvement was crucial. The then Director, John Trim, called a meeting of interested parties to envisage the possibility. Thereafter CILT provided meeting space and invaluable advice for the working party which prepared the ground. The new association was launched in January 1990.

The Association today

Today, the Association's close on 7,000 members benefit from a thriving and dynamic organisation. They receive a regular newsletter, *Language*

World as well as the *Language Learning Journal,* which has earned an international reputation, and language specific journals. The activities of the numerous local branches are the focus for the dissemination of ideas in their areas. Through its central administration ALL organises a broad range of day, weekend and longer conferences both in the UK and abroad. It has a growing range of publications on practical teaching matters. At a national and international level it is consulted and initiates debate on all relevant matters. In the MFL world, its annual conference is the biggest forum for the exchange of ideas and the accompanying publishers' exhibition the largest showcase of teaching/learning materials in the UK. The Association has close links with other organisations which support language teaching (including English as a Foreign Language) in order to maintain a high profile for language learning and improve the national capability. Although two thirds of the members are secondary school teachers, the membership as a whole covers the whole spectrum of language teaching and learning from early learners to university and the adult sector. The Association is therefore well placed to work for a national MFL policy and improved conditions and facilities through making representations to Government ministries and other decision-making bodies.

The in-service training function of ALL is all the more precious now that local systems based on LEAs and language advisers are so much reduced. In an increasingly nationally centralised and locally fragmented education service, ALL provides one of the few channels by which ideas can be discussed, receive wide attention and gain influence and recognition.

The festivals of languages and Young Linguists' awards

The initial impetus was again provided by John Trim, then Director of CILT, who arranged a meeting representing a wide range of language, educational, examination and business interests to discuss the possibility of a Young Linguist's competition loosely based on a German model but with a festival attached. Sponsors were found, the major one being the National Westminster Bank supported by cultural institutes and embassies, professional bodies, trusts, colleges and LEAs as well as industry and commerce. A committee was formed chaired by the then Gloucestershire adviser, Martin Ash. Christine Wilding, now Secretary General of ALL, was appointed National Co-ordinator. A pilot project was carried out in 1983 and thereafter a national event was held biennially from 1986 to 1992.

There were heats in five regions and a national final. In the process, the young candidates, who had to operate in at least two languages, were involved in a series of life-like language activities which broke new ground in testing techniques. The finalists were all very good multi-linguists indeed. In many areas teachers were not entirely happy with the competition idea but held festivals anyway and these assumed the greater importance for most young people. They usually involved the co-operation of local institutions and firms with schools and language advisers as well as the Festival's regional organiser. The national Festival, held in excellent facilities at the University of Warwick, became a huge event. Thanks to the energy and imagination of all concerned – and not least the National Co-ordinator – thousands of young people and their teachers were involved in exhibitions, theatrical performances of every conceivable kind – plays, choirs, dance, mime, etc. The atmosphere was terrific – hosts of young people using MFL and enjoying it (see John Trim's note, p327). The last national festival in 1992, which received substantial funding from the Department for Education and Science, the Scottish Office for Education, the Department for Education in Northern Ireland and the European Union, involved over 8,000 people. Unfortunately sponsorship has been increasingly difficult to find and there has been no national event since 1992. Local festivals continue however. The North East festival, inspired by its organiser Stella Marsh, had in 1995 its most successful event ever. The idea has been much admired and copied abroad and now festivals are held in half a dozen countries throughout Europe. It is to be hoped that the still flourishing regional network will one day again find sponsors to give it national expression.

Part

eight

Three decades of research

1966-1996 30 YEARS

Research and the teacher

It seems to me that language teaching, like all teaching, is an activity that has its own momentum, in which good practice is rather like the sea coming in and eroding a land mass . . . The sea is constantly probing; so too teaching constantly tries to advance learners' competence by going for the points where access is easiest . . . And just as the sea does this, so good language teaching practice consistently tries to improve itself . . . and the theory of language teaching is not about changing that process necessarily but about understanding it . . . The theory may consist of better and better understanding of what teachers, the best teachers, are doing anyway.

Even research aimed at teaching is not concerned with finding a way of telling teachers (whether ourselves or others) what to do. It is not, as Stephen Krashen (1983) claimed, identifying the best psycholinguistic model and applying it; rather it is understanding what the best practising teachers are doing, and accounting for what that is in terms of the theories that are around derived from other language teaching situations, from studies of language learning, sociolinguistics and other relevant areas. I would not want to suggest that the process is entirely one way, from practice to theory, but I think it is more that direction than the reverse . . . **Chris Brumfit, from concluding talk at CILT Research Forum, Cambridge, January 1996 (Wright P (ed),** *Current research into language teaching and learning, 1993–95* **(CILT, 1996))**

29

Research in the UK and Europe

Richard Johnstone and John Trim

Both CILT and the Modern Languages Projects of the Council of Europe had their origins in the optimism of the 1960s. In this chapter we follow these two tracks in research in language teaching from their optimistic beginnings to more recent work, and try to summarise the lessons to be drawn from them. The chapter therefore falls into two sections:

- Research initiatives in the UK as recorded in CILT's Research Register;
- Modern Languages Projects of the Council of Europe.

We limit our account of research to these two tracks because (thanks largely to the informative role of CILT) they have remained closely in tune with each other and proved mutually supportive. Some important research projects in the UK must inevitably fall outside our account, if they are not listed in the CILT Register. We have not attempted to include research in other English-speaking countries such as the USA, Canada, Australia, or in Eastern Europe, Russia or the Far East.[1]

The early 1960s saw a remarkable awakening of interest in British universities in the way that languages are learned and taught. The awakening was encouraged by the creation of a number of new universities and polytechnics, many of which set up 'Language Teaching Centres' breaking away from traditional patterns of degree and non-degree language studies (see James Coleman's account of this movement, Chapter 5).

Until 1960, university courses in modern languages were almost exclusively conducted in the mother tongue and were devoted to the history of the language and literature concerned. My syllabus as a student of German in the University of London in the forties was 'German language and literature from their beginnings to the present day'. In the atmosphere

---

1 Information on research outside the UK can be obtained from ERIC, an information system established in 1966 and designed to provide users with ready access to an extensive body of education-related literature.

ERIC Clearinghouse on Languages and Linguistics
1118 22nd Street, N.W., Washington, D.C. 20037

URL: http://ericir.syr.edu/Eric/

and conditions of the Second World War and its aftermath, present-day German language and culture were not highly valued, indeed almost totally ignored. Literature effectively ended with the naturalists around 1875. The German language was studied only in its medieval forms according to neogrammarian methods, again of about 1875.

Postgraduate research in modern languages generally was almost exclusively literary history, with few theses on language topics. Though interest in historical philology faded, there was next to no research on contemporary language except by some dedicated lexicographers. Linguistics was virtually unknown, confined to postgraduate studies at SOAS, with phonetics taught, but with no postgraduate school, in a handful of centres, notably University College, London. When, from 1960, central policy promoted applied linguistics at first in EFL and then, with the creation of CRDML, in foreign languages, there was no established body of linguistic knowledge and theory to call upon, nor structures to support teaching and research on any scale.

By the end of the decade, there were seventeen departments of linguistics in British universities, strongly oriented towards EFL. The few professionals in the field found themselves called upon to found departments, recruit and train staff, develop courses – and at the same time to commit themselves to ambitious programmes of applied research. Modern language departments were also pressed to engage in research for which they were totally unprepared. The stream was apparent and it is not surprising that the quality of some early projects did little to raise the respect of colleagues in more established fields. Nevertheless a great deal was achieved during the sixties and under the energetic leadership of HMSI Riddy the steps taken in Britain to carry out the programme set out by the Council of Europe were equal to any. In addition to the setting up of CILT, the teaching of a modern language – almost inevitably French – to all pupils from eleven in the comprehensive schools, the equipment of all secondary schools with language laboratories, the development of the Nuffield Foreign Languages programme and defined syllabuses, the experiment in primary language teaching, the Emmans/Hawkins and James/Rouve surveys of needs, all were in tune with the European programme and contributed greatly to its development. It is simply a great pity that once the infrastructure was in place in the universities and polytechnics and was producing potential research of quality, and measures had been put in place in the schools which desperately needed strong intellectual support for both material and methodological development, funding was abruptly withdrawn and, despite the efforts of the National

Council for Modern Languages (NCML) never effectively replaced. CILT, which was confined by its statutes to an informational role, was in no position to take on other functions of NCML. Its Research Information Section carefully monitored research, and its colloquies, reports and papers were designed to promote interaction among researchers and spread the results of their work among practitioners. However, this could not replace active stimulation backed by adequate funding. The result was a severe setback, leading to the 'Crisis in Modern Languages' of the seventies until the grassroots renewal in the Graded Objectives movement of the late seventies and eighties.

John Trim

~

RESEARCH INITIATIVES IN THE UK AS RECORDED IN CILT'S RESEARCH REGISTER

Throughout its thirty years, CILT has provided information on research into language, language use, language teaching and language learning. A first step was to support the introduction of *Language-Teaching Abstracts*, compiled by the English-Teaching Information Centre of the British Council and CILT. Volume 1 number 1 appeared in January 1968. Published by Cambridge University Press, this international journal is still with us, now entitled *Language Teaching*. The next major development was the publication of the *Register of current research in Britain: language and language teaching*. The first volume covered 1971–72; a second covered 1972–75 and a third 1975–77, all three published by Longman and edited by Helen Lunt. A register of research for 1977–86 was made available on five microfiches. There appears to have been a gap between 1986 and 1992, apart from continuing support for *Language Teaching Abstracts*, until the publication of a different register of *Current research in language teaching and learning: results of a survey of research*, the product of a CILT advisory group on research that had been established in 1989 by Alan Moys.

Readers of the initial registers cannot fail to be struck by the astonishing range and variety of research activity. The 1971–72 volume recorded 640 projects encompassing language, particular languages, language teaching, sociolinguistics, psycholinguistics and educational psychology. The 1972–75 volume recorded 763 projects, of which 423 were new since 1972, with entries for 72 different languages and the teaching of 29. The 1975–77 volume recorded 730 current projects of which 354 were new, with entries for 76 different languages and teaching of 28. A visible strand running through these documents is language development and use in a broad sense, including summaries of projects in progress that were to achieve prominence when subsequently published. It is possible for present purposes to name only a few examples: Joan Tough's pre-school language project and her research on language development and the environment; Gordon Wells' study of language development in pre-school children; Barbara Tizard and colleagues on the characteristics of adult–child dialogue at home and at school; Tom Gorman's adult literacy project; and several projects on the language needs of what at the time were called immigrant groups, including Harold Rosen's survey of linguistic diversity in ILEA schools; David Crystal's research on the diagnosis of language disorders of children.

From this point on, attention will be directed to research on the teaching and learning of foreign or second languages. Given the large numbers of projects recorded, only a small number can be highlighted. These have been selected as reflecting important trends, but it is not suggested that they necessarily represent the best research by the best researchers.

The 1968–71 abstracts indicated 98 projects on audio-lingual methodology or language laboratories, 49 on the visual element in language teaching, and nineteen on foreign languages at primary school. These of course were not the only themes. Among others were *School and university co-operation in modern language studies* (1967) and *Intensive courses, some possible patterns* (1970), both registering the name of Eric Hawkins. A dominant concern, though, was audio-lingual/visual methodology: e.g. *The new audio-visual student* (H Monod-Cassidy, 1967), *The language laboratory and the audio-visual student* (D Friedemann, 1967), *Closed-circuit television in the language laboratory* (R Smith, 1969), *Towards programmed language laboratory courses* (Klaus Bung, 1969) and *The place of the language laboratory in a university French Department* (Brian Farrington, 1969). This is not to suggest that these innovations were uncritically accepted even in those early days. Several abstracts were already asking questions, e.g. *What's wrong with pattern practice?* (F Johnson, 1969), *The return of the paradigm* (R Brend, 1967), *The contextualisation of language drills* (Michael Buckby, 1967), *The psychological evaluation of audio-lingual techniques and the modification of basic precepts* (L Cole, 1968, containing the insight *it is difficult to make spontaneous variations in the basic patterns learned*). At a more fundamental level there was Pit Corder's (1967) seminal *The significance of learners' errors,* in which the abstract notes that *the author considers errors as indications of a learning strategy and feels that teachers should adapt to the needs of the pupil rather than impose on them their own ideas of how he ought to learn and what and when.*

The registers: 1971–86

Among the key themes to be observed in CILT's first register (1971–72) were languages for young learners, bilingual education, comparative studies and the needs of employers. The main project on languages for young learners was the NFER evaluation led by Claire Burstall, concerned with French in the primary school. As already indicated, though, the reader of the 1971–72 register is able to place this in a wider range of research on primary school children and languages, including the projects by Joan Tough and Gordon Wells. The Welsh language featured strongly in projects concerned with bilingual education, e.g. the *Bilingual Education Project* of the Schools Council (Richards, Price and Dodson) which was intended for pupils at school in Wales who were monoglot speakers of English, and an initiative under the auspices of the Welsh Joint Education Committee consisting of *Research to establish an interim model of standard spoken Welsh as the basis of all Welsh-teaching in schools*. These projects reflected a strategy of supporting the Welsh language in schools, building on grass-roots initiatives in pre-school playgroups that were coming into place at the same time, and placing Welsh ahead of other Celtic languages in promoting language maintenance and revival through initiatives in school education.

Two key projects reflected the prominent national role played by the University of York. One was a comparative study involving Peter Green and Eric Hawkins in which three matched classes were learning German by different methods (Green, 1975). The other was a three-year enquiry by Keith Emmans, Eric Hawkins and Adam Westoby, funded by the Nuffield Foundation, into *The language needs of employers in the UK* (Emmans et al, 1974). Consciously in close co-ordination with the Emmans et al study was the Vaughan James and Sonia Rouve *Survey of curricula and performance* in relation to French, German, Spanish, Italian and Russian. The mention of Russian is noteworthy. Compared with present times in the mid-1990s, the abstracts of 1968–71 and the initial CILT registers in the early 70s point to an abundance of research geared to this language.

The register covering 1972–75 revealed a sharp drop in the number of research projects on audio-lingual methodology or the use of language laboratories but signaled the emergence of two major new themes. The first concerned language syllabuses, e.g. David Wilkins' (1974) *Semantic syllabuses* which justified semantic (or, notional) criteria in designing foreign or second language syllabuses, accompanied by John Trim, Jan van Ek, David Wilkins, René Richterich and others on a *European unit-credit system in modern languages for adults*. The second had to do with the by then problematical innovation of 'modern languages for all' in the early years of secondary education in state schools, e.g. *The less able learner of French* (H J Ford, 1974), *Research on tests and testing and examinations* (Ann Harding, 1975) exploring issues in the assessment of pupils aged 11–15 using Schools Council materials in French, German, Spanish and Russian, and a *Survey of French materials used in the first two years of secondary school in Scotland* (Richard Johnstone, 1975) which was the first in a long series of research on modern languages in schools funded by the (then) Scottish Education Department.

In addition, research on bilingual education in Wales continued apace, e.g. *Bilingual education in Welsh secondary schools* (Carl Dodson) which extended the primary school initiative into secondary, and *Concept and language development of nursery and infant-school children aged 3–7* (Carl Dodson again) in which comparisons were intended between monoglot English-speaking, monoglot Welsh-speaking and bilingual Welsh/English-speaking children.

The register of research covering 1975–77 revealed an increase in the number of projects on languages for vocational or specific purposes, e.g. *German for music students, French teaching for the police, Languages and international law*, and *The language needs of a group of interrelated technological communities.* In similar vein there was a follow-up study by Keith Emmans on *The subsequent use of French and German in employment by 'A' level candidates.* It also identified projects that were exploring new, more learner-centred approaches to the teaching or learning of languages, e.g. *Investigation into group-work procedures in the teaching of English as a second/foreign language* (Christopher Brumfit, 1976,), *Self-directed/autonomous language learning* (Les Dickinson, 1977), *The construction of support systems for adults learning languages for radio and television* (S Rybak, 1977), and an early sign of learning strategies in *Strategies employed by learners of French to facilitate the language learning process* (G D Thomas, 1977).

Research designed to investigate aspects of the teaching modern languages to the full range of learners at secondary was clearly gathering momentum, e.g. a first mention of graded objectives in *Graded series of examinations for foreign languages* (Michael Buckby, 1977), a *Survey of language teaching in 176 secondary schools in Yorkshire* (Brian Page, 1977), *Towards criteria for the assessment of foreign language teaching materials in the classroom* (Rod Hares, 1977) and *Modern languages teaching skills and strategies* (Richard Johnstone, Rosamond Mitchell and Brian Parkinson, 1978), an SED-funded project which developed a new approach to the systematic analysis of classroom events and explored the potential of mastery learning for enabling slow learners in Scottish comprehensive schools to achieve language objectives that would otherwise have been considered beyond their grasp.

In the microfiche version of the register covering 1977–86, there was evidence of a developing Scottish tradition of collaborative research and development on languages in HE: e.g. *Communication skills in French at final honours level* (Sam Taylor, Tony Lodge, Robin Adamson, Margaret Lang and John Devereux). Elsewhere, Peter Dyson evaluated *The year abroad* by students taking degree courses in French, German and Spanish in British universities and polytechnics – measuring their performance in listening and speaking before and after the year abroad. There was a study of *Attainment and progress of students in written French from 'A' level to the BA honours degree* (J C Ireson, 1980) – a precursor of James Coleman's recent (1995) major study.

Research on the technology of language learning was well beyond language laboratories, e.g. *Elaboration of models for a computer-based learning of French post-'A' level*, based on self-instruction (Brian Farrington, 1980); *A multifaceted language laboratory – CALL with speech synthesis and computer-controlled video* (P Jarratt, 1985); the *Development of a scheme of observation in a modern languages classroom with one or more microcomputers present* (Sue Hewer, 1985), the *Potentialities and limitations of the microcomputer in foreign-language learning* (Richard Johnstone, 1983). Apart from computers, there was research on *The use and effectiveness of broadcast language courses* (Brian Hill, 1980). The research investigated why adults dropped out of broadcast courses and aimed to suggest strategies for combating this. The language needs of industry continued to receive attention: *Foreign language use, services and needs in West Midlands industry and commerce* (Dennis Ager, 1979), assessing the needs, demands and services required in the interaction between providers and users. 1984 witnessed the first appearance in the register of research by Steven Hagen through his *Survey of foreign language use in northern commerce and industry*, involving up to 3,000 companies.

There were several important entries in relation to research on secondary schools. In England, David Westgate (1980) was exploring *Patterns and processes of classroom interaction identifiable in the context of foreign language lessons,* and David Sanderson through his *Language teaching research project* (1980) was locating and studying examples of successful foreign-language teaching in comprehensive schools. The register also recorded a number of studies on aspects of cultural learning and languages, e.g. *The effect of language teaching on young people's perceptions of other cultures* by Michael Byram and Pam Allatt, 1984, exploring the contribution of foreign-language learning at school to pupils' understanding and tolerance of foreign cultures. There was a first indication of APU research in foreign languages through *Monitoring of performance in French, German and Spanish* (Peter Dickson at NFER, 1981) involving the development of assessment instruments for thirteen-year-old pupils.

In Scotland, the Scottish Office continued its substantial funding in support of a series of policy-related research projects on language-teaching at school. *Communicative interaction in elementary foreign language teaching* (Rosamond Mitchell and Richard Johnstone, 1980–83) explored teachers' views about the nature and feasibility of a communicative approach and supported a small group of committed teachers in action research on particular aspects of communicative methodology. *The Independent evaluation of the national S1–S2 French course* (Brian Parkinson, Donald McIntyre and Rosamond Mitchell, 1982) reported on how a nationally sponsored curriculum development project was understood and implemented in secondary schools. *The School-based assessment of communicative foreign-language skills in S3 and S4* (Richard Johnstone, Mary Kilborn and Diana Kent, 1983–84) explored with teachers their first attempts at developing, implementing and evaluating the use of the oral interview as an assessment instrument within the context of the new Standard Grade examination that was coming into place. In respect of Scottish Gaelic, Donald McIntyre and Rosamond Mitchell (1975–81) investigated *Processes, context and outcomes of bilingual education in the Western Isles.*

There were several entries that had important implications for aspects of foreign or second language acquisition. Among these were: *Vocabulary acquisition in a second language* (Paul Meara, 1980), consisting of a biographical survey and a series of experimental investigations; the *Relationship between language teaching and language learning* (Dick Allwright, 1984) which explored the interpretive procedures that learners used in order to makes sense of language data and forms of guidance in typical language lessons; a study of *Ab initio foreign and second language learning in higher education classrooms* (Rod Ellis, 1985) that followed the acquisitional routes of three sets of learners. Of particular interest in a *Comparison of first and foreign language-learning ability* (Peter Skehan, 1984) was that it followed the children whose pre-school language development and early school achievement had been monitored by Gordon Wells' Bristol project and who were now learning a foreign language in secondary school classrooms.

The new registers: 1992–96

The first volume in the new format for the register was published in 1992, presenting the results of a survey conducted in 1991. A 1993 volume presented findings from 1992, a 1994 volume presented findings from 1993 and a 1996 volume presented findings from 1994–95. Compared with the initial registers, the new format was restricted to the teaching and learning of foreign or second languages, with relatively little emphasis given to research on first languages, linguistics or language-related aspects of psychology. Each of the four versions of the revised form of the Register has maintained a fairly standard format beginning with an article that provides an overview of research as evidenced in the responses received in the survey of the particular year. This is followed by a quantitative analysis of survey returns. There is a summary of each new research project and a list of theses and dissertations related to the teaching of modern foreign languages in Britain completed in the period of the survey. The questionaire for the 1992 Register elicited 156 positive replies of which 77 represented research as opposed to curriculum or materials. The 1993 version recorded 71 research projects of which 41 were new, while the 1994 version recorded 21 new research projects, suggesting a decline in the volume of new research projects being undertaken during this period. Below, some of the key themes are set out that appear to emerge from the register in its new format since 1992.

In higher education, work continued that related a modern language to substantive areas of learning, e.g in *Science with language* (Sam Taylor, Tony Lodge and Robin Adamson), relating science language teaching to the teaching of science itself. Cecilia Roberts and Michael Byram were developing an ethnographic approach in relation to cultural learning among students on language degrees. In combination with Barcelona University, Nigel Reeves and colleagues were investigating how students of the *Fine Arts* used language in their learning and, on a different project entitled *Business Language Workbench*, were developing a language auditing toolkit for English, Dutch, Portuguese and Greek. The largest-scale piece of research in HE appears to have been *the European language proficiency survey* (James Coleman) which investigated the proficiency, progess, background, aims, motivations, attitudes, language anxiety and transferable skills of advanced language learners, based on a proficiency test and questionnaire to 25,000 students of French, German, Spanish, Russian and English in seven European countries. The findings suggest a failure of university departments to define proficiency levels, uneven rates of progress and the key role of residence abroad.

Applications of technology continued to receive research interest: *The potential of interactive multimedia*, using CD-ROM, in the teaching of languages was investigated by Brian Hill, Graham Cook and Paul Slater. Other topics included *The value of teletext subtitled programmes* (T Vanderplank) and the *Telephone-only tutorial programme* (Anne Stevens and Sue Hewer).

Some of the research in schools was based on specially-funded projects. Among these were a major international study: *The ILEA*

language education study (Barbara Lee and Peter Dickson, NFER) in Phase
1 of which national profiles were being developed for 27 countries, taking
account of social, demographic, educational, economic and other background information, with the aim of compiling descriptions of policy,
provision and access to language teaching in all sectors of mainstream
education. With reference to schools in England, two ESCR-funded
projects involving the University of Southampton are of particular significance. The first, on *Knowledge about language* (Christopher Brumfit and
Rosamond Mitchell), studied the beliefs of secondary school teachers of
modern languages and English about language and its role in education,
their practices in class in relation to explicit knowledge about language,
and their pupils' beliefs. The second, a joint project between Southampton
and NFER (Rosamond Mitchell and Peter Dickson) is investigating
Progression in foreign language learning by pupils in the early years of
secondary education, including pupils' development of vocabulary,
grammar and conversational skills, the role in classroom learning of
unanalysed chunks, is exploring the links between children's learning and
their classroom experiences and is evaluating critically the progression
proposed in the National Curriculum.

At the University of Durham the tradition of research on culture and language learning continued, e.g. a study of *Cultural awareness* (Michael
Byram and Carol Morgan, in collaboration with the Institut National de
Recherche Pédagogique in Paris), focusing on sixth form teaching with the
aim of widening the linguistic and literary basis of the current syllabus to
include a deeper awareness of culture, and there was collaboration with
researchers at the University of Braunschweig, Germany, on the analysis of
textbooks for English in Germany and German in England. Another international study was undertaken in relation to *The evaluation of in-service
courses for language teachers in the target country* (Michael Byram and
Geneviève Zarate), including England, Spain, France, Portugal and Ireland.

The Scottish Office continued to fund policy-related research in
modern languages at school. In a study of *Differentiation,* Mary Simpson
focused on three different subjects, including a modern language. A
research team at Stirling (Richard Johnstone, Sally Brown and Lesley
Low, 1990–1995) completed the independent evaluation of the national
pilot projects for modern languages in Scottish primary schools. A review
was undertaken (Richard Johnstone) of the impact of current developments designed to promote the Gaelic language in education, the
media, the arts and economic development at a time of apparently
severe demographic decline for the language, and a three-year study

(Richard Johnstone, Wynne Harlen, Morag MacNeil and Graham Thorpe) has begun into the attainments of pupils receiving their primary education through the medium of Gaelic.

To complement the above projects that have received substantial external research funding, it is encouraging to note several projects based on personal, institutional or trans-institutional initiatives. Among these are: an investigation (Anne Convery) into the *European dimension*, whether its inclusion in the curriculum helps change attitudes to Europe, and a related study (Anne Convery, Simon Green, Ernesto Macaro and Jane Mellor) into *Pupil perceptions of Europe*, in which 1292 teenagers aged 14–16 were surveyed in France, England, Germany, Italy, the Netherlands and Spain. In secondary schools in several countries in western Europe *a foreign language* is being used *as a means of learning other subjects*, and so it is encouraging to note research in this area in England (Do Coyle), e.g. teaching science through the medium of French and geography through the medium of Spanish.

There are several projects that are investigating pupils' learning, e.g. Mike Grenfell and Vee Harris are seeking to identify pupils' *Language learning strategies*, to develop a working taxonomy and to develop appropriate research methodologies. They are exploring the sequences in which learning strategies emerge in Years 7–9 learners and the extent to which the development of these strategies can be influenced by teaching. Denis Ager and colleagues are studying the attitudes and motivations of schoolchildren learning French and English as foreign languages in England and France. Terry Lamb is studying the development of *Metacognitive strategies* in modern foreign language learning at Key Stages 3 and 4, and Violante Lujan-Ortega the use of *Compensatory strategies* by English learners of Spanish. Jane Jones is exploring *Early modern language teaching and interculturality*, including EFL at primary school in Italy and Spain and various foreign languages at primary school in England, with a focus on intercultural learning and the development of positive attitudes. Luned Anne Ainslie is studying learning strategies used by 11–16 year-old learners of Welsh as a second language. Margaret Wells is conducting a longitudinal study of parallel classes of Year 9 modern language pupils in a 13–18 comprehensive school, focusing on different styles of *Grammar* teaching. Janeen Leith is investigating *The development of spontaneity* in the first year of foreign language learning, and Philip Hood is exploring the role of groupwork in *Strategy development for reading*.

Overview

What then is to be learned from this peregrination through CILT's registers of research? It does not provide us with large amounts of findings – partly because of problems of space, partly because the registers mainly record research in progress rather than research that has been completed and published. What the registers do achieve is to document what researchers were interested in investigating and to build up a picture of how these topics have changed and developed over the years. Two trends stand out fairly clearly.

310

First, a trend towards learner-centred research. In the initial abstracts and registers there was a strong research interest in different methods of teaching and in the uses of equipment as a reflection of these methods, e.g. language laboratories as a reflection of audio-lingual teaching. By the 1980s the focus had changed to communicative methodology and the challenges of teaching a modern language to a wide range of learners. In turn this has led by the mid-1990s to a much greater emphasis on learners, at all levels from primary school to university. Perhaps by the mid-1990s the profession has begun to catch up with Pit Corder. A small number of UK researchers are making a contribution to fundamental aspects of acquisition research, e.g. by documenting the course of progression in learners' language development, several are exploring different aspects of learner strategies, including learners' perceptions of what is involved in the process, and several are exploring how learners may progress towards autonomy by developing strategies for accessing and processing language through combinations of the new technologies that they find to be helpful.

Second, a trend towards internationalisation, with UK researchers increasingly gathering data not only from UK contexts but also from other countries in Europe, as they participate in transnational groups or networks. In this respect it is evident that the EC LINGUA programme and the Council of Europe have helped enormously in creating a supportive infrastructure.

Much of the research recorded in the registers has been undertaken by staff in Education, Modern Languages, Applied Linguistics and Language Centres in universities. Given the other competing pressures on their time, it is to their credit that they have been able to make so much of the relatively limited financial resources at their disposal. Most staff in UK universities are keen to do both research and teaching – but it remains to be seen whether government funding policy will permit them to do so or will force them into one camp or the other. With regard to funding from those government agencies responsible for schools, there appears to have been particularly strong support for policy-related research in Scotland and Wales, covering modern foreign and heritage Celtic languages as appropriate.

It may be fitting to conclude with a thought about the format of the old and new registers. The old style of register allowed readers to gain a sense of how research into foreign/second-language teaching fitted into a much broader picture of research in education, linguistics, and the psychology and sociology of language. The reader interested in a particular foreign-language topic was able to see what else was going on in these broader areas of research for the same age-group. On the other hand, the old model contained much that many busy schoolteachers would not consider relevant to their concerns. The new style of register has a much clearer focus. It is mainly about foreign and second languages in the UK; it provides a useful descriptive overview of recent developments and an invaluable quantitative analysis of returns. It may, however, possibly re-inforce an impression that foreign and second-language learning and use are in a special category of their own, unconnected to other aspects of education and language. It is not clear, though, that one register can serve both general and specific purposes, and for future historians of languages research it will be fascinating to learn what sorts of information CILT will choose to include in its registers of research over its next thirty years.

References

CILT, *Language and language teaching: current research in Britain, 1971–72* (Longman, 1973)
CILT, *Language and language teaching: current research in Britain, 1972–75* (Longman, 1975)
CILT, *Language and language teaching: current research in Britain, 1975–77* (Longman, 1978)
CILT, *Language and language teaching: current research in Britain, 1977–1986* (CILT, 1987)
Krashen S D, 'Second language acquisition theory and the preparation of teachers: towards a rationale' in Alatis J E, H H Stern and P Strevens (eds), *Applied linguistics and the preparation of second language teachers: towards a rationale*: 255–263 (Washington D.C.: Georgetown University Press, 1983)
Wright P (ed), *Current research into language teaching and learning 1993–95* (CILT, 1996)

Richard Johnstone

MODERN LANGUAGES PROJECTS OF THE COUNCIL OF EUROPE

Although the Council of Europe was founded in 1949, it was not until 1961 that the first Symposium in the modern languages field was held. It took place in Paris at the invitation of the French Government to present internationally the work of the Centre de Recherche et Diffusion du Français (CREDIF), which had recently produced *Le français fondamental,* a statistically-based linguistic specification of an objective for the early study of French, and based upon it an audio-visual course *Voix et images de la France,* employing the 'structuro-global' methodology proposed by Professor Guberina in Zagreb. This Symposium stimulated the setting up of a ten-year Major Project in Modern Languages, supervised by HMSI D Riddy (UK), Prof M Gorosch (Sweden) and Prof B Pottier (France), later joined by Prof G Nickel (Germany).

By 1969 an intensive programme of activities had been undertaken and many more planned covering all educational sectors from primary through to higher education and research as well as adult education and dealing with the organisation and structure of modern language teaching, modern methods of teaching, the training and further training of teachers, textbooks and other teaching materials, assessment techniques (tests, examinations, certificates, guidance) and teaching technology (hardware and software problems). These themes were dealt with by means of consultative meetings of experts, commissioned studies and enquiries and governmental courses (workshops and symposia). On 25 January 1969 the Committee of Ministers adopted Resolution R(69)2 setting out the objectives for *an intensified modern language teaching programme for Europe',* many of which are still valid.

Resolution (69)2 bases itself on some basic principles with which the Council of Europe has always been identified: the need for the lowering of language barriers for full understanding to be achieved among the countries of Europe, leading to the strengthening of links and exchanges upon which economic and social progress depends; the value of linguistic and cultural diversity as a source of mutual enrichment; the need for knowledge of a modern language, no longer as a *luxury reserved for an élite, but as an instrument of information and culture which should be available to all.* The Resolution then recommended to Governments an *intensified programme.* In primary and secondary schools it recommended: *to the maximum extent possible* the teaching of at least one widely-spoken European language to all pupils from the age of about ten, modern facilities, courses and materials (emphasising the *full and systematic use of audio-visual means*) and examination reform *to give due prominence to auditory and oral skills.* It stopped short of recommending the introduction of a modern language into the primary curriculum, preferring *systematic experimentation into the feasibility* of doing so. For institutions of higher and other forms of post-secondary education it advocated: the *modernisation* of courses of study by specialists to ensure proficiency in present-day use of the language and a sound knowledge of the civilisation of the country; installation of equipment for practising language; arrangements for study visits and exchanges; the provision of language centres to cater for the general and professional needs of non-specialists. Facilities for *permanent education* for adults were also supported.

With regard to the initial and in-service training of modern language teachers, the Committee of Ministers recommended the *organisation, for all future and serving modern language teachers, of courses on recent developments in teaching methods, on such findings of linguistic science as are relevant to language teaching and on ways of using modern teaching apparatus efficiently.* It also recommended study visits abroad *at regular intervals* and special training for teachers of adults.

An important place was given to research, specifying:

- research into the factors affecting language acquisition, learning and teaching at all ages and with all categories of learner;
- research into the development of the most suitable syllabuses, materials and methods of teaching for all categories of pupils and students;
- definitions of criteria of language proficiency leading to the production of tests for evaluating the results of language learning;
- preparation of basic lists of words and structures of the European language (spoken and written) to facilitate the construction of study materials appropriate to modern aims and methods of language teaching, and examination of the possibility of furthering the study of less widely known European languages.
- analysis of the specialised language of science and technology, economics, etc.

Finally member Governments were urged *to nominate or create national centres specialising in such fields as:*

i) *systematic collection and distribution, to language teachers and others, of information on the findings of research having a bearing on language teaching;*

ii) *documentation on the specialised use of languages particularly in science and technology;*

iii) *techniques of testing proficiency in modern languages;*

to examine whether any existing institutes or centres for modern languages could, with advantage, take over certain tasks of common European benefit.

Its last recommendation clearly envisaged CILT as a model to be followed by all member-states and amounted to an invitation to HM Government to nominate CILT as co-ordinating centre in a European research information network. This duly happened and was perhaps the most concrete outcome of R(69)2. Otherwise, the response of DES to the admittedly over-generalised and unfocused plea for the intensification of applied linguistic research was to abolish, early in the following year, the Committee on Research and Development in Modern Languages (CRDML) which it had set up for that very purpose in October 1964.

On the European scale, the Council of Europe continued its ten-year programme until the mid seventies, but then changed direction. In September 1971, following an Intergovernmental Symposium held at Rüschlikon, Switzerland, largely organised by the Foundation for European Language and Educational Centres (Eurocentres), the Committee for Out-of-School Education (EES) convened a small expert group to investigate the feasibility of developing and introducing a European unit-credit scheme for adult language learning. This work was at first a side-growth from the Major Project, (it is not mentioned in Riddy's survey), set up with the aim of providing a pan-European test-bed for the ideas of Bernard Schwarz for structuring '*éducation permanente*' through a system of 'unités capitalisables' which adult learners could pro-gressively accumulate and carry with them from one educational context to another.

The situation in 1971 presented the EES Expert Group with a unique opportunity. The accelerating internationalisation of life was at its point of take-off as technical developments in the communications and informa-tion industries massively transformed social life in many interconnected aspects. Multinational industries; global financial markets; mass tourism and entertainment science and medicine created a mass demand for practical proficiency in modern languages, particularly for English, which was rapidly establishing itself as the first foreign language in schools and the primary medium of international communication outside the Soviet bloc. However, the (possibly excessive) discrediting of Skinnerian behav-iourism and post-Bloomfieldian structuralism (which Chomskyan grammarians had no intention of replacing) and disillusion with mechanistic audio-lingual and audio-visual methodologies meant that the teaching profession was in need of a new approach to meet the challenge. The Expert Group, because of its marginal position was able to develop a new approach without the political constraints to be expected in a large intergovernmental organisation, but was in a position to exert consider-able influence should its ideas gain the support of the Council's decision-making bodies.

The intellectual and experiential backgrounds of the members of the

Group enabled it to draw upon and attempt to synthesise a wide range of influences. The aims and purposes of the Council of Europe provided the ideological base: the encouragement of personal mobility and interaction, the need for intensified international co-operation, respect for human rights, implying on the one hand understanding and tolerance of cultural (and hence linguistic) diversity as a source of mutual enrichment and on the other the democratisation of education, with languages for all rather than for a social or professional élite and the participation in decision-making of all those affected by the decisions. We have seen already the networks and working methods inherited from the Modern Languages Major Project of the Sixties and the guidelines laid down in Recommendation (69)2. The project on permanent education contributed the concept of lifelong learning as a coherent and purposive development, as well as learner centredness, learner autonomy, and the demystification of objectives, breaking down global subjects into transparently describable sub-parts. From the Eurocentres came the proposals for an approach based upon the analysis of situations and also the articulation of learners' needs, which had also been developed in the Hawkins and Vaughan James enquiries in UK. From DVV (deutscher Volkshochschulverein) and the associated International Certificate Conference (ICC) came a model for fully explicit syllabuses, based on *Le français fondamental* developed by CREDIF. The detailed syllabuses of the Nuffield Foundation were an important input, the *Sprechintentionen* of its *Vorwärts* syllabus being a valuable contribution to the classification of speech functions, together with the 'In the Air' syllabus developed by Svanta Hjelmström for the Swedish experimental media-based school at Linköping as well, of course, as the work of Austin and Searle on speech-acts (and Roget's *Thesaurus*!). The work of Tony Becher at the National Council for Educational Technology provided the basis for a 'systems approach' in which the analysis of needs and resources, the specification of objectives, the development of materials and methods, and the processes of assessment and evaluation form a coherent system, in which the transparent formulation of worthwhile and feasible objectives has a central role. Educational technology also brought realism and concern with human and material resources, especially media, and an understanding of their possibilities and limitations. In linguistics, the socio-anthropological, ethnographic approach of Firth and Malinowsky and particularly the concept of 'communicative competence' developed by Del Hymes together with the virtual withdrawal of a rejuvenated grammar from concern with applications, facilitated – indeed made almost inevitable a re-orientation of applied linguistics and language didactics from structural formalism to pragmatic functionalism (though of course the legacy of the detailed descriptions of English Grammar by Jespersen, Zuidema and others was known and available). The socio-linguistic schemata of the German followers of

Habermas (Wunderlich, Ehlich, Rehbein) and the early work of Candlin
provided models for the description of interactional strategies. As to the language teaching methodology itself, the abiding influence of the work of
316 Harold Palmer on British EFL was strongly felt and, in particular, the functional analysis embodied in Palmer and Blandford's *Everyday sentences in
spoken English*. More generally the perspectives of the Group were clearly
within the paradigm of the reform movement of the 1880s with its roots in
the neogrammarian linguistic revolution of the 1870s.

There was thus no shortage of relevant ideas, knowledge and experience for the Expert Group to work upon. Its task (clearer perhaps in
retrospect than at the time) was to distil from it a coherent set of basic
principles, to give them concrete expression in the form of models which
practitioners could adapt and apply to their own situations and to develop
strategies of educational innovation leading to syllabus and examination
reform, to improved course design and materials production to corresponding forms and content of initial and in-service teacher education and
training and thus to deep and permanent changes in classroom practice
and – what is of ultimate importance – the experience of language learning itself. Evidently, such a process of educational innovation requires
coherent and convergent decisions by a very large number of policy
makers and practitioners at many different levels. It is important for a
framework to be provided which can sustain effort and provide continuity
over a period long enough for deep and lasting reform to take effect. At the
same time the process must be dynamic and responsive to changes.

To provide such a framework, successive Projects have sought to gain
general acceptance for a small number of basic aims, directly related to
the general educational and political aims of the Council of Europe:

- to facilitate the free movement of people, information and ideas in
  Europe with access for all and to encourage closer co-operation by providing the linguistic means of direct interpersonal communication,
  both face-to-face and at a distance;
- to build up mutual understanding and acceptance of cultural and
  linguistic diversity in a multilingual and multicultural Europe, with
  respect for individual, local, regional and national identities, developing
  a common European intercultural identity by unforced mural influence;
- to promote the personal development of the individual as a learner
  and user of a language with growing self-awareness, self-confidence
  and independence of thought and action combined with social
  responsibility as an active agent in a participatory, pluralist democratic society;

- to make the process of learning itself more democratic by providing the conceptual tools for the planning, construction, conduct and evaluation of courses closely geared to the needs, motivations and characteristics of learners and enabling them so far as possible to steer and control their own progress.

In pursuing these aims, Projects have advocated, promoted and exemplified a 'systems development' approach emphasising the interrelation of aims, objectives, methods, materials, assessment and evaluation. A clear **317** specification of objectives, accepted as common goals by all the 'partners for learning', is seen as central to the planning of learning and teaching. Objectives should be **appropriate** in the light of the learners characteristics, **desirable** in the light of the vocational, recreational, cultural and personal needs of learners and the interests of society and **feasible** in the light of the human and material resources which can be brought to bear. Methods and materials for teaching and testing should be selected, produced and used which are appropriate to the learners and teachers and to the learning situations so as to achieve, or assess the achievement of, the agreed objectives. Clearly, there can be no universal 'best' method any more than there can be one objective for all learners. Choices should be made and decisions taken as close to the point of learning as possible, by consultation and agreement among all the relevant partners. The approach to language learning and teaching should be learner-centred, rather than subject-centred or teacher-centred, the function of teachers and other support personnel being to facilitate appropriate and effective learning and progressively to promote independent learning in a permanent education perspective, as the developing individual learns to understand and communicate in diverse ways for diverse purposes in a multilingual and multicultural world.

Having formulated these principles in the early seventies, the EES Group's next step was to develop and exemplify a new model for the specification of objectives. In 1974, drawing on a number of previous studies, J A van Ek elaborated *The threshold level,* a detailed specification of the minimum language requirements of *people who want to prepare themselves, in a general way, to be able to communicate socially on straightforward everyday matters with people from other countries who come their way, and to be able to get around and lead a reasonably normal social life when they visit another country.* This concept and in particular the shift of attention from form to function was warmly welcomed by the field and the apparatus of situations, functions, themes and notions was soon adopted as an analytic framework by EFL syllabus designers for curricula, textbooks and public examinations, as well as for the hugely successful multimedia course *Follow me.* Versions have since been produced for French, German, Spanish, Italian, Danish, Dutch, Swedish, Norwegian, Catalan, Basque, Portuguese and Welsh, while others are in preparation for Russian, Latvian, Estonian, Lithuanian, Maltese, Irish and Greek.

In 1976, the Committee on General and Technical Education commissioned adaptations of *The threshold level* and *Un niveau-seuil* for schools and decided to concentrate resources on the development and propagation of the new approach, which was also recommended to member Governments by the Committee of Ministers in Recommendation R(87)18. A 'Schools Interaction Network' was organised between 1977 and 1987, in which small teams of persons engaged in innovative projects visited other member states for discussions with colleagues in schools similarly engaged as well as with ministry officials involved in national curriculum development. The Network produced a strong sense of common purpose, as did the series of 37 workshops for teacher trainers held between 1984 and 1987. In the current Project *Language learning for European Citizenship,* support is being given to the new member states in Central and Eastern Europe in the reform of language teaching and teacher training along similar lines. In addition, a further series of workshops has been organised, dealing with new sectors and themes. Most of these are 'new-style' workshops, in which an international programme of action research is initiated at one workshop and received at a second some two years later.

In a long-term perspective, particular importance may attach to the current development of a *Common European descriptive framework for language learning and teaching* and an associated *European language learning portfolio, in* which individuals may record their language learning achievements and experiences of all kinds throughout their lives. The *Framework,* which presents the parameters and categories for a comprehensive model of language use and the user's activities and competences, together with proposals for scaling proficiency and methodological options, is now circulating in draft for field consultation.

The Council of Europe has no directive powers and very little money. Its moral authority rests on the quality of work carried out by the thousands of teachers, researchers, teacher trainers, course developers, examiners and administrators in over 40 countries who have worked together to produce its findings, models, recommendations and other documents. The language teaching profession causes a high responsibility for guiding a new generation through the dangers of featureless uniformity on the one hand and xenophobic backlash on the other into a new century of borderless opportunity and equipping them with the cultural awareness and communication skills they need to meet its challenges. The work of the past thirty years will, one may trust, provide them with a useful springboard for that task.

John Trim

Part

nine

A postcript

1966-1996 **YEARS**

In 1966, coinciding with CILT's opening its doors, a pamphlet from
the Incorporated Association of Headmasters suggested that

> *the effects upon education that will follow (from imminent closer
> collaboration with Europe) are at present only dimly perceived.
> How are we to face the enormous amount of . . . hard, detailed, poly-
> glot discussion that . . . this will entail not only on the part of
> specialist translators and interpreters . . . but . . . at all levels and in
> all professions and trades?* (Incorporated Association of
> Headmasters, *Modern languages in the grammar school*, 1966)

Euphoric hopes of important *effects upon education* may now,
to the cynic, seem to have been sadly misplaced. But though it may
be questioned whether the average British adult is much better
equipped than in 1966 for the *hard, detailed discussion* in a foreign
language that the Headmasters foresaw, yet a great deal has been
gained.

In Part 9 an old campaigner who steered CILT through some
very rough seas, reflects on lessons to be learned from battles lost
as well as from the many won.

30

A view from the bridge

John Trim

Asked by his grandson what exploits he had accomplished in the wars of his youth, a French veteran is said to have replied: *I survived!* Looking back on my Directorship of CILT from 1978 to 1987, I must confess to a similar feeling. The 'bridge' from which I can give a view was not so much the control centre of a mighty vessel sailing a steady course, as a foot-bridge under fire, leading from the secure territory of the 1960s and 1970s to the more verdant pastures of CILT today.

CILT was founded in the optimistic and expansive atmosphere of the early to middle sixties in the context of Britain's realisation after Suez that its economic future lay in Europe rather than as a world power and its first unsuccessful attempts to join the Common Market. The Annan Committee on the Teaching of Russian (1962) took up a proposal from the Hayter Report (1961) for a National Language Institute, with specific recommendations for its role and staffing. Whilst this recommendation was not implemented, in October 1964 the Secretaries of State for Education and Science and for Scotland set up a Committee on Research and Development in Modern Languages (CRDML) in association with the Trustees of the Nuffield Foundation, the University Grants Committee, the British Council and the Federation of British Industries. The terms of reference of the Committee, under the Chairmanship of Dr L Farrer Brown, Director of the Nuffield Foundation, were:

> *To examine the need for research and development in modern languages (including English as a Second Language) and in the teaching of these languages to keep in touch with what is being done in these fields in educational institutions and elsewhere and to make information readily available to interested parties; to advise on such proposals and suggestions as may be submitted to the committee and, where necessary, to stimulate research and development.*

The setting up of CILT was announced on 27 July 1966 by the Secretaries of State acting on the recommendation of CRDML, with Dr Farrer Brown as its nominal founder. CILT was established as an independent charitable foundation, maintained principally by central Government grants, to take on part only of CRDML's remit, namely *to collect, co-ordinate and disseminate information about all aspects of modern language teaching and learning for the benefit of teachers and others professionally concerned in Great Britain.* Regrettably, CILT was not given a role in the stimulation of research and development or in the co-ordination of its funding, which was abandoned upon the demise of CRDML in 1970, with a clear lowering of the priority given to language research by the various funding bodies and the newly established Research Councils. For many years none of the Research Councils found a place for language research in spite of the best efforts, first of John Galleymore, CRDML's dedicated research advisory officer and then of the National Council for Modern Languages (NCML), set up by a number of academic modern language associations in an attempt to fill the gap. The information function of CILT was parallel to that of the British Council's English Teaching Information Centre (ETIC), the Director of which, George Perren, moved across to set up CILT as its first Director, Dr Farrer Brown serving as Chairman of Governors from the foundation until 1972. CILT was alongside ETIC first in State House, High Holborn and from 1974 in Carlton House Terrace. A joint CILT/ETIC Language Teaching Library was developed and soon enjoyed a high reputation as a unique resource with open access to its collection for the language teaching profession at home and overseas. Volume 1 of *Language Teaching Abstracts*, with summaries of the more important articles from the periodicals held in the library was published in 1968. The series still continues as *Language Teaching.*

Another regular activity of CILT in its early years, inherited from CRDML, was a register of Research in Progress, looked after with loyal devotion by Helen Lunt until her untimely death from cancer in March 1987, assisted by June Geach from 1972 until she became responsible for English as a second language. George Perren's conception of CILT's role was strictly informational. In that perspective he believed strongly that the most effective way for CILT to reach its constituency was through publication rather that through labour-intensive personal outreach. Many publications were designed to draw on the information sources held in CILT (most especially the Language Teaching Library), in order to make their content more accessible to teachers unable to come to London. *Language Teaching and Linguistics: Abstracts* was of this nature, as were the general and specialised Language Teaching Bibliographies and the annotated annual catalogues of newly accessed courses and audio-visual materials in the major school languages. The Research Register was published at intervals as an independent publication and new entries (including those from Europe) in *Abstracts* meanwhile. Conferences were held on topics of current interest, usually on a seminar scale, with the papers and discussion published in the series *CILT Reports and Papers,* which also contained some commissioned collections. The appointment of C Vaughan James as Deputy Director created some more space for outreach activity, but for the most part the informational remit of CILT's Charter was fairly strictly observed until George Perren's retirement in 1978.

My association with CILT goes back to its pre-natal stage. I served on the Fundamental Research Sub-Committee of CRDML, chaired a working party on the effectiveness of language laboratories and organised a colloquy on post-A-level German. In 1965–69 I took part in CILT conferences on languages for special purposes and on language teaching methods; aims and techniques, thus contributing to the first two volumes of *CILT Reports and Papers.* However, it was in the framework of the Council of Europe that I came into closest contact. Encouraged by Donald Riddy, HMSI, and by Professors Peter Strevens and Eric Hawkins, CILT took a full part in the Council's first ten-year Major Project in Modern Languages. In 1967 CILT conducted under contract a European Survey of Research into Spoken Language and negotiated for a co-ordinating role in a European network of national information centres. In its Resolution (69)2 'on an intensified modern language teaching programme for Europe', the Committee of Ministers included an invitation to 'each Government member states as soon as possible, to nominate or create national centres specialising in such fields as:

(i) systematic collection and distribution, to language teachers and others, of information on the findings of research having a bearing on modern language teaching;
(ii) documentation on the specialised use of languages particularly in science and technology;
(iii) techniques of testing proficiency in modern languages;
(iv) use of modern technical equipment for teaching languages'.

The model recommended was clearly CILT, and when the recommendation continued:

. . . to examine whether any existing institutes or centres for modern languages could, with advantage, take over certain tasks of common European benefit;

the finger pointed at CILT as clearly as in a National Lottery advertisement! After further negotiation DES provided CILT with additional funding to strengthen the Research Information Section to enable it to take on the co-ordination of (i) above, research information. This entailed a change in the Centre's title (though not its acronym) to 'Centre for

Information on Language Teaching and Research' and to the title of *Language Teaching: Abstracts* to *Language Teaching and Linguistics: Abstracts.*

My own involvement with the Council of Europe came in 1967, when the University of Essex withdrew from its commitment to host the Second AILA Congress and I saw an opportunity to demonstrate in a practical way that applied linguistics was relevant to the full range of language problems in society. I was unaware at the time that AILA had been set up by the Council of Europe to promote closer interaction between academic researchers and the teaching profession following the failure to get backing for a European Centre for Modern Languages (recently set up, at last, in Graz, Austria). In fact, the success of the 1969 Congress, with 649 participants from over 40 countries world-wide, established AILA as a world organisation, moving its affiliation from the Council of Europe to UNESCO. However, BAAL charged George Perren and me with the editorship of Applications of Linguistics, a selection of Conference papers. I quickly grew to appreciate George's critical acumen and editorial skills. When in 1971 I was asked to chair a Council of Europe Working Party to investigate the feasibility of a European Unit-credit Scheme for Modern Languages in Adult Education, George Perren was a member of the Working Party. His cool judgement as well as his gift for clear exposition and for recognising and exposing empty rhetoric and intellectual incoherence were invaluable to us in formulating basic principles and concrete proposals in those formative years.

In the mid-seventies, though the work of the Council of Europe and in particular the 'Threshold Level' developments were warmly received on the Continent and in EFL (English as a Foreign Language) circles generally, the public support for modern language teaching in this country waned. Technology, in the form of audio-visual or audio-lingual courses in language laboratories, had not transformed language learning, at any rate to the extent which would justify the heavy expenditure involved and the Burstall Report killed the Nuffield Foundation's hope that starting the first foreign language at the age of eight would make space for a second foreign language from eleven. The Brezhnev years did not encourage the learning of Russian. Mainstream linguistics, under the influence of Chomsky, came to pride itself on its distance from observable language behaviour and its irrelevance to the language teaching profession. The irresistible rise of English as a vehicle for international communication made it easy to argue that the educational cost of producing a low level of communicative skill was too high to be justified in a curriculum under pressure from physical and human sciences. The motivation of the 'new' learners when a modern language, almost always French, was made compulsory in the comprehensive school, was low, with a 60% drop-out rate, which had a catastrophic effect on the morale of teachers used to teaching in selective grammar schools only. By 1976, George Perren wrote of waves beating on a stony beach and a conference convened at King's College London was held in an atmosphere of doom and gloom.

I succeeded George Perren on his retirement in 1978 and, at the same time, Alan Moys succeeded Vaughan James, who left to set up the Pergamon Institute of English, as Deputy Director. We felt that whilst we must continue and in fact intensify the Centre's publications output, our task must go well beyond this. We should go out actively into the field and give support and encouragement to a hard-pressed profession, to bring it out of isolation and fragmentation and reverse the reputation modern languages seemed to have acquired for being difficult, formal, boring and irrelevant to the real needs of young people and society more generally. We were greatly helped in this task by the energetic determination of the profession to put its own house in order. At the end of the 1970s groups of teachers in Oxfordshire began to use the Nuffield defined syllabuses and the Council of Europe 'threshold level' specifications to produce their own early learning objectives, selected so as to be clearly of direct practical use for communication in the most common situations of daily life. The movement, chronicled by Brian Page, its guiding spirit, elsewhere in this volume (see Chapter 7), spread rapidly. The University of York responded by awarding certificates of achievement – often the first recognition the 'new constituency' of learners in comprehensive schools had achieved. The effect on motivation and on drop-out rates was dramatic. From 1980 – when we organised a first national conference on GOML (Graded Objectives in Modern Languages), whilst leaving direction entirely in the hands of the teachers – CILT provided secretarial and other services to groups involved in the GOML movement, including the publication of a regular newsletter. In time, more university Departments of Education and Examining Boards gave support and offered services. For a time it looked as though a dual system might develop. In fact, however, when government introduced the Common Curriculum, modern languages were in a better position to give a rapid and coherent response than most other subjects. The communicative ideology brought other benefits, too. Its acceptance helped to heal the rift between the 'modernist' British Association for Language Teaching (BALT) and the 'traditionalist' Modern Languages Association (MLA) and prepared the ground for the re-unification of the language teachers' associations into the Association for Language Learning (ALL). Reunification of the smaller language-specific associations was also assisted by the end of French-only College of Education courses in favour of degree courses, usually involving at least two languages, plus a PGCE year. The year abroad has also made teachers much more competent and confident in handling classroom teaching in the target language and using communicative methods.

326

Attempts to build bridges with English teachers

The communicative approach also provided a common focus for language teaching of different kinds; modern foreign languages, EFL and ESL (English as a foreign/second language), minority mother tongues development and even the language component of mainstream English teaching. In the preceding period, modern language teaching was mainly concerned with correctness of linguistic form and English teaching took mother tongue competence for granted and was concerned with the individual's expression of experience and appreciation of imaginative literature. The two groups of teachers had little to say to each other. In 1973, George Perren brought 100 modern languages and English teachers together, reported in CILT Reports and Papers no 10 with the significant title *The space between . . . English and foreign languages at school*. As James Brittain put it (p45):

> *As English teachers we have tended to regard teachers of foreign languages as having less concern with the cause we are promoting than have the teachers of most other subjects in the curriculum.*

Harold Rosen's penetrating criticism of Del Hymes conception of communicative competence appeared to point in a quite different direction from that in which it had proved so fruitful in the modern languages field. However, some common ground emerged in the language problems of ethnic minority children and also in the proposal by Eric Hawkins for the introduction of language awareness into schools on a cross-disciplinary basis (see Chapter 10). Perren persisted and I fully concurred. Language studies should find their appropriate place within a coherent universe, calling upon a common theoretical base though developing in different directions in accordance with their diverse functions and audiences. Our dream was to develop the CILT/ETIC Library as a common resource. It seemed that the National Congress on Languages in Education (after an inauspicious start in 1978 when modern linguists and English mother tongue specialists again conducted a 'dialogue of the deaf') might provide a common framework as a basis for the development of a common information service and for the kind of fruitful interaction which characterised the Royal Society of Arts' Language Committee. Alas, this

dream-boat was soon dashed against the rocks of the
made it impossible to maintain existing activities,
initiatives. First, ETIC was abolished as the English
the British Council had to make 25% cuts at 48 hou
1983 the Language Teaching Library was remodell
and Media Resource Centre, it was doomed even b
opened by the Queen. In 1984 the dreaded mid-term
in a rent rise of some £1m p.a. for Spring Gardens
Terrace. DES would not fund this and CILT had t ___.,, fortunately
finding accommodation in Regent's College and taking its library holding
with it. The British Council immediately closed its library to the public and
dispersed the holdings when English Language Division moved to
Manchester. Until 1986 CILT was funded to service NCLE and common
interests, especially in developing language awareness, but CILT then
came under pressure from DES to cut expenditure whilst NCLE chose to
distance itself from CILT and seek independent government funding,
which was not forthcoming. Cross-disciplinary co-operation between the
language disciplines in schools thus suffered a serious set-back. It must
now be for another generation to realise the essential unity of the development of a young person's communicative potential and to find forms of
organisation which will assure its coherence.

Enthusiasm of young linguists

Our attempts at bridge-building thus had mixed results. The internal
fragmentation of the modern language teaching profession was overcome,
but disciplinary isolation much less so. The communicative approach had
done much to establish that language learning need not focus on form but
rather on the sharing of meanings and thus could be both relevant and
successful for mainstream learners. Activity-based learning itself went far
to remove the 'boring' image. In addition, we promoted the Festival of
Languages and Young Linguists Competition as an appropriate British
counterpart to the German *Wettbewerb Fremdsprachen* (see p295). The
response was exhilarating, with some 8,000 schoolchildren and parents
thronging the Arts Centre of Warwick University of present work and play
in 36 languages. My daughter took a multi-ethnic group from a middle
school in Ealing to perform *Cendrillon,* immediately following a highly
polished performance of a scene from Chekov in Russian by the sixth form
of St Paul's School. The boys had loyally agreed to sacrifice a football
match and Alison's day was made when going back on the coach one of
the boys exclaimed: *Cor! That were better 'an football, wannit!* Clearly the
image presented was one of fun and enjoyment, as HMI Betty Parr had
foreseen. Her support was invaluable, as were the organising skills and
perseverance of Christine Wilding and the generous support of National

estminster Bank. But above all, the enthusiastic response of teachers and pupils at regional level throughout the UK justified all the effort and expense. We also saw how strongly young people were attracted to the new technology – especially when older children produced the programmes! From an early stage we had encouraged practitioners in CALL (Computer-Assisted Language Learning) and supported an annual conference and newsletter.

Indifference of employers

Our task over these years was not made easier by the fact that, while language teachers were recovering their self-confidence and sense of purposive direction, the prevailing public mood remained one of indifference, bordering on hostility. Two anecdotes may provide illustrations. To support and stimulate the learning of less widely-taught languages, we produced a series of *Language and Culture Guides*. No 1, *Arabic*, was published in 1985. To publicise the Guide and to promote Arabic we invited 100 from the educational side and 100 from trade and industry with commercial interests in the Arab world to come to CILT for its launch. Almost all the invitees from education came; from the user side only one, a junior training officer from Shell. A similar disproportion in the so-called two-sided conferences on languages in industry gave the impression of a one-sided love affair. In July 1985 CILT organised a three-day conference on *German in the United Kingdom: issues and opportunities*. The Conference was attended by 423 participants. More than 50 applications had to be declined for lack of room. Sixty papers were presented and discussions, ranging over the whole field of policy and teaching methodologies was both serious and lively. In opening the Conference the German Ambassador pointed out – as a predecessor had done some years before – that unlike English, German was not a world language. Germans were quite ready to use English when selling their goods abroad, but when buying from abroad expected to negotiate in German. However, his words went unreported. The non-specialist Press ignored the invitations sent to them. Instead, the following day the Times published a leading article proposing that modern languages should be dropped from the school curriculum and computer language taught instead. After all, they and English alone were the languages of modernity! It was, of course, the Silly Season, but in general at that time public pronouncements on language matters were ignorant and self-opinionated, demonstrating how badly courses in language awareness were needed as part of a general education.

Perhaps in tune with this public mood, government policy kept the Centre continuously under threat from the time in 1979 that the newly-elected Conservative administration declared an open season on Quangos. A disproportionate part of directorial time and effort went to explaining and justifying our existence, refuting draconian and uncomprehending management reviews. Four years were spent 'under review' with a reduced budget and a veto on planning beyond the current year, with the Governing Board in abeyance. HMSI muttered the Pope quotation: 'willing to wound and yet afraid to strike'. Fortunately for CILT and for the future of modern languages, the language teaching profession stood solidly behind the Centre, particularly in response to a consultation letter sent by the Secretary of State to CILT's clients in order to seek their views on the future direction of CILT services, with a view to 'improving value for money'. In April 1986 Sir Keith Joseph formally announced the end of the review, writing to Dr Albert Sloman, Chairman of Governors:

I have been impressed by the number and quality of the consultative responses. They are a clear indication of the importance which CILT's clients attach to the Centre's continued and effective operation.

Sir Keith defined CILT's future agenda:

I have in mind that the main focus of each of the Centre's activities should be the teaching of languages in schools. However, I am persuaded of the desirability of CILT's continuing to provide information services to further and higher education and to foster communication among the different sectors. I would encourage CILT to emphasise aspects of its work which relate to language teaching for the purposes of practical communication; and also to consider whether more can be done to provide appropriate support for industry and commerce and indeed to seek support from them.

This apparent endorsement of CILT's role and policy over the years (though with no reference to its international role) was accompanied by clear directions on finance and organisation, involving a new Board of Governors, a re-organised staff structure and new financial arrangements. The new regime coincided with my attainment (with allowance for wartime infantry service) of the retiring age – though retirement has in effect meant simply an intensification of my work as Project Director in Modern Languages for the Council of Europe. I felt in leaving very confident that CILT had safely crossed over the perilous bridge, which had swayed but not broken, and that it was once again on firm ground, in the competent and experienced hands of Alan Moys. My abiding feelings are of gratitude and affection for a loyal and dedicated staff, serving a great profession, whose highest responsibilities and achievements still lie in the future as we all strive to equip young people to face the challenges and seize the opportunities of an increasingly international society. I am delighted to see how, in a more aware and supportive atmosphere, CILT is in a flourishing condition, enriched by the network of Comenius Centres. We shall all do well to remember and follow the precepts and example of that wise, humane, courageous and far-sighted teacher: 'Let all things come of free will. No violence in human affairs!'

330

References

CILT, *Languages and culture guides: 1. Arabic* (CILT, 1985)

CILT, *German in the United Kingdom: issues and opportunities,* papers from a conference held at Regent's College, London, 11–13 July 1985 (CILT, 1986)

Harding A, B Page and S Rowell, *Graded objectives in modern languages* (CILT, 1980)

Perren G E and J L M Trim (eds), *Applications of linguistics: selected papers of the Second International Congress of Applied Linguistics, Cambridge 1969* (Cambridge: CUP, 1971)

Perren G E (ed), *The space between . . . English and foreign languages at school,* papers from a conference on language in the middle years of secondary education held at the Manchester Teachers' Centre, 20–22 November 1973, CILT Reports and Papers 10 (CILT, 1974)

Van Ek J A and L G Alexander, *Threshold level English* (Oxford: Pergamon, 1980)

Part

ten

**Dreams and
challenges**

1966-1996 30 *YEARS*

We tend to forget that our (westernised) educational systems had their foundations laid in an age of relatively small independent nation-states. They transmit a largely national culture and are primarily vernacular systems with much emphasis on national traditions, national values, and a national language.

They are, even today, still in the main monocultural, monolinguistic and ethnocentric, even if they do not go in for the more blatant national self-advertising of a few decades ago. This applies to the whole system from the primary school to the university . . .

The introduction of a foreign language into this limited monoglot world has far-reaching consequences. We are, in fact, breaking with the nineteenth-century tradition of literacy in terms of a national language if we propose to introduce into the concept of fundamental literacy the mastery of another language . . . it has repercussions which are not confined to the primary (and the secondary) stage . . . Just as we take it for granted that the ordinary man and woman in all westernised countries is literate and numerate in terms of his own society, in about fifty or a hundred years' time it might perhaps be regarded as a matter of course that he has the command of at least one other language.

(Stern H H: paper read to the *International Conference on Modern Language Teaching*, West Berlin, September 1964. Quoted in Hoy P H (ed), *The early teaching of modern languages* (Nuffield Foundation, 1977))

Lid King

There is a (rather mediocre) French comedy film starring the late lamented Coluche and called *Le maître d'école*. In perhaps the only memorable scene Coluche is being inducted into his new role as a primary teacher by a rather pompous *Inspecteur d'Académie*. To the *Inspecteur*'s litany of lofty abstractions – vocation, sacerdos, and the like – Coluche has only one often repeated question:

> *Oui, Monsieur, mais qu'est-ce que je dois faire?*

The *Inspecteur* gives no answer.

As we too contemplate the complexities and uncertainties of the future there is a perhaps inevitable pressure to answer such a simple and urgent question. What indeed are we to do?

What national policy?

The inspector's dilemma – for of course he has no answer to the question – is also a real one. As teachers we often have an idea of a destination – the kind of competence for example which we would wish our pupils to attain – but despite all the efforts of the planners, the publishers and indeed the inspectors we find it difficult to actually describe the route which they will take. What indeed will they do?

There is a parallel in our contemplation of the future of our subject. It is actually not too difficult to define the kind of framework for languages which we would like to see. Eric Hawkins himself put forward such a plan over fifteen years ago. More recently there has been considerable impetus for and interest in the idea of a 'national policy' on languages, taking inspiration from developments in other countries and argued most forcefully by Professor Gareth Thomas in 1993. Indeed within the pages of the current volume there are certain common assumptions about the nature of such a strategy for languages (Hawkins, 1981). In looking to the future the problem may be not so much **what** to do as **how** to get there.

We could perhaps have recourse to an old and respected tradition – the oracular predictions found throughout the world: Apollo and the Sybil, the Revelation of St John, Nostradamus and Agathangelos and, more recently, rather less cataclysmic forecasters such as Old Moore and Mystic Meg. The persistence of such faith in oracles suggests a deep seated need in humans for certainty about the future , a need not belied by the wonderful obscurity of the oracles themselves. *And behold on the left side there shall be a serpent and a blonde man shall arise speaking tongues and with a mark upon the sixth finger* . . .

Until now there have been no known examples of oracles predicting the future state of education.

We can therefore rely only on our own expectations and dreams – and such imaginings as the following 'Report on languages' from the year 2026.

1996 2001 2006 2011 2016 2021 2026

LANGUAGES IN THE UK
A REPORT OF THE HAWKINS COMMISSION

Pre-school (Language development stage)

Following detailed investigation between experts in Child Development, Linguistics, First Language Acquisition, English, Community Languages, Foreign Languages, Teachers and Parents Groups, a coherent framework has been worked out for language development in pre-school pupils.

In addition to appropriate exposure to L1 discourse (for example daily conversation with adult role model helpers) this seeks to stimulate curiosity in language through songs and play and some exposure to other cultures and the sounds of other languages.

The success of this programme is guaranteed by the reform of the nursery vouchers scheme and the extension of full-time free nursery education for all children from the age of three. Target PTR 8.

The 2003/5 Johnstone/Coyle research on bilingual immersion learning has in addition provided the basis for funded bilingual centres in every major town.

Primary (Preparatory Stage)

Building on the success of the pre-school programme LANGUAGE AWARENESS has been developed as a core part of the primary curriculum. Based on Professor Hawkins' earlier work and the experience of previous primary language projects, in particular the Scottish programme of the early 1990s, this new curriculum has at its centre:

- Education of the ear
- Learning about language
- Cultural awareness
- Exposure to foreign language (from age six for all pupils)

In addition to the core programme a Special Needs support strand has been put in place — targeted in particular at those pupils who had not benefited from the still voluntary pre-school language provision. Support for all pupils is also available in after school 'TALKING AND READING CLUBS' staffed 80% by teacher, student and parent volunteers.

The introduction of this programme had proved possible because of detailed curricular planning involving the NCAA, CILT and the subject bodies which took place between 1996 and 1999 and was followed by the major teacher training and INSERVICE programme supported by the TTA and national Inspectorates and funded by the Millennium Fund (1999–2002).

Prior concerns about teacher supply and language competence were discovered to be ill-founded after the Wragg Committee's award on teacher's pay significantly eased the supply problem. The expansion of European funding for languages in education after Maastricht 2, coupled with the introduction of compulsory language competence modules in all first degrees (Nott Committee 1998) has also greatly improved the foreign language capabilities of primary school teachers.

8–13 (Apprenticeship Stage)

The Language Awareness programme continues to age eleven and includes the introduction of formal learning programmes about grammar and discourse in L1.

From age eight all pupils (except a small minority of disapplied pupils) include one of the NC languages in their programme which is based on the now well-researched Scottish Model. All pupils continue with their first foreign language and the majority begin a second language at age eleven.

The new Accreditation Authority has accordingly carried through a revision of the National Curriculum Order in England, Wales and NI (Dearing IX). The programmes have been made more relevant for younger pupils, in particular through a revision of the curriculum content. The content of primary language courses now mirrors the general primary curriculum as has been the case in Scotland for a number of years. Also revisions to the programmes of study and attainment targets have increased the weight given to a range of specifically linguistic competences.

336

It is expected that most pupils should reach level 4 of the revised MFL curriculum by age eleven. About 20% of the cohort are already attaining level 6. The majority of pupils should reach GCSE equivalent (New Standard Grade in Scotland) in at least one language at age fourteen.

In a number of schools throughout the UK bilingual sections are being developed. The expansion of the Content Oriented Language Teaching programme has resulted in the introduction of at least one combined course (predominantly Geography/MFL) into all schools in the post-11 curriculum. The Combined Universities Assessment Board and the Scottish Examination Authority have dropped all previous objections to assessment in languages other than English.

The 2009 Revision of the School Day Orders have freed up the organisation of the timetable and enabled schools to introduce new models of curricular provision. In addition to the recommended minimum of four hours foreign language study equivalent per week, increasing numbers of establishments are using new European and UK funding opportunities to introduce intensive language exchanges in Year 7 (S1 in Scotland). Initial OFSTED reports show no dilution in progress across the curriculum and the national targets (50% of pupils to engage in at least three months study abroad by the year 2026) appear eminently realisable.

The linking of all schools to Optic Fibre Cable and recent breakthroughs in ATM switching have provided the basis for widespread real-time video conferencing and joint use of multi media materials. All UK schools are now linked to partner schools throughout the EU and in the Pacific Rim. Joint multilingual curricular projects are specifically timetabled from the end of Key Stage 3.

(14–19) Preparatory Stage

The sound basis in linguistic and language competence established by the 3–14 curriculum is reflected in the now well established 'modular triple pathway' of the 14–19 phase.

Foreign language learning is a compulsory part of the 14–19 curriculum. In particular each subject pathway comprises relevant language modules. The prime objective of this stage is to develop more advanced language skills which are appropriate for the subject content of each pathway and eventually the career aspirations of all learners.

The *Bedford report* gives the following profile of nineteen-year-old language learners:

Higher levels (specialist linguists, translators, etc). No significant change in numbers for 40 years. Anecdotal evidence (from examiners and lecturers) of significantly increased facility with and appreciation of language and its effect, competent manipulation of appropriate technology, e.g. machine translation programmes. Major problems reported over grammatical accuracy (particularly irregular verbs and agreements).

Intermediate levels (language competence applied to other specialisms, also known as 'vocational'). Vastly increased numbers. Linguistic abilities and levels commensurate with group 1 above but less specialised (e.g. little translation or text manipulation competence). Strategic and Com-municative competencies excellent even when learning *ab initio*.

Foundation levels (occupational and functional language use). As general educational levels have risen this group has declined in numbers. Problems remain over disaffected students on pre-vocational courses (especially boys). General competence much improved, however, especially in languages of maximum 'employability' (Japanese, German, Korean, Standard Australian).

The 1999 reform of all advanced and vocational qualifications (New Advanced Diploma) has greatly aided the spread of linguistic competence in this sector. Of particular importance has been the simplification of accreditation procedures undertaken by the new accreditation body.

All 14–19 (and surviving 16–19) establishments are also involved in joint curricular projects on the Worldwide EduNet and — in conjunction with HE Language Centres — provide individualised (including remedial) support for language learners. A key tool for developing this support has been the expansion of self-access centres and open and distant learning programmes (often linked to the Virtual Open University).

The link with higher education has also enabled this sector to expand provision of tailored *ab initio* courses in non-core languages (languages other than French; German, Spanish, Japanese and Urdu). These count for equal credit with previously learned languages.

Higher education

The re-introduction of a language entry qualification for HE (this time set at NLS level 3 or equivalent) has had the effect on the one hand of increasing language studies pre-19 and on the other of radically altering the nature of language learning in universities.

Compared with the situation described by James Coleman in the pre-Reform mid-1990s there is now very little provision for *ab initio* language learning in higher education. This is now the role of schools. and the newer Tertiary Colleges often working in collaboration with a university Language Centre.

The expectation is that all undergraduates will be competent in two languages. They will also have partial competence (perhaps NVQ reading skills) in at least one other. The internationalisation of the curriculum and of working life has meant that there are now very few courses which do not include at least one module which is taught and assessed in a language other than English. Increased mobility between teaching and research staff has helped this process considerably.

By removing the pressure on universities to provide basic language courses for a wide range of specialisms resources have been released for a number of new purposes:

* the development of joint courses with universities overseas;
* the strengthening of language competence in lecturing staff;
* research and development of educational technology for language learning.

In this latter area in particular enormous progress has been made. It is a striking fact that 75% of language learning and use of foreign languages at HE level now takes place in the absence of a live teacher. Increasingly the applications being developed in this sphere are having an effect also on younger learners.

The reform of Initial Teacher Education in the early part of the century, in particular the introduction of compulsory foreign language competence and applied linguistics studies for all trainee teachers, have had a significant effect on the language pool among teachers at all levels. Great significance is attached to the recently accredited International Diploma in Secondary Teaching, requiring subject fluency in at least three world languages.

Finally there has been a significant expansion in research activity thanks in no small part to the increase in Euro and Pacific funding opportunities. It is still too early to say with confidence whether the compulsory research sabbatical for teachers and lecturers has had a significant effect on outcomes. Some older researchers have claimed that current research into language learning is too output-related.

Working life — the adult learner

The resolution of the funding crisis of the late twentieth century through a combination of governmental, European and industrial investment has lead to a new phase in Adult Language Learning. A key factor has been the adoption of the Council of Europe 'portfolio' of language competence and the corresponding lifelong occupational validity of language capabilities. In this respect also the promotional work of the former Languages Lead Body (now Languages Occupational Training Council) was of vital importance. The DTI's (now DIEE's) espousal of the Investor in Languages award and the effect of this on the recruitment and training policies of major companies has raised the status of language competence in the industrial sphere.

The drive to make language learning relevant and accessible to adults and to improve the qualifications of language teachers and trainers (NatBLIS programme) has brought Adult Language Learning into the mainstream. Despite the overall growth of language competence throughout the UK there remains a central role for the Adult trainers — the introduction of new languages for occupational and also social purposes. Notwithstanding recent advances in psycho-occupational testing it remains impossible to predict which language any individual might need at any particular stage in her or his life. Here the adult/business trainer (for the two are now virtually indistinguishable) remains of paramount importance.

One interesting consequence of progress has been the decline of traditional languages in this sector. In 2024 the most popular language for adults was Korean.

Another important development has been the introduction of the Advanced Language Teaching Diploma and the Central Bureau's relatively new programme of Business Trainer Exchanges with the emerging countries of Southern Africa and Oceania.

The increasing professionalisation of this sector and its integration with the needs of business has not entirely altered the traditions of adult language learning. Although the permanent beginner may be becoming a phenomenon of the past the latest statistics still show that 25% of learners in the over 55 age range were learning languages for cultural or leisure purposes. Most of these regarded themselves as beginners and considered the conviviality of their language class as one of the main reasons for continuing their studies.

In sum

The UK now has a coherent and effective languages policy for all stages of society which is relevant to the country's economic needs and to the aspirations of its citizens, and which is furthermore cost-effective and responsive to change. The long term objectives of this Commission and of support organisations such as CILT have been achieved. We propose immediate dissolution in order to go home and *cultiver notre jardin*.

2026 2021 2016 2011 2006 2001 1996

Waking from the dream . . .

It might of course be so. But even if we agree on the destination we can not predict the detailed course of events – which languages, what technology, which systems and above all what resources will be available.

And since we do not share the arcane confidence of a Nostradamus we can offer no such definite prescription for the future, but just a dream. It does however seem likely that many of the concerns of the past thirty years which have been documented in this volume will provide a guide to future developments, whether they are to indicate possible solutions or be the genesis of new challenges.

Rather than presenting a blueprint, then, let us speculate about those existing and new challenges that will face our discipline and about some of the most likely outcomes. For if it is to be of value any account of the past must not simply be a celebration. We have undoubtedly achieved a great deal since the 1960s and it is right that we record this, but as Eric Hawkins points out in his introduction and as our contributors underline in their different ways, the future of foreign language learning in the UK is neither clear nor assured.

A characteristic of the preceding pages is the diversity of views expressed within the framework of a common commitment to the importance of language learning. This may in itself be a reflection of the fundamental importance of language – the uniqueness of our subject to refer again to Eric's words. It also makes the task of drawing out common threads even more unlikely to satisfy everyone or perhaps anyone at all. Let us nonetheless make our way through the labyrinth and seek some answers to Coluche's plaintiff request.

Qu'est-ce qu'on va donc faire?

Four fundamental challenges

Of one thing we can be certain. The future will not develop either smoothly or as we expect. There is a common image of progress which is a road – or in technological terms a superhighway. While appealing it is also a misleading representation. Things develop not in smooth straight lines but through conflict and contradiction. We may as teachers and examiners be attracted by the idea of a regular progression of levels. As educators and as linguists we also know that in reality learners advance in contradictory, often surprising and rarely linear ways. After months or years of apparent inactivity they may take off into the stratosphere. It seems that life is not dissimilar – and the way that we meet the challenges which exist now will determine the shape of our future.

Let us therefore address these existing challenges – challenges which in many respects have been the story of this book and which we have still not resolved.

1 Why learn languages – the role of International English

The first challenge is the simplest and the most intractable. It is the challenge faced in the opening section of our book – do we need linguists at all?

It seems that periodically this question is resolved, only for it to be raised again – probably in the pages of a national newspaper:

ENGLISH NOW THE WORLD LANGUAGE
says Professor Pangloss

The article/letter/speech argues that the 'triumph' of English on a world scale makes redundant our efforts to inculcate the rudiments of French/German Spanish in recalcitrant pupils. Better by far to teach them 'correct' English.

Such views are compounded by the petty nationalism of 'sceptics' of various hues. They are reflected, often in more subtle mode, in key parts of the academic world and also (perhaps even more so) in business. Their persistence suggests that despite the advances made in the last thirty years the argument for foreign language learning still has not been won (*The Times*, 1994).

There is of course some truth in the premise – English **is** for many purposes an international language and the tendency is probably increasing. Anyone who has worked in international contexts will know this from direct experience. To win the argument dreams and fine words will not be enough. Why indeed should we learn languages?

In earlier chapters Jim Beale and Nigel Reeves have given one convincing answer. Our recent experience of the role of languages in business has underlined the 'bottom line' significance of language competence – not least on the switchboards of our major companies. This is now becoming accepted wisdom. Perhaps even more interesting has been an apparent convergence between such sternly instrumental views of language learning – we learn German to sell more sprockets – and the more humanist traditions of linguists from Comenius to the editor of the current book. In line with the 'softer' approaches of modern business management theory the importance of human **communication** is increasingly stressed (Handy, 1993).

342   Language – including foreign language – is key to such communication and real interchange.

One, perhaps not fully comprehended, aspect to this – the 'humanistic bottom line' – is the development of employee (i.e. people's) interest in language learning. This may indeed be the key to the future expansion of languages in the world of work, as suggested in our fantasy report from the twenty-first century. Employees rather than employers may be the driving force of increased language use and competence. In this sense 'business' becomes just one (important) aspect of human interaction and language is seen as an even more fundamental need.

It is certainly this need which underpins the 'educational' arguments for foreign language learning advanced so forcefully by Eric Hawkins on pp21ff. We must undoubtedly transcend the strictly instrumental arguments about language learning for they are limiting and incomplete. Not least they can not be justified for all of our people. Some will **not** need languages for economic purposes. Some may not even work. And yet – we have seen it – some of the most moving and relevant examples of language learning in practice have been the attempts of the very young and the striving of those with learning difficulties to communicate in foreign tongues. Through it they have learned – about themselves, about the world, about their own language. There is not only a point. There is also a deep seated need (NCC, 1993).

The existence of this need brings us to the second challenge.

2 Who learns languages – the uneven playing field

The transformation in language learning from a subject for the elite to a subject for all – what we might call the democratisation or normalisation of language learning – is only partially complete. The past thirty years have shown both the desirability and the possibility of making foreign language learning a meaningful experience for all. Yet there remain many pupils in schools who resist language learning and who significantly underachieve. Proportionately more of these are in the 14–19 age group, in particular working class children and above all working class boys.

Despite the growing and documented enthusiasm among adults for languages there remain many for whom language learning is an arcane mystery. The permanent beginner still roams the land (or rather the classrooms of our colleges and adult centres).

In this area our balance sheet can show only partial progress. There is more than a suspicion that our subject, as it is currently taught and resourced, favours the prejudices of what some call the chattering classes. The experience of Gites on the Loire and nights at the opera are advantages for young students of languages. As a result foreign languages learning retains an element of elitism. That this is not inevitable is documented above (for example in Bernardette Holmes's account in Chapter 8). The challenge nonetheless remains.

The challenge is the normalisation of language learning recounted in our future fantasy. The question we still have to answer is whether this can be done.

In many ways the conditions are now far more propitious than they have ever been for such a significant shift in British attitudes and expectations. The very existence of the National Curriculum – with all its imperfections – provides a powerful institutional context for normalisation in language learning. Other influences – the European Union's insistence on multi-competence in languages, the concerns of exporters and their promoters in the DTI , the pressures from adults for language competence as a need in the multi national workplace – all provide strong support for the dream of multilingualism (DES/WO, 1990; EC, 1996).

And yet the problems remain. If we are really to break though the monolingual loop we will have to build further on the progress made in the recent past. When Brian Page records the efforts of teachers to establish meaningful programmes for all pupils (the GOML movement, see Chapter 7) we should not forget the essential characteristic of those efforts. Not only did they involve teachers working together, taking ownership of the curriculum, they also sought meaningful content for learners who might not always wait patiently for the deferred reward of an examination grade.

There is no *potion magique* in any branch of learning – far less in languages, but the search for relevance. for contact with the target culture will continue and will be at the centre of all our endeavours. In this respect it is fascinating to note the recent recrudescence of interest in two aspects of language learning – the learning of serious subject matter 'through the medium' and the study of language 'for itself' (Hawkins, 1988).

If we are to progress it seems likely that these two approaches , or indeed a combination of the two will be at the centre of our thinking in the coming period. The simple point may be that unless our learners see the 'point' of language learning – both/either because language study is of relevance in its own right, and/or because its provides access to knowledge and understanding of value to the learner, then 'languages for all' will remain an aspiration rather than a reality.

We know that it can be so. To achieve it will require continued discussion, debate, training and curricular development. The spiral will continue . . .

344   3 How are languages learned – reforming the system

If the future promises further debate on the content of learning, it will also require change in the mechanics of the curriculum. If language learning (perhaps any learning?) is to be really 'for all' then the systems which we have inherited from the 1950s will inevitably need to change.

Consider just one example – the timetable. The division of learning into short chunks of time – the drip feed method – which we have often demanded may actually prevent effective learning. How long is it since Eric Hawkins first provided us with the image of the gardener in the gale? And what have we sought to do about it? And what is the effect of the 'divided timetable' on what we know can be the most effective way to acquire language competence – the intensive course and extended study visit?

As the number of pupils, students, learners increase and the complexity of their demands and needs expands the present set up will come under greater and greater tension. A radical rethink of the learning day, the nature of learning activities, the role of the teacher and of technology will be inevitable. Better that it should be sooner – and with the participation of teachers and learners – than later and imposed by necessity or government.

We are also – perhaps uniquely in the developed world – bedevilled by continuing debate about the ways in which we divide up our pupils (selection by attainment, income, geography). Whatever the rationale for the differing views and whatever their outcomes, the existence of such uncertainty is a continuing threat to the normalisation of language learning.

What after all could be easier and more dangerous than to justify the restriction of language learning opportunities to the highest attainers, which in turn brings us back to our first challenge? Why learn languages at all?

Beyond this discussion on purpose and principle we also need further debate about the ways in which we organise language learning. This must be more than a discussion about teaching organisation. It implies continued reflection about how different learners learn – the role of the group, individual learning, whole class teaching. It implies reassessing the way we make use of resources and attacking the fundamental question of how we deliver better and more learning with the same or sometimes even less. It involves examining the possibilities for self-tuition of various kinds (learning how to learn). It involves some radical thinking about boys and girls and mixed groups and single sex groups and appropriate styles of teaching and learning.

The agenda is a long and rich one. The answers will not necessarily come quickly and those who seek them will often be overwhelmed by systems they did not choose and confronted by learners they did not ask for . . . But unless we can break through at some point in the organisation of learning then 'languages for all' will remain a dream (or worse a pretence).

4 The challenge of technology – numbers, phobes and freaks

The fourth challenge is both a threat and an opportunity.

We have already seen (see Chapters 19–21) how the promises of technology – the 'glittering streams' referred to by Peter Green – have impacted on language learning. Whatever the proposed medium – tape recorder, video machine, computer – the potential seems never to have been matched in reality. As we now enter the Information Age some would say that nothing has really changed. Technology is still no more than an adjunct, the provider of tools which may or may not be of use in simple tasks; the Internet is no more or less important than the printing press.

For others there is a qualitative change – the Knowledge Society is at hand. The new information technology will hold the key to the problem of numbers and needs. It will provide solutions to the constraints of time and space and resource. The speed with which information can be accessed, the possibilities for distant communication will provide endless new possibilities and needs for language learning.

Whatever the future holds, and let us here avoid the seductive dangers of prophecy, it does seem that the ways in which we address this issue will be of major significance for language learning in the next century.

There are two main strands in the impact of the new information technology on learning, what Professor Terry Mayes has categorised as improvements in efficiency and improvements in effectiveness. By efficiency we might understand doing more of the same and by effectiveness doing it better. Both – the quantitative and the qualitative – have implications for language learning (Esch, 1994).

We need greater efficiency – because we are committed to the delivery of greater language competence to greater numbers of people (languages for all). Unless we believe in almost infinite resourcing, endless supplies of trained teachers (and tooth fairies) we must find technological solutions to the challenge of numbers. Anything else is likely to take us back to our elitist history. In doing so, however, we will need to rethink a great deal of our current practice – not least the roles of teacher, learner, resources and programme. Such change is already taking place, mainly in the better resourced institutions of academia, and the newly established Language Colleges may well provide a valuable testbed for such developments in the secondary sector. If we are to succeed such experience must become more generalised over the next decade.

Re-examining current practice should bring us inexorably to the second strand – effectiveness. Inasmuch as we are passionate about our subject this is likely to excite us somewhat more than simply the question of numbers, as we seek to make language learning more relevant and rewarding to greater numbers of people. What is exciting to some about the new technologies is the potential which they seem to hold for doing just that. Whether it be through the interactive potential of electronic communications or the learner centredness of recent CD developments there seems to be something about current technological developments which is qualitatively different from what has gone before. If this is the case, and not simply the amazement of simple folk in front of the *camera obscura*, it is because the new information technology is about choice, about content, about interaction. It is, in a word, communicative.

This in itself will present us – language educators – with new challenges. What is the relationship between teacher and resource? What is the effect of virtual (as opposed to real) communication? How do learners access information? Will English dominate the Internet (and what kind of English will it be?). Which brings us back full circle to our first fundamental challenge. And so the spiral continues.

The future for CILT – a kind of conclusion

It is somehow fitting that we end with unresolved questions. This reflects the real nature of progress and says something about, not just CILT but all of those whose efforts and aspirations make up the story of languages in the UK. The more immediate future – subject inevitably to the vagaries of politics and resourcing – will not be so much an apocalypse as a progression (sometimes steady, sometimes unexpected). Existing challenges will be solved, new ones will appear, the spiral will continue.

It is of course our hope and our intention that CILT should continue to play a key role in such change – reflecting, supporting, sometimes provoking. Above all it must continue its key function, which is not to be an oracle or fount of all wisdom but something more humble (and hopefully more effective). The image is that of a gatekeeper – filtering and passing on not so much people as information. Its function is that of transmitting ideas and possibilities, between learners and teachers, practitioners and policy makers, researchers and educators.

My own view is that so long as communication remains central to human development, so long as we retain our fascination with the ways we interact, so long as we look beyond ourselves to other people, other cultures, other traditions, then there will be a place and a need for such 'guardians at the gate'. Indeed as the quantity of available knowledge increases exponentially the gatekeepers come into their own. Without them even Nostradamus gets confused.

We must of course admit to some degree of failure. It seems inherently unlikely that we will ever fully answer Coluche's opening plea – what will we do tomorrow? On the other hand it may be that the patient reader will have found many possibilities within these pages, relating to her/his own concerns and looking not only backwards but to the future. We might also remember that the certainty of the prophet is a suspect certainty. Far better perhaps the knowledge and experience which is able to react to change with some confidence . . . In the final analysis we can not say what is to be done. for we can only guess at the future. Who in 1966 would have predicted the PC on which these words are being written? The most interesting developments have not yet been imagined. When they face us we shall no doubt think of something.

References

CILT conference, *Quality and standards* (Cambridge, December 1995)

CILT seminar, *Through the medium* (July 1996)

The common European framework of reference for language learning and teaching (Council of Europe, due to be launched in 1997)

Coyle D and G Fruhauf, *Teaching content in the foreign language: practical perspectives in European models of bilingual education* (Alkmaar: Stichting Europrint, 1996)

DTI Languages for Export Campaign, Joint Export Promotion Directorate, tel: 0171 215 8146

Edelenbos P and R Johnstone, *Researching languages at primary school: some European perspectives* (CILT/Scottish CILT, 1996)

Esch E (ed), *Self-access and the adult language learner* (CILT, 1994)

'Eurosceptics and foreign languages' in *Education* (29 September 1995)

Handy C, *The empty overcoat* (Hutchinson, 1993)

Hawkins E W, *Modern languages in the curriculum* (CUP, 1981; revised 1987)

Hawkins E W, *Intensive language teaching and learning* (CILT, 1988)

'Here's one Euro fight we won, Mr Major' in *The Times* (28 July 1994)

Language World (ALL journal), June 1996

Modern foreign languages for ages eleven to sixteen (DES/WO, October 1990)

NCC, *Modern foreign languages and special educational needs: a new commitment* (February 1993)

Peters T, *The pursuit of WOW!:* 213–5 (Vintage Books, 1994)

'Students shun languages' in *Education* (24 September 1995)

Teaching and learning towards the learning society (European Commission, 1996)

Thomas G, *The Threlfold Lecture* (April 1993)

Epilogue

Lid King

As society becomes more complex, in many respects harsher and more divisive, language, communication and the desire to relate to others remain the essential mortar holding us together. This is understood by nobody more acutely than Eric Hawkins, for whom this volume has been a herculean labour (and we hope a labour of love) and whose erudition, wisdom and deep humanity speak from its pages. We are of course immensely grateful to all of those who have worked to make sense of languages over the last thirty years, but none should feel diminished if the final word is for Eric who has inspired (still inspires) generations of language teachers with his vision of a multilingual and humane society and for whom, in this year when England did not win the European Cup, the level playing field remains a central aspiration.

Appendices

1966-1996 YEARS

Appendix I

CILT's first 30 years in context — a calendar of events

compiled by Gill Tench

The context	CILT

1961

Hayter Committee (on place of non-European languages) recommends establishment of a 'National Languages Institute' (p321).

APRIL
Second conference of European Ministers of Education in Hamburg sets out programme for reform of modern language teaching. Council of Europe launches ten-year major project. HMSI D Riddy plays a leading role (p323).

1962

Report of the Annan Committee on teaching of Russian (p154) :
- repeats Hayter call for National Languages Institute for research and teaching;
- recommends feasibility study of early start to FL in primary school;
- calls for reform of 16+ exam.

Secondary Schools Examination Council (SSEC) abolished by Government. Replaced by *Curriculum Study Group*.

The context	CILT

354

First school 'language laboratory' established in Salford Grammar School, Lancashire. (Five years later. 200 language labs in schools.) (p211)

1963

Higher education: Robbins report to Prime Minister gives statistics on access to university:
45% from higher professional homes;
4% from skilled manual homes.
Selection at age 11+ widely seen as major factor in 'uneven opportunity'.

Secondary schooling: Newsom Report, CACE(E), *'Half our future': on education of 'non-academic' pupils* (p200).

Joint Council of Language Associations (JCLA) is formed.

French from eight Pilot Scheme launched by Sir Edward Boyle (p155). Nuffield Foundation funds production of teaching materials *En avant!* under Sam Spicer, initially at Leeds, from 1967 at York.

1964

The first GCE 'O' level in MFL with optional translation from English launched by the AEB (p200).

Schools Council for Curriculum and Examinations replaces both Curriculum Study Group and SSEC.

Audio Visual Language Association formed, as professional body for language teachers pioneering new methods and examinations.

OCTOBER
Committee for Research and Development is set up by the Secretary of State for Education and Science and the Secretary of State for Scotland, in association with the trustees of the Nuffield Foundation, the University Grants Committee, the British Council and the Federation of British Industries. Its terms of reference include . . . *to examine the*

The context	CILT

Central Bureau for Educational Visits and Exchanges given responsibility for Language Assistants Scheme (see Appendix III).

DES issues Circular 2/64, stipulating *the need to bring about a major development in the teaching of languages if this country is to maintain its competitive position in overseas markets.*

Gougenheim et al, *L'élaboration du français fondamental* (Paris: Didier).

need for research and development in modern languages and the teachers of these languages. It recommends the establishment of a *Centre for Information on Language Teaching* (p321).

1965

Government issues circular 10/65 requesting LEAs to submit plans for *comprehensive re-organisation of secondary education* (p82).

Standing Conference on University Entrance (SCUE), abolished the requirement of a foreign language for entrance to university in England and Wales (p78).

Alternative syllabus for GCE 'O' level accepted by JMB at request of schools in Lancashire and Cheshire. No translation into the FL. Candidates chose two books from a list of 100 recommended by JMB. 44% of marks given for oral work (p200).

1966

25 AUGUST
CILT's Declaration of Trust agrees the following objectives:
. . . the promotion of education by means of the collection of information on all aspects of modern languages and the teaching of modern languages and the making

The context

CILT

available of such information to such persons or bodies of persons as may be concerned with the educational interests of the people of the United Kingdom (p322).

20 SEPTEMBER
George Perren appointed first Director of CILT.

Eleven Governors formally appointed including:
* John Davies, CBI
* Professor Strevens, University of Essex
* R A Becher, Nuffield Foundation
* Eric Hawkins, Director, Language Teaching Centre, York
* Dr Leslie Farrer-Brown as first Chair (Dr Farrer-Brown, Director of the Nuffield Foundation and one of the promoters of the *French from eight* Pilot scheme.)

29 SEPTEMBER
CILT officially opens at State House, High Holborn in London. Premises comprise 700 square feet, attached to *English Teaching Information Library*, seven offices and a 432 square feet room for use as an *Audio-Visual Library.*

NOVEMBER
First plans developed, including production of a *Register of current research*, liaison with other centres and organisations, and a modest publications programme. It was decided not to develop publicity materials . . . *until the Centre could offer real services.*

The context	CILT

1967

Schools Council joins Nuffield Foundation to fund Materials Project at York producing three new courses for secondary schools. (*Vorwärts*, ¡*Adelante*! and *Vperyod!*) to supplement *En avant* (p156).

DES initiates ten-week intensive training courses in French for volunteer teachers of eight- to thirteen-year-olds, in an attempt to meet teacher demands of Pilot Scheme (p160).

Plowden Report on Primary Schooling (Lady Plowden, Chairman. *Children and their primary schools*, HMSO, January 1967). Stressed crucial influence of the 'encouraging home'. Expressed doubts about the Pilot Scheme (*French from eight in the primary school*) (p155).

JULY
H H Stern, Reader, Language Department, Essex University, appointed to CILT Board of Governors. Agreement reached with CUP to publish *Language Teaching Abstracts.*

OCTOBER
John Galleymore appointed Deputy Director and Research Adviser.

AUTUMN
A number of enquiries received from companies seeking advice including *Ford Motors, Michelin, EMI* and *Linguaphone.*

1968

JMB launches reformed GCE 'O' level in MFL with a structured oral test, recorded and marked centrally. It represents 35% of the total marks.

MARCH
CILT Audio-Visual Library fully operational.

JUNE
Discussions with the *Council of Europe* on co-ordination of information relating to language teaching and research.

DECEMBER
Languages for special purposes event at CILT. 50 invited participants.

The context	CILT

1969

JANUARY
Committee of Ministers of Council of
Europe issues Resolution (69)2
proposing reforms at national level,
including the creation of national
information centres on language
teaching (p323).

DES issues Circular 18/69 requiring
Modern Languages graduates to complete a course of professional training
to teach in maintained schools (p269).

20 AND 21 MARCH
First CILT conference on *Aims and
techniques: language teaching
methods and their comparative
assessment* at State House. 30
invited participants.

OCTOBER
Research into spoken language
completed on behalf of the Council
of Europe.

1970

*Interim report on pilot scheme (French
from eight)* launched in 1963.
Dr Clare Burstall, National Foundation
for Educational Research (NFER),
shows consistent 'linear correlation'
between pupil performance and status
of parental occupation (p127).

Schools Council Working paper no 28
(edited by E Hawkins), *New patterns
in sixth form modern language studies*
aims to encourage language take-up
of non-specialists and diversification
of languages studied in sixth forms
(pp86–87).

APRIL
Agreement reached with the
National Association of Language
Advisers to run joint *Information
days* for teachers.

AUGUST
John Galleymore leaves the Centre
(p322).

1 NOVEMBER
J A Corbett appointed Deputy
Director.

1971

SEPTEMBER
Council of Europe embarks on
Programme 4, an expert group set up
under the chairmanship of John Trim,
to investigate the feasibility of a

JUNE
Following the demise of the
*Committee on Research and
Development in Modern Languages*
and the transfer of some of its

European unit-credit system of adult language learning. The Group lays down basic principles for the systematic planning of language learning and teaching. (p314)

Scottish Education Department publication 'Alternatives to French as a first foreign language in Secondary Schools' argues the case for diversification.

responsibilities to CILT, CILT renamed *Centre for Information on Language Teaching **and Research**.* (p322).

1972

'From birth to seven' (Davie et al, Longman). First report of National Child Development Study. Showed percentages of 'poor readers' at age seven (i.e. after two years of infant school) from different home back-ground: 8% poor readers from Class I ('administrative class') homes; 48% poor readers from Class V ('unskilled manual workers') (p124).

The place and aims of modern language teaching in secondary schools (SED, HMSO, 1972) by Scottish Central Committee on Modern Languages notes growing needs of industry and commerce, explosion of leisure travel and move towards European community (p94).

JUNE
Agreement with the Council of Europe to undertake European responsibilities, involving the maintenance and dissemination of information about research into language and language teaching.

Dr Farrer-Brown resigns as Chair after six years in office. G R Potter, Director of Education, West Sussex County Council, appointed as new Chair.

NOVEMBER
Retirement of Dr Corbett, Deputy Director.

1973

Britain enters the European Economic Community (EEC) (p35).

SEPTEMBER
Mr C V James appointed Deputy Director.

OCTOBER
Director reports little progress in the *European Information Exchange Scheme.*

The context

CILT

NOVEMBER
National conference in Manchester on *Language in middle years of secondary education,* an attempt to promote dialogue and cooperation between English teachers and foreign language teachers (p326).

1974

Systems development in adult language learning by John Trim promotes theory of 'unit/credit' modular syllabus for adult learners, tailored to specific adult language needs. (p324)

Publication of final NFER Report on Pilot Scheme *Primary French in the balance.* Government decides against further support for the scheme (p160).

An alternative to 16+ by Brian Page makes case for 'graded objectives' (p99).

Foreign languages in industry (Emmans, Hawkins, and Westoby at Language Teaching Centre, York), a three-year study funded by Nuffield Foundation, highlights neglect by industry of language skills (p36).

OCTOBER
CILT moves from State House to 20 Carlton House Terrace.

Publication of *The space between,* comprising papers from the 1973 national conference (pp126, 326). (Includes proposal for study of language in curriculum as bridge between English and FL teaching.)

1975

Bullock Committee Report, *A language for life* (London: HMSO) (p124), recommends:
• whole-school policies of 'language across the curriculum';
• teacher training for **all** teachers should include a course on 'language';

- recruitment of 'language aides with one year's training' to help teachers provide individual dialogue with an adult for pupils deprived of it at home.

The results of the Council of Europe MFL *Programme 4* begin to be published:

Van Ek J, *The threshold level* (Strasbourg: Council of Europe) (p324)

Establishment by Scottish Consultative Council on the Curriculum of national curriculum development project, aimed at making French accessible to full range of ability in early years of secondary education (p94)

1976

National Congress on Languages in Education (NCLE) established as an 'Association of Associations'. Its objective is to draw up recommendations for policy and action by Central Government. CILT provides Secretariat and publishes the Assembly's papers.

FEBRUARY
Development of policy on conference programme (two to three conferences per year). Mainly to invited participants.

DECEMBER
CILT invited by Directorate XII of the EEC to develop a proposal for a network of information centres on modern language teaching.

1977

Nuffield Foundation publishes *The early teaching of modern languages* (edited by P Hoy), an appraisal of the Government's Pilot Scheme, in response to unduly negative NFER Report of 1974 (p161).

HMI publish *Curriculum 11–16* ('The red book') putting case for 'core

MAY
Report of limited effect of Council of Europe proposal for network. Little progress on EC project.

1977/78
CILT organises meetings of the *National Congress on Languages in Education* and publishes in 1978

362

The context

CILT

curriculum' to include a foreign language (four periods a week in a 40-period week).

HMI Survey of 'Modern Languages in Comprehensive Schools' based on study of one in ten sample of 83 schools in 40 LEAs. Finding that two out of three pupils starting at FL at age eleven dropped it at age fourteen. Only one in ten reached GCE 'O' level pass after five years (p84).

Working Party papers for the first assembly (Durham) *Foreign languages in education* (edited by E Hawkins) and *The mother tongue and other languages in education* (edited by Sam Spicer) (p326).

1978

'Crisis conference' *Does Britain need linguists?* called by British Overseas Trade Board, University of Surrey and Royal Society of Arts.

In response to HMI Survey of 1977, three-year study funded by Nuffield at Language Teaching Centre, York, to identify good practice in language teaching (see 1982).

MAY
John Trim appointed Director of CILT (from Summer of 1978) following the retirement of George Perren. From 1971 John Trim has been the Director of two successive major Council of Europe Projects. His appointment therefore strengthens CILT's international profile (p323)

Mr C V James retires as Deputy Director.

SEPTEMBER
Mr Alan Moys appointed Deputy Director.

1979

British Overseas Trade Board follows 1978 conference with Study Group chaired by HRH The Duke of Kent. Publishes *Foreign languages for overseas trade*, showing adverse effects of neglect of language skills.

JANUARY
Dr A E Sloman, formerly Professor of Spanish, Liverpool, and Vice-Chancellor of Essex University, succeeds Mr Potter as Chairman.

The context	CILT

CILT

MARCH
EEC decides not to proceed with the proposal to establish a language information network. Instead general network of Educational Policy Information Centres (EPIC) is established with the NFER operating the UK terminal.

APRIL
First CILT conference on *Graded Objectives*, at which GOML Coordinating Committee is established (p99).

CILT support for *British Overseas Trade Board Study Group* on *Foreign Languages for Overseas Trade*.

1980

The Schools Council carries out a study on the Diversification of modern languages in schools. CILT provides the Secretariat. Study is published in 1981 as *Languages other than French in the secondary school* (edited by C G Hadley).

University Grants Commission recommends closing of six university Russian departments and phasing out of thirteen others, due to severe decline in numbers of Russian entries.

The Association for Language Learning (ALL) is established.

JANUARY
Prime Minister announces to Parliament a cut in CILT's grant to take effect until 1984. CILT sets up a *Grants and Services Fund*. Donations come from British Petroleum, Shell, Longman Group, Thorn EMI and RTZ.

John Trim, Director of CILT, meets with representatives of language learning associations to explore collaboration. The seven principal UK MFL associations set up a working party to arrange amalgamation which results in the establishment of the Association for Language Learning (ALL).

1981

Secretary of State for Education and Science issues *The School Curriculum*, which states *Most pupils should have*

Directory of organisations and centres for language teachers and students published as a handbook.

The context

CILT

the opportunity to learn a foreign language . . . at least two, or, if possible, three years of language teaching should be provided as a minimum. Wherever possible pupils should be encouraged to keep up a modern language until the end of the fifth year of secondary education.

Future of 16+ examinations under debate.
Report of Rampton Committee set up by Shirley Williams to enquire into the education of children from ethnic minorities: Rampton A (Chairman), *West Indian children in our schools* (London: HMSO). Shows performance of different ethnic groups in (written) English at age sixteen in the six LEAs with largest numbers of immigrant pupils. Percentage scoring good pass (A–C): West Indian pupils 9%; Asian pupils 21%; other pupils 29% (p124).

CILT increases its support for English as a Second Language. Other areas of major expansion include initial and in-service teacher education.

1981/2
Annual workshops on Computer Aided Language Learning (CALL) begin.

1982

The second foreign language in secondary schools: a question of survival is published by the Schools Council.

September
Following piloting of principles in *Programme 4* and the publication *Modern languages 1971–81*, the Committee of the Council of Europe issues Recommendation R(82)18, advocating generalised reform of language teaching in secondary education in accordance with communicative principles.

CILT liaises with other bodies to establish a UK scheme to promote foreign language learning to schoolchildren, based on a West German model: *Young Linguists Festival and Competition*. NALASW offers to run the one-year pilot project (p295).

Report of York (Nuffield) Study:
Modern language teachers in action
(Sanderson D (ed), Language
Teaching Centre, York).

1983

DES/WO issue consultative paper on
*Foreign languages in the school
curriculum* (HMSO) (p85).

Following a pilot project, the Foreign
Languages at Work scheme is
launched by the British Overseas
Trade Board and the London
Chamber of Commerce and Industry.

APU (Assessment of Performance Unit
within NFER) survey of French,
German and Spanish in secondary
schools.

The Queen formally opens the joint
British Council/CILT Resources
Centre in Carlton House Terrace,
London.

1984

DES (HMI Discussion document)
English from 5 to 16, Curriculum
Matters 1. DES makes controversial
proposal that the aims of English
teaching should include *to teach
pupils about language*.

DES Circular 3/84 sets up Council for
the Accreditation of Teachers (CATE)
and calls for closer cooperation
between teacher training institutions
and schools to ensure higher
proportion of teacher trainers with
recent and relevant teaching
experience and to increase the length
and value of school experience (p275).

FEBRUARY
With financial support from the
Economic and Social Research
Council (ESRC), CILT hosts a
national conference, *Second language learning: research needs and
priorities*. The event aims to encourage researchers to identify ways in
which they could advance the understanding of language learning, to
the benefit of teachers and learners.

September
Major rent increases oblige CILT to
relocate to Regent's Park to occupy
space (in the form of two large
library rooms) in Regent's College,

The context

CILT

a new institution taking over the premises of the former Bedford College.

National conference on *Languages in adult education* at Nottingham University. Over 100 participants attend. A plan of action is agreed.

NOVEMBER
CILT Language Teaching Library re-opens to the public.

1984/5
Major review of CILT undertaken by Secretary of State (p329).

1985

DES *Better schools* document *the great majority of pupils should receive a course in a foreign language designed to be of lasting value and . . . a second foreign language should be offered from the second or third year to those pupils who can benefit from it.*

DES (HMI document) *Modern languages in the sixth form: . . . should provide opportunities for students to take more responsibility for their own learning and to develop habits of independent study.*

Swann report *Education for all* (London: HMSO). (Committee of Inquiry on education of children of ethnic minorities) 'Use of home language for early school learning would be ethnically divisive'. Support for 'awareness of language' as helpful for pupils in multi-ethnic communities

JANUARY
CILT hosts Open Day to introduce its new location and operation to its constituency. With a variety of talks and demonstrations, the event is attended by teachers from all over the country.

CILT publishes the educational video-film *Languages at work,* produced under the auspices of Rowntree Mackintosh.

Education Secretary, Sir Keith Joseph, issues a statement announcing the present Government will continue to fund CILT, but with reduced funding (p329).

Publication of *Language awareness* (edited by B G Donmall) NCLE Papers and Reports 6, providing case studies of 'awareness of language because all pupils (and their families) can make equally valid contribution to discussion from their own language experience (p135).

1985/6
Dispute over teachers' salaries has marked effect on applications for teacher training. CILT forced to postpone or cancel many INSET courses.

courses' in a number of schools and results of national survey.

FEBRUARY
CILT forms agreement with Trinity College, Dublin to promote in the UK the *AUTHENTIK* series of newspapers in French, German, Spanish and Italian.

CILT collaborates with the Goethe-Institut to run a major national conference *German in the UK: issues and opportunities,* which is sponsored by the Embassy of the Federal Republic of Germany. The event attracts well over 400 participants.

CILT begins to publish papers for BAAL annual meetings.

Publication of *Language and culture guides* starts, for less widely taught languages including Bengali, Gujarati, Punjabi, Urdu and Hindi (28 *Guides* published from 1985–87).

1986

DES/WO *Foreign languages in the school curriculum,* a *draft statement of policy* comments on APU findings announcing . . . *signs of widespread low achievement.*

OCTOBER
First National Festival of languages and young linguists competition takes place at Warwick University. (Organisation co-ordinated by Christine Wilding) (p295).

CILT's conference programme continues its support for GOML and CALL.

JANUARY
Launch of a new initiative to provide for LEAs packaged INSET programmes on vocational languages. Its first year of operation attracts training requests from fourteen LEAs in London.

MARCH
Publication of first edition of CILT *Languages and careers* information pack for Heads of Department and teachers in secondary schools.

The context

CILT

Launch of *NETWORD*, a scheme whose main aim is to promote the local networking of AE tutors.

CILT collaborates with the BBC in providing support documentation for its radio series *A taste of* . . . for minority languages.

APRIL
New framework established by Secretary of State for CILT's work. Reconstitution of Governing body.

DECEMBER
Sir Hugh Byatt succeeds Sir Albert Sloman as Chairman of CILT.

1987

Publication of Standard Grade Arrangements for Modern Languages (in Scotland): syllabus has as its primary aim the development of communicative competence and confidence among pupils; strong encouragement of the use of the foreign language in class; curriculum and assessment at three levels (Credit, General and Foundation), covering six grades (p94).

The European Economic Community (EEC) becomes the European Community (EC).

DES Modern foreign languages 11–16 Consultative Document (HMSO). The proposed 'foundation subjects' in the new National Curriculum should include a modern foreign language.

JANUARY 1987
First publication of *NETWORD News*.

CILT and Scottish Education Department agree to establish a CILT Scottish Liaison Group.

PICKUP programme (Professional and Commercial Updating and Training) by DES supported by Department for Trade and Industry. Twenty Language-Export Centres set up offering language and export-related skills of FE and HE to the business world. Secretariat based at CILT.

APRIL
Alan Moys, CILT's Deputy Director, succeeds John Trim as Director of CILT.

The context	CILT

The context

ERASMUS (European Schemes for the Mobility of University Students) approved by European Council of Ministers.

Revision of Higher Grade and Sixth Year Studies courses in Scotland: amounting to a further development of practical language skills begun at Standard Grade.

CILT

JULY
Following the Government's review a new Board of Governors meets for the first time and the structure of the Centre is re-organised.

SEPTEMBER
An additional Language Teaching Liaison Officer appointed with special responsibility for languages in FE, HE and in the world of work.

NOVEMBER
Conference on *The learning of Japanese in the UK* in secondary and adult education, in collaboration with the Japan Information Centre, Japan Foundation and SOAS.

1988

The context

GCE 'AS' papers set for the first time, representing half the value of GCE 'A' level (see Appendix II, Table 6).

Office for Standards in Education (OFSTED) takes over HMI role of inspecting schools, but do not take over HMI's additional role of providing in-service advice and courses (p289).

Report of Committee of Inquiry into the Teaching of English, Kingman Report. Accepts case for teaching about language (p125).

CILT

1988/89
CILT provides administrative and information support for the ten LEAs selected by Government to undertake experimental work on the diversification of the first foreign language in secondary schools.

Three national conferences include *Beyond GCSE in languages: new post-16 developments,* reflecting the renewal of 'A' level syllabuses.

1989

The context

DES *English for ages 5–16* (The Cox report – NC English working group) (London: DES) restates the case for teaching pupils about language (see Chapter 10).

CILT

DES asks CILT to provide a London base for the Language Export (LX) network of centres providing services to the business world.

The context

CILT

WO Cardiff, Education Department's Welsh for ages five to sixteen published, makes NC proposals for Welsh: the only bilingual education available under the NC (p136).

EC ministers launch the five-year LINGUA programme, starting in 1990. Six pilot projects launched in Scotland for language teaching at primary school at a cost of £500,000 over four years. 36 primary and six secondary schools involved. Languages introduced: French, German, Spanish and Italian.

DES Circular 14/89 Initial Teacher Training further develops the themes of Circular 3/84.

Circular 11/89 (Scottish Education Department) recommends that: the study of a modern language should normally be pursued by all pupils during first four years of secondary education; that this aim should be achieved by 1992 (pp95, 387).

Development of National Certificate Modules (SCOTVEC) encourages languages to be taught within TVEI.

APRIL
Following completion of project 12, *Modern languages for communication'*, DES organises national conference for 71 decision-makers who make recommendations for action of '*Languages for communication: the next stage'*, edited by HMSI Michael Salter.

JANUARY
In conjunction with the CBI, CILT hosts a national conference *Languages mean business* at Centre Point, London.

| **1990** |

DES/WO *Modern foreign languages for ages 11–16* (London: HMSO). Proposals of the Secretary of State and Secretary of State for Wales (Final Report of National Curriculum Working Group, chaired by Martin Harris, Chairman of CILT) (pp108, 121).

House of Lords Select Committee on the European Communities. Thirteenth report *European schools and language learning in UK schools* warns that shortage of teachers . . . *the most serious concern with regard to the future of modern language teaching in the UK* . . . Call on Government to launch a campaign (p1).

HMI report on Effective Learning and Teaching in Scottish Secondary schools': identifies and illustrates characteristics of good practice in ML classrooms and departments.

SEPTEMBER
The Isle of Man launches scheme to teach a foreign language form the age of nine and eventually from age seven (p165).

Bursaries of £1,500 introduced for PGCE language students.

JANUARY
The *UK LINGUA Unit* is established in London and managed jointly by CILT and the Central Bureau for Educational Visits and Exchanges (CBEVE).

A residential national conference in High Wycombe *Autonomy in language learning*. A follow-up conference is held the same year at Dyffryn House, Cardiff, the results of which are later published by CILT under the title *Letting go – taking hold* (p258).

FEBRUARY
CILT national conference in London: *Action for a national capability in languages*.

MAY
HRH The Prince of Wales addresses an invited audience of some 200 senior representatives of the business, training and educational world at a CILT event in collaboration with the CBI.

SEPTEMBER
Professor Martin Harris, Vice-Chancellor, University of Essex, appointed Chair of CILT Governors, succeeding Sir Hugh Byatt.

AUTUMN
CILT provides the Secretariat for the newly formed Languages Lead Body (LLB), established by the Department of Employment (as part of a national programme to establish a framework for standards for National Vocational Qualifications) (p44).

The context	CILT

Publication of the first title in the Pathfinder series for language teachers.

1991

CILT runs a project funded by the National Curriculum Council (NCC) on *Languages and special educational needs.*

DECEMBER
CILT's three-year Development Plan 1992–95 *Promoting a national capability in languages: an agenda for progress* is endorsed by the Minister of State.

Scottish CILT (SCILT) is established as a joint project between CILT and the University of Stirling with support from the Scottish Office Education Department (SOED) and with Professor Richard Johnstone as Director.

1992

SEPTEMBER
DfE circular 9/92 *Initial teacher training* (secondary phase) lays down requirements regarding teacher training (students' experience in school, defines competencies required to qualify and distributes substantial proportion of budget to be transferred to schools as contribution to teacher training (pp275, 280).

Launch of the first six Comenius Centres, involving partnerships with HE and TT institutions and FE colleges. This initiative also involves all the major national agencies and cultural institutes in the field.

MARCH
Alan Moys retires as Director, to be succeeded by Dr Lid King, Head of the Centre's Professional Services Section.

The context	CILT

October
Publication of results of CILT's 1990 follow-up conference on Autonomy under the title *Letting go – taking hold* (p256ff).

1993

Opening of Single European Market (p55ff).

Publication of National Guidelines for Modern European Languages 5–14 by Scottish Office Education Department: identifies attainment outcomes, attainment targets, programmes of study and principles of assessment and recording for early years of secondary education. Does not yet make specifications for modern languages at primary level.

January
One world in Europe conference on the European dimension attracts nearly 300 participants.

February
CILT relocates to 20 Bedfordbury, Covent Garden.

The CILT Library undergoes radical remodelling. Facilities include two purpose-built rooms for IT and audio, satellite and video, plus a Reading Room which offers a free meetings point.

The *CILT Resources Library* launches a new programme of extended opening hours to cater more fully to the needs of its constituency.

A programme of on-site events *CILT at CILT* is established at CILT's London premises.

Publication through Scottish CILT of evaluation report on initial years of national pilots of modern languages in Scottish primary schools.

Publication by CILT, in collaboration with Scottish CILT, of SOIED-funded review of impact of current developments to promote the Gaelic language.

Peter Boaks appointed Deputy Director of CILT.

The context

CILT

1994

The European Commission (EC) becomes the European Union (EU).

Dearing Report School Curriculum and its assessment. Final Report. In response to widespread criticism and teacher industrial action, Report recommends slimming down of curriculum and allowing more scope for curricular initiative in schools.

Introduction of modular GCE 'A' and 'AS' courses (for examination in summer 1966) in order to facilitate teaching for the two levels in parallel in sixth forms.

DTI launches Government's *Languages for export* initiative to raise awareness and promote regional networking (p44).

Start of national training programmes designed to equip primary school teachers in Scotland with skills and knowledge for teaching a modern language, as the initiative is generalised to primary schools beyond the pilot samples (p174).

Five further Comenius Centres open, bringing the total number to eleven.

An external review of SCILT takes place. Conclusions are extremely encouraging.

CILT participates in the DTI-led national *Languages for Export* campaign (p44).

CILT's *National Business Languages Information Service* (NatBLIS) is launched at the beginning of the campaign and its first product – a database of business languages trainers – is established at the end of the period.

JANUARY
CILT conference on grammar in language teaching is followed by a publication by the same name; *Grammar!* (edited by L King and P Boaks, CILT).

18 MARCH
In collaboration with the French Embassy, the Chamber of Commerce and the DTI, CILT hosts a conference *Doing business with the French.*

AUGUST
A new, high-profile scheme to facilitate more immediate and targeted access to CILT's information resources – *CILT Direct* – is launched.

375

NOVEMBER
European Dissemination Project
(EDP): feasibility study begins with
NCET and various European
partners to establish a European
languages database on the Internet.

1995

LEONARDO begins, new EC
programme for training. Unifies
COMETT, EUROTECNET, FORCE,
PETRA and Lingua Action 3 under
one programme.

A *European Modern Languages Centre*
is set up under a Council of Europe
Partial Agreement in Graz, Austria
(p324).

Final year of national and regional
pilots for modern languages in
Scottish primary schools.
Generalisation phase now underway
(p174).

Publication of outline framework for
modern languages within the national
Higher Still programme in Scotland:
brings different post-16 systems
(National Certificate modules, Higher,
Sixth Year Studies) into one framework at five levels.

MARCH
SOCRATES, new EU programme for
education, formally adopted. Comes
into immediate effect and due to
continue until end 1999. *

Secretary of State Gillian Shephard
announces a scheme to establish a
network of specialist Language
Colleges.

JANUARY
Three further Comenius Centres
are established, bringing the total
to fourteen Centres.

The *National Comenius Centre of
Wales, Canolfan Genedlaethol
Comenius Cymru* opens on three
sites: two in Cardiff and another in
Bangor.

Publication through Scottish CILT
of final evaluation report on national pilots of modern languages in
Scottish primary schools.

MARCH
NatBLIS develops a second
product: a database of translators
and interpreters.

CILT *Modern languages in primary
schools report* publishes findings of
survey.

APRIL
A new publications series is
launched called *The Young
Pathfinder Series* for teachers of
young learners.

MAY
EDP Pilot Project complete. Report
submitted to EC to set up a
European database on language
teaching and learning.

The context

CILT

SEPTEMBER/OCTOBER
The first six Language Colleges are designated.

OCTOBER
CILT undertakes a survey on *Diversification of the first foreign language in the 11–16 sector* in partnership with the *Times Educational Supplement.*

1996

September
With implementation of the National Curriculum, all pupils in Year 10 now required to study an accredited modern foreign languages course (p2).

AUGUST
Automation of CILT Resources Library at its Covent Garden premises finally completed.

OCTOBER
CILT and NCET launch pilot project – *Lingu@net*, a virtual language resource centre, on the Internet.

Professor Martin Harris ends his term of office as Chairman of CILT.

Appendix II

A statistical picture of modern language studies

Eric Hawkins

A statistical overview of modern language studies at school and university in the past 30 years. Unless otherwise stated, the sources of the statistics are the Department of Education and Science (DES) and Department for Education and Employment (DfEE) Annual Statistics of Education, the Reports of the GCE Examining Boards and GCSE Examining Groups and statistics issued by the Universities' Statistical Record (USR) and the Higher Education Statistics Agency (HESA). Scottish statistics are drawn from the Statistical Bulletins, Education Series, of the Scottish Office, Edinburgh.

List of tables

378

Numbers of boys and girls aged sixteen and eighteen in years 1965, 1975, 1985 and 1995 in England/Wales, Scotland and N Ireland

The tables of numbers studying languages at school and university in this Appendix should be seen against the fluctuating population figures in the period under review. The Table below shows numbers of sixteen- and eighteen-year-olds in England/Wales, Scotland and Northern Ireland, at years 1965, 1975, 1985 and 1995. Source: Office for National Statistics (ONS) and Government Actuary's Department, Demography Division.

Population (in thousands) at ages 16 and 18 in years shown					
		1965 [1]	1975	1985	1995 [2]
England and Wales					
Aged 16	Male	386.7	373.6	403.2	324.0
	Female	368.9	356.8	380.6	305.0
	Total	755.6	730.4	783.8	629.0
Aged 18	Male	369.7	356.9	418.5	295.4
	Female	352.6	340.5	397.2	278.0
	Total	722.3	697.4	815.7	573.4
Scotland					
Aged 16	Male	42.4	44.5	44.0	33.0
	Female	41.3	43.2	41.8	31.0
	Total	83.7	87.7	85.8	64.0
Aged 18	Male	40.5	41.5	45.6	30.0
	Female	39.5	40.3	43.2	28.0
	Total	80.0	81.8	88.8	58.0
Northern Ireland					
Aged 16	Male	13.7	13.0	14.7	13.0
	Female	13.0	12.9	14.0	13.0
	Total	26.7	25.9	28.7	26.0
Aged 18	Male	13.6	12.3	15.3	12.0
	Female	12.3	12.3	13.8	11.0
	Total	25.9	24.6	29.1	23.0

1 Figures for 1965 are estimates calculated from 5 year totals for ages 15–19.
2 Figures for 1995 are projections issued by the Government Actuary's Department (Demography Division). These figures reflect a fall of some 20% in the UK annual birth rate in the late 1970s.

1 Entries for Modern Languages in first public examinations (age sixteen) 1965–1995

380 A England and Wales (and, in 1995, N Ireland)

The School Certificate (SC), the first nationally recognised public examination system, was introduced in England and Wales following the post-war Education Act of 1918. Broadly it catered for pupils in selective 'grammar' schools and streams. It served both to sanction entry to sixth form studies and as the gateway to the majority of clerical and professional careers which then recruited at age 16+.

SC was a 'group' exam; the certificate was awarded for passes in five subjects, which must include a foreign language, as well as English and Maths or a science. Two of the five passes had to be at 'credit' level. Students who obtained 'credit' level in all five subjects were awarded a 'matric' certificate, signifying 'exempt matriculation examination' for university entrance. Normally all candidates entered for six to eight subjects. It is interesting that in 1938, out of a total subject entry of 531,445, entries for French were 72,466 and for German 9,935 (together 15.5% of total entry). Entries for English language (taken by nearly all candidates) totalled 77,358. The figures thus show that virtually all candidates took a modern language.

In the same year entries for Latin were 28,735 (or 5.4% of total entry).

SC gave way, in 1950, to the General Certificate of Education (GCE) 'O' level. This was a 'single subject' examination. Certificates merely recorded passes in individual subjects. There was no requirement to pass in specific 'groups' of subjects, such as foreign languages or sciences. Most universities continued, however, until the mid 1960s, to demand a GCE 'O' level pass in a foreign language as a minimum requirement for entry to most degree courses (and certainly all 'Arts' courses), in addition to three passes at GCE 'A' level (see Table 3).

In 1965 a new 16+ examination, the Certificate of Secondary Education (CSE) was introduced, to supplement GCE 'O' level, and catering for those pupils for whom GCE was considered too demanding. A 'Grade 1' pass in CSE was generally reckoned the equivalent to a pass at GCE 'O' level. In many schools pupils were entered for both GCE 'O' level and CSE, as an insurance against failure at GCE.

In 1988 both GCE 'O' level and CSE were replaced by the General Certificate of Secondary Education (GCSE). This is, like GCE and CSE, a 'single subject' examination, with no 'group' requirement, but designed to cater for the whole 16+ age group. GCSE mark schemes gave credit for a significant element of 'course work' (modules of work done in the candidate's own time, not under examination conditions).

The following table shows entries for the five modern languages most commonly studied in schools, and, for comparison, entries for English, Maths, Latin and Greek, for GCE 'O' level and CSE in the years 1965, 1975, 1985 in England and Wales and for GCSE in 1995 in England, Wales and N Ireland.

Figures in italics show entries for each subject as percentage of total entries in exam concerned.

		1965 GCE 'O' & CSE	1975 GCE 'O'& CSE	1985 GCE 'O'& CSE	1995 GCSE
Total subject entries	GCE CSE **Total**	2,170,019 230,977 **2,400,996**	2,591,246 2,355,515 **4,946,761**	3,066,764 3,231,017 **6,297,781**	 **5,431,625**
English [1]	GCE CSE	348,688 *16.0%* 41,487 *17.9%*	425,020 *16.4%* 440,045 *18.6%*	519,684 *16.9%* 666,125 *20.6%*	(language only) 648,987 *11.9%*
Maths	GCE CSE	234,289 *10.8%* 38,804 *16.8%*	260,433 *10.0%* 353,566 *15.0%*	318,625 *10.3%* 419,238 *12.9%*	 678,445 *12.5%*
Latin	GCE CSE	52,420 *2.4%* 20 *0.008%*	29,775 *1.1%* 3,571 *0.1%*	19,928 *0.6%* 5,018 *0.1%*	 12,958 *0.2%*
Greek	GCE CSE	2,647 *0.1%* NIL	4,400 *0.1%* *	1,303 *0.04%* *	 1,143 *0.02%*
French	GCE CSE	163,651 *7.4%* 8,345 *3.6%*	152,137 *5.7%* 113,303 *4,8%*	147,657 *4.7%* 163,326 *5.0%*	 350,027 *6.4%*
German	GCE CSE	32,737 *1.5%* 986 *0.4%*	43,374 *1.6%* 19,009 *0.8%*	42,616 *1.3%* 31,855 *0.9%*	 129,386 *2.3%*
Spanish	GCE CSE	9,776 *0.4* 235 *0.1*	12,147 *0.4* 4,228 *0.1*	11,749 *0.3* 6,020 *0.1*	 40,762 *0.7*
Italian	GCE CSE	2,895 *0.1%* NIL	4,456 *0.1%* 472	2,389 *0.07%* 646	 5,610
				0.01%	*0.1%*
Russian	GCE CSE	2,374 *0.1%* 19 *0.008%*	2,290 *0.08%* 359 *0.01%*	1,375 *0.04%* 179 *0.005%*	 1,882 *0.03%*
Other MLs [2]	GCE CSE	4,672 *0.2%* 158 *0.06%*	7,708 *0.3%* 1,851 *0.07%*	7,142 *0.2%* 934 *0.02%*	 19,557 *0.3%*
All modern languages	GCE CSE	216,105 *9.9%* 9,743 *4.2%*	222,112 *8.5%* 139,222 *5.9%*	212,928 *6.9%* 202,960 *6.2%*	 547,224 *10.0%*

1 In GCE: English Language not Literature; in CSE: English all modes; in GCSE: English language only.
2 Including Welsh as a foreign language.

Appendix II

B   Scotland

In Scotland pupils sit the Scottish Certificate of Education, Standard Grade (previously Ordinary Grade) at age 16, after a four-year secondary course starting at age twelve, and the Higher Grade, on which university places are awarded, at seventeen or eighteen.

The Table shows entries for Ordinary/Standard Grade 1965 to 1995. Italics show entry for each subject as percentage of total subject entries.

	1965	1975	1985	1995
Total subject entries	199,167	406,936	446,008	490,112
English	30,037 *15.1%*	66,470 *16.3%*	72,952 *16.4%*	61,107 *12.5%*
Maths	22,527 *11.3%*	39,953 *9.8%*	43,554 *9.7%*	62,364 *12.7%*
Latin	6,003 *3.0%*	5,719 *1.4%*	2,885 *0.6%*	1,292 *0.2%*
Greek	325 *0.1%*	173 *0.04%*	72 *0.02%*	14 *0.003%*
French	17,231 *8.6%*	27,351 *6.7%*	24,574* *5.5%*	41,672 *8.5%*
German	3,541 *1.7%*	6,518 *1.6%*	6,300* *1.4%*	15,849 *3.2%*
Spanish	699 *0.3%*	1,130 *0.3%*	1,340* *0.3%*	2,210 *0.4%*
Italian	167 *0.08%*	613 *0.1%*	514* *0.1%*	554 *0.1%*
Russian	271 *0.1%*	224 *0.06%*	193* *0.04%*	47 *0.009%*
Gaelic (learners)	59 *0.02%*	116 *0.04%*	414 *0.09%*	440 *0.09%*
Other MLs	15 *0.007%*	68 *0.02%*	42 *0.009%*	No longer examined
Total MLs	21,983 *11.3%*	36,070 *8.8%*	33,377 *7.4%*	60,772 *12.3%*

*   Total entries, traditional and 'alternative' papers.

2 Boys' and girls' performance in first public examination compared

A England and Wales (and, in 1995, N Ireland) 1965–1995

Entries for English, Maths, Latin and Modern Languages in GCE 'O' level, and CSE in 1965, 1975 and 1985 and GCSE in 1995. Figures in italics show passes (Grades A to C in GCE and GCSE, Grade 1 only in CSE) in each subject as percentage of entries for that subject. It will be noted that figures shown separately for boys and gilrs do not always tally exactly with total figures. This is because the examination boards are not always able to distinguish between boy/girl entrants.

		1965	1975	1985	1995
Total subject entries	**GCE 'O' level**				
	Boys	1,201,930	1,322,229	1,509,639	
		55.4	*58.1*	*56.57*	
	Girls	968,089	1,269,017	1,557,125	
		61.2	*60.8*	*57.57*	
Total subject entries	**CSE**				**GCSE**
	Boys	140,202	1,229,697	1,626,847	2,679,592
		12.4	*13.8*	*14.95*	*48.9*
	Girls	90,775	1,125,908	1,604,170	2,751,527
		11.9	*15.4*	*17.88*	*57.1*
English	**GCE** [1]				
	Boys	194,776	202,458	242,200	
		48.9	*55.4*	*48.43*	
	Girls	153,912	222,562	277,484	
		61.9	*66.4*	*55.13*	
	CSE [2]				**GCSE**
	Boys	23,676	220,157	333,887	325,682
		8.9	*11.4*	*14.59*	*48.8*
	Girls	17,811	219,888	332,238	323,265
		17.7	*19.8*	*22.48*	*65.7*
Maths	**GCE**				
	Boys	145,284	152,424	166,490	
		60.4	*59.3*	*59.97*	
	Girls	89,005	108,009	152,135	
		57.4	*52.8*	*51.86*	
	CSE				**GCSE**
	Boys	25,572	191,118	264,875	334,550
		16.2	*14.6*	*16.26*	*45.5*
	Girls	17,490	186,108	269,575	343,872
		8.2	*10.9*	*14.31*	*44.3*
Latin	**GCE**				
	Boys	28,500	13,984	9,913	
		60.3	*67.2*	*75.6*	
	Girls	23,920	15,791	10,015	
		67.8	*71.7*	*78.6*	
	CSE				**GCSE**
	Boys	9	1,476	2,004	6,776
		77.8	*39.9*	*45.7*	*90.2*
	Girls	11	2,095	3,014	6,182
		90.9	*51.1*	*55.9*	*92.7*

1 English language (not literature).
2 All modes and all English syllabuses.

		1965	1975	1985	1995
French	**GCE**				
	Boys	83,799	67,109	58,962	
		53.8	*56.8*	*58.87*	
	Girls	79,852	85,028	88,695	
		62.5	*63.4*	*60.47*	
	CSE				**GCSE**
	Boys	3,736	43,965	59,860	163,694
		9.9	*11.8*	*17.63*	*42.9*
	Girls	4,609	69,338	103,466	186,323
		19.2	*18.2*	*22.69*	*56.2*
German	**GCE**				
	Boys	15,941	18,302	16,128	
		53.0	*56.6*	*64.39*	
	Girls	16,796	25,072	26,488	
		62.0	*60.2*	*65.53*	
	CSE				**GCSE**
	Boys	472	7,401	12,024	60,692
		11.0	*13.4*	*13.98*	*47.5*
	Girls	514	11,608	19.931	68,694
		17.9	*18.5*	*20.46*	*61.6*
Spanish	**GCE**				
	Boys	4,182	4,128	3,790	
		53.1	*57.5*	*65.01*	
	Girls	5,594	8,019	7,959	
		62.0	*64.1*	*65.99*	
	CSE			**GCSE**	
	Boys	139	1,372	2,070	15,955
		18.0	*13.3*	*12.71*	*50.7*
	Girls	96	2,856	3,950	24,807
		17.7	*18.2*	*17.57*	*63.9*
Italian	**GCE**				
	Boys	1,135	1,345	720	
		41.0	*56.2*	*69.86*	
	Girls	1,760	3,111	1,669	
		60.8	*63.4*	*75.19*	
	CSE				**GCSE**
	Boys	NIL	108	230	1,895
			20.4	*26.09*	*73.8*
	Girls	NIL	364	416	3,715
			25.8	*32.45*	*80.1*
Russian	**GCE**				
	Boys	1,382	1,125	620	
		58.9	*66.9*	*79.68*	
	Girls	992	1,165	755	
		73.1	*70.2*	*82.52*	
	CSE				**GCSE**
	Boys	6	138	74	864
		16.7	*23.2*	*28.38*	*76.0*
	Girls	13	221	105	1,018
		7.7	*30.3*	*40.95*	*83.0*

		1965	1975	1985	1995
Other MLs [3]	**GCE**				
	Boys	2,848	3,491	3,632	
		56.0%	*60.7%*	*73.46%*	
	Girls	1,824	4,217	3,510	
		65.6%	*69.9%*	*76.13%*	
	CSE				**GCSE**
	Boys	73	717	588	8,920
		5.7%	*5.9%*	*20.75%*	*69.7%*
	Girls	85	1,134	346	10,598
		8.5%	*12.7%*	*33.24%*	*78.7%*
Total MLs entries	**GCE**				
	Boys	109,287	95,500	83,852	
		53.6%	*57.1%*	*61.09%*	
	Girls	106,818	126,612	129.076	
		62.5%	*63.1%*	*62.59%*	
	CSE				**GCSE**
	Boys	4,426	53,701	74,846	252,020
		10.3%	*12.1%*	*16.97%*	*45.8%*
	Girls	5,317	85,521	128,114	295,155
		18.9%	*18.2%*	*22.26%*	*59.3%*

3   including Welsh as a Foreign Language

B   Scotland 1996–1995

Entries for Scottish Certificate of Education, Ordinary/Standard Grade, 1966 to 1995. (1966 is the earliest year in which boys and girls results were published separately).

Figures in italics show passes (all passes in 1966, A to C in 1975 and 1985, 1 to 3 in 1995) in each subject as percentage of entries for that subject.

		1966	1975	1985 [1]	1995 [2]
Total subject entries	Boys	114,847	202,906	212,753	244,207
		71.6%	*61%*	*63%*	*56%*
	Girls	95,408	204,030	233,255	245,905
		73.2%	*60.9%*	*65.2%*	*64%*
English	Boys	16,612	31,982	34,939	30,954
		69.3%	*54.5%*	*51.6%*	*65%*
	Girls	15,166	34.488	38,013	30,153
		80.1%	*67.1%*	*62.9%*	*80%*
Mathematics	Boys	15,184	22,856	22,350	31,637
		67.5%	*54.7%*	*63.4%*	*50%*
	Girls	7,854	16,422	21,204	30,727
		73.2%	*57%*	*62.1%*	*50%*
Latin	Boys	2,841	2,231	1,202	531
		75%	*82.8%*	*80%*	*74%*
	Girls	3,166	3,488	1,683	761
		82.5%	*85.1%*	*80.7%*	*81%*

		1966	1975	1985 [1]	1995 [2]
French	Boys	7,964	10,953	6,738	20,060
		69.5%	*57.5%*	*70.4%*	*40%*
				Alt 1,949	**W** 8,104
				68.4%	*46%*
	Girls	9,585	16,398	12,002	21,612
		77.6%	*62.8%*	*70%*	*59%*
				Alt 3,885	**W** 12,386
				68.9%	*60%*
German	Boys	1,111	1,849	1,385	7,717
		76.8%	*61.4%*	*68.9%*	*49%*
				Alt 636	**W** 3,794
				61.1%	*49%*
	Girls	2,581	4,669	3,009	8,132
		84.4%	*71.6%*	*74.7%*	*67%*
				Alt 1,270	**W** 5,313
				68.3%	*64%*
Spanish	Boys	307	358	261	864
		77.1%	*58.4%*	*65.1%*	*45%*
				Alt 89	**W** 367
				—	*35%*
	Girls	475	772	743	1,346
		78.9%	*65.6%*	*70.8%*	*72%*
				Alt 247	**W** 917
				68.8%	*51%*
Italian	Boys	66	165	120	198
		84.8%	*66.7%*	*78.3%*	*48%*
				Alt 2	**W** 88
				—	*32*
	Girls	149	448	370	356
		85.9%	*71.7%*	*76.7%*	*74%*
				Alt 22	**W** 254
				—	*52%*
Russian	Boys	113	83	59	24
		69.9%	—	—	*34%*
				Alt 2	**W** 6
				—	*50%*
	Girls	159	141	118	23
		74.2%	*71.6%*	*86.5%*	*73%*
				Alt 14	**W** 15
				—	*73%*
Gaelic (learners)	Boys	33	77	176	223
		75%	—	*64.2%*	*52%*
					W 65
					73%
	Girls	28	89	238	217
		78.5%	—	*75.3%*	*67%*
					W 109
					84%

		1966	1975	1985	1995
Other MLs	Boys	12	22	18	—
	Girls	4	29	24	—
All ML entries					
	Boys	9,606	13,507	11,435	29,086
	Girls	12,981	22,546	21,942	31,686

1   in 1985 ML candidates could take either the 'traditional' or the 'alternative' (**Alt**) paper
2   in 1995 all ML candidates took speaking, reading and listening elements of the examination. A fourth element, 'writing' was optional. Entries for 'writing' (**W**) are not additional to main subject entries.

The more equal balance of boy/girl entries in 1995 should be seen in conjunction with Scottish Office Circular 11/89 (effective from 1992) requiring all pupils to study their foreign language up to age sixteen. A similar requirement in England and Wales comes into effect in September 1996.

3   Entries for Modern Languages in second public examinations

A   England and Wales: HSC 1938; GCE 'A' level 1965–1995

Note: GCE 'A' level replaced Higher School Certificate in 1950. For comparison, figures are given for HSC in 1938.

The figures in italics show entries for the various languages as percentage of total subject entries in each year.

It is worth noting that in the period 1938 to 1965, following the 1944 Education Act, which offered free secondary schooling to all, but before comprehensive re-organisation of secondary education, the number of entries for GCE 'A' level, which sanctioned entry to university, and to the professions, rose to approximately ten times the 1938 HSC figure. Over the next thirty years the total approximately doubled again.

The tenfold rise between 1938 and 1965 was the more remarkable when it is remembered that the official school-leaving age remained at fifteen until 1967, when it was raised to sixteen.

The comparative drift away from modern languages was marked. In 1938 entries for French in HSC were 12.8% of total entries. By 1965 entries for French in GCE had fallen to 6.9% of total entries, by 1985 to 3.6% of total entries, recovering slightly to 3.7% in 1995. Other languages gained ground against French. In 1938 entries for other languages were only 22% of French entries; in 1965 they represented 42.6%, by 1985 58% and in 1995 73.8%. It is notable, also, that, in 1938, entries for Greek approximately equalled entries for German, and there were three entries for Latin for every one in German, while even as late as 1965 there were more entries for Latin than for German.

	HSC	GCE 'A' level			
	1938	1965	1975	1985	1995
Total subject entries	36,951	370,435	498,883	609,215	730,415
Latin	2,589 7.0%	7,901 2.1%	3,117 0.6%	2,216 0.3%	1,625 0.2%
Greek	881 2.3%	1,322 0.3%	583 0.1%	469 0.07%	283 0.03%
French	4,752 12.8%	25,599 6.9%	24,421 4.8%	22,140 3.6%	27,563 3.7%
German	899 2.4%	7,107 1.9%	7,810 1.5%	7,949 1.3%	10,634 1.4%
Spanish	138 0.3%	2,213 0.6%	2,581 0.5%	2,615 0.4%	4,837 0.6%
Italian	2 0.005%	585 0.1%	833 0.1%	668 0.1%	913 0.1%
Russian	NIL —	602 0.1%	619 0.1%	307 0.05%	426 0.05%
Other languages	103 0.2%	422 0.1%	1,225 0.2%	1,320 0.2%	3,547 0.5%
All MLs	5,894 15.9%	36,528 9.8%	37,489 7.4%	34,999 5.7%	47,920 6.5%

B   Scotland: Certificate of Education Higher Grade 1965–1995

Entries in Scottish Certificate of Education, Higher Grade. Higher Grade is normally taken at age seventeen, one year after the 'Standard Grade', unlike the two-year sixth form course leading to GCE 'A' level in England/Wales. (Some pupils remain at school after 'Highers' and take the Certificate of Sixth Form Studies. In 1995 only some 450 pupils took French in this examination).

It will be noticed that the drift away from modern languages after the age of sixteen is similar to that in England and Wales. In 1994 some 39,000 pupils presented French at Standard Grade, of whom nearly 19,000 scored good passes, grades 1–3. Yet one year later only 5,000 presented French in the Higher Grade examination. Modern language entries as percentage of total subject entries declined from 16.1% in 1965 to 5.2% in 1995. All languages except Gaelic (learners) lost ground over the thirty years surveyed.

It will also be noted that total entries in all subjects for Scottish Highers doubled in the decade 1965 to 1975 but did not show the same increase between

1975 and 1995 as entries for GCE 'A' levels in England and Wales (but see tables of population at relevant ages, p379).

In the table below, figures in italics show each subject entry as percentage of total entries for year concerned.

	1965	1975	1985	1995
Total subject entries	74,969	149,170	168,309	160,925
Latin	3,014 *4.0%*	2,715 *1.8%*	1,004 *0.6%*	442 *0.3%*
Greek	325 *0.4%*	128 *0.09%*	44 *0.03%*	13 *0.008%*
French	9,267 *12.3%*	12,042 *8.1%*	8,351 *5%*	5,111 *3.2%*
German	2,199 *2.9%*	3,275 *2.2%*	2,355 *1.4%*	2,170 *1.3%*
Spanish	379 *0.5%*	705 *0.5%*	589 *0.4%*	653 *0.4%*
Italian	106 *0.1%*	340 *0.2%*	317 *0.2%*	214 *0.1%*
Russian	131 *0.1%*	136 *0.09%*	64 *0.04%*	14 *0.008%*
Gaelic (learners)	—	84 *0.06%*	131 *0.08%*	140 *0.09%*
Other MLs	6 —	15 *0.01%*	23 *0.01%*	6 —
All MLs	12,082 *16.1%*	16,597 *11.1%*	11,830 *7%*	8,308 *5.2%*

4 Boys' and girls' performance in second public examination compared

A England and Wales (and, in 1995, N Ireland): GCE 'A' level 1965–1995

Entries and percentage passes in GCE 'A' level compared, in: English, Mathematics, Latin and Modern Languages, 1965 to 1995. Figures in brackets show percentage of entry for each subject scoring A to E pass grade. Figures in italics show subject entry as percentage of total entry for all subjects.

Note: In the following table, 'English' in 1965 meant specifically English Literature; in 1975 and 1985 only 'English' was set. In 1995 'English Language' was distinguished from English Literature. The 1995 figures in the table refer to the language paper. Entries for English Literature in 1995 were: Boys: 17,730

Girls: 40,111

		1965	1975	1985	1995
Total subject entries	Boys	243,819 (67.6%)	286,751 (67.6%)	320,236 (70.8%)	344,128 (83.7%)
	Girls	126,616 (71.1%)	212,132 (69.5%)	288,979 (69.5%)	386,261 (84.6%)
	Total	**370,435**	**498,883**	**609,215**	**730,415**
English	Boy	16,959 (66.8%) 4.5%	21,965 (68%) 4.4%	17,738 (73.33%) 2.9%	8,411 (83.2%) 1.1%
	Girls	23,222 (76.0%) 6.2%	41,543 (72.3%) 8.3%	41,745 (74.93%) 6.8%	20,215 (87.2%) 2.7%
Mathematics	Boys	50,164 (70.7%) 13.5%	54,950 (65.1%) 11.0%	68,946 (69.94%) 11.3%	41,199 (86.2%) 5.6%
	Girls	8,647 (74.5%) 2.3%	14,809 (69.7%) 2.9%	28,058 (70.14%) 4.6%	22,281 (88.7%) 3.0%
Latin	Boys	4,164 (74.2%) 1.1%	1,383 (85.0%) 0.2%	911 (88.0%) 0.1%	762 (94.8%) 0.1%
	Girls	3,737 (78.2%) 1.0%	1,734 85.4% 0.3%	1,305 83.7% 0.2%	863 (96.3%) 0.1%
French	Boys	11,221 (67.4%) 3.0%	8,014 (67.7%) 1.6%	6,047 (76.81%) 0.9%	8,169 (89.2%) 1.1%
	Girls	14,378 (73.1%) 3.8%	16,407 (70.0%) 3.2%	16,093 (75.03%) 2.6%	19,394 (88.7%) 2.4%
German	Boys	3,572 (71.0%) 0.9%	2,734 (76.5%) 0.5%	2,208 (86.32%) 0.3%	3,381 (90.2%) 0.4%
	Girls	3,535 (78.5%) 0.9%	5,076 (81.4%) 1.0%	5,741 (80.14%) 0.9%	7,253 (88.7%) 1.0%
Spanish	Boys	1,197 (74.2%) 0.3%	862 (76.5%) 0.1%	715 (84.9%) 0.1%	1,456 (92.0%) 0.2%
	Girls	1,016 (77.3%) 0.2%	1,719 (78.8%) 0.3%	1,900 (79.47%) 0.3%	3,381 (89.0%) 0.4%
Italian	Boys	258 (81.8%) 0.06%	271 (67.5%) 0.05%	211 (81.9%) 0.03%	276 (96.0%) 0.03%
	Girls	327 (91.7%) 0.09%	562 (77.6%) 0.1%	457 (86.0%) 0.07%	637 (96.2%) 0.08%
Russian	Boys	350 (80.3%) 0.09%	247 (81.8%) 0.05%	132 (95.4%) 0.02%	199 (95.0%) 0.02%
	Girls	252 (82.9%) 0.06%	372 (82.3%) 0.07%	175 (93.1%) 0.02%	227 (96.5%) 0.03%
Other MLs	Boys	233 (67.8%) 0.06%	621 (72.5%) 0.1%	611 (77.1%) 0.1%	1,525 (89.4%) 0.2%
	Girls	189 (76.2%) 0.05%	604 (78.2%) 0.13%	709 (80.1%) 0.1%	2,018 (91.5%) 0.3%
Total MLs	Boys	16,831 (69.2%) 4.5%	12,749 (70.7%) 2.5%	9,924 (79.9%) 1.6%	15,006 (89.9%) 2.0%
	Girls	19,697 (74.7%) 5.3%	24,740 (73.5%) 4.9%	25,075 (77.0%) 4.1%	32,910 (89.1%) 4.5%
	Total	**36,528** **9.3%**	**37,489** **7.4%**	**34,999** **5.7%**	**47,920** [1] **6.5%**

1 It will be noted that figures shown separately for boys and girls do not always tally exactly with total figures. This is because the examination boards are not always able to distinguish between boy/girl entrance.

B Scotland: Certificate of Education Higher Grade 1966–1995

Boys' and girls' entries and percentage passes compared in Scottish Certificate of Education, Higher Grade, 1966 to 1995. (1966 is the earliest year in which boys and girls results were published separately.)

Figures in brackets show percentage in each subject awarded pass grade in 1966, A–C pass in 1975–1995. Figures in italics show subject entry as percentage of total entry, all subjects.

Note: NP = percentage passes not published

		1966	1975	1985	1995
Total subject entries					
	Boys	44,565 (72.5%)	77,202 (63.3%)	79,711 (65.9%)	73,771 (67%)
	Girls	34,906 (76.7%)	71,968 (64.3%)	88,598 (66.3%)	87,154 (72%)
	Total	**79,471**	**149,170**	**168,309**	**160,925**
English	Boys	10,831 (70.8%) *13.6%*	17,357 (59.3%) *11.6%*	17,087 (62.3%) *10.1%*	14,706 (65%) *9.1%*
	Girls	10,264 (79.4%) *12.9%*	18,782 (65.6%) *12.5%*	21,611 (66.4%) *12.8%*	19,249 (71%) *11.9%*
Mathematics	Boys	6,499 (72.8%) *8.2%*	11,581 (56.5%) *7.7%*	13,378 (61.1%) *7.9%*	10,708 (65%) *6.6%*
	Girls	2,918 (75.2%) *3.6%*	6,639 (58.1%) *4.4%*	10,176 (63.3%) *6.0%*	9,554 (70%) *5.9%*
Latin	Boys	2,841 (75%) *3.5%*	886 (87.0%) *0.5%*	428 (85.3%) *0.2%*	183 (83%) *0.1%*
	Girls	3,166 (82.5%) *3.9%*	1,829 (93.8%) *1.2%*	576 (87.3%) *0.3%*	259 (82%) *0.16%*
French	Boys	4,120 (74.7%) *5.2%*	3,861 (64.9%) *2.5%*	2,080 (73.4%) *1.2%*	1,297 (80%) *0.8%*
	Girls	5,602 (81.5%) *7.0%*	8,181 (64.6%) *5.4%*	6,271 (70.4%) *3.7%*	3,814 (79) (79%) *2.3%*
German	Boys	718 (80.2%) *0.9%*	770 (63.8%) *0.5%*	463 (65.4%) *0.2%*	569 (74%) *0.3%*
	Girls	1,713 (85.2%) *2.1%*	2,505 (61.5%) *1.6%*	1,892 (61.9%) *1.1%*	1,601 (76%) *0.9%*
Spanish	Boys	214 (80.3%) *0.2%*	212 (70.8%) *0.1%*	135 (68.9%) *0.08%*	153 (86%) *0.09%*
	Girls	282 (81.2%) *0.3%*	493 (70.8%) *0.3%*	454 (72.7%) *0.2%*	500 (83%) *0.3%*
Italian	Boys	49 (79.5%) *0.06%*	91 (NP) *0.06%*	91 (NP) *0.05%*	54 (78%) *0.03%*
	Girls	111 (82.3%) *0.13%*	249 (70.3%) *0.16%*	226 (74.3%) *0.13%*	160 (75%) *0.09%*
Russian	Boys	72 (88.8%) *0.09%*	30 (NP) *0.02%*	24 (NP) *0.01%*	2 (100%) *0.001%*
	Girls	91 (84.6%) *0.1%*	106 (73.6%) *0.07%*	40 (NP) *0.02%*	12 (92%) *0.007%*

		1966	1975	1985	1995
Gaelic [1]	Boys	—	33	51	48
		—	(NP) 0.02%	(NP) 0.03%	(92%) 0.02%
	Girls	—	51	80	92
		—	(NP) 0.03%	(NP) 0.04%	(92%) 0.05%
Other MLs	Boys	7	9	8	4
		(NP)	(NP)	(NP)	(NP)
	Girls	6	6	15	2
		(NP)	(NP)	(NP)	(NP)
Total MLs	Boys	5,180	5,006	2,852	2,127
		6.5%	3.3%	1.6%	1.3%
	Girls	7,805	11,591	8,978	6,181
		9.8%	7.7%	5.3%	3.8%
	Total	12,985	16,597	11,830	8,308
		16.3%	11.1%	7.0%	5.1%

1 Gaelic learners.

5 Boys' and Girls' performance compared across the curriculum in first and second examinations

A England and Wales 1995

Entries and pass rates compared in GCSE, GCE 'A' and 'AS' levels, in Mathematics, English, Latin and five foreign languages. Figures in italics show the percentage of passes (A–C at GCSE, A–E at 'A' and 'AS' level).

		GCSE	'A'	'AS'
All subjects	Boys	2,679,592	344,128	27,233
		48.9	83.7	73.2
	Girls	2,751,527	386,261	26,484
		57.1	84.6	74.8
Mathematics	Boys	334,550	41,199	5,702
		45.5	86.2	72.3
	Girls	343,872	22,281	3,306
		44.3	88.7	75.3
English	Boys	325,682	8,411 [1]	750 [1]
		48.8	83.2	87.5
	Girls	323,265	20,215	1,263
		65.7	87.2	89.3
Latin	Boys	6,776	762	66
		90.2	94.8	69.7
	Girls	6,182	863	75
		92.7	96.3	89.3
French *	Boys	163,694	8,169	1,289
		42.9	89.2	82.9
	Girls	186,323	19,394	1,678
		58.2	88.7	74.3

		GCSE	'A'	'AS'
German *	Boys	60,692	3,381	522
		_47.5_	_90.2_	_84.9_
	Girls	68,694	7,253	672
		_61.6_	_88.7_	_79.3_
Spanish *	Boys	15,955	1,456	196
		_50.7_	_92.0_	_78.6_
	Girls	24,807	3,381	334
		_63.9_	_89.0_	_80.8_
Italian	Boys	1,895	276	90
		_73.8_	_96.0_	_92.2_
	Girls	3,715	637	134
		_80.1_	_96.2_	_88.8_
Russian	Boys	864	199	11
		_76.0_	_95.0_	_100.0_
	Girls	1,018	227	15
		_83.0_	_96.5_	_93.3_
All syllabuses in language area	Boys	252,020	15,006	2,108
		_45.8_	_89.9_	_83.5_
	Girls	295,155	32,910	2,833
		_59.3_	_89.1_	_77.0_

1   English Language paper, not Literature.

B   Scotland

Entries and pass rates compared in Scottish Certificate of Education, Standard Grade (normally taken at age sixteen) and Higher Grade normally taken one year later, in Mathematics, English, Latin and five foreign languages.

Figures in italics show percentage of passes (1–3 at Standard Grade, A–C at Higher Grade).

		Standard Grade		Higher Grade	
All subjects	Boys	244,207	_56%_	73,771	_67%_
	Girls	245,905	_64%_	87,154	_72%_
Mathematics	Boys	31,637	_50%_	10,708	_64%_
	Girls	30,727	_50%_	9,554	_70%_
English	Boys	30,954	_65%_	14,706	_65%_
	Girls	30,153	_80%_	19,249	_71%_
Latin *	Boys	531	_74%_	183	_82%_
	Girls	761	_81%_	259	_81%_
French *	Boys	20,060	_40%_	1,297	_80%_
	Girls	21,612	_59%_	3,814	_79%_
German	Boys	7,717	_49%_	566	_74%_
	Girls	8.132	_67%_	1,601	_76%_
Spanish *	Boys	864	_45%_	153	_86%_
	Girls	1,346	_72%_	499	_83%_

		Standard Grade		Higher Grade	
Italian *	Boys	198	48%	54	78%
	Girls	356	74%	169	76%
Russian *	Boys	24	34%	2	100%
	Girls	23	73%	12	91%
All MLs	Boys	29,086		2,127	
	Girls	31,686		6,181	

Note: The Scottish Tables show interesting correlations with those for England/Wales/N Ireland.

In languages marked * girls outscore boys in GCSE/Standard Grade (age sixteen) while boys' pass grades are higher in GCE 'A' level/Higher Grade. Where boys do have a higher pass percentage this generally correlates with a smaller (and so more selective?) entry. In English language, however, this equation does not hold. Girls' consistently outperform boys in English. (The imbalance in the top marks in English is even more marked: 14.2% of girls score an 'A' grade in English in GCSE against only 7.7% of boys. In the Scottish Certificate, Standard Grade, similarly 13% of girls scored pass '1' in English, against only 7% of boys).

In both Tables, girls' higher performance in English correlates with higher performance across the board at secondary school.

The imbalance in mastery of English begins with girls' more rapid physiological and neurological development, pre-puberty. There may also be cultural factors which have not been widely discussed. Burstall (1974; p.61) quotes Preston (1972) showing that whereas in America girls outscore boys in reading comprehension, the reverse is true in Germany, where 'reading and learning' are approved masculine activities, and where the teaching force, at elementary level, was predominantly male when Preston made his study. After adolescence the linguistic imbalance becomes less marked, but, by then, many career decisions have been made. The effect of girls' marked (though temporary) linguistic precocity on the career choices that boys and girls make at age sixteen raises crucial questions about the teaching of the mother tongue at primary level, and about the wisdom of co-educational schooling at adolescence.

Table 6

A   Entries for GCE 'AS' level in 1995

GCE 'AS' level papers were introduced (Exam Boards in England/Wales/N Ireland) in 1988. Like the former Higher School Certificate Subsidiary papers, they are meant to be taken at age eighteen, and to call for approximately half the study time required for GCE 'A' level. As with the old HSC Subsidiary papers, a pass at 'AS' level is intended to represent half the value of a GCE 'A' level pass, for purposes of university entrance.

Comparison of entries for the 'AS' level papers with entries for the old HSC Subsidiary papers is difficult because national statistics of Subsidiary entries were not published annually. However the Schools Council (Working Paper No. 28, 1970) published figures for the Northern Joint Matriculation Board, one of the largest Boards, showing entries for French Main and Subsidiary papers, in 1939 and 1949:

		1939	1949
JMB Entries for French	HSC MAIN	1,669	3,076
Entries for French	HSC SUBSID.	2,433	3,756

From these figures it is safe to conclude that, nationally, entries for the HSC SUBSIDIARY papers in French outnumbered entries for the MAIN papers. The contrast with the present relationship of 'AS' to 'A' papers is marked.

Entries for 'AS' papers compared with 'A' level in 1995

Figures in italics show entries for 'AS' level as percentage of entries for 'A' level in the subject concerned.

		'A' level	'AS' level	
All subjects	boys	344,128	27,233	*7.9%*
	girls	386,261	26,484	*6.8%*
English language	boys	8,411	750	*8.9%*
	girls	20,215	1,263	*6.2%*
Maths	boys	41,199	5,702	*13.8%*
	girls	22,281	3,306	*14.8%*
Latin	boys	762	66	*8.6%*
	girls	863	75	*8.6%*
French	boys	8,169	1,289	*15.7%*
	girls	19,394	1,678	*8.6%*
German	boys	3,381	522	*15.4%*
	girls	7,253	672	*9.2%*
Spanish	boys	1,456	196	*13.4%*
	girls	3,381	334	*9.8%*
Italian	boys	276	90	*32.6%*
	girls	637	134	*21.0%*
Russian	boys	199	11	*5.5%*
	girls	227	15	*6.6%*
Total languages	boys	15,006	2,108	*14.0%*
	girls	32,910	2,833	*8.6%*

B   Dropout from languages after age sixteen

i   in England and Wales

The Table shows numbers of sixteen-year-old pupils scoring good grades in French, German and Spanish in GCSE in 1993, compared with numbers taking 'A' and 'AS' levels two years later in 1995 (but see note below).

		1993		1995	
		GCSE entries	Passes (A–C)	'A' level entries	'AS' level entries
French	boys	130,883	52,274	8,169	1,289
	girls	152,894	78,381	19,394	1,678
German	boys	45,082	21,577	3,381	522
	girls	53,434	32,303	7,253	672
Spanish	boys	9,191	3,875	1,456	196
	girls	13,670	7,681	3,381	334
All languages	boys	191,548	81,644	15,006	2,108
	girls	227,341	123,718	32,910	2,833

Note: the true extent of the dropout from languages in school sixth forms is disguised in the table by the fact that though only sixteen-year-old candidates with good passes in GCSE are listed, a considerable number of 'A' and 'AS' level entries shown in the table are mature candidates from further education colleges, not from sixth forms.

Against this must be set some 45,000 of eighteen-year-olds who (in 1995) entered for the General Studies paper set by one Board (NEAB) which tests (by multiple choice questions) a limited reading competence in a foreign language (10% of the paper).

ii   in Scotland

The Table shows numbers of sixteen-year-olds scoring good passes in the Scottish Certificate of Education, Standard Grade, in French, German and Spanish in 1994 compared with entries for the Higher Grade Examination in 1995.

		1994		1995
		Standard Grade entries	Passes (1–3)	Higher Grade entries
French	boys	18,902	7,349	1,297
	girls	20,546	11,508	3,814
German	boys	6,689	3,569	566
	girls	7,243	4,733	1,601
Spanish	boys	682	317	153
	girls	1,022	679	499

		1994		1995
		Standard Grade entries	Passes (1–3)	Higher Grade entries
Spanish	boys	682	317	153
	girls	1,022	679	499
All languages	boys	26,551	11,364	2,127
	girls	29,262	17,247	6,181

7 Entries for GCSE and GCE 'A' level in main community languages in 1994

England and Wales

Numbers of candidates for GCSE and GCE 'A' level in main community languages, 1994:

GCSE		GCE 'A' level	
Welsh L2	6,393	Chinese	901
Urdu	5,995	Urdu	808
Welsh	2,824	Welsh L2	545
Chinese	1,931	Welsh	361
Bengali	1,826	Greek	249
Panjabi	1,482	Panjabi	159
Gujerati	1,370	Turkish	140
Arabic	903	Bengali	137
Greek	846	Hindi	41
Turkish	606		
Hindi	376		

Source: SCAA

In Scotland two papers ('Gaelic' and 'Gaelic Learners') can be taken in the Scottish Certificate of Education, at Standard and Higher Grade.
Entries for these papers in 1995 were as follows:

Standard Grade	Gaelic	102
	Gaelic Learners	440
Higher Grade	Gaelic	40
	Gaelic Learners	140

Accounts of the position of Welsh and Gaelic in the school system can be found at pp135 and 138. See also Johnstone R, *The impact of current developments to support the Gaelic language* (CILT/Scottish CILT, 1994).

8 Language students at university

A UK domiciled students studying Modern Languages at university (former UFC-funded establishments only) 1993/4

	Men	Women	Total
French	1,022	3,087	4,109
German	482	1,248	1,730
Hispanic Studies	295	694	989
Russian	217	289	506
Other European languages	685	1,664	2,349
Chinese	118	118	236
Other oriental/ Asian/African langs	407	435	842
Other and combined languages and related studies	3,620	9,816	13,436
Total MLs and related studies	6,846	17,351	24,197

Source: Universities Statistics 1993/94 Part 1 (USR)

The figures must be read with caution; combined honours students and students studying a language as a minor subject are not fully represented (see Coleman, 1996: 34).

B First year Modern Languages students, all HE institutions, December 1994

First year students on full-time and sandwich courses, all higher education institutions, as at 1 December 1994. (Numbers on part-time courses are shown in italics.)

	Men		Women		Total	
French lang. lit. and culture	838	*261*	2,229	*407*	3,067	*668*
German lang. lit. and culture	217	*148*	536	*199*	753	*347*
Italian lang. lit. and culture	60	*59*	161	*110*	221	*169*
Spanish lang. lit. and culture	141	*154*	329	*169*	470	*323*
Portuguese lang. lit. and culture	7	*34*	7	*36*	14	*70*
Latin American langs. lit. and culture	43	*0*	66	*0*	109	*0*
Scandinavian langs. lit. and culture	28	*114*	23	*67*	51	*181*
Russian lang. lit. and culture	95	*107*	99	*154*	194	*261*
Slav./E. Euro. langs. lit. and culture	17	*89*	24	*100*	41	*189*
Other Euro. langs. lit. and culture	389	*75*	791	*129*	1,180	*204*
Chinese lang. lit. and culture	38	*109*	40	*122*	78	*231*
Japanese lang. lit. and culture	49	*139*	41	*103*	90	*242*

	Men		Women		Total	
Other Asian langs. lit. and culture	20	*3*	16	*4*	36	*7*
Mod. Middle-E. langs. lit.and culture	79	*89*	70	*132*	149	*221*
African langs. lit. and culture	11	*0*	40	*0*	51	*0*
Other language studies	50	*24*	137	*44*	187	*68*
Other or unspecified mod.langs.	336	*211*	1,066	*387*	1,402	*598*
Total FT and PT 1st yr. MLs	2,418	*1,616*	5,675	*2,163*	8,093	*3,779*

Source: HESA Services Ltd. Data Report July 1995. Students in Higher Education Institutions

Note that students not majoring in above languages are excluded from the Table. According to HESA figures, out of some one and a half million students in universities and HE colleges in UK:

* approximately 936,000 are on full-time courses;
* one third of new full-time undergraduates are over 21 years of age;
* one in ten students comes from overseas.

9   Number of HE institutions offering particular languages in 1963 and 1996

	Number of institutions listed			Number of institutions listed	
	1963 entry	1996 entry		1963 entry	1996 entry
French	38	106	Danish	6	2
German	37	98	Serb/Serb-Cr Studies	4	2
Spanish	27	77	Romanian	3	1
Italian	23	46	Provençal	8	0
Russian	26	39	Pali	3	0
Japanese	3	32			
Portuguese	17	16	**Linguistic/cultural groups**		
Arabic	12	11			
Chinese	5	11	Latin American Studies	14	13
Dutch	7	6	African Studies	3	5
Catalan	11	5	Asian Studies	3	5
Persian	6	5	Oriental Studies	5	4
Modern Greek	5	5	Slavonic Studies	3	3
Turkish	6	4	Scandinavian Studies	2	5
Czech	4	4	Semitic Studies	5	1
Hindi	0	4	East Asian Studies	0	3
Swedish	10	3			
Polish	6	3	(excludes languages taught in fewer than		
Slovak	3	3	three institutions)		
Korean	0	3			

Table compiled by David Nott from data in Stern H H (ed), *Modern languages in the universities* (Macmillan, 2nd edition, 1965); Universities and Colleges Admissions Service; *UCAS Handbook 1996* entry (UCAS, 1995).

10 Graduate teachers in schools: 1966 and 1995

A   England and Wales

400 *i   Graduate teachers in full-time service in grant-aided schools and establishments*

	1966	1993
Men	55,957	86,637
Women	25,951	121,768
Total	**81,008**	**208,405**

ii Modern Languages graduates in full-time service in grant-aided schools and establishments

with ML as first named subject of degree		
	1966	**1993**
Men	6,583	4,522
Women	4,912	9,768
Total	**11,495**	**14,290**

with ML among degree subjects	
	1993
Men	7,070
Women	15,503
Total	**22,573**

iii Graduate teachers in full-time service in maintained nursery and primary schools, all subjects

	1966	1993
Men	2,725	16,199
Women	3,192	59,957
Total	**5,917**	**76,156**

iv Modern Languages graduates in full-time service in primary schools

with ML among degree subjects	
	1993
Men	582
Women	3,577
Total	**4,159**

Notes:

i. The tables reveal a marked change in the balance between men and women graduate teachers. Whereas in 1966 men graduates outnumbered women graduates by more than two to one in the State system, in 1993 the ratio was three women to two men.

ii. In primary schools, women graduates now outnumber men by some four to one, whereas in 1966 there was near parity.

iii. Among modern language graduate teachers with a ML as the first-named degree subject, the number of men has fallen by one third since 1966, while the number of women has doubled.

iv. It is significant that there are now over 4,000 graduate teachers in primary schools whose degree included a modern language. It would be interesting to know how many of them currently teach a language.

B Scotland

Comparable tables for Scotland are not available but the latest available figures of secondary teachers in Education Authority schools, in September 1992, were as follows:

Main teaching subject	Full time equivalent	%age of total	
		Male	Female
All subjects	23,971	52	48
English	3,025	37	63
Mathematics	2,782	57	43
French	1,541	28	72
German	369	27	73
Spanish	65	38	62

11 Modern Languages teachers in training

A England and Wales: UG AND PGCE, 1993

Numbers recruited for Secondary Phase Language Courses, 1993					
	Male		**Female**		**Combined**
Subject	**UG ***	**PGCE ***	**UG ***	**PGCE ***	**Total**
French	12	194	46	863	**1,115**
German	2	77	8	273	**360**
Spanish	3	30	10	98	**141**
Italian	0	2	0	9	**11**
Russian	0	3	0	17	**20**
Welsh	8	5	12	33	**58**
Other MLs	4	26	12	71	**113**
Total MLs	**29**	**337**	**88**	**1,364**	**1,818**

* UG = degree courses giving qualified teacher status; PGCE = one year post graduate certificate courses

(Source: Dept for Education and Employment, 1996)

For comparison: numbers recruited for English and Maths:

Subject	Male		Female		Combined
	UG *	PGCE *	UG *	PGCE *	Total
English	24	406	35	1,188	**1,653**
Maths	306	913	174	819	**2,212**

* UG = degree courses giving qualified teacher status; PGCE = one year post graduate certificate courses

B   Scotland

Figures in italics show totals graduating in 1992.

Students completing pre-service secondary training, 1993				
	Male	Female	Total	(1992)
French	15	87	102	*91*
German	4	11	15	*20*
Spanish	6	16	22	*8*
Russian	1	1	2	*1*
Gaelic	0	4	4	*2*
Other MLs	1	4	5	*10*
Total MLs	27	123	150	*132*
For comparison: numbers qualified in English and Maths:				
English	37	124	161	*134*
Maths	89	62	151	*123*

(Source: Scottish Office. Government Statistical Bulletin. Educational Series Edn/G1/1995/1)

Appendix III
The main support organisations

Central Bureau for Educational Visits and Exchanges

10 Spring Gardens, London SW1A 2BN. Tel: 0171 389 4004
3 Bruntsfield Crescent, Edinburgh EH10 4HD. Tel: 0131 447 8024
1 Chlorine Gardens, Belfast BT9 5DJ. Tel: 01232 664418

The Central Bureau is funded in the UK by the Government Education Departments. It forms part of the British Council. Its principal aim is to promote and support the international dimension in all sectors of the education system. The teaching and learning of modern foreign languages are vital to this purpose.

The Central Bureau is the national agency for several European Union actions under the EU Socrates and Leonardo programmes and publishes a range of guides, directories and information sheets. It administers the Foreign Language Assistants Programme and a wide range of teacher exchange and study visit options. Support for curriculum linking and other international projects is also provided. The Central Bureau organises courses abroad and also provides courses in this country for teachers from abroad.

National Council for Educational Technology

Milburn Hill Road, Science Park, Coventry CV4 7JJ. Tel: 01203 416 994 (enquiries
to Enquiries Desk). E-mail: Enquiry_Desk@ncet.org.uk
URL: http://ncet.csv.warwick.ac.uk/index.html

NCET is a registered charity funded by the UK Education Departments (DfEE, WOED, DENI and SOED) to develop and promote the use of information technology in every area of education and training. NCET researches and evaluates the relevance of new technologies to enhance learning and raise standards in teaching and learning: it promotes their effective use across all sectors of education.

National Foundation for Educational Research

The Mere, Upton Park, Slough, Berkshire SL1 2DQ. Tel: 01753 574123

The National Foundation for Educational Research in England and Wales is Britain's leading educational research institution. It is an independent body undertaking research and development projects on issues of current interest in all sectors of the public education system. Its membership includes all the local education authorities in England and Wales, the main teachers' associations and a large number of other major organisations with educational interests.

By means of research projects and extensive field surveys, it has provided objective evidence on important educational issues for the use of teachers, administrators, parents and the research community. The major part of the research programme relates to the maintained educational sector – primary, secondary and further education. A further significant element has to do specifically with local education authorities, teacher training institutions and other agencies concerned with education and training.

The Foundation's research activities are backed up by an extensive network of supporting services in computing and statistics, in survey administration, in information and in the development and use of tests.

French Embassy, Bureau de Coopération Linguistique et Educative

23 Cromwell Rd, London SW7 2EL. Tel: 0171 838 2055. Fax: 0171 838 2088
13 Randolph Crescent, Edinburgh EH3 7TT. Tel: 0131 225 5366. Fax: 0131 220 5080
188 Oxford Rd, Manchester M13 9GP. Tel: 0161 273 1524. Fax: 0161 272 8123 (will move in 1997)

The BCLE collaborates with CILT and other national agencies in offering courses in French language and culture and teaching methodology. Through the Comenius Network the professional staff of the BCLE are involved in the provision of advice, support and information to language teachers. It also provides an educational service – documents, teaching ideas – on the Internet called 'France à la Carte' (http://www.campus.bt.com/CampusWorld/pub/FranceALC/).

Goethe-Institut

50 Princes Gate, London SW7 2PH. Tel: 0171 411 3400. Fax: 0171 581 0974
3 Park Circus, Glasgow G3 6AX. Tel: 0141 332 2555. Fax: 0141 333 1630
Churchgate House, Fourth Floor, 56 Oxford Street, Manchester M1 6EU.
Tel: 0161 237 1077. Fax: 0161 237 1079
County House, 32–34 Monkgate, York YO3 7RQ. Tel: 01904 611 122.
Fax: 01904 612 736
URL: http://www.goethe.DE/

The Goethe-Institut is an independent, non-profit making organisation, funded by the German government, which aims to promote the study of the German language abroad and to encourage international cultural co-operation. The Goethe-Institut provides the following services for teachers of German: in-service training, seminars, workshops and weekend conferences on methodology and contemporary German issues, short courses in Germany, refresher courses, grants and scholarships. The Goethe-Instituts in London, Manchester and York also organise in-service training events in collaboration with the Comenius Centres in the UK.

The Goethe-Institut runs its own web site on the internet, 'Click Deutsch' (see URL above), and produces teaching materials in conjunction with British partners such as the BBC and Kent County Council.

The Italian Cultural Institute

39 Belgrave Square, London SW1X 8NX. Tel: 0171 235 1461. Fax: 0171 235 4618
E-mail: italcultur@martex.co.uk

The Italian Cultural Institute promotes the Italian language and culture in the UK and organises lectures, exhibitions, seminars, concerts and language courses.

The Institute makes available:

* scholarships for teachers of Italian who wish to attend the refresher course organised in Italy every summer by the Italian Ministry of Education;
* bursaries, scholarships and research grants for British citizens.

A well stocked reference and lending library is open to the public Monday to Friday.

Spanish Embassy Consejería de Educación

20 Peel Street, London W8 7PD. Tel: 0171 727 2462. Fax: 0171 229 4965

The Spanish Embassy Education Office offers a range of services in support of Spanish teaching at all levels in the UK, including:

* courses and in-service days for teachers;
* publications;
* resources centres;
* training and support for language assistants;
* examinations in Spanish as a foreign language;
* information;
* survey on the situation of Spanish as a foreign language in the UK.

Association for Language Learning

150 Railway Terrace, Rugby CV21 3HN. Tel: 01788 546 443. Fax: 01788 544 149

The Association for Language Learning (ALL) is the major UK subject teaching association for those involved in the teaching of modern foreign languages in all sectors of education, both state and independent, and at all levels from five to eighteen to further, higher and adult education and training.

As well as supporting its members' work through the Association's journals, newsletters and other publications, it provides a range of language specific INSET training days and courses, as well as courses on general language topics, and *Language World*, the Association's annual three-day conference with the largest UK language exhibition running alongside. There are also numerous evening and day events organised by ALL branches throughout the UK.

The Institute of Linguists

24a Highbury Grove, London N5 2DQ. Tel: 0171 359 7445

The Institute of Linguists is the leading professional language body in the UK with over 6,500 members, including language teachers and educationalists in schools, colleges and higher education. Founded in 1910 with the aim of promoting high standards in the use of foreign languages in industry and commerce, the Institute has been providing recognised language qualifications for over 80 years. The Institute offers public examinations in over 70 languages for both the general and the specialist user which have been developed to meet the needs of industry, commerce and the public services.

In the past eight years, the Diploma in Translation and the Diploma in Public Service Interpreting have become established as proof of professional competence in these disciplines while the Examinations in Languages for International Communication have achieved their aim of ensuring the highest standards of testing of linguistic competence.

National Association of Language Advisers

Stella Marsh, Membership Secretary
Broadway EDC, Springwell Rd, Sunderland SR4 8NW. Tel: 0191 553 5600.
Fax: 0191 553 5633

NALA exists to provide professional support for those whose work is mainly concerned with advice, in-service training, or inspection for MFLs in schools and colleges in the UK. Members include freelance consultants, and those employed in the public services.

BBC Education

White City, 201 Wood Lane, London W12 7TS. Tel: 0181 746 1111
URL: http://www.bbc.co.uk/education/languages/

BBC Education provides multimedia language learning resources for use in formal and informal learning situations and for learners from age nine to adult.

Schools programmes and support materials (for pupils aged nine to eighteen) are provided in French, German and Spanish. Television programmes provide resources appropriate to the specific age range and are linked closely to curricular need. These are further developed through photocopiable activities in the published resource packs, which also contain transcripts and notes to teachers.

Adult resources are published in fourteen languages from survival level through to multimedia self-study packages with additional tutor support. These resources are appropriate for learners in adult, further and higher education following institution-wide language modules.

Channel 4

PO Box 100, Warwick CV34 6TZ. Tel: 01926 433 333 (Information line).
Fax: 01926 450 178

Resources for modern language teaching have an important role in Channel 4 Schools programming and the output will continue to support the teaching and learning of languages. As well as a commitment to Continental Europe languages, there are also series to support the learning of Gaelic and Irish.

Instituto Cervantes

22–23 Manchester Square, London W1M 5AP. Tel: 0171 235 1487. Fax: 0171 235 4115
The University, 169 Woodhouse Lane, Leeds LS2 3AR. Tel: 0113 246 1741.
Fax: 0113 246 1033
324–330 Deansgate, Manchester M3 4FN. Tel: 0161 237 3376. Fax: 0161 228 7467

The Instituto Cervantes is the official Spanish government centre for the promotion of the Spanish language and culture. Its aims are:

- **Promotion of the language:** Spanish language courses at different levels; special courses, e.g. business Spanish; preparation of the *Diploma de Español como Lengua Extranjera;* courses for teachers of Spanish; assistance to Hispanists and researchers; seminars to promote the study of present day Spanish and teaching methodology.
- **Promotion of culture:** cultural events such as exhibitions, concerts, lectures on literature, films, theatre and aspects of contemporary Spain.

Canning House

Education Department, 2 Belgrave Square, London SW1X 8PJ.
Tel: 0171 235 2303/7. Fax: 0171 235 3587

Canning House is the home of the Hispanic and Luso-Brazilian Council, which was founded in 1943 to promote understanding between Britain, Spain, Portugal and Latin America. Its services to teachers include a library; a newsletter to schools; information and research; courses and conferences; cultural events; Portuguese evening classes at various levels.

Appendix IV
Glossary of acronyms used in the text

Eric Hawkins

ACACE	Advisory Council for Adult and Continuing Education
AEB	Associated Examining Board
AILA	Association Internationale de Linguistique Appliquée
AL	Awareness of Language (see **LA** below and Chapter 10)
ALL	The Association for Language Learning founded in 1990 from the merger of existing foreign language associations (see Chapter 28)
A-LM	Audio-Lingual Materials
ALTL	Association of Language Testers in Europe
APTAB	Access to Primary Teaching for Asian and Black People
ASTCOVEA	Aston, Coventry and East Anglia Universities project
AUPHF	Association of University Professors and Heads of Department of French
A-V	Audio-Visual
AVLA	The Audio-Visual Language Association founded in 1962 (see Chapter 27). Name changed in 1974 to British Association for Language Teaching; merged in 1990 in **ALL** (see above)
BAAL	British Association of Applied Linguistics
BALT	British Association for Language Teaching (see **AVLA** above)
BEd	Bachelor of Arts in Education
BOTB	British Overseas Trade Board
CACE(E)	Central Advisory Council for Education (England)
CALL	Computer-Assisted Language Learning
CAT	College of Advanced Technology
CATE	Council for the Accreditation of Teachers
CBEVE	Central Bureau for Educational Visits and Exchanges (see p403)
CERCLES	Conférence Européenne de Centres de Langues dans l'Enseignement Supérieur
CKS	Cambridgeshire, Kent and Southampton project
CL	Community Languages

CILT	Centre for Information on Language Teaching and Research
COLT	Content Oriented Language Teaching (see Chapter 23)
CREDIF	Centre de Recherche et Diffusion du Français (Paris)
CRDML	Committee on Research and Development of Modern Languages; set up 1964 (see Chapter 31)
CSE	Certificate of Secondary Education first set in 1965 (see Appendix II, Table 1)
CTI	Computers in Teaching Initiative (University of Hull)
DELTA	Developing European Learning Through Technical Advance
DULC	Directors of University Language Centres
DVV	Deutscher Volkshochschulverein (Germany)
EBLUL	European Bureau for Lesser Used Languages (see Chapter 5)
EEC	European Economic Community
EFL	English as a Foreign Language
EPC	Educational Publishers Council (see Chapter 17)
ESL	English as a second language
ESRC	Economic and Social Research Council
ETIC	English Teaching Information Centre
ETML	The early teaching of modern languages
EU	European Union
FE	Further Education (see Chapter 9)
FEFC	Further Education Funding Council
FLAW	Foreign Languages at Work (see Chapter 1)
FLES	(in USA) Foreign languages in the elementary school.
FLIC	Foreign languages in the curriculum
GCE 'A' level	GCE Advanced level (see Appendix II, Tables 3 and 4)
GCE 'AS' level	GCE Advanced Supplementary (name changed to Advanced Subsidiary in 1996) (see Appendix II Table 6)
GCE 'O' level	General Certificate of Education Ordinary level (see Appendix II, Tables 1 and 2)
GCSE	General Certificate of Education, examination replacing both GCE 'O' level and CSE (see above) in 1988 (see Appendix II, Tables 1 and 2)
GMU	Gaelic Medium Units in which teaching is in Gaelic
GOML	Graded Objectives in Modern Language teaching (see Chapter 7)
GTV	Gaelic Television
HEFC	Higher Education Funding Council
HEI	Higher Education Institution
HESA	Higher Education Statistics Agency
HMI	Her Majesty's Inspectorate

HMSI	Her Majesty's Staff Inspector (i.e. senior HMI for one curriculum subject)
HRB	Humanities Research Board
HSC	Higher School Certificate (see Appendix II, Tables 3 and 4)
IAAM	Incorporated Association of Assistant Masters in Secondary Schools
IAHM	Incorporated Association of Headmasters
ICC	International Certification Conference (see Chapter 5)
ILEA	Inner London Education Authority
INRP	Institut National de Recherche Pédagogique (Paris, rue d'Ulm)
INSET	In-service education of teachers
IoL	Institute of Linguists (see p406)
IT	Information Technology
ITE	Initial Teacher Education
ITT	Initial Teacher Training
IWLPs	Institution wide language programmes
JCLA	Joint Council of Language Associations
JMB	(Northern Universities) Joint Matriculation Board (see **NUJMB** below)
LA	Language Awareness (see Chapter 10)
LINGUA	See p371
LAD	Language Acquisition Device (see Introduction and Chapter 10)
LASS	Language Acquisition Support System (see Chapter 10)
LCCIEB	London Chamber of Commerce and Industry Exam Board
LEA	Local Education Authority
L1	First (native) language
L2	Second (target) language
MEG	Midland Examining Group
MFLE	Maîtrise Français Langue Etrangère (see Chapter 23)
MFLs	Modern foreign languages
MLs	Modern languages
MLA	Modern Language Association, founded 1892. Merged 1990 in **ALL** (see above)
MLPS	Modern Languages in the primary School (Scotland)
NAHT	National Association of Head Teachers

NALA	National Association of Language Advisers founded 1969 (see Chapter 27)
NALDIC	National Association for Language Development in the Curriculum
NatBLIS	National Business Language Information Service (see Chapter 1)
NC	National Curriculum
NCC	National Curriculum Council, advising the Secretary of State on curriculum
NCET	National Council for Educational Technology
NCLE	National Council for Languages in Education
NCML	National Council for Modern Languages (superseded by **UCML**, see below)
NCW	National Curriculum Council for Wales, advising the Welsh Office
NCWG	National Curriculum Working Group for MLs (Chair: Martin Harris)
NCVQ	National Council for Vocational Qualifications responsible for defining and administering National Vocational Qualifications (NVQ) and General National Vocational Qualifications (GNVQ)
NEAB	Northern Examinations and Assessment Board (see **NUJMB** below)
NFER	National Foundation for Educational Research
NIACE	National Institute for Adult and Continuing Education
NICCEA	Northern Ireland Council for the Curriculum, Examinations and Assessment
NLS	National Language Standards set up by NCVQ to accompany NVQs and GNVQs where appropriate
NVQs	National Vocational Qualifications (see Chapter 18)
NUJMB	Northern Universities Joint Matriculation Board, one of the regional Boards setting examinations, now the Northern Examining and Assessment Board
OCSEB	Oxford and Cambridge Schools Examinations Board
OFSTED	Office for Standards in Education
OHP	Overhead Projector
OU	Open University
PC	Personal Computer
PE	Physical Education
RSA	Royal Society of Arts
RE	Religious Education
SC	School Certificate (see **GCE 'O' level** above)
SCAA	School Curriculum and Assessment Authority

SCHML	Standing conference of heads of MLs in Polytechnics and other colleges
SCITT	School centred Initial Teacher Training (see Chapters 25–26)
SEG	Southern Examinations Group
SEM	Single European Market
SEN	Special Educational Needs (see Chapter 8)
SHAPE	Supreme Headquarters Allied Powers in Europe (see Chapter 19)
SHS	Social handicap score, in Plowden Report (see Chapter 10)
SMEs	Small- and medium-sized companies/enterprises (see Chapter 1)
SOAS	School of Oriental and African Studies
SODS	Specialists in other disciplines (see Chapter 5)
SOED	Scottish Office of Education
SSEC	Secondary Schools Examinations Council (gave way 1962–4 to Schools Council for Curriculum and Examinations, largely funded by LEAs and more open to fresh thinking)
SWOT	Strength, Weakness, Opportunities, Threats (see Chapter 1)
TAVOR	Teachers Audio-Visual and Oral Aids (see Chapter 19)
TELL	Technologically enhanced language learning
TES	Times Educational Supplement
TLTP	Teaching and Learning Technical Programme
UCAS	Universities Central Council on Admissions
UCLES	University of Cambridge Local Examinations Syndicate
UCML	Universities Council for Modern Languages
ULEAC	University of London Examinations and Assessment Council
UODLE	University of Oxford Delegacy of Local Examinations
WG	Working Group
WJEC	Welsh Joint Education Committee
WLC	Welsh Language Council
W-MU	Welsh medium units, in which teaching is in Welsh (see Chapter 11)

Appendix V

A selective index

Eric Hawkins

This selective index lists the themes and individuals (other than contributors) most frequently cited in the text. References are to pages. All publications cited in the text are listed alphabetically at the end of each chapter.

417

Appendix VI
The contributors

Lore Arthur is a lecturer with the Open University and responsible for its German Programme. She began her career as a part-time tutor for German in adult education and industry before becoming head of languages at Goldsmiths College, School of Adult and Community Studies in 1984, where she developed training courses for foreign language tutors. She has researched and published in foreign language learning and adult education theory and is course designer for the BBC series *Deutsch Plus* and has worked with CILT over a number of years.

Jim Beale was educated at George Heriot's School, Edinburgh, and Edinburgh University, where he gained an Honours Degree in French and Spanish.

Following graduation in 1957, he was commissioned into The Royal Scots. Thereafter he joined Procter and Gamble before joining the PA Consulting Group in 1964. He became Director of the Western European operating arm of the Company in 1974. In the early 1980s, operating from PA's Brussels office, he was made responsible for all PA's operations in the Benelux countries, including all the European institutions.

He was National Chairman of the Chartered Institute of Marketing in 1991 and President of the European Marketing Confederation in 1993, when he retired from PA. He has been a Governor of CILT, and a member of the Languages Lead Body, since 1990.

Madeleine Bedford taught languages for twenty years in grammar and comprehensive schools, and has been head of department and a deputy head. She worked in Hampshire as modern languages adviser, then as a post-16 inspector before taking up her current post as an inspector for the Further Education Funding Council in England. She has worked closely with many organisations, including the Welsh Joint Education Committee and the former SEC 18+ modern languages committee. She is a former Chair of NALA and served for six years as a Governor of CILT. She is currently President of ALL.

Jim Coleman is Professor of Foreign Language Learning at the University of Portsmouth. Co-author of *Le français en faculté* and *Lyon à la une*, and now co-editor of the series *Current issues in university language teaching*, he has published widely on many aspects of language teaching, as well as books and articles on French literature.

Do Coyle worked for sixteen years in a variety of comprehensive schools in the UK and France. She currently co-ordinates the Franco-British *Maîtrise*/PGCE in initial teacher education at the School of Education, University of Nottingham. She is completing a doctoral research in content-based classroom practice in the UK. She has worked closely with CILT and ALL in setting up a national network of schools and institutions interested in bi-lingual and cross-curricular language learning. She is joint author and editor of the latest publication supported by the European Commission on 'Teaching Content in a Foreign Language: Practice and Perspectives in European Bilingual Education', and will co-ordinate the opening of the first bilingual secondary PGCE course in the UK for students of History, Geography and Science through the medium of French and German in 1997.

Rosemary Davidson studied Modern Languages at Oxford and began her career with the Ernst Klett Verlag in Stuttgart (1952–53), in a team creating new English textbooks after the Second World War. After working on the German dictionary project at Harraps, she went to work with Mary Glasgow and Baker (later Mary Glasgow Publications), started the German and English magazines there and became a director. She later moved to Longmans, where she spent fourteen years (1964–78) on modern language publishing, bringing the list into the audio-visual era. For the final eleven years of her publishing life she was in charge of the educational publishing group of Cambridge University Press. She served for two years as the (first woman) Chair of the Educational Publishers Council and also as the Chair of the ALL publishing committee. Since retiring from publishing in 1989, she has been writing for children on art, working for the National gallery as educational publishing consultant and running her own gallery in Cambridge.

June Geach joined CILT as Research Information Officer in 1972. From 1982 to 1990 she was Linguistic Minorities Information Officer, responsible for the collection, storage and dissemination of information relating to the language concerns of linguistic minorities in Britain, including English as a second language, community languages, and issues in bilingualism and bilingual education. She is a founder member of Multilingk, and continues to serve on the committee.

Peter Green studied in Cambridge and Lund, Sweden, and taught German and French in British schools. From 1965 he was lecturer, then senior lecturer at the Language Teaching Centre, University of York (Director 1979–84), where he was mainly concerned with language teacher training. He has conducted research and published in the fields of acoustic phonetics, effectiveness of language laboratories, aptitude testing and interlanguage analysis. He is a textbook author. He is a former school governor and Governor of CILT.

Louis Greenstock is currently Head of Teaching Resources at CILT, having worked in the Centre's Resources Library since 1978. He previously worked in private and public libraries.

Vee Harris is PGCE Modern Languages tutor at Goldsmiths College. Since 1989, she has been working with teachers in schools to explore ways of setting up independent learning in the classroom. Her publications include textbooks for teachers as well as a book on equal opportunities in the CILT Pathfinder series and contributions relating to learner autonomy and learner strategies in a number of CILT publications. She is a member of several CILT working groups, including the Teacher Training Working Group.

Eric Hawkins studied at Cambridge and in Republican Spain in the 1930s where he heard Garcia Lorca read his poetry. Teaching was interrupted by six years army service (infantry) in North Africa and Italy. After fifteen years as a grammar school head he went to York in 1965 to set up the Language Teaching Centre responsible for teacher training, 'service courses' and research in language teaching. Elected emeritus on retirement, he went to China for a term to teach English. He chaired the School Council ML committee and served on the Plowden and Rampton committees (primary schooling and education of ethnic minority children).

Sue Hewer has taught foreign languages to students in the 11–18 age group for 25 years. For the last twelve years she has worked with practising and intending teachers of foreign languages in the primary, secondary and HE sectors to promote the use of new technologies in language learning. Her research interests lie in the potential of the characteristics of new media to promote development and use of effective language learning strategies, with particular reference to reading and writing. She is series editor for CILT of *InfoTech*, a forthcoming series concerned with new media and language learning.

Brian Hill is Professor and Head of the Language Centre at the University of Brighton and is responsible for the organisation of language training to some 4,000 students. He has for many years been involved via research and authorship of published material in promoting effective exploitation of media technology in language teaching and learning. Amongst other activities, he is editor of the CILT series *Making the most of technology* and of the Macmillan *Breakthrough* series comprising audio and video courses at various levels in ten languages. His current interests involve exploring the potential of interactive multimedia and telematic technology.

Bernardette Holmes has worked with pupils of all abilities in a number of urban comprehensive schools. She has particular interest in developing appropriate curricula for pupils in special schools and has been actively involved with the work of CILT in supporting the development of effective teaching and learning strategies for pupils with learning difficulties in both special and mainstream education. She is currently a general inspector with responsibility for modern languages in Essex.

Geraint Hughes is a native of Harlech in North Wales. He was educated at Ysgol Ardudwy, Harlech and University College, Cardiff. He was a teacher of Welsh at Llanrumney High School Cardiff and Head of Department at Cowbridge Comprehensive School. Since 1982 he has been Officer for Welsh and Assistant Secretary (Welsh) at the WJEC's National Language Unit of Wales, responsible for developing materials for teaching and learning Welsh (mother tongue) and Welsh as a Second Language.

Barry Jones taught French and German in Birmingham and Hertfordshire in Technical, Grammar and Comprehensive schools before becoming a teacher trainer at Homerton College, Cambridge. He has published computer software and books on modern language learning, the most recent of which is on Creativity, the use of the target language, and Cultural awareness in the CILT Pathfinder series. He is co-writing a French course, *Spirale*, published by Hodder and Stoughton. He was co-director of a three-year joint French Embassy/DfE project which produced a book, a cassette and four TV programmes, *Learning strategies*, designed to offer distance training for returners to language teaching. At present he is co-directing a second three-year project designed to teach English as a Foreign Language and French, German and Spanish to primary school children.

Richard Johnstone is Professor and Head of the Department of Education, University of Stirling, and Director of the Scottish Centre for Information on Language Teaching and Research (Scottish CILT). He has directed many research projects for SOIED on the teaching and learning of second languages, and has written several books on the subject. His most recent work has included responsibility for the evaluation of national pilot projects in modern languages in Scottish primary schools.

Lid King, a graduate in Languages at Cambridge University with a PhD in Socio-Linguistics, has extensive experience as teacher, examiner and writer of publications at secondary and post-secondary levels. He joined CILT in 1988 as a Teacher Liaison Officer, becoming Director in 1992. Since then he has played a key role in developing a national network of resource and information centres in the UK, languages consultancy services to British business, and the establishment of European information networks.

Alan Moys' career in language education spanned the first 28 years of CILT's existence, and included experience as a teacher, teacher trainer, and LEA adviser before he joined CILT, first as Deputy Director and later as Director. He started teaching in 1959, and from an early stage became involved in the flurry of exciting new developments such as audio-visual courses and the language laboratory. His first experience of in-service training was to attend the Besançon CREDIF course on audio-visual techniques, in 1962. From 1965–69 he worked in Bristol as an initial teacher trainer (St Matthias College, Fishponds). In 1969 he moved to Derbyshire, first as Modern Languages Adviser to the Derby LEA, and from 1974 as County Modern Languages Adviser for Derbyshire and Derby area General Secondary Adviser. He joined CILT in 1978 and became Director in 1987.

David Nott is Senior Lecturer in French Studies at Lancaster University, having previously trained future language teachers at University College Bangor (1981–85), and taught at the Manchester Grammar School (1963–80). He was co-author with J E Trickey of the 'A' level course *Actualités francaises* (1971), and is author of the first-year undergraduate course *Points de départ* (1993); as well as editions of Sartre's *Les mots* (1981) and of Vailland's *325,000 francs* (1975 and 1989), he has since 1977 published several articles on French language and literature, and on language syllabuses, teaching and examining.

Brian Page was a secondary school teacher for fifteen years before going to the University of Leeds to direct the Language Centre. He chaired the GOML National Coordinating Committee for several years and was the first president of ALL. He has always worked closely with secondary school language teachers throughout the UK and, through the British Council and the Council of Europe, with many other countries.

Cathy Pomphrey is course tutor to the PGCE Modern Languages at the University of North London. She has taught in various London schools and was Head of Languages and senior teacher at Hampstead School for a number of years.

Nigel Reeves is Pro-Vice-Chancellor and Professor of German at Aston University. He graduated from Oxford with First Class Honours in German and French in 1963, and took his DPhil in 1970. He lectured at Lund University in English from 1966-68, at Reading University in German from 1968-74 and was Professor of German and Head of Linguistic and International Studies, University of Surrey 1975-89, and Dean of the Faculty of Human Studies 1986-90. He was appointed Professor of German at Aston University in 1990, was Head of Department of Languages and European Studies 1990-96 and was appointed Pro-Vice-Chancellor (External Relations) from August 1996.

He has been President of the National Association of Language Advisers, Chairman of Council of the Institute of Linguists, of which he is Vice-President, and President of the Association of Teachers of German. He is Chairman of the London Chamber of Commerce Foreign Languages at Work Management Committee and International Languages Consultant to the Chamber, a member of the Academic Advisory Council to the Linguaphone Institute, and Vice-President of the Conference of University Teachers of German of Great Britain and Ireland. He is consultant to the LCCI-Hong Kong Government Vocational English Programme.

Peter Satchwell taught French and German in comprehensive schools for twenty years before becoming Languages Adviser for Surrey LEA in 1981. His advisory work brought him into regular contact with a large number of primary schools in the county, all of which have taught French to 8–12-year-olds since the 1970s. The writing of two sets of county Guidelines for teaching foreign languages in the primary school (1983 and 1993) and his work as chairman of the national Primary Languages Network have sustained his keen interest in promoting an early start to language learning in this country. He was recently Modern Languages Tutor for the PGCE course at Sussex University and is currently involved in writing/editing two CILT books on teaching languages in the primary school.

John Trim graduated in German at UCL in 1948 and taught phonetics there from 1949 to 1958, when he was appointed university lecturer in phonetics at Cambridge. There he set up the Department of Linguistics as its first Director and was Fellow of Selwyn College from 1962 to 1978, when he was appointed Director of CILT. He retired in 1987, since when he has mainly been engaged in the work he has carried out as Director of the Modern Languages projects of the Council of Europe since 1971. He is an *Officier dans l'Ordre des Palmes Académiques* and holds honorary doctorates from Dublin and Prague.

Maurice Whitehead is a Senior Lecturer in Education and Director of the Centre for Languages in Education at the University of Hull. A graduate of the University of Durham, he taught modern languages in London for eleven years before taking up the post at Hull in 1987. He is currently editor-elect of the *European Journal of Teacher Education.*

Colin Wringe gained his BA in Modern Languages at Oxford and his PhD at the University of London Institute of Education. He has taught in secondary schools and further education and is currently a Modern Languages tutor and reader in Education at Keele. He has written a number of books and articles on both modern languages teaching and wider aspects of education, and was Editor of the *British Journal of Language Teaching* and founding Editor of the *Language Learning Journal.*